SAMS Teach Yourself

Crystal Reports® 9

Joe Estes
Neil FitzGerald
Kathryn Hunt
Steve Lucas
Ryan Marples

in 24 Hours

SAMS 800 East 96th St., Indianapolis, Indiana, 46240 USA

Sams Teach Yourself Crystal Reports® 9 in 24 Hours

Copyright © 2003 by Sams Publishing

International Standard Book Number: 0-672-32090-8

Library of Congress Catalog Card Number: 00-109102

Printed in the United States of America

First Printing: September 2002

06   05   04   7   6   5

Trademarks

Warning and Disclaimer

Bulk Sales

Sams Publishing offers excellent discounts on this book when ordered in quantity for bulk purchases or special sales. For more information, please contact:

U.S. Corporate and Government Sales
1-800-382-3419
corpsales@pearsontechgroup.com

For sales outside of the U.S., please contact:

International Sales
1-317-428-3341
international@pearsontechgroup.com

ASSOCIATE PUBLISHER
Michael Stephens

ACQUISITIONS EDITOR
Michelle Newcomb

DEVELOPMENT EDITOR
Mark Renfrow

MANAGING EDITOR
Charlotte Clapp

PROJECT EDITOR
Andy Beaster

COPY EDITOR
Rhonda Tinch-Mize

INDEXER
Kelly Castell

PROOFREADER
Abby VanHuss

TECHNICAL EDITOR
Marc Borbas

TEAM COORDINATOR
Lynne Williams

INTERIOR DESIGNER
Gary Adair

COVER DESIGNER
Aren Howell

PAGE LAYOUT
Ayanna Lacey

GRAPHICS
Oliver Jackson
Tammy Graham

Contents at a Glance

Contents

PART VII Supplemental Crystal Reports Technologies 447

APPENDIX A Crystal Reports for Visual Studio .NET 449

APPENDIX B Common Crystal Reports FAQs and Tips 463

Index 473

Foreword

Information Drives the Internet

When people hear the word "report," chances are that they think of some relatively boring, corporate financial information. Well welcome to the world of Crystal Reports, in which a report can be anything from a telephone bill to a bank statement, a customer invoice to a list of out of stock products, a portfolio of market equities to an airline timetable, an analysis of file space on a hard drive to a list of top selling books—the list is limited only by your imagination.

Since its first release in 1992 and its bundle as the reporting engine in Visual Basic in 1993, Crystal Reports has been used by millions of people to take information from almost every conceivable data store and format it to allow people to more easily and quickly view and understand that data.

By coincidence, 1992 was also the year that the Internet moved away from being solely a defense and academic network with the appearance of the first commercial Internet service providers. In the 10 years since its inception, the Internet has dramatically changed the way we think about and use information, but we have still only just scratched the surface. With the maturing of wireless broadband and PDA technology, the next five years will see the Internet make more difference to our everyday lives than ever before. Every one of us will expect all the information we receive as consumers (bills, statements, payment histories, appointment, schedules, and more) to be delivered over the Internet, and literally, into the palm of our hands. We will then expect more details and analysis of this information to be available via a variety of devices—PDAs, cell phones, and home PCs.

Hence, two technologies that had very separate beginnings more than 10 years ago have now converged. Crystal Reports has evolved from a Windows report writer to a full-fledged Web technology that can deliver information from server-side databases, easily and seamlessly, within new and existing Web sites. If you consider how much of the content on the Web is underpinned by data coming from various databases, you will then start to imagine the huge return on investment that can be made using a tool like Crystal Reports—which makes many additional people much more productive at creating the Web pages that service millions of Internet users every day.

Version 9 of Crystal Reports is a huge step forward for Windows and Web report writers alike, and this book will help those of you already acquainted with Crystal Reports understand just how big that step forward is. However, one of the best things about Crystal Reports 9 is that although it is simple enough for the novice user to start using immediately, it also has a huge depth of functionality that will service you well as the information you are trying to present gets more complex and the users consuming your reports get more demanding. So if you have never used Crystal Reports before, this book will help you understand just how valuable it will be to you, both immediately and into the future.

The Internet revolution is far from being over and is really just picking up the pace. Its future will be dominated by the challenge to deliver information from a tremendous collection of disparate data stores spread across the globe to millions of end users seeking accurate and reliable information. I can think of no better way to take up the challenge than by arming yourself with this book and a copy of Crystal Reports 9.

Donald MacCormick, Director of Crystal Applications at Crystal Decisions

About the Lead Author

JOE ESTES has been in the information technology industry for more than eight years. He currently manages the Midwest Pre-Sales Team at Crystal Decisions, working with some of the company's largest customers. Prior to working for Crystal Decisions, Joe has been focused on the data reporting, information delivery, and analytical aspects of Data Warehousing and Business Intelligence initiatives exclusively during the past six years. Throughout his career, Joe has held positions varying from system analyst and consultant at large consultancies, to system engineer and project manager at various Business Intelligence software companies. Joe is an avid enthusiast of running, snowboarding, in-line skating, and squash.

About the Contributing Authors

NEIL FITZGERALD has 7+ years experience working with information delivery, business intelligence, and enterprise reporting tools. He has combined this experience with his Bachelor of Computer Science degree from Queens University in Kingston, Canada, and his MBA from the Ivey School of Business at the University of Western Ontario, London, Canada, to help provide information solutions to an array of Fortune 500 companies throughout NYC and the Northeastern United States. Neil is currently managing a top-shelf group of technical consultants in the NY/NE region for Crystal Decisions. He can be contacted at nf_cr24@hotmail.com.

Born, raised, and educated in Vancouver BC, KATHRYN (also known as KAT) HUNT has been working at Crystal Decisions since 1994. During that time, she has held many roles that have brought her both customer-focused and report design experience. She is now considered one of the elite "report design gurus" at Crystal Decisions. She's frequently referred to as the "Reporting Goddess." In her current role as program manager, charged with the Crystal Reports Designer and its features, she has experienced many aspects of how Crystal technologies are designed, marketed, implemented, and supported.

STEVE LUCAS has been in the information technology industry for more than 10 years. He currently manages the Strategic Pre-Sales Team for North America at Crystal Decisions, working with some of the company's largest customers worldwide. Steve regularly speaks on current and future Crystal technology at significant events and trade shows for Crystal. Prior to Crystal, Steve focused on Microsoft technology and consulting for the better part of his career. He is currently based in Denver.

RYAN MARPLES is a program manager at Crystal Decisions responsible for delivering new and powerful developer tools as part of the Crystal Reports product. In addition to this book, Ryan has been involved in the authoring and editing of various other books and magazine articles. In addition to writing, Ryan has been a speaker at software conferences around the world.

About the Technical Editor

MARC BORBAS has worked in the enterprise software industry for five years in a variety of marketing and product management roles. He is currently the product marketing manager for Crystal Enterprise, Crystal Decisions' core information delivery technology. Marc works regularly with analysts, media, and customers to communicate the value and functionality of the Crystal product set. He is an avid enthusiast of snowboarding and sailing.

Dedications

To the single most important person in my life: my beautiful wife Aimee. You are my daily inspiration, my guiding light, and the foundation of all I do.

–Joe Estes

To Arlene, Mom, Dad, and the entire Family FitzGerald (Katherine, Deirdre, Bernie, Nora, Terry, Linsey, Connor, Matthew, and Christopher).

–Neil FitzGerald

To my mother Patricia. Always believing in me and helping me be the best I can, makes you not just my mom, but my inspiration. Love you lots.

- Kathryn Hunt

To the most important people in my life: my wife Shelley and my two kids, Lynnie and Kenny.

–Steve Lucas

To every person at Crystal Decisions: Your hard work and passion for our company over the years has not only helped make this book possible, but has also provided me with a lifetime of learning, experiences, and friendships.

–Ryan Marples

Acknowledgments

Joe Estes: With utmost veneration and gratefulness, I want to thank my wife, Aimee, for her unwavering encouragement and support through all my endeavors. Special thanks to my mother and father, who have taught me the value of perseverance and hard work.

A special thank you to Steve Lucas for your guidance and wisdom, and for completing the vision behind so many ideas that you inspire everyone around you to succeed. To Michelle Newcomb and the entire team at Sams Publishing, thank you for providing me with the opportunity to lead this authoring project. I also want to thank each contributing author and technical editor—Neil, Kat, Ryan, Donald, and Marc—who has dedicated themselves to making this book a reality. It could not have been possible without your hard work and support. Finally, thank you Crystal Decisions for creating exceptional products and allowing us to write this book, and to many of my colleagues who are as enthusiastic and excited as I am when it comes to providing world-class Business Intelligence solutions.

Neil FitzGerald: Thanks to Steve Lucas, Michelle Newcomb, Joe Estes, Kathryn Hunt, Ryan Marples, and Marc Borbas for the opportunity and experience of participating in this great endeavor with you guys—you are all truly world class.

Special recognition goes to a few people who have made this possible without even knowing it: Arlene for inspiring and tolerating me throughout; Paul Sochan, Mike Voloshko, Tim Weir, Gravy Man (Steve Holzgraefe), Larry Skiscim, and the entire technical Crystal team for exposing me to creative uses of the Crystal products and all the brains in Vancouver and Ipswich responsible for shaping this world class product—specifically the top notch Product and R&D teams.

Kathryn Hunt: There are so many people to thank, where do I begin? At the beginning, I guess. Mom and my brothers, David and Mark: "Love ya for who you are and who you are destined to be. All the best!" Recently passed away Bob Brassington—VE7BBB: "Grandpa, if it wasn't for you letting me play on that computer when I was 8, who knows where I'd be today. I miss you." Areni Kelleppan and Matteusz van Wollen: Thanks for keeping me going through requests for progress on my writing and words of wisdom during this adventure. "Through everything, you've kept me grounded and you've reminded me of who I am. No matter what." "

Thanks to Joe, Neil, and Ryan. I've so enjoyed working with you on this. Thanks for making it so much fun. From "pink." Thank you Steve, for asking me to contribute in the first place and for reminding me of the light at the end of the tunnel. Thanks to Marc for being our technical editor. And thanks to Michelle and the whole team at Sams Publishing.

Thanks to everyone at Crystal Decisions who I've had the pleasure and honor to work with over the past 8 years. I've had such a great time with the people and the products, that I can't imagine having as much fun anywhere else. Thanks for keeping life challenging.

And finally, I'd like to thank all my family and friends; you know who you are. If it wasn't for your love, laughter, and support, I wouldn't have been able to accept Steve's invitation to write.

Steve Lucas: Thank you Shelley for being the best friend and companion I could ask for and more. You are amazing. Thanks to my family and friends for all your support and encouragement.

Thank you Joe, Kat, Ryan, and Neil for keeping me involved in this book: You are all very talented individuals. Thank you Michelle and everyone from Sams Publishing who were involved in this book: You are incredible professionals.

I also want to thank some very intelligent and inspiring people at Crystal Decisions who I've worked with over the last three years: Roger Sanborn, Tim Weir, Steve Holzgraefe, James Church, Sandra Lutz, Donald MacCormick, Nigel Stoodley, Fred Tummonds, Bev Coxford, and James Luiken.

Paul, you are a true Wozniak!

Ryan Marples: I'd like to thank the other authors and the team at Sams, including Michelle Newcomb, for their patience and drive to make this a great book. I'd also like to acknowledge our Research and Development team, who put endless long hours into this product. It's all paid off with a great product.

We Want to Hear from You!

As the reader of this book, *you* are our most important critic and commentator. We value your opinion and want to know what we're doing right, what we could do better, what areas you'd like to see us publish in, and any other words of wisdom you're willing to pass our way.

As an associate publisher for Sams Publishing, I welcome your comments. You can email or write me directly to let me know what you did or didn't like about this book—as well as what we can do to make our books better.

Please note that I cannot help you with technical problems related to the *topic* of this book. We do have a User Services group, however, where I will forward specific technical questions related to the book.

When you write, please be sure to include this book's title and author as well as your name, email address, and phone number. I will carefully review your comments and share them with the author and editors who worked on the book.

Email: `feedback@samspublishing.com`

Mail: Michael Stephens, Associate Publisher
Sams Publishing
800 East 96th Street
Indianapolis, IN 46240 USA

For more information about this book or another Sams title, visit our Web site at `www.samspublishing.com`. Type the ISBN (excluding hyphens) or the title of a book in the Search field to find the page you're looking for.

Introduction

If you've picked up this book, undoubtedly you have heard of or are interested in Crystal Reports—the world's most popular reporting product from Crystal Decisions. If you are looking for a comprehensive guide to all the major features that Crystal Reports has to offer, and you don't have time for a one week course, this is the perfect book for you.

The reason Crystal Reports is so popular is because today's organizations are looking for fast, efficient ways to make sense of their data. Crystal Reports can be found everywhere, bundled in products from ERP solutions, such as SAP and PeopleSoft, to developer products such as Visual Basic and Visual Studio.NET. Crystal Reports is used to solve almost any type of reporting or information access problem imaginable, from creating sales reports for field-based account reps, to summary reports for organizational executives.

You might not know this, but some of the bills you get in the mail every month, as well as your online 401(k) statement accessible via the Web are often Crystal Reports. Crystal Reports has been in the market for 15 years, which has contributed significantly to its position as the market standard for enterprise reporting.

Over the past 15 years, Crystal Reports has evolved from providing presentation quality, paper-based reports to the current, highly interactive Web reporting solution we know today. This evolution, primarily driven by the Internet, has reshaped what most people perceive Crystal Reports to be. The Internet has given organizations a new medium by which to track and capture data about almost everything we do online, which has resulted in a massive increase in the amount of data available to the average organization. Accessing this data, and more importantly, turning it in to meaningful information is what Crystal Reports does best.

Sams Teach Yourself Crystal Reports 9 in 24 Hours was written to help you get the most out of Crystal Reports in the shortest amount of time. This book contains 24 lessons, each lasting about an hour if you complete all the reading and exercises available. After each lesson, a short quiz is provided to help you retain some of the key concepts you'll learn.

We've included two appendices as well, which will help you use some of the additional tools related to Crystal Reports that will enrich your reporting experience. Although Crystal Reports has an endless stream of business problems that it can solve, we've kept the book focused on some of the following topics:

- An overview of Crystal Reports, how to install it, and some of the reporting issues you can address by using it.
- Discussions on how to understand your corporate data because we think this is as much of a challenge as reporting itself.

- Hours that cover the fundamentals of reporting from a Crystal Reports developer perspective.

- Detailed sections on how to create aesthetically pleasing reports that provide valuable information for business users and managers.

- Information on how to share and distribute your reports with others.

All the preceding topics are based on the real-world experiences of the authors of this book, so it's not only informational, but also realistic.

What's in This Book?

The book is logically separated into six parts that cover broad topics.

Part I: "Introduction to Crystal Reports 9.0"

Part I is intended for you to become familiar with Crystal Reports, as well as for you to be up and running as quickly as possible. It is critical for someone who is new to Crystal Reports. It provides an introduction and an overview of how to quickly install and begin using the product. Even if you think you know what Crystal Reports is all about, you'll want to read this section because version 9 of Crystal Reports is a major update.

Part I includes

- Hour 1, "The Value of Crystal Reports 9" —This is where you'll find out what Crystal Reports is all about and what features you can expect to find in version 9. Even if you haven't decided that Crystal Reports is the product for you, this hour provides the information you'll need to make an informed decision.

- Hour 2, "Getting Started With Crystal Reports 9" —This hour covers how to prepare your system to install Crystal Reports, the actual installation, and some housekeeping functions you'll need to be aware of to navigate the application.

- Hour 3, "Accessing Your Data" —This hour is arguably the most important in the book. Although Crystal Reports is a great product, understanding the types of data you will access, how you are going to access it, and what Crystal Reports can do with it are the basis for success. A number of Crystal Reports features will help you in your data access efforts, and they are introduced here as well.

- Hour 4, "Using the Default Report Wizards" —Although Crystal Reports is used for a vast array of reporting solutions, many of the features available are used in almost every report. Those features are encapsulated in a set of easy to use Report Wizards. The Report Wizards will have you accessing your data and creating interactive Web reports in a flash.

Part II: "Fundamentals of the Crystal Report Design Environment"

Part II answers the most common question that anyone new to Crystal Reports asks: "How do I create a report from scratch?" This section answers this question and includes some fundamental report design concepts, which you'll use for the rest of your Crystal Reports career.

Part II includes

- Hour 5, "Creating and Designing Basic Reports" —This hour introduces you to the process of creating a new Crystal Report from scratch. The key word for this hour is process because planning a report before actually developing it will ensure success each and every time you need to create a report. Effective planning will also reduce the amount of time you invest in a report because not every report you develop will be like the examples in this book.

- Hour 6, "Selecting and Grouping Data" —Understanding the various objects that reports might contain, as well as how to organize those objects, are introduced in this hour. Two fundamental, yet major, concepts, selecting and grouping, are introduced here. This hour reviews how to refine data queries using selections as well as how to organize it in the most understandable fashion through grouping. If you've heard the buzzword Drill-Down report and want to find out what this means, this is the hour for you.

- Hour 7, "Filtering, Sorting, and Summarizing Data" —Three additional core reporting concepts are introduced in this hour, as indicated by the title. This hour reviews concepts that will help you further refine and organize you reports. Each of these topics will help you make the reports you create more relevant to business end users.

Part III: "Formatting Reports"

Part II focused on some of the mechanics of report design, such as data organization and filtering. Part III covers what is often missed in report design: effective formatting. Without proper formatting, reports can be hard to understand and often times rendered useless.

Part III includes

- Hour 8, "Fundamentals of Report Formatting" —Some of the obvious report formatting techniques, such as field and object sizing and positioning, have many subtle tips and tricks that we cover here. All the basics of formatting, such as fonts, colors, highlighting, and page properties can be found here as well.

- Hour 9, "Working with Report Sections" —Report Sections are one of the most fundamental concepts to report design, and mastering them will make you a proficient report developer. Any given Crystal Report will include numerous Report Sections that segment a report in to logical sections that can behave independently based on certain triggers and settings. This hour covers some of the finer aspects of working with reports sections, such as how to suppress or hide sections based on certain criteria.

- Hour 10, "Understanding and Implementing Formulas" —Formulas can be a very powerful feature in your reports. They enable you calculate fields and summaries, as well as determine outcomes of what a report will look or act like based on almost anything. This hour introduces the concept of what a formula is and how to leverage them in almost any Crystal Reports you create. This hour also reviews some of the updates to the formula editor that you'll find with Crystal Reports version 9 because the formula editor has received a significant face-lift from previous versions.

- Hour 11, "Visualizing Your Data with Charts and Maps" —Very few reports make it out the door without some type of visual representation of the data in the report itself. Crystal Reports contains a number of charting and geographic mapping features, which separate it from any other reporting tool on the market. This hour reviews how to use the various types of charts and maps available, as well as how to customize them to your organizational needs.

- Hour 12, "Implementing Parameters for Dynamic Reporting" —Seldom does one report meet all the needs of a given group of users. Parameters provide a way to make reports dynamic—whereby the outcome of what the report looks like or what type of data it contains is driven by a user-specified parameter before the report is processed. You'll learn how to create parameters and integrate them within the reports you create.

Part IV: "Enhancing Crystal Reports"

Part IV takes the concepts you have learned from the prior parts of the book and extends them even further. Topics such as additional formatting techniques and analytic report design are discussed. Intermediate report design features, such as subreports and the Report Component Repository, are reviewed here as well.

Part IV includes

- Hour 13, "Custom Formatting Techniques" —This hour covers many formatting techniques that you will use in almost any report. Beyond the standard formatting you'll learn prior to this, such as fonts and colors, this hour introduces topics such as conditional formatting and ToolTips.

- Hour 14, "Using Cross-Tabs for Summarized Reporting" —A cross-tab report is a highly formatted report set in a grid object. This type of report is very similar to a Microsoft Excel worksheet. This hour reviews the various uses for cross-tab reports, how to use the Cross-Tab Wizard, and what's new in Crystal Reports 9 that's related to cross-tab reports.

- Hour 15, "Using Record Selections and Alerts for Interactive Reporting" — Although most reports you create will provide a wealth of information for the end user, requirements will undoubtedly arise for reports that draw attention to certain informational elements. Hour 15 covers two common ways to narrow down the amount of data presented to a user through record selections and alerting.

- Hour 16, "Using Subreports" —Subreports allow existing reports to be embedded inside other reports. This opens up a wide variety of solutions using Crystal Reports, such as aggregating data from multiple sources into one "container" report. Hour 16 introduces the concept of subreports, how they can benefit you as a report developer, and how to use them.

- Hour 17, "Using Formulas and Custom Functions to Implement Complex Business Logic" —One of the most useful features of Crystal Reports is the ability to build your business rules and logic into reports themselves through the use of formulas and custom functions. Both features have been introduced in prior hours, but not explored to their full potential.

- Hour 18, "Working with the Report Component Repository" —The Report Component Repository, a central store for various components of a report, is arguably the most significant new feature of Crystal Reports version 9. Although the repository was used in prior hours, because it is now a core feature of Crystal Reports, this hour reviews it in detail and explains its significance in any report you will create. The hour demonstrates how to use the repository to control objects, such as report header images, that are commonly used in all reports you create.

- Hour 19, "Designing Effective Report Templates" —Crystal Reports version 9 introduces a powerful new feature in which existing reports can be used as templates for other reports. This hour explores how this dramatically reduces the amount of time required to format reports to a specific corporate look and feel. You'll find out how to use any of your reports as templates and what the most effective methods are to do so.

Part V: "Advanced Report Design Concepts"

Part V introduces a host of advanced report design concepts, which revolve around different types of data access and methods. For most Crystal Reports developers, these topics are not the traditional data access methods you'll use, such as ODBC. By reading the hours in this part, we hope to open your eyes to a world of possibilities with Crystal Reports and extend your report design knowledge even further.

Part V includes

- Hour 20, "Multidimensional Reporting Against OLAP Data" —Multidimensional reporting, commonly referred to as *OLAP (Online Analytical Processing)*, is gaining wide acceptance as an effective way to stage data for optimum reporting and analysis performance. For organizations that are using OLAP data sources, such as Microsoft SQL Server Analysis Services and Hyperion Essbase, Crystal Reports provides an effective means to capture and deliver valuable information to business users. Hour 20 reviews basic OLAP concepts as well as how Crystal Reports retrieves data from an OLAP data source. This hour also provides an introduction into creating Crystal Reports from OLAP data sources.

- Hour 21, "Additional Data Sources for Crystal Reports" —Crystal Reports version 9 introduces a host of powerful new data access mechanisms, including JavaBean connectivity and updated XML and COM provider (.dll) connectivity. This hour introduces you to how Crystal Reports can connect to a dynamic data source, such as a .dll, and read data. This hour also introduces you to a variety of specialized connectivity for third-party products such as SAP, BAAN, and Seibel.

- Hour 22, "Optimizing SQL Queries in Crystal Reports" —As you will figure out by this hour, Crystal Reports is actually writing *SQL (Structured Query Language)* for you when you create a report. As this hour discusses, a good understanding of SQL is a must for the advanced Crystal Reports developer. This hour reviews what SQL is, how to understand the SQL that Crystal Reports generates, as well as introduces some optimization techniques to keep in mind when developing reports.

Part VI: "Sharing And Distributing Crystal Reports"

Part VI covers the topic that will seem most important to you after you've actually created your reports: sharing them. This part explores a variety of options for sharing your reports with others, from solutions provided by Crystal Decisions to programmatic solutions that any savvy developer can achieve.

Part VI includes

- Hour 23, "Distributing Crystal Reports" —This hour covers the laundry list of options available for distributing Crystal Reports. This includes common methods, such as email, to developer specific solutions such as Active Server Pages. A major topic, Crystal Enterprise is also introduced in this hour. Crystal Enterprise is a powerful solution from Crystal Decisions for sharing Crystal Reports in a secure,

manageable fashion. This hour reviews every option available and provides a number of examples.

- Hour 24, "Crystal Reports in Applications—A Developer's Perspective" —This
  hour provides a discussion on how to use the *Software Developers Kits (SDKs)*
  available for Crystal Reports. Crystal Reports functionality is often embedded in
  custom-built applications using technologies such as Microsoft Visual Basic or
  Java. In this hour, you'll learn about the developer tools available to you in Crystal
  Reports 9 and how to get started developing applications that incorporate Crystal
  Reports.

Part VII: "Supplemental Crystal Reports Technologies"

Part VII introduces some technologies that might be useful to you in your reporting
efforts.

Part VII includes

- Appendix A, "Crystal Reports for Visual Studio .NET" —Crystal Reports for
  Visual Studio .NET is a .NET developer-focused edition of Crystal Reports and
  provides a comprehensive reporting solution for Visual Studio .NET developers.
  This edition of Crystal Reports is seamlessly integrated with both the Visual Studio
  .NET development environment (IDE) and the .NET Framework. This appendix
  overviews Crystal Report's unique functionality and features in Visual Studio .NET
  and is targeted at developers working within the Visual Studio .NET application
  development environment, as well as readers interested in obtaining an introduction
  to this custom version of Crystal Reports.

- Appendix B, "Common Crystal Reports FAQ's and Tips" —This Appendix acts as
  a reference for some of the common questions we get from report designers and
  developers, both novice and advanced. It includes various tips on how to better use
  the Crystal technologies and additional resources available to you from Crystal
  Decisions.

The appendixes will provide you with supplemental material—not required reading.
Also, we encourage you to look at Crystal Enterprise for your report distribution and
sharing needs because it is the most powerful and popular option for doing so. Crystal
Enterprise is a scalable server platform for managing and sharing Crystal Reports over
the Web. It is a leading standard for enterprise reporting and business intelligence, and
you can use Crystal Enterprise to publish reports to an Internet/intranet site without programming to securely share reports with large groups of users.

Equipment Used for This Book

We have made available to you various supporting material that will assist you in the completion of the exercises in this book, as well as supplemental documentation on related topics.

Web Resources

We've provided all the source code for the examples in the book, as well as the appendixes to the book, at an easy to find Web site. Just go to www.samspublishing.com. You'll find easy to download report samples and code for you to leverage in your report design and sharing efforts. Also, a great deal of additional product related information on Crystal Reports can be found at www.crystaldecisions.com.

Intended Audience

We wrote this book to appeal to beginner and intermediate level users of Crystal Reports. You'll find this book useful if you've never used Crystal Reports before or if you are looking to explore some of the new features found in version 9. You don't have to be an expert, but you should have a basic understanding of the following concepts:

- Database systems such as Microsoft SQL Server, Oracle, Sybase, and Informix
- Operating system functions in Windows NT/2000/XP
- General Internet/intranet-based concepts such as HTML, DHTML, ActiveX, and Java

The parts of this book build on each other, so skipping around isn't the best approach unless you have some familiarity with Crystal Reports 9. Even if you are familiar with Crystal Reports, many new features have been introduced in version 9, so we encourage you to read the whole book so that you don't miss anything.

Assumptions Made for This Book

For this book, we assume that you have access to a computer that has at least a Pentium II or equivalent processor, 128MB of RAM, and a Windows NT Workstation, 2000 Professional, Advanced Server, or Windows XP Professional.

All reports are based on sample data that is installed with Crystal Reports, so you will have access to the same data that we use in this book. You'll need to install Crystal Reports to get the most out of the examples included in each hour.

Conventions Used in This Book

Several conventions are used within this book to help you get more out of the text. Look for special fonts or text styles and icons that emphasize special information.

- Formula examples appear in mono, and they can be found on the Sams Publishing Web site as well.

- Objects such as fields or formulas normally appear on separate lines from the rest of the text. However, there are special situations in which some formulas or fields appear directly in the paragraph for explanation purposes. These types of objects will appear in a special font like this: `Some Special Code`.

- In some cases, we might refer to your computer as *machine* or *server*. This is always in reference to the physical computer on which you have installed Crystal Reports.

- You'll always be able to recognize menu selections and command sequences because they're implemented like this:

  Use the File, Open command.

- URLs for Web sites are presented like this: `http://www.crystaldecisions.com`.

Notes help you understand principles or provide amplifying information. In many cases, a note emphasizes some piece of critical information that you need. All of us like to know special bits of information that make our job easier, more fun, or faster to perform.

Tips help you get the job done faster and more safely. In many cases, the information found in a tip is drawn from experience rather than through experimentation or documentation.

Coffee Breaks and sidebars spend more time on a particular subject that could be considered a tangent, but will help you be a better Crystal Reports developer as a result.

PART I

Introduction to Crystal Reports 9.0

Hour

HOUR 1

The Value of Crystal Reports 9

Crystal Reports is a design application for creating powerful and compelling reports that transform data, from virtually any data source, into meaningful information. Hundreds of thousands of business users and application developers alike have discovered the power and flexibility of Crystal Reports. Not just a tool for application developers, Crystal Reports is also an application for a wide variety of organizational users who need to analyze and interpret important information for better presentation and decision making. Many corporate business users get their information from a variety of *legacy* mechanisms that are still prevalent today—custom applications, mainframe reports, ASCII files, and so on. But, these mechanisms do very little to maximize the investment that organizations often make in their corporate Information Technology systems, such as *Enterprise Resource Planning (ERP)*, *Customer Relationship Management (CRM)*, and other critical data systems.

Considered to be the world standard for report writing, Crystal Reports has more than seven million licenses distributed worldwide. A contributing factor to this great success is that Crystal Reports is packaged within some of the most predominant software solutions in the world, including Microsoft's .NET platform, SAP, PeopleSoft, and others. As a result, users of these best-in-class solutions also benefit from the tightly integrated and highly powerful Crystal Reports technology. Partnerships such as these are perhaps the biggest endorsement any particular software product could hope for. Figure 1.1 shows an example of a Balance Sheet report created using Crystal Reports.

FIGURE 1.1

A sample Balance Sheet report created using Crystal Reports.

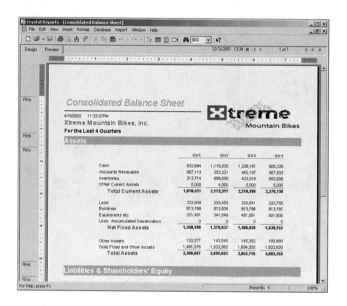

The proliferation of Crystal Reports as the most common reporting application in the world is in large part because of its intuitive design environment that enables beginners to create simple reports, as well as its capability of empowering more experienced users to design sophisticated reports to satisfy more complex requirements. This hour introduces the concepts of report design and the components of Crystal Reports that aid in the planning and creation of reports. The hour will also cover many of the new features made available in this latest release of Crystal Reports (version 9.0).

In this hour, the following topics are covered:

- Transforming data into information with Crystal Reports
- Key benefits of the Crystal Reports application
- Crystal Reports as a Content Creation application
- New features and enhancements in Crystal Reports 9

Transforming Data into Information with Crystal Reports

Businesses in every industry now collect and maintain data relevant to their operation. For example, manufacturing companies collect and maintain information about inventories and production, retail shops record sales and order information, health care organizations maintain patient medical records, and publishing companies track book sales and inventories. Nonetheless, storing data is not enough! Businesses, and their management staff, must use this data to make well-informed business decisions on a regular basis. The data collected must be transformed into information, and then it must be properly organized, easily accessible, and shared among various individuals—both internal employees and external affiliates and customers. The transformation and dissemination of this data facilitates analysis that can reveal business-critical information, such as sales trends or potential inventory shortages. To make this possible, corporations and application developers use reporting software, such as Crystal Reports, to enable the presentation of stored data sources. Crystal Reports was the first reporting software in the market to fully recognize this need, and was released in 1992 as a Windows-based report writer.

A common business concern for many organizations is how to effectively report against multiple data source systems simultaneously, merging sales data that resides in an Oracle database with inventory data that resides in an IBM DB2 database. One distinct feature unique to Crystal Reports is that you can easily create reports that connect to such disparate databases, join the data together within your reports, and transform the otherwise isolated data into meaningful information that now displays such items as average days between the sales order entered versus the shipping date and provides dynamic alerting if inventory levels are dangerously low. Whatever industry, business unit, or technological ability of the user, most people seek information that allows them to make more informed decisions. Crystal Reports is the most common tool in the world that provides users with the information they need. Whether these reports include customer invoices, billing statements, account transaction listings, financial statements (as shown in Figure 1.1), or cross-tabular summaries of sales by month, Crystal Reports can service your need.

When thinking about all the various sources of data within most organizations and how diverse the collection of sources can be, it quickly becomes important to consider a common toolset for accessing, analyzing, and sharing the information produced from these sources among a wide audience of organizational users. This is often where the value of spreadsheet applications diminish and where the value of a robust reporting application begins. In this manner, Crystal Reports can access nearly any source of data, interpret and analyze the data to present meaningful information, and share the resulting reports with users throughout the organization. These sources might include sales data, inventory data, customer call center data, and an organizational data warehouse of centralized historical data. Perhaps the most immediate value of using a common reporting tool in conjunction with organizational data sources is that decision makers will be looking at the same information and performance measures across all of their reports. This helps eliminate the concern that one manager might be looking at different performance results than another manager, or that the various managers are defining a commonly used calculated value in slightly different ways, such as variance or margin.

It's not unusual for a sales meeting to take place where various sales professionals have different forecast numbers. Each sales manager might use his own spreadsheet to manage and forecast his projections. As a result, discrepancies often exist among these professionals when using independent, unmanaged spreadsheets for reporting purposes, and this can become a very serious concern when it involves financial and performance measurement analysis. Providing these managers with meaningful and accurate reports that access a centralized data source can prevent this scenario.

Crystal Reports also offers greater organizational value than that offered by many of the application-specific reporting tools, such as those offers by database software vendors. Crystal Reports extends the power of reporting well beyond a single database or application environment to allow report designers to access virtually any data source, as well as merging multiple sources of data together in a single report—regardless of where the actual data resides. The remainder of this section discusses the value Crystal Reports offers as a corporate standard for reporting and various system integration issues.

Standardization

Most organizations want one common reporting solution that is able to work with all their data sources and support a broad base of audience-specific reporting requirements. Such standardization also facilitates the acquisition of a consistent skill set across the organization and increases the availability of expertise needed to support the organizational use of the application. Rather than having many different report file formats created from different applications (and of varying versions), an organization that standardizes with a professional reporting solution, such as Crystal Reports, can help ensure that information consumers will receive the right information, in the right format, and at the right time.

Why choose Crystal Reports as the standard for reporting within an organization? It is the most mature and widely accepted reporting application in the market. Crystal Reports supports virtually all data sources, can merge data of differing sources together, and offers advanced technological features that are compatible and forward thinking to support other technological and industry standards (XML, COM, and Java, for example). It is also a solution that is easy to administer and manage after it is deployed. As an example, for much the same reason that corporations use Microsoft Office for common word processing and spreadsheet applications, they also use Crystal Reports for all organizational reporting because it has established itself as the world standard.

System Integration

The topic of integration speaks to how well a product coexists and, ultimately, complements other technology and organizational standards. It's critical that a reporting solution, such as Crystal Reports, integrate into standard solutions already deployed within most organizations. This includes technologies such as Microsoft Office, Lotus Notes, and others.

Crystal Reports offers the flexibility and power to complement virtually any technology deployed within any organization.

This includes

- Exporting reports to various file formats and destinations
- A powerful *Software Developer's Kit (SDK)* that provides developers control over report layout and formatting within custom Web and Windows applications
- The means to access transitory data streams, such as XML, at runtime to pass information between objects in report applications

A core consideration when planning to create reports for a large audience is what file format the users need and what capabilities various formats can offer. The presence of specific software applications on most corporate workstations can vary from group to group and from user to user. With this in mind, Crystal Reports has been designed to support a wide variety of formats to accommodate any organizational demand, as shown in Figure 1.2. A sample collection of various file formats from which Crystal Reports can export to includes, but is not limited to, the following:

- DOC—Microsoft Word format
- XLS—Microsoft Excel format
- PDF—Adobe Acrobat's Portable Document Format
- XML—Extensible Markup Language

- HTML—Hypertext Markup Language
- RTF—Rich Text Format
- CSV—Comma Separated Values format
- Text—Simple text format
- ODBC sources—ODBC database sources, such as Microsoft Access and SQL Server 2000

> PDF format is a good delivery format for sharing sensitive information that should not be modified by the user. Unlike Excel, data within PDF files cannot be changed and are most commonly used for formatted data display purposes only.

Thus, Crystal Reports can complement and integrate with most standard corporate applications, such as Microsoft Word, Excel, and Acrobat Reader. By combining Crystal Reports with these other best-of-breed applications, organizations can offer a very robust and widely usable reporting solution.

FIGURE 1.2

The Export window in the Crystal Reports designer provides export capabilities to popular applications such as Microsoft Word and Excel.

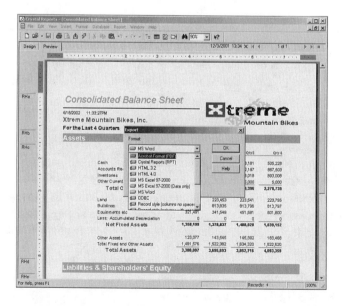

When deciding on the best alternative for sharing report files with other users, it is important to be aware of some distinct advantages of using the Crystal Reports (.RPT) file format in contrast to those listed previously. Crystal Reports files offer highly interactive report navigation and viewing, permitting users to quickly find the information they are looking for in a very intuitive way. For example, let's assume that you are viewing a World Sales report for a large organization that shows a pie chart of aggregated sales figures by country at the top of the report, and you want to find out more about the specific product sales in the city of Chicago. The report can be designed so that all you would need to do to locate Chicago is click on the U.S. slice of the pie chart, which then presents a second-level bar chart showing the national sales numbers for each of the states, where you would then click on the bar representing Illinois. As a result, you have quickly located the Chicago sales figures within a large and comprehensive report. This highly interactive example is often referred to as drilling-down on information, and creating reports that facilitate such simple navigation are very easy. As we explore the Crystal Reports application, Hour 6, "Selecting and Grouping Data," and Hour 11, "Visualizing Your Data with Charts and Maps," will both address this specific example.

Other notable characteristics unique to the Crystal Reports file format include the capability to offer a highly formatted and professional looking report, hyperlinks within reports that can provide for a variety of actions (link to other reports, initiate an email, or navigate the business user to a Web site), and compatibility with the Crystal Enterprise solution (discussed in Hour 23, "Distributing Crystal Reports") for enterprisewide delivery and management of reports. As an example, hyperlinks are often used to create a navigation path for business users between multiple related reports.

After a report is designed and created, organizations then need to distribute this content among the information consumers who need access to the reports. Just as there are a variety of file format options, there are also a wide variety of supported export destination options for sharing Crystal Reports content. Crystal Reports supports report destinations such as disk locations, Microsoft Exchange folders, Lotus Domino databases, and email. In addition to directly exporting report files to these destinations, Crystal Reports content can also be distributed via a variety of Web and Windows (client/server) applications. See Hour 23 for further information.

Key Benefits of Crystal Reports

Perhaps the greatest benefit of using Crystal Reports for report creation is its simplicity and ease of use. The report design interface is extremely user friendly and accommodating for users of different skill levels. The Crystal Reports application is extremely visual based, allowing users to intuitively construct reports with the support of several Explorers or development components per se. Figure 1.3 shows an example of this. See Hour 5, "Fundamentals of Report Creation and Design," for more details on design Explorers.

FIGURE 1.3

The Explorer design components enable the report designer to quickly and intuitively create meaningful reports.

With the release of Crystal Reports 9, designers now have a truly object-oriented design environment that allows them to intuitively create powerful report content. Crystal Reports also supports such industry and technology standards as *Extensible Markup Language (XML)*, *Open Database Connectivity (ODBC)*, and *Object Linking and Embedding for Databases (OLE DB)*. In addition to adhering to such data connectivity standards, Crystal Reports can also support virtually any application (Web or Windows) and device (PDAs and cell phones). This makes Crystal Reports a very flexible solution for organizations and developers who need to support a wide range of specific information delivery requirements. Examples could include a Web interface for executive management through a *digital dashboard* application, an expense tracking and reporting application for finance, and a product catalog Internet application for customers. Crystal Reports can support all these application needs as a reliable and flexible means to access most any underlying data, transform the data into meaningful information, and present the contents in a professional manner to the information consumers via any device. For more details with application integration, see Hour 24, "Integrating Crystal Reports in Applications."

Connecting to Corporate Data

One of Crystal Reports' core strengths is its capability to connect to virtually any data source via a variety of data connectivity methods. These data sources can include *relational database management systems (RDBMS)*, spreadsheets, text files, custom data sources (Enterprise JavaBeans, or EJBs, and COM objects), and *Online Analytical*

Processing (OLAP) structures. Crystal Reports can recognize and report against tables, views, system tables, synonyms, and stored procedures within a RDBMS environment to better incorporate various database strategies into the overall report design process. Furthermore, Crystal Reports is quite unique in its capability to directly connect to multiple data sources within any single report. If commonality does exist in the data between two or more sources, such as Sales or Order information, it might be advantageous to construct an amalgamated display that merges this information into one report.

For more details on data connectivity options, see Hour 3, "Understanding Your Data."

When selecting a data connectivity mechanism with Crystal Reports, it is often necessary to consider the inclusion of a metadata layer that can shield report designers from the physical structure of the end database. A metadata file acts as an intermediary between the report and the data source. The decision to use a metadata source for reports rather than connecting directly to the database is often based on several possible considerations, including the skill level of the report designer, complexity of the database, necessity to provide report designers with custom calculations or formulas that do not exist in the database, and the need to reorganize or restructure the displayed data for easier use. For example, metadata files are often used to preestablish table linking and rename fields and tables to make them more logical and friendly to report designers because report designers often aren't familiar with the complex naming conventions of the data source system. Essentially, a metadata file can demystify the data source by making it more user friendly for the report designer.

Crystal Dictionary files are available to service this metadata role. Crystal Dictionaries are simply an optional offering and are not a required component to Crystal Reports. Crystal Reports supports both direct database connectivity (the primary data access method for this book) as well as metadata deployment options.

A Crystal Dictionary file (.DC5) is an optional source of data for Crystal Reports. The dictionary file is a structured and simplified view of organizational data that report designers or application administrators can create for any of the individuals in an organization that use Crystal Reports. Using a dictionary file as a data source, end users only see the appropriate subset of tables and fields they require. It is often used to clarify and simplify (via logical field names and groupings) complex data access techniques for report designers who are not familiar with the underlying database. See *Crystal Dictionary* in the Crystal Reports Help files for further details on this topic.

Crystal Reports as a Content Creation Application

The measure of any report's value is in its capability to provide the most accurate and timely information to assist the business user in making a more effective business decision. By allowing users to make more informed decisions, reports can increase the competitiveness of organizations, identify and reduce operational costs, and focus an organization's attention on specific performance measures. Crystal Reports offers a powerful design environment for creating highly dynamic and interactive content that aids information consumers in making better decisions—everyday. When you create reports with Crystal Reports, you are creating information content that facilitates action.

What Is Content Creation?

The process of report creation is commonly referred to as *content creation*. This includes the process of stating the report objective, identifying the required information for a report, accessing the appropriate data source(s), incorporating the necessary data fields and elements, constructing any required elements (such as formulas and calculations), and formatting the report for presentation purposes. For example, to create a new sales report, you will need to know several things:

1. Objective of the report—Display sales by region for each of the three major product lines.

2. How the intended audience will use the report (level of interactivity)—Sales managers will need to quickly locate regional sales dollars and units sold for each unique product item.

3. Where the data resides (data sources)—The primary Sales data resides in an Oracle database, but will need to be combined with data from a Microsoft Access database as well.

4. Understand what the report will be communicating (data fields and elements)—Sales dollars, units sold, region, product line, and product item.

5. Format the report for presentation purposes—Add a stacked bar chart at the top of the report showing product line sales figures by region.

Planning Reports

In most business scenarios, reports perform the role of a management tool to help business users quickly grasp the essential elements and relationships found in various organizational data sources. Reports should be well planned with an objective in mind, assisting the targeted users of the report to make more educated and informed decisions.

Reports also need to present accurate data in a logical way to be effective. Reports that present inaccurate data or present data in an illogical manner could actually lessen the effectiveness of the decision-making process. It is also important to keep the *consumers* of a report in mind throughout the development process. Because each consumer of a report has a unique interest and perspective on the data, it is necessary to include the information each one is looking for, and to employ the appropriate mechanisms (prompts, calculations, and so on) to efficiently service the intended audience.

When beginning the report development process, it is good practice to first identify the objective of the report. The report objective should include the anticipated audience for the report, as well as provide both a starting point and a final goal for the report development process.

> Using charts and maps within reports is a good method for quickly and intuitively communicating information to the business users of a report.

Some examples of report objectives are

- The objective of this report is to show quarterly and annual call volumes by employee, compare this quarter's numbers to last quarter's numbers, and identify the employees whose call volumes are greater than the specified company standards. The audiences for this report are various departmental and cost center managers.

- The objective of this report is to show weekly sales revenue, cost, and margins by store location and highlight actual sales revenue figures based on their deviation from identified expectations. The report also needs to include alerts that detect and notify the user if sales margins are less than expected. The audiences for this report are North American sales management and various store managers.

Defining report objectives before you begin the report development process is a critical step in the overall success of the report. For more details on how to effectively plan, design, and implement reports, see Hour 5.

New Features in Crystal Reports 9

Crystal Reports (CR) 9 includes many extraordinary product enhancements from its earlier release, version 8.5, and could quite possibly represent the greatest single improvement of the Crystal Reports application from one release to another. Table 1.1 outlines the key enhancements by feature value and provides a brief introduction to each feature.

The specifics of each feature will be addressed throughout the topics of the book, as they are related to the appropriate hours.

TABLE 1.1   A Quick Reference of the New or Enhanced Features Within Crystal Reports 9

Feature Value	Feature Name	Feature Description
Productivity	Report Component Repository	A central library of report components that report designers can share among all reports within the report design process. These components include text objects, images, custom functions, and commands. A sample repository, including prebuilt functions and objects, is provided with the CR 9 release.
Productivity	Report Parts and Navigation Improvements	Report parts provide a mechanism to deliver report content to wireless devices and integrate content into Web applications, portals and Office XP. Select pieces of information (parts) in a report can now be delivered to the specific device required by business users—report information is no longer bound to the page view. Report parts can interact with the parent report or other report parts via links. Enhanced navigation within and between reports allows for linking between report objects (parts) .
Productivity	Custom Functions	Custom functions permit report designers to define their own functions that can be used and shared between multiple reports. Custom functions are mapped to data fields to create formulas in reports, and these functions can then be stored within a Report Component Repository.

TABLE 1.1   continued

Feature Value	Feature Name	Feature Description
Productivity	Unicode Support	A feature to support International standards to save time and space for required code, and includes the ability to run reports created in any language version of the product on any language version operating system. All International languages are represented in one 16-bit character set, and the previous 254-byte character limit has been removed.
Productivity	Wireless Report Viewing	CR 9 now offers three new wireless viewers: WML, simple HTML 3.0, and Pocket PC. These viewers will support the HTML, cHTML (compact-HTML), IPAQ, Windows CE, WML, and Palm OS languages.
Productivity	Query and Database Engine Re-architecture	Improved SQL (Structured Query Language code) generation from the graphic design interface, capability to create and add queries from inside the designer, support for additional database join types, new database connectivity options, and an improved user interface.
Usability	Formula Enhancements	New formula workshop user interface, improved error tracking, and auto-complete formula creation feature.
Usability	General Usability Enhancements	New object-oriented report and repository Explorers, new and improved report wizards and experts, custom templates, Microsoft Excel financial functions, application menu and toolbar improvements, and the capability to lock objects and set read-only properties.

TABLE 1.1   continued

Feature Value	Feature Name	Feature Description
Usability	Charting and Cross Tab Enhancements	New chart types (Gantt and Gauge), formatting improvements for date/time and numeric x-axis values. Cross Tab support for running totals, vertical and horizontal summary display, percent summaries, Top N, suppression of rows, and relative position within a section.
Usability	OLAP Reporting Enhancements	Increased support for OLAP data sources, new OLAP worksheet, filter and page dimension parameters, and a drill-down feature in report preview view.
Usability	Interactive Report Viewing	Zero-client report viewing for the report consumer. Advanced searching, navigation, and enhanced exporting. While viewing reports, business users can perform Boolean searches and link to the parent report from search results, zoom and highlight, and export reports to Microsoft Word and Excel formats as well as directly to email.
Power and Flexibility	Exporting Enhancements	New Excel and HTML exporting, improved support for RTF and PDF formats, and improved support for exporting images and charts.
Power and Flexibility	Report Application Server	New functionality that enables report consumers to interactively view reports. This includes improved control over x/y object placement, full section formatting, view-time security, and support for alerting and consolidation reporting.

TABLE 1.1 continued

Feature Value	Feature Name	Feature Description
Power and Flexibility	Java, COM and .NET Application Interfaces	Separate object models are provided to support Java, COM, and .NET development environments. These interfaces are focused on providing application programmers with tools to integrate reporting into custom applications created in the Java, COM, or .NET environments.

Summary

You should now understand the value of Crystal Reports as a design application for creating powerful and compelling reports that transform data, from virtually any data source, into meaningful information. Crystal Reports is used by hundreds of thousands of business users and application developers to service a wide array of reporting demands. Crystal Reports is widely accepted as the de facto reporting application in the market and can complement any corporate business and technology environment that requires reporting—from custom applications to mainframe reports, ASCII files, and so on—to maximize the investment that organizations make in their corporate Information Technology systems.

The proliferation of Crystal Reports is in large part because of its intuitive design environment that enables beginners to create simple reports, as well as empowering more experienced users to design sophisticated reports to satisfy more complex requirements. This hour has introduced the concepts of report design and the components of Crystal Reports that aid in planning and creating reports. The latest release of Crystal Reports, already considered to be the world standard for reporting, now offers even greater productivity, usability, power, and flexibility for report designers to deliver information. Whether you are creating reports for yourself or supporting an entire organization's information demands, Crystal Reports can service your report design requirements. We will now move into how you can get started using the Crystal Reports application in the next hour, "Getting Started with Crystal Reports 9."

Workshop

Here's a brief quiz to help you review this hour's terminology.

Quiz

1. What is the advantage in standardizing on one tool for all organizational reporting needs?

2. What is content creation?

3. What is the new Report Component Repository in Crystal Reports 9?

Quiz Answers

1. Most organizations want one common reporting solution that is able to work with all their data sources and support a broad base of audience-specific reporting requirements. This in turn facilitates the attainment of a consistent skill set across the organization. Crystal Reports is the most mature and widely accepted reporting application in the market. It supports virtually all data sources, can merge data of differing sources together, and offers advanced technological features that are compatible and forward thinking to support other technological and industry standards (XML, COM, and Java, for example). It is also a solution that is easy to administer and manage after it is deployed.

2. Content creation is the process of report creation. This includes stating the report objective, identifying the required information for a report, accessing the appropriate data source(s), incorporating the necessary data fields and elements, constructing any required elements (such as formulas and calculations), and formatting the report for presentation purposes.

3. The report component repository is a central object-oriented library of report components (often called *objects*) that report designers can reuse and share between reports when creating report content. These components include text objects, bitmaps, custom functions, and commands. A sample repository database is also provided with Crystal Reports 9.

HOUR 2

Getting Started with Crystal Reports 9

Building on the discussion of Crystal Reports as a content creation application for designing interactive, actionable reports, it's now time to install and explore the Crystal Reports designer application. The installation of Crystal Reports is a very straightforward process, making installation simple for even novice users with limited technical experience. The Crystal Reports Installation Wizard presents various options throughout the installation process that will affect the function of the designer. This hour covers the planning considerations prior to the installation of Crystal Reports, options available during the install, and minimum systems requirements necessary to run Crystal Reports 9.0.

As an introduction to the Crystal Reports designer, this hour also provides a high-level review of the more important and immediately useful components within the Crystal Reports application. Although brief, this introduction to the Crystal Reports design environment will prepare you for the subsequent hours and activities you will complete throughout the book.

In this hour, we will cover the following topics:

- Preparing for the installation of Crystal Reports
- Installation and configuration of Crystal Reports
- Introduction to standard report features such as report sections, toolbars, and menus

> If you are unfamiliar with the Crystal Reports application, you will want to closely review the section in this hour covering report sections because this topic is central to understanding how to build and format Crystal Reports.

Preparing for the Installation

In general, there are two communities of Crystal Reports users within most organizations: report designers and report *consumers*. The report designer group is usually smaller in number. These individuals are focused on creating the actual report content, whereas the report consumer group consists of the end organizational audience viewing the reports. Thus, these are distinctively different roles, with the smaller group of designers supporting the greater group of viewers. Although this book is focused more on providing the report designers with the information and skills required to create reports, it is also very important to consider the needs of the report consumer group and how they will be using the end reports.

Depending on your situation, you might be one of a number of Crystal Report designers within a large organization or an individual report designer in a small company. In any case, Crystal Reports is a graphical report design application that needs to be installed locally on your workstation in order to create reports. If you're a member of a large organization, you might have a supporting Information Technology group who will perform the installation of Crystal Reports for you. Regardless, Crystal Reports can be installed on a local PC residing on a corporate network in very much the same manner as a home PC or workstation. In this aspect, installing Crystal Reports is much like installing other popular PC applications, such as Microsoft's Word and Excel, your preferred Web browser, and Adobe's Acrobat Reader.

The consumers of information and reports created by Crystal Reports includes a wide range of individuals and corporate professionals. For example, common users of Crystal Reports include corporate business personnel in departments such as finance, human resources, and sales for operational reporting purposes, organizational performance measurement, and sales analysis. In addition to the business community demands, IT groups often have specific development requirements to embed reporting capabilities into custom applications and corporate Web pages. Not only do corporate personnel use Crystal Reports, but it is also a highly used application for individuals who require an easy-to-use and intuitive tool for creating attractive and meaningful reports.

> I assume that you will need to perform the installation of Crystal Reports yourself, so you will be guided through the installation process in this hour.

During the report design phase, it is common for reports to be processed on the report designer's local workstation, which in turn requires resources on the local workstation. Before installing Crystal Reports on your local PC, you should verify and properly configure certain system settings, such as

- At least 64MB of RAM is installed. You can locate your system RAM amount on the General tab within the Windows System Properties dialog (located at Start, Settings, Control Panel, System).

- At least 300MB of hard disk space is available. To locate your available disk space, open Windows Explorer, right-click on the appropriate drive letter (for example, C:), and select Properties from the pop-up window.

- Windows system virtual memory should equal the amount of physical RAM on the local PC, plus 11MB. For example, reports that perform substantial aggregation, grouping, or calculating of data will use more operating system resources. This is simply a general recommendation that helps ensure that your personal workstation will have adequate resources available.

> *Virtual memory* is the amount of space, in kilobytes, committed to memory for any process running on the workstation. Crystal Reports requires the use of such operating system resources, and it's important that enough virtual memory is available to support the processing of reports that are run locally on the report designer's workstation.

- Confirm that the Temp variable and directory is set up on your Windows system—the Temp variable is a system environment variable that specifies the location where programs place temporary files. The Temp variable can be configured within the System Properties dialog (located at Start, Settings, Control Panel, System) and by selecting the Environment Variables button on the Advanced tab, as shown in Figure 2.1.

- Before installing Crystal Reports, it is important to consider which data sources you will need to access. Based on what data sources you will need to access during the report creation process, you might then want to install various components from the available database connectivity options that are packaged within the Crystal Reports installation. For more details on these database connectivity options, see Hour 3, "Accessing Your Data."

FIGURE 2.1

The Windows 2000 system settings.

Reviewing the System Requirements for Crystal Reports 9

As with previous releases, multiple editions of the Crystal Reports 9 application are available from Crystal Decisions. Specifically, there are four distinct editions of Crystal Reports 9:

- Standard
- Professional
- Developer
- Advanced

The Advanced Edition is new to the version 9 release of Crystal Reports. This edition primarily includes additional server software licensing. The only feature difference in addition to what the Developer Edition provides is that the COM and Java data connectivity drivers are only available in the Advanced edition. The Advanced Edition provides components for embedding dynamic content from custom, legacy, and enterprise data sources into wireless and Web applications for zero-client, end-user report interaction.

Nearly all of the exercises in this book can be completed using any of these editions. However, the developer-focused exercises covered in the later hours might require either the Developer or Advanced Editions—though these topics can still be reviewed and include valuable information on advanced report design concepts. The edition that best serves your needs is dependent on your specific reporting and technical requirements. For example, for users who only need to access data sources to create simple reports via the Crystal Reports designer, the Standard or Professional editions will most likely meet their requirements. However, report designers or application developers who require the added ability to embed reporting functionality within custom applications (such as applications created with the Visual Basic, .NET, and Java programming languages) will require either the Developer or Advanced Editions of Crystal Reports.

> The Developer and Advanced Editions of Crystal Reports include additional components to assist application developers with embedding reporting capabilities into custom applications. For example, developers who create custom Java applications can benefit from the *Java Software Developer Kit (SDK)*, which will aid them with embedding reporting functionality directly within their applications. Separate SDKs are provided to specifically support the three most common development environments—Java, .NET, and COM.

The key minimum system requirements are necessary to ensure that the Crystal Reports application has sufficient local resources available on the report designer's workstation. Regardless of which edition of Crystal Reports 9 you will be installing, the minimum system requirements for a local workstation installation (from CD-ROM) are as follows:

- Microsoft Windows 98 (Second Edition), ME, NT 4.0, 2000 and XP. (Note: Windows 95 is no longer supported for the version 9 release of Crystal Reports.)
- Minimum of 32MB RAM (64MB required for Windows NT). 64MB RAM is recommended for all operating systems.
- Minimum 60MB of hard drive space. Approximately 200MB maximum for English and up to 400MB for other languages.
- An additional 100 MB of free disk space is also recommended on your C: drive for use by Windows during the installation.
- Pentium or higher system processor required.
- CD-ROM drive.

If you plan to perform a network installation of Crystal Reports 9, the preceding minimum requirements should be adjusted as follows:

- Typical hard drive space required on a network server: 217MB
- Typical hard drive space required on a workstation: 105MB

The Crystal Reports 9 design application does not support the Macintosh operating system. Viewing shared reports through a Web browser is possible on multiple platforms, including Windows, Unix, and Macintosh.

The ReleaseNotes.doc file, located in the root directory of the Crystal Reports 9 CD, includes a listing of all known issues and other important notes that users should be aware of before installing Crystal Reports 9. It is recommended that users read this document before installing Crystal Reports 9.

Installation and Configuration of Crystal Reports

When you insert the Crystal Reports 9 CD into the CD-ROM drive of the workstation, the autostart program should present the Crystal Reports splash screen, as shown in Figure 2.2. From the lower-right corner of the splash screen, select the Install Crystal Reports option. You should now see the Crystal Reports Setup Wizard and the Welcome screen, as shown in Figure 2.3.

FIGURE 2.2

The Crystal Reports 9 splash screen presented via the autostart program on the CD-ROM.

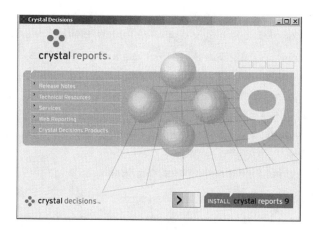

FIGURE 2.3

The Welcome dialog screen within the Crystal Reports Setup Wizard.

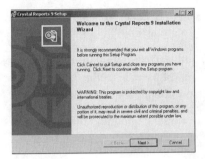

If the splash screen does not automatically appear after inserting the CD-ROM, navigate to the root of the CD-ROM to locate the setup.exe file. Double-click on this file to launch the Crystal Reports Installation Wizard.

From the introductory splash screen, you can learn more about the Crystal Reports 9 application by selecting to view the Crystal Reports 9 release notes, technical resources, services overview (technical support, training, and consulting), Web Reporting resources, or the Crystal Decisions product overview. These informational sources are intended to provide you with additional details around the Crystal Reports technologies and related resources available to you.

New for Crystal Reports 9 is the use of an *install-on-demand* technology for some of the application's components. Install on demand means that certain Crystal Reports components are only installed when needed. As a result, there might be a short delay for the install-on-demand features to load upon the first use of a respective component after the installation. However, this delay will only occur once for each of the features for new installations of the software.

Typical Installation Type

Regardless of which installation type (Typical, or Custom) you want to perform, the initial default installation process leads to the Setup Installation Type Options screen (see Figure 2.4). From the Welcome screen, follow these brief steps:

1. Select Next from the Welcome screen.

2. Read the license agreement and select Next if you agree with the terms of this agreement.

3. Enter an authorized product key code, located on the back of the Crystal Reports CD-ROM disc jacket, and select Next.

At this point, the Select Installation Type screen appears. The Typical installation type is most appropriate for the majority of users installing Crystal Reports. The Typical installation option will install the most commonly used components of Crystal Reports, such as

- Support for various export formats
- A collection of sample reports
- Data connectivity components for frequently accessed data sources, such as Microsoft Access and SQL Server

Within this screen, you can also specify the desired installation directory path for the application's program files to be installed on the local workstation. However, it is strongly recommended that you accept the default directory structure—C:\Program Files\Crystal Decisions\Crystal Reports 9\.

FIGURE 2.4

Two Installation Types are available: Typical and Custom.

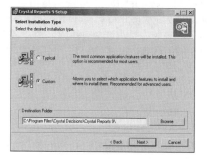

Even if the default directory path is modified, the installation program will still install approximately 70MB of files into the default directory location, consisting mostly of necessary program *.DLL (Dynamic Link Library)* files.

If you have selected to perform the Typical installation type, you will then be presented with the Start Installation screen. Selecting Next at this screen will begin the actual installation of Crystal Reports. After the installation of Crystal Reports is complete, you will be asked to register the product. By following the wizard to register your installation, the entire installation process of Crystal Reports is complete. You have now successfully installed Crystal Reports 9.

The Registration Wizard will create your user profile, which will ensure that you then receive access to important updates and support, including technical support topics, enrollment in Crystal Decision's online user community, online documentation, online tutorials, free samples, and product updates.

For further information on the specific application component options, refer to the later section on the Custom installation type. If you have now completed your installation and you are not interested in reviewing the Custom installation options, you can skip ahead to the section "Preparing to Access Your Data."

Ensuring that adequate hard drive space is available on the local workstation is perhaps the most common problem that individuals installing Crystal Reports experience during the Typical and Complete installation processes.

Custom Installation Type

The Custom installation type is most suitable for individuals who want to explicitly ensure which application components will be installed on their personal workstation, such as report designers who might have specific data access requirements, or if you would like to quickly install all the available application components. For example, the Crystal Reports 9 Installation Wizard does not install the Geographic Mapping and Custom Charting components as part of the Typical installation option, and you might want to add these components to support particular reporting needs.

From the Crystal Reports Welcome screen, follow the same steps as outlined earlier for the Typical installation type:

1. Select Next from the Welcome screen.

2. Read the license agreement and select Next if you agree with the terms of this agreement.

3. Enter an authorized product key code, located on the back of the Crystal Reports CD-ROM disc jacket, and select Next.

At the Select Installation Type screen (see Figure 2.4), select the Custom option from the installation type list. By choosing to perform a Custom installation, you will be identifying which specific product components you want to install on your local workstation. A list of the Crystal Reports product components is presented in the Select Features dialog screen, shown in Figure 2.5.

FIGURE 2.5

The Select Features screen provides a list of available product components.

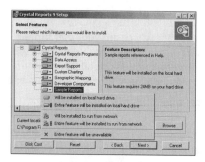

You can further specify the manner in which each of the listed components will be installed on to your local PC by selecting from up to six installation alternatives. These alternatives include

- Will be installed on local hard drive
- Entire feature will be installed on local hard drive
- Will be installed to run from CD
- Entire feature will be installed to run from CD
- Feature will be installed when required
- Entire feature will be unavailable

As Figure 2.5 displays, by selecting the Sample Reports item from the component list you will then be presented with a fly-out list of installation alternatives for this component.

For example, if you want to make use of the entire collection of Crystal Reports sample report files but do not want to occupy additional hard drive space on your local PC, click on Sample Reports within the feature list and select the Entire Feature Will Be Installed to Run from CD option. In doing so, you will need the Crystal Reports CD-ROM available to access the entire sample report collection when it is required.

The fifth of the six preceding options, "Feature will be installed when required," is convenient when you want to avoid the unnecessary consumption of hard drive space; yet it provides for the component to be available when it is required for use by Crystal Reports, while simultaneously eliminating the need to use the CD-ROM to access the material. An icon consisting of a small yellow number 1 denotes this option.

Even though the Select Features screen allows you to choose the desired installation directory path for the application's program files to be installed on your local workstation, it is recommended that you accept the default directory structure for your Crystal Reports installation. Even if the default directory path is modified, the installation program will still install approximately 70MB of files into the default directory location, consisting mostly of necessary program .DLL files.

During the installation process, you can quickly evaluate the amount of local disk space required for the product components that you have selected to install by selecting the Disk Cost button in the lower-left of the Select Features screen. An example of the Disk Cost screen is shown in Figure 2.6. The Disk Cost screen will provide a warning if the hard drive containing the chosen directory path has insufficient space available.

FIGURE 2.6

The Disk Cost screen permits you to evaluate the amount of local disk space required for the product components that you have selected to install.

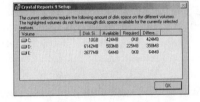

You can reset the selection of available application components to their default settings by selecting the Reset button within the Select Features screen at any time. This resets everything to their default status at the initial screen.

After you are satisfied with the chosen application component options, select Next to proceed to the Start Installation screen. By selecting Next from the Start Installation screen, you will then begin the actual installation of the application files on to your local workstation.

Preparing to Access Your Data

Now that you have successfully installed Crystal Reports, it can be used to access data for report creation. A major challenge that many organizations face when attempting to access and retrieve data from corporate data sources is selecting the best connectivity option for each particular source among a collection of disparate data sources.

Crystal Reports provides a wide variety of data connectivity options designed to provide you with the best mechanisms that support the retrieval of data from an array of distinct data sources. You still need to determine the most efficient way to access your specific data sources for each report that you will be creating. Establishing a strategy for connecting to your data and evaluating your connectivity options for each report is of paramount importance, and both can have a significant impact on the performance of your reports.

Crystal Reports provides an array of connectivity options that support virtually any data source environment, including relational, flat-file, and multi-dimensional (that is, OLAP—Online Analytical Processing) data sources. Crystal Reports also supports the use of database-specific client software, such as Oracle's SQL Client application, that are designed to be used when accessing the respective vendors' database environment. Additional data access information is covered in Hour 3.

> If appropriate, any necessary database client software should be installed and configured prior to installing Crystal Reports. However, if you've installed Crystal Reports before installing the database vendor's client software, follow the directions located in the Crystal Reports Help files to ensure correct configuration of the Crystal Reports system *Data Source Names (DSN)*.

When designing reports, you will be presented with data connectivity options at the start of the report design process. Selecting the connectivity option that best meets the business and technical requirements for your reports is an important consideration.

Locating the Crystal Reports Application

After Crystal Reports is installed, you can locate the installed programs by navigating to the Start, Programs, Crystal Reports 9 Tools listing. Depending on what options were selected during the installation process, this program listing might vary. Regardless of the exact selections, the Crystal Reports designer application will be accessible from this listing.

The specific applications available under the Crystal Reports 9 Tools listing will depend on what application components you choose to install during the installation process. These could include the Crystal Registration Wizard, Crystal Reports License, Crystal Dictionary, and Crystal SQL Designer applications. The Crystal Reports License application is a very simple program used solely for managing Crystal Reports licenses. The Crystal Dictionary and the Crystal SQL Designer are no longer included as part of the product installation with Crystal Reports 9. However, these components can be installed separately from the Crystal Reports 9 CD.

Both the Crystal Dictionary and Crystal SQL Designer programs extend the Crystal Reports application to add additional value in the event that you need to employ the use of a file-based metadata layer (Crystal Dictionaries) or SQL queries to serve as report data sources rather than accessing database systems directly. Additional details on Crystal Dictionaries and the SQL Designer can be found in the Crystal Reports Help files.

Introduction to the Crystal Reports Designer

Now that you have successfully installed Crystal Reports, it is time to open the application and familiarize yourself with the design environment. This section briefly introduces you to the following components of the application interface:

- Report sections
- Application toolbars
- Application menus

Although creating a useful Crystal Report is not a difficult task, we will defer actually building a report with data until Hour 4, "Using the Default Report Wizards."

Upon first opening the application, you might be required to register your installation if you did not do so during the installation process. Complete this task if necessary.

Assuming that you have already registered your installation, you should first be presented with the Welcome to Crystal Reports screen, as shown in Figure 2.7. This screen provides quick access to existing Crystal Reports files while also allowing you to begin designing new reports via the Report Expert Wizard or from a blank report template. In order to provide a quick introduction to the layout of the design application, the remainder of this hour is focused on selecting the As a Blank Report option from the Welcome screen.

Learning About Report Sections

From the Welcome dialog window, select Using the Report Wizard item (listed under Create a New Crystal Report Document) and then click OK. You should now see the Crystal Report Gallery dialog —select As a Blank Report and click OK. At this point, you'll see a window labeled Data Explorer—click Cancel. If the Field Explorer window is also displayed, click Close.

FIGURE 2.7

The Welcome screen provides quick access to existing Crystal Reports files as well as the Report Expert Wizard.

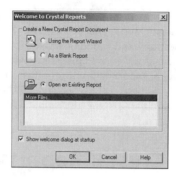

You are presented with a blank report template that is divided into numerous report sections. As Figure 2.8 illustrates, report sections are identified by name on the left side of the design area. These sections segment the Crystal Reports design environment, and hence a report, into logical areas to facilitate more intuitive report creation, including the Report Header, Page Header, Details, Report Footer, and Page Footer sections. Each of the various sections has unique properties and printing characteristics that you can modify. When creating reports, you will place objects, such as a corporate logo image or data field, into various sections and organize the objects based on your report design requirements. If a report object, such as an image, is placed in the Report Header section, the image will display and print only once per report, on the first page. If the same image is placed in the Page Header section, the image will then display and print once per page. The same holds true for custom sections, such as Group Headers and Group Footers. The Details section implies that whatever is placed in this section will display and print once for each and every row retrieved from the data source.

FIGURE 2.8

Report sections provide for an intuitive way to create and organize your data when designing reports.

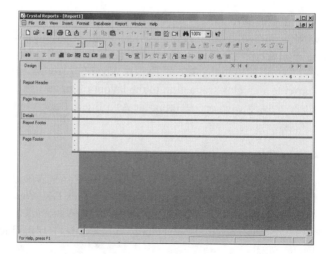

Although Crystal Reports is commonly used for Web reporting initiatives, the design environment is built on a paper metaphor with *pages* as a concept to facilitate the presentation of information.

Report sections can contain a variety of different object types, including database field, text, picture, chart, and map objects. Additional objects, such as formula and sub-report objects, are also positioned within report sections and will be covered later in the book in greater detail.

The Section Expert is used to view or modify the properties of the report sections. To access the Section Expert, perform one of the following actions:

- Right-click on the section's label (or name, located on the left sidebar) you want to work with, and then select Section Expert from the pop-up menu.
- Click on the Section Expert button.
- Select the Section Expert option from the Format menu.

When designing reports, you should consider the following items when working with report sections:

- It is good practice to print a test page of each report you are designing.
- Consider keeping all font sizes the same within each section.
- Print preprinted forms on the same machine to avoid discrepancies in the interpretation of the report layout by different print drivers and printers.

Crystal Reports also provides for some more advanced section formatting options, reviewed later in the book, such as underlaying and suppressing sections based on certain criteria (formulas). These features are accessible from the Section Expert dialog.

Using Toolbars and Menus

Toolbars are the graphical icon bars at the top of the Crystal Reports application environment, containing various buttons that you can click to activate the most frequently used application commands. Toolbars act as shortcuts to access commonly needed functions of the design application, and they can be enabled and disabled to appear at the top of the application area by selecting Toolbars from the View menu, which is located in the upper-most area of the application. As Figure 2.9 shows, there are four main toolbars that you can use within the Crystal Reports design environment:

- Standard—The most commonly used application functions, including New, Open, Save, Print, Preview, Export, Copy, Cut, Paste, and Help.

- Formatting—Functions that pertain specifically to modifying object properties with regard to Font, Font Size, Bold, Italics, Underline, Alignment, Currency, and Percentage formats.

- Insert Tools— Quick access to report-enhancing and advanced features. The items found on this toolbar are consistent with the commands listed under the Insert menu.

- Expert Tools—Functions that allow you to quickly access the main application experts, such as the Database, Group, Select, Section, Formula Workshop, and Highlighting Experts.

FIGURE 2.9

The Toolbars dialog provides for an intuitive way to enable quick and easy access to commonly used application commands during report design.

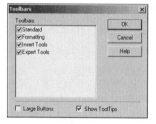

ToolTips are pop-up descriptions that appear when your cursor rests over any of the toolbar buttons. To view ToolTips on your toolbars, select the Show ToolTips check box from within the Toolbars dialog. ToolTips are enabled by default.

In much the same way that the toolbars offer quick and easy access to commonly used commands, the Menu items at the top of the application environment provide listings to virtually all the application functions available in Crystal Reports. The Menu items act as shortcuts to all the commands within the design application, and they include the following items:

- File menu—The File menu includes file-specific commands to create a new report file, open an existing report, close a current report, save a report, save a report as an alternative filename, export to a different file format, save the current data set with a report, and secure a report so that it cannot be opened by other users. In addition, the File menu contains commands that enable you to preview a report before printing, send a report to a printer, select a specific printer, modify the page setup and margins, and add summary information to a report.

- Edit menu—The Edit menu includes commands used to modify various aspects of a report, including commands to undo and redo actions, as well as to cut, copy, and paste report and OLE objects. Additionally, you can edit fields, formulas, summaries, and sub-report links.

> *Object Linking and Embedding (OLE)* enables you to insert objects (OLE objects) into a report from other applications and then use those applications from within Crystal Reports to edit the objects if necessary. If Crystal Reports did not make use of OLE, you would have to exit Crystal Reports, open the original application, change the object, return to Crystal Reports, delete the object originally inserted, and then insert the newly revised object.

- View menu—The View menu includes commands used to customize the user interface of the Crystal Reports application. The View menu commands enable you to navigate between the application's Design and Preview views, access the three main explorers (Field, Report and Repository Explorers), access the Toolbars dialog, zoom in and zoom out of a report, as well as to turn on and off the application rulers, guidelines, grids, and group tree from both the Design and Preview views of the report.

- Insert menu—The Insert menu includes commands used to insert text objects, summaries (counts, sums, medians, and so on), groups, sub-reports, lines, boxes, pictures, charts, maps, and other objects into your report. The Insert menu becomes very convenient when designing reports that will include a variety of objects, such as a corporate logo and summary figures.

- Format menu—The Format menu provides easy access to a variety of commands useful in formatting your reports for presentation purposes. This menu includes commands used to change the characteristics of the objects in a report. The Format menu provides quick access to commands for modifying font properties (color, size, borders, background color, and drop shadows for example), chart and hyperlink properties, and formatting for entire sections of the report. The Format menu also provides commands to arrange report objects (move, align, and size) and to specify desired highlighting characteristics via the Highlighting Expert.

- Database menu—The Database menu includes commands used to access the Database Expert: from which you can add and remove data source tables for use within reports, specify links between data source tables, and modify table and field alias names. This menu also provides easy access to the set database location, log on and off SQL and ODBC servers, browse field data, and display and edit the report SQL syntax. In general, the Database menu allows you to maintain the necessary specifications for the report with regard to the data source(s) the report interacts with.

- Report menu—The Report menu includes commands used to access the main application Experts (also referred to as *wizards*), identify the desired records or groups to be included in a report via the Select Expert and Selection Formulas (often referred to as applying reports *filters*), construct and edit formulas, create and view alerts, specify report bursting indexes, modify grouping and sorting specifications, refresh report data by executing the query to run against the database, and view report performance information.

- Chart menu—The Chart menu is only visible after selecting a chart or map object and includes specific commands used to customize your charts and maps. Depending on the type of chart you select, the Chart menu includes commands to zoom in and out of charts; apply changes to all instances of a chart; discard custom changes made to the chart; save the chart template to a file; apply and modify template specifications for the chart; change the titles, numeric axis grids, and scales of the chart; and auto-arrange the appearance of the chart. After selecting a map object, the Chart menu then includes additional commands used to configure the overall style of the map, reorganizing the layers of report elements, changing the geographic map, and hiding or showing the Map Navigator.

- Window menu—The Window menu includes commands used to rearrange the application icons and windows, as well as providing a list of report windows that are currently open and a command that allows you to close all report windows at once.

- Help menu—The Help menu includes commands used to quickly access the Crystal Reports online help references, commands to register Crystal Reports and locate the Welcome screen, and quick access to the About Crystal Reports dialog and several key Crystal Decisions Web sites for technical support and product information.

Many application commands that are available from the Toolbars options can also be located from one of the menus. In these cases, the respective icon for these commands is presented within the Menu listing to the left of the command name, indicating that it can also be found on one of the application Toolbars.

Summary

In this hour, you have installed Crystal Reports and started exploring the core concepts of creating reports at a very high level. The installation of Crystal Reports is a very straightforward process after you have reviewed the appropriate system requirements and identified which edition of the product you will be using. The introduction to the design environment presented you with several of the more important components of the application—report sections, toolbars and menus—and should have educated you on how the design environment is structured. Of particular importance, you will need to understand report sections in order to proceed through the book and perform virtually every forthcoming activity. Based on the material covered in this hour, you are now ready to move ahead and begin using the Crystal Reports application.

Workshop

Here's a brief quiz to help you review this hour's terminology, as well as activities for you to try on your own.

Quiz

1. What is virtual memory?
2. What is the recommended amount of virtual memory on your local system to install and run Crystal Reports?
3. Where can you locate your local system's Temp variable configuration settings?

Quiz Answers

1. Virtual memory is the amount of space, in kilobytes, committed to memory for any process running on the workstation. Crystal Reports requires the use of such operating system resources, and it's important that enough virtual memory is available to support the processing of reports that are run locally on the report designer's workstation.

2. The recommended size for the system's virtual memory is equal to the amount of physical RAM on the machine plus 11MB.

3. To confirm that the Temp variable and directory is set up appropriately on your Windows system, you can locate the Temp variable settings within the System Properties dialog. Navigate to Start, Settings, Control Panel, System, and select the Environment Variables icon on the Advanced tab.

Activities

To further introduce report sections, open the Crystal Reports application and select Open from the File menu. Within the Open dialog, navigate to the following directory path and open the Inventory report that is installed with the Crystal Reports Samples:

```
C:\Program Files\Crystal Decisions\Crystal Reports
9\Samples\En\Reports\General Business
```

After you have opened the Inventory report, click the Design tab. Notice all the various report sections required to create this report. Each section contains specific objects, such as a corporate logo, product picture and numerous database fields (product description, product ID, and units in stock) necessary to achieve the desired report structure and format. If desired, right-click on any of the section listings on the left side of the design view. Various options are available from the resulting pop-up menu—one of which is the Selection Expert item as discussed earlier in this hour. Select this option to open the Selection Expert dialog. At this point, you can explore the section properties.

After you have explored this report and feel that you have a basic understanding of report sections, close the report without saving any changes you might have made.

HOUR 3

Accessing Your Data

The first step in creating a report is always to identify a data source. Although much of the complexity of the database and the interaction with it is hidden by Crystal Reports, effective report developers will understand their data and how to bring it into Crystal Reports.

In this hour, we will discuss the following topics:

- Types of Data Sources
- Introduction to the Data Explorer
- Database Objects
- Linking

Understanding the Different Types of Data Sources

Crystal Reports was originally designed as an add-on reporting package for an accounting program. However, it was its expansion into the world of mainstream data sources that led to its current popularity. Today, Crystal Reports supports more than one hundred different types of data sources. Some of these data sources are what would be considered traditional databases such as Microsoft SQL Server, Oracle, IBM DB2, and Microsoft Access. Other Crystal Reports data sources are more abstract forms of data such as log files, email, XML, and multidimensional (OLAP) data.

In order for Crystal Reports to support such a multitude of data sources while preserving a consistent user experience, the support for each data source is provided via a *database driver*. The role of a database driver is to act as a gateway between Crystal Reports and a specific type of database or data access technology. These database drivers have a *pluggable* architecture, meaning that each has the same type of user interface and functionality. When creating the report, one or more drivers are selected, along with the location of the actual data. When the report is executed and it comes time to load data from the database to the report, the driver performs the actual query.

To determine which database driver to use to connect to a certain data source, it's best to understand the different types of database drivers. The following sections discuss direct and indirect access database drivers.

Direct Access Drivers

Direct access database drivers are built solely for reporting from a specific type of database such as Oracle. If a direct access driver (sometimes called a *native* driver) exists for the database that you intend to report from, it is generally the best choice. Although they follow the standard model of a database driver, direct access drivers are tailored for that specific database. For example, if you choose the Microsoft Access direct access driver during the creation of a report, you will be prompted for the filename of the Access MDB file. Whereas if you are using the Oracle direct access driver, you will be prompted for a server name. Not only is the user experience more specific to that database, a direct access driver will often result in better performance than other methods of connecting to the same data. Table 3.1 lists some of the most common direct access database drivers.

TABLE 3.1 Common Direct Access Database Drivers

Direct Access Driver	Description
Microsoft Access	Used to access Microsoft Access databases
Microsoft Excel	Used to access Microsoft Excel spreadsheets
Oracle	Used to access Oracle database servers
DB2	Used to access IBM DB2 database servers

Indirect Access Drivers

As you might guess from the name, an indirect access driver is one that connects indirectly to an actual data source. Indirect access drivers are not built for any one type of database, but rather are built to read data from a variety of data sources via a standard data access mechanism. The purpose of these drivers is to allow Crystal Reports to use data sources for which direct access drivers do not exist. The two major indirect access drivers provided are ODBC and OLE DB.

ODBC, which stands for Open Database Connectivity, is a long standing technology built to connect various applications to various data sources via a common mechanism called an ODBC driver. Just as Crystal Reports has a concept of database drivers that allow data access to report developers, ODBC has a concept of ODBC drivers that allow data access to any application. The Crystal Reports ODBC database driver communicates with an ODBC driver, which in turn communicates with the actual database. ODBC drivers are generally developed by the database vendors themselves and often come bundled with the database software. Crystal Reports comes with the following ODBC drivers developed by DataDirect Inc.: Oracle, Informix, Sybase, DB2, and XML.

OLE DB, pronounced "*OH-lay-dee-bee*," is the evolution of ODBC. Like ODBC, OLE DB has a concept of database drivers, but calls them OLE DB providers. Crystal Reports can read most OLE DB providers. Figure 3.1 illustrates the various ways to connect to your data.

FIGURE 3.1

Crystal Reports data access architecture.

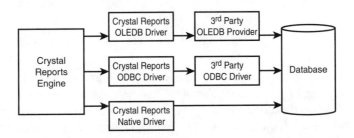

If appropriate, any necessary database client software should be installed and configured prior to installing Crystal Reports. However, if you've installed Crystal Reports before installing the database vendor's client software, follow the directions located in the Crystal Reports Help files to ensure correct configuration of the Crystal Reports system Data Source Names (DSN).

Introduction to the Data Explorer

Now that you've got a basic understanding of what database drivers are and an idea of which one you might use to access a particular data source, let's look at the user interface for specifying the data source of a report. Because this is the first step in the creation of a report, it is only natural that this is the first step in the Report Wizard. This is shown in Figure 3.2. The Data Explorer is a tree control hosted inside the Report Wizard that allows the report developer to identify the following things:

- Which Crystal Reports database driver you want to use
- Which data source you want you use
- Which database objects you want to use

FIGURE 3.2

The Data Explorer.

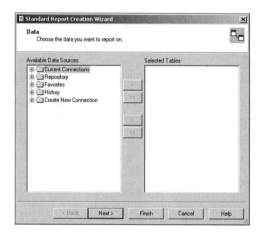

To bring up the Data Explorer, select File, New and click OK to create a new report using the Report Wizard. The Data Explorer represents data source connections organized into the following categories: Current Connections, Repository, Favorites, History, and Create New Connection. The following sections describe each of these categories, with the exception of the repository, which will be discussed later in the hour.

Create New Connection

To specify a new connection, expand the Create New Connection node in the Data Explorer. The following data sources correspond to the database drivers installed on the system. By default, the following drivers are preinstalled:

- Access/Excel (DAO)
- Crystal Queries

- Dictionary/Infoview
- ODBC (RDO)
- OLAP
- OLE DB (ADO)

If during the installation of Crystal Reports, a typical install was selected, you will notice a node for each of these drivers. There are also two additional nodes: Database Files and More Data Sources.

The Database Files node doesn't represent a specific database driver, but rather, when expanded, will allow you to select a variety of database files such as Access (.mdb), XML (.xml), and Universal Data Link files (.udl). This is simply a shortcut. Selecting an Access MDB file via the Database Files node is functionally equivalent to selecting it under the Access/Excel (DAO) node.

The other node of interest is More Data Sources. When this is expanded, it will list all database drivers that are available but not installed.

Crystal Reports 9 supports *install on-demand*. This means that various features will always appear as being available, even if they are not installed. When an *advertised* feature is selected, it will be installed and become available for use immediately.

When you expand one of the database drivers' nodes selections under the More Data Sources node, that driver would be installed on-demand. After this is done, the next time the Data Explorer is loaded, it would list that driver directly under the Create New Connection node.

Now that you understand what data sources are listed where, let's look at the process of creating a connection:

1. To create a connection, expand the node that corresponds to the appropriate database driver. An easy one to play with is the Xtreme sample database that comes with Crystal Reports 9. To create a connection to this database, expand the ODBC (RDO) node.

2. You will notice that when a node is expanded, a dialog is presented that allows for the specification of connection information. In the case of ODBC, the DSN is the only thing required. In this list of available DSNs, Xtreme Sample Database 9 should be visible. This is pre-installed with Crystal Reports. Select this and click Finish.

3. Focus will return to the Data Explorer, and there should be a node below the ODBC (RDO) node called Xtreme Sample Database. Below that node is the list of available tables and views, as well as the Add Command option for adding a SQL command. (This will be discussed shortly.)

The Xtreme Sample Database could also have been used via the OLE DB or direct Access driver. Note that when prompted for connection information when using one of these drivers, the report developer is asked to provide different information. In the case of ODBC, a DSN needed to be selected; whereas with OLE DB, a provider would need to be specified.

Current Connections

The Current Connection node lists all database connections that are currently open. In other words, if a report is currently open or was recently open, that connection will be listed under the Current Connections node. The first time the Crystal Reports designer is opened, the Current Connection node will be empty because no connections have been initiated. This will be indicated by a "...no items found..." item shown when the Current Connections node is expanded. This is a quick way to select the same connection as another report currently open.

Favorites

The Favorites node lists all connections that have been designated a favorite. This is analogous to favorites and bookmarks in a Web browser. If you have a certain database connection that is used often, adding it to the favorites will make it quick and easy to find in the future.

To accomplish this, create a connection to a database (you can use the Xtreme Sample Database to try this out), and select Add to Favorites when right-clicking on that connection. Be sure to right-click on the connection and not the driver or table name. Figure 3.3 illustrates the Xtreme Sample Database connection being added to a user's favorites.

History

Under the Favorites selection in the Data Explorer is the History node. It lists recent database connections that have been made. This is useful for quickly locating and using a connection that has been recently used, but not added to the Favorites list. The history list will store the last few connections. If you find yourself using connections from the History node frequently, it might be better to add the connection to your favorites list.

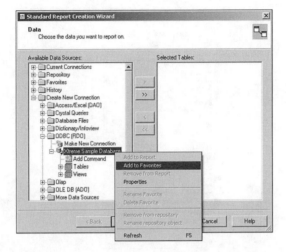

Adding Database Objects to Your Report

The term *database objects* is used to describe the various forms of data that can be added to a report. Specifically, Crystal Reports can use the following types of database objects as data sources for a report:

- Tables
- Views
- Stored procedures
- SQL Commands

Database objects are listed underneath connections in the Data Explorer and are grouped by object type. In Figure 3.4, the various database objects are shown for the Xtreme Sample Database. In this case, there are tables, views, and stored procedures. The Add Command node gives you the ability to add SQL Commands to this report.

The following sections describe each of these database object types in further detail.

Reporting Off Tables

Tables are the most basic form of a data structure. Although different vendors' databases have different concepts and terminologies, a table is pretty universal. Simply put, a table is a set of fields bound together to represent something in the real world. A Customer table might exist with fields that describe all the customers a given business has. An Employee table might exist that stores information about a corporation's employees such as name, title, or salary.

Figure 3.4

The Data Explorer
groups database
objects into categories.

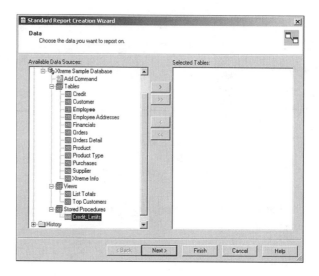

To add a table to a report, select the table in the Data Explorer and click the arrow (>)
button. The table is added to the Selected Tables list on the right side of the dialog below
its corresponding connection. Most database administrators will give the tables meaningful names; however, sometimes tables can have quite archaic names, such as
RM564_321. A name like this isn't very descriptive, so it would be useful to rename this
table to something more meaningful. This is accomplished by selecting the table in the
Selected Tables list and pressing the F2 button (F2 is a standard convention for renaming
things in Windows). In Crystal Reports, renaming a table is referred to as *aliasing* a
table.

Reporting Off Views

A *view* is a query stored by the database that returns a set of records that resemble a
table. Views often perform complex query logic, and good database administrators will
create them to simplify the job of people (like report developers) extracting data out of
the database. For example, the Top Customers view in the Xtreme Sample Database
returns all customers who have sales of more than $50,000. From a report developer's
perspective, views act just like tables and can be added to the report in the same way.

Reporting Off Stored Procedures

Stored procedures, in the context of Crystal Reports, are similar to views in that they are
predefined queries in the database and return a set of records. The major difference is
that a stored procedure can be parameterized. This means that rather than having a preset
query that will return the same data every time it is run, stored procedures will return
different data based on the values of parameters passed in.

Adding a stored procedure to a report works much the same way as tables and views. However, if the stored procedure has a parameter, a dialog will appear when attempting to add the stored procedure to the report. This is shown in Figure 3.5. The dialog will ask the report developer to provide values for each of the stored procedures' parameters. After this is completed and the OK button is clicked, focus returns to the Data Explorer and the stored procedure is shown in the list of selected tables. At this time, a parameter is created in the report that corresponds to the stored procedure parameter, and any values that parameter is given will be passed to the underlying stored procedure.

FIGURE 3.5

Adding a stored procedure with a parameter invokes the Enter Parameter Values dialog.

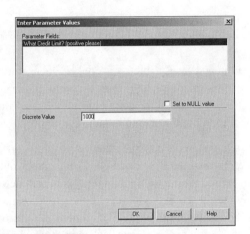

3

Reporting Off SQL Commands

When reporting from tables, views, and stored procedures, Crystal Reports generates a query behind the scenes using the *Structured Query Language (SQL)*. This is beneficial because the report developer does not need to understand the complexity of the SQL language, but rather can just drop fields on to the report and get data back that matches those fields. However, sometimes report developers are quite experienced with databases and specifically, the SQL language. Because of this, they sometimes prefer to write their own SQL query rather than have Crystal Reports generate it for them. To learn about the SQL language, refer to Hour 22.

SQL Commands are a new feature in Crystal Reports 9. They allow the report developer to use his own prebuilt SQL query and have the Crystal Reports engine treat the query like a *black box*. What this means is that any query, whether simple or very complex, that returns a set of records can be used as a data source for a Crystal Report. To create a SQL Command, select the Add Command item under the database connection, and then click the arrow (>) button. This initiates a dialog that allows the user to type in a SQL query. Figure 3.6 illustrates a typical query.

FIGURE 3.6

Adding a typical SQL Command to a report.

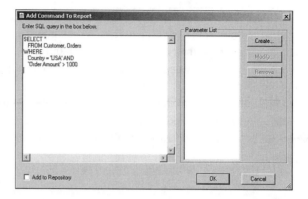

After the query is typed in and the OK button is clicked, focus returns to the Data Explorer and the newly created command is represented as 'Command' underneath its corresponding connection. As with all database objects, selecting the command and pressing the F2 button will allow the user to rename the object.

A key feature of SQL Commands is parameterization. If the report developer had to create a static SQL query, much of the power of SQL Commands would be lost. Fortunately, SQL Commands in Crystal Reports 9 support parameters. Although parameters can be used in any part of the SQL Command, the most common scenario would be to use a parameter in the WHERE clause of the SQL statement to restrict the records returned from the query. To create a parameter, when in the Add Command to Report dialog, click the Create button. This initiates a dialog that allows the user to specify a name for the parameter, text to use when prompting for the parameter value, a data type, and a default value. After the OK button is clicked, the parameter will appear in the Parameter list. To use this parameter, place the cursor where the parameter should be used in the SQL query, and double-click the parameter name. Figure 3.7 illustrates a simple SQL Command with a parameter.

FIGURE 3.7

Using a parameter in a SQL Command.

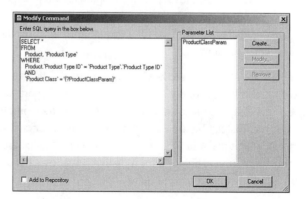

When a SQL Command is created with a parameter, the report developer will be prompted for a parameter value. This works much the same way as parameterized stored procedures in that a parameter will automatically be created in the report that will map to the SQL Command parameter.

Adding SQL Commands to the Repository

You might have noticed that there is an Add to Repository check box on the Add Command to Report dialog. The repository is a new feature of Crystal Reports 9. It will be discussed in detail in a later hour, but a brief description follows.

The *repository* is a central database that holds various elements of reports. Its purpose is two-fold: reuse and maintenance. When an element is published to the repository, it can then be reused across reports. Then when that element is modified, all reports using that element can be easily updated. In the context of the Data Explorer, the repository is used to store SQL Commands.

Adding a SQL Command to the repository makes a copy of the SQL Command and its associated connection and stores this in the repository database. This is indicated by a special icon next to the connection that resembles a network connection.

> A default repository database is set up during installation of Crystal Reports 9 with a name of Crystal Repository. This database is stored as a Microsoft Access database on the local machine. To take advantage of the repository's central storage, it's best to set up a repository database on a central machine in your network.

The SQL Command in the report maintains a link to the SQL Command in the repository. Each time a report is opened, the report developer has the option of updating any repository objects. This is enabled by checking the Update Repository Objects check box within the Open file dialog. Crystal Reports will then check for any updates to that SQL Command, and if any are found, the SQL Command in the report will be updated to reflect those changes. Publishing SQL Commands to the repository provides reuse and maintenance and will provide for a more efficient reporting process. For more information on the repository, see Hour 18, "Working with the Report Component Repository."

Joining Database Objects Together

Up until this point, only reports based on a single table, view, stored procedure, or SQL Command have been discussed in this hour. However, it is quite a common occurrence to have several database objects in the same report. Crystal Reports treats all types of database objects as peers, which mean that a single report can contain multiple tables, views, stored procedures, and SQL Commands. Because all database objects are treated as peers, the term table will be used from now on to describe any of these database objects.

Because of Crystal Reports' inherent basis on relational data, any time multiple tables are used, they must be linked together so that the sum of all database objects is a single set of relational records. The good news is that most of the time, Crystal Reports will take care of this automatically, and the report developer need not worry about linking.

To see this in action, create a connection to the Xtreme Sample Database and add both the Customer and Orders tables to the report. When clicking Next in the Report Wizard, the linking between those tables is displayed as shown in Figure 3.8. Each table is represented by a window. In addition to the name, each field in the table is listed inside the window, and those fields that are defined as indexed fields in the database are marked with colored arrows. Any links defined between tables are represented as arrows connecting the key fields from two tables. Based on general database theory, linking to a field that is indexed will generally result in a better performing query.

FIGURE 3.8

Linking multiple tables together.

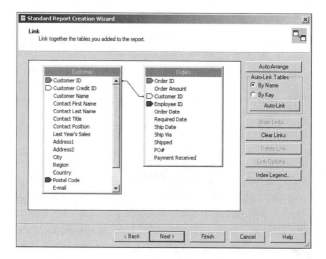

By default, Crystal Reports creates links based on name. In this case, both tables have fields with a name of Customer ID, so a link is already created. To accept this link, simply click Next to move to the next step in the Report Wizard. If there were not a common field name, selecting the By Key option and clicking Auto-Link would attempt to create a link based on the fields defined in the database as keys. If neither of these methods of automatic linking work, the link must be manually created. This is very simple to do: Simply drag the field to link from one table and drop it on to the field from a second table.

After links are created, they can be configured by clicking on the link arrow connecting two tables (it will turn blue when selected), and then clicking the Link Options button. Links have two options: join type and link operator. These settings determine how Crystal Reports matches records from both tables. The default join type is an inner join, which means that only records with a matching key in both tables are included. The default link type is equal. For most cases, these two settings will not need to be modified.

Understanding the Different Join Types

In Crystal Reports, the Link tab of the Report Wizard (and Database Expert) provides a visual representation of the relationship between multiple database objects. Defining the appropriate join strategy for any given report should be reflective of the data within the database objects and on how the report needs to read and display that data. Join type settings allow you to more precisely control the query results based on your unique requirements. The following is a description of the most common types of joins:

- Inner—The resultset includes all the records in which the linked field value in both tables is an exact match. The Inner join is the standard type of join for most reports, and it is also commonly known as the Equal join.

- Left Outer—The resultset includes all the records in which the linked field value in both tables is an exact match. It also includes a row for every record in the primary (left) table for which the linked field value has no match in the secondary (lookup) table. For example, if you would like your report to display all customers and the orders they have each placed—including the customers who have not placed any orders at all—you can use a Left Outer join between the Customer and Orders tables. As a result, you would see a row for every customer who has not placed any orders.

- Not Equal—The resultset includes all records in which the linked field value in the primary table is not equal to the linked field value in the secondary (lookup) table. For example, if you needed to report on all orders that were not shipped on the same date that they were ordered, you could use the Not Equal join type to join the OrderDate field in Orders table with the ShipDate field in the OrderDetails table.

- Full Outer—The resultset includes all records in both of the linked tables—all records in which the linked field value in both tables is an exact match, in addition to a row for every record in the primary (left) table for which the linked field value has no match in the secondary (lookup) table, and a row for every record in the secondary (lookup, or right) table for which the linked field value has no match in the primary table. The Full Outer join is a bi-directional outer join, which essentially combines the characteristics of both the Left Outer and Right Outer joins into a single join type.

Using the Database Expert

After the report is created, to return to the Data Explorer, select Database Expert from the Database menu. Here tables can be added, removed, and renamed just as they could from the Data Explorer in the Report Wizard.

To modify a SQL Command, double-click on the command object in the Selected Tables list. If the SQL Command is stored in the repository, it must be disconnected before it can be edited. To do this, right-click on the command object and select Disconnect from Repository. After a SQL Command is disconnected, the icon next to the connection will not show the network connection picture.

A SQL Command disconnected from the repository can be edited by double-clicking the same as with regular SQL Commands. To save the changes back to the repository, check the Add to Repository check box when editing the command. When prompted for a location to save the command in the repository, select the same folder and name as the existing SQL Command to be updated. This is shown in Figure 3.9. Crystal Reports will ask for confirmation of updating the command.

FIGURE 3.9

*Updating a command
in the repository.*

Summary

In this hour, you have learned about the wide variety of data sources that Crystal Reports supports. You should now understand the concept of database drivers and how Crystal Reports uses them to connect to these various data sources—some of them directly, and some through industry standard data access layers like ODBC and OLE DB.

You have also had an introduction to the first step in the Report Wizard: the Data Explorer. You have learned how to specify a database driver and database connection information, as well as add tables, views, stored procedures, and SQL Commands to a report.

You have learned how to publish SQL Commands to the repository for future use and maintenance. Finally, because multiple database objects can be added to a report, you've learned how to define links between the tables.

Workshop

Here's a brief quiz to help you review this hour's terminology, as well as activities for you to try on your own.

Quiz

1. What are the two types of Crystal Reports database drivers?
2. What is the Data Explorer used for?
3. Why would you want to use a SQL Command versus a table in a report?

Quiz Answers

1. The two types of Crystal Reports database drivers are direct access and indirect access drivers.
2. The Data Explorer is used to specify a database driver, a connection to a database, as well as for adding various database objects to a report including tables, views, stored procedures, and SQL Commands.
3. You would use a SQL Command instead of a table if you have a good understanding of SQL and wanted to use a complex query or a query that Crystal Reports does not inherently support.

Activities

To ensure that you are comfortable with the topics discussed in this hour, try to perform the following tasks:

- Create a blank report from the Xtreme Sample Database using the ODBC database driver. Add the Customer, Orders, and Order Details tables to the report and ensure that links are defined between those tables.

- Create a blank report from the Xtreme Sample Database using the direct access driver. Add a SQL Command to the report using the following SQL: `"SELECT * FROM Customer"`. Add this SQL Command to the repository.

- Create a blank report from the SQL Command stored in the repository from the previous task. After the report is created, change the SQL Command to use the following SQL: `"SELECT * FROM Customer WHERE Country ='Canada'"` and update the SQL Command in the repository.

HOUR 4

Using the Default Report Wizards

Now that you have been introduced to the Crystal Reports 9 development environment and reviewed different strategies for accessing your data, you are ready to begin creating reports using the default report wizards. The report wizards are provided to expedite the report design process for report designers of all skill levels, but they are especially useful for new users of Crystal Reports.

The report wizards, also commonly referred to as *report experts*, provide a simplified interface and guided path to constructing the fundamental elements found within most reports. As a result, designing interactive, professional looking reports can be achieved in a matter of minutes.

In this hour, we will cover the following topics:

- Understanding the Crystal Reports Gallery
- Using the Standard Report Creation Wizard
- Working with the Report Design Explorers

 Using the default report wizards as a starting point for most reports is a good idea. The report wizards offer a shortcut to establishing the core elements required for most reports. Hour 5, "Creating and Designing Basic Reports," builds on many of the principles covered in this hour.

Understanding the Crystal Reports Gallery

The Report Gallery is a special dialog that is presented when you select to create a new report file. The Report Gallery acts as a shortcut to various report creation wizards, which then provide the guided, visual creation of reports.

As Figure 4.1 illustrates, the Crystal Reports Gallery is a dialog that serves as the gateway to accessing and using the various report creation wizards. From the Report Gallery dialog, you can select from one of the four provided report wizards:

- Standard—Used to create traditional columnar-styled reports.
- Cross-Tab—Used to create summary styled cross-tab reports.
- Mail Labels—Used to create reports with multiple columns, such as address labels.
- OLAP—Used to create summary styled cross-tab reports that are based on an *OLAP (Online Analytical Processing)* data source.

The remainder of this hour focuses on exploring and using the Standard Report Creation Wizard. In general, this is the most commonly used report wizard, and it provides a good introduction to the components of the report design process. However, if you are interested in learning more about the other wizards, an exercise on creating a cross-tab report using the Cross-Tab Wizard is provided in Hour 14, "Using Cross-Tabs for Summarized Reporting."

FIGURE 4.1

The Crystal Reports Gallery dialog provides quick access to the various report creation wizards.

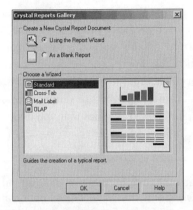

Crystal Reports 9 provides enhanced Cross-Tab and OLAP reporting capabilities as compared to the previous version. Crystal Reports 9 developers can perform more advanced summary-styled reporting against a variety of OLAP sources, including Microsoft's OLE DB provider for OLAP (such as SQL Server), IBM DB2 OLAP server, and Hyperion Essbase server. See Hour 14, and Hour 20, "Multidimensional Reporting Against OLAP Data," for further information.

Using the Standard Report Creation Wizard

The Standard Report Creation Wizard is the most often used design assistant in Crystal Reports. It provides multiple dialogs common to creating reports that are based on conventional corporate data sources. The Standard Report Creation Wizard guides you through selecting a data source, linking data source tables, adding data source fields to the report, specifying field groupings, identifying summary (total) fields, and setting the desired sort criteria for your report.

Additionally, the Standard Report Creation Wizard walks you through creating chart objects, applying record selection criteria (data filters), and applying predefined templates (layouts) to your report.

The term *filter* is commonly used to describe data selection criteria that narrow the scope of the data being extracted by the report from the underlying data source. For example, by using a filter such as Country = USA, you can easily limit your report to include only the information you are interested in extracting.

In total, the Standard Report Creation Wizard consists of nine dialog screens that allow you to specify the criteria mentioned previously to quickly create a professional looking report. The sequence of the wizard's dialog screens is dynamic and directly associated with the items selected in each of the progressive screens. For example, if you do not choose to identify any summary items for your report, you will not be presented with a Chart dialog screen. In general, charts apply best to summarized data, so if you have not identified any summary fields, the wizard assumes that you do not want to include a chart object in your report.

> Charts can also be created from base-level data, although to do this you must appropriately specify the On Change Of option and use the Advanced settings with the Chart Expert. Generally, it makes more sense to base chart objects on summary-level data, such as regional sales by quarter—where you are charting the total sales for each quarter rather than each sales transaction in each quarter.

It's now time to practice using the Standard Report Creation Wizard. In the following exercises, we will discuss each of the steps in the wizard and build a sales report to display last year's sales by country. By making use of the Standard Report Creation Wizard, we will include the country, city, customer name, and last year sales database fields, graphically display a summary of last year sales by country, and apply professionally styled formatting to the report.

1. From the Report Gallery dialog, select Using the Report Wizard in the upper portion of the screen, and then select Standard from the wizard list in the lower portion of the screen. Click OK to initiate the Standard Report Creation Wizard.

2. As shown in Figure 4.2, you should now be presented with the first dialog—labeled Data—as part of the Standard Report Creation Wizard. From the Data dialog screen, expand the Create New Connection node and then expand the ODBC listing as well. This should present the ODBC Data Source Selection dialog.

> To expand the listing items (also commonly known as *nodes*), click the + sign to the left of each particular item.

FIGURE 4.2

The Standard Report Creation Wizard begins by requesting a data source for your report.

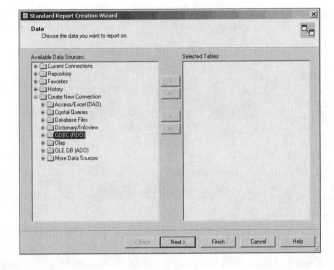

3. From the ODBC Data Source Selection dialog, scroll to the end of the Data Source Name list and select the Xtreme Sample Database 9 item, as shown in Figure 4.3. Click Next to continue.

FIGURE 4.3

The ODBC Data Source Selection dialog allows you to select a valid connection to access your ODBC data sources.

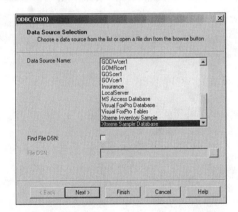

4. As illustrated in Figure 4.4, verify that the Data Source Name is correct and click Finish from the ODBC Connection Information dialog. No password is necessary to access this database.

FIGURE 4.4

The ODBC Connection Information dialog asks you to verify the connection information to access your ODBC data sources.

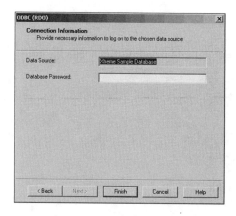

5. After you have successfully identified and connected to Xtreme Sample Database 9, you should see this item listed under the ODBC node in the Available Data Source area of the Data dialog screen, as shown in Figure 4.5. Upon expanding the Xtreme Sample Database item, you should see three distinct data source items listed: Tables, Views, and Stored Procedures (shown in Figure 4.6) .

FIGURE 4.5

The Xtreme Sample Database will be listed under the Available Data Sources area of the Data dialogscreen.

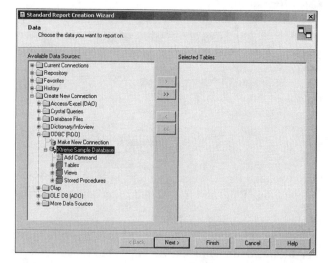

6. Within the Data dialog screen, select the Customer and Orders tables so that they are listed in the Selected Tables area on the right (as shown in Figure 4.7). After these two tables are selected, click Next to continue.

FIGURE 4.6

Upon expanding the Xtreme Sample Database item, you will notice multiple database items listed.

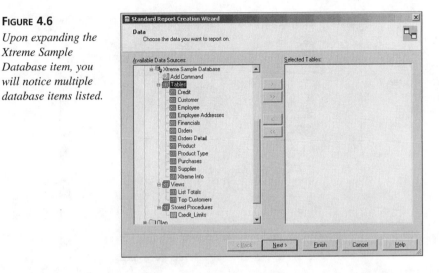

There are multiple ways to include tables in your report from within the Data dialog screen. From the list of available tables on the left side of the dialog, you can perform any one of the following actions to populate the Selected Tables list on the right side of the dialog area:

- Double-click on each desired table item
- Drag-and-drop each desired table item
- Highlight the table item on the left and click on the respective arrow icons (> or >>)between the two listing areas to populate the listing on the right

7. The Link dialog screen presents a visual representation of the relationship between these two tables and permits you to modify the defined relationship by specifying the exact *Join* links that you require to accurately report on the data within the selected tables. As shown in Figure 4.8, you should now see the Link dialog screen. For our purposes here, we will accept the default Join condition. Click Next to continue.

Figure 4.7

The Customer and Orders tables should now be listed in the Selected Tables area.

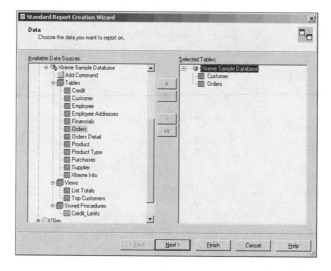

Figure 4.8

The Customer and Orders tables are linked together via the Customer ID field.

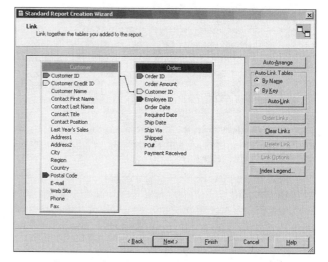

What Is a Link?

A *link* is often described as a field common to two or more database tables, which serves as a connecting point between those database tables. Crystal Reports uses the link to match up records from one database table with those from one or more other database tables. For example, if two database tables each contain a Customer ID field (even though the fields might have different names), Crystal Reports can use these fields to electronically connect the records in one database table with the corresponding records in the other table. As a point of reference, the term *link* in Crystal Reports is equivalent to the term *relationship* in Microsoft Access. See Hour 3 for more details on Join types.

8. After specifying the table linking, you will see the Fields dialog screen, shown in Figure 4.9. Select the Country, City, Customer Name, and Last Year's Sales fields so that they appear under the Fields to Display area on the right. If necessary, you can use the up and down arrows to modify the order of these fields in the list. Click Next to continue.

FIGURE 4.9

The Country, City, Customer Name, and Last Year's Sales fields should appear under the Fields to Display area.

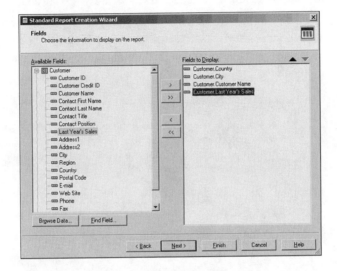

9. You should now see the Grouping dialog screen. This dialog allows you to identify logical groups of information within your reports. For this example, select to group by the Country field only, as shown in Figure 4.10. Click Next to continue.

FIGURE 4.10

The Grouping dialog allows you to create structured groupings of information within your report.

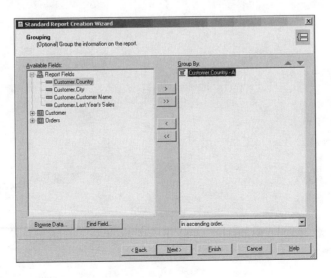

The Summaries dialog screen allows you to identify summary values to complement the report's structure and how you want to present the information within your reports. If you do not identify any grouped items in a report, you will not see the Summaries dialog because summaries are only applicable to grouped data. For example, if you are grouping your report according to the country field, you might want to see a sum of last year's sales figures for each country group.

10. You should now see the Summaries dialog screen. To apply a summary object to the report, select the Last Year's Sales field so that it appears under the Summarized Fields list on the right. This is shown in Figure 4.11. Click Next to continue.

As you might notice, Crystal Reports automatically chooses a summary for you if you choose to group your report data. It will examine the detail information you've specified for the report and build a summary on the first available numeric field. However, this default summary criteria can easily be modified.

FIGURE 4.11

The Summaries dialog screen allows you to create summarized values that are frequently used in coordination with the grouping structure within reports.

By default, the Last Year's Sales field that appears under the Summarized Fields area on the right is aggregated as a Sum of the actual field value. As shown in Figure 4.11, the drop-down list located in the lower-right area of the Summaries dialog screen allows you to select from a variety of summaries, including Sum, Average, Maximum, Minimum, Count, Correlation, Covariance, and Standard Deviation.

11. We will now sort the report based on last year's sales of the top five countries. The Group Sorting dialog screen allows you to sort the grouped fields based on the summarized totals. From the Group drop-down list, select the Country field (the only option in our example here) and select the Top 5 Groups option from the Group Ordering choices. Also, select the Sum of Last Year's Sales item from the Comparing Summarized Values drop-down list, as shown in Figure 4.12. Click Next to continue.

FIGURE 4.12

The Group Sorting dialog allows you to sort your report based only on the Group values that you want to include in the report results.

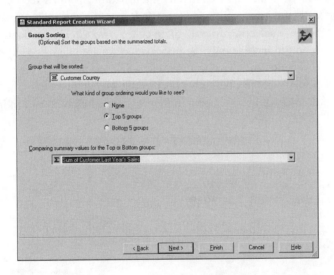

12. Let's add a chart to visually display the top five performing countries according to last year's sales. From the Chart dialog screen, you can select a chart object to be included in the report based on the group and summary items you identify here. For our example, we will add a bar chart and select the Country field from the On Change Of drop-down list and the Sum of Last Year's Sales item from the Show Summary drop-down list. Change the chart title to read, `Last Year's Sales by Country`—see Figure 4.13 for additional guidance. Click Next to continue.

FIGURE 4.13

The Chart dialog allows you to select a chart object for your report based on the previously identified group and summary criteria.

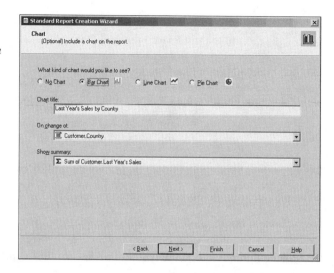

13. Let's assume that we are only interested in customer records in which last year's sales are greater than $1,000. The Record Selection dialog screen allows us to identify selection criteria, often called *data filtering*, to isolate the resultset of the report to include only the information we are interested in returning. We make this distinction by selecting Last Year's Sales as the Filter Field, choosing Is Greater Than from the filter operators drop-down list, and typing in `1000.00` in the value drop-down list, as shown in Figure 4.14. Click Next to continue.

FIGURE 4.14

The Record Selection dialog permits you to narrow your resultset based on the selection criteria identified here.

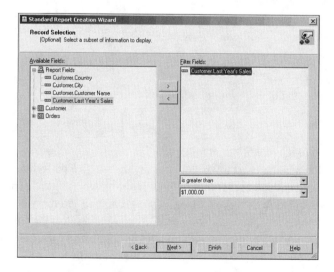

14. Finally, we will apply a predefined style to our report. From the Template dialog screen, you can select predefined styles to be applied to your report for formatting purposes, as shown in Figure 4.15. The Available Template list includes various sample templates that are included with the Crystal Reports 9 installation. However, you can also create your own templates to be used for report formatting. For this example, select the Block Sample (Blue) template. For additional details on how to design and implement your own templates, see Hour 19, "Designing Effective Report Templates."

This now concludes the Standard Report Creation Wizard example. After you click Finish, you will execute the report that you have just created and will be presented with the preview of the corresponding resultset. At this point, you can click Finish if you are satisfied with the report design criteria. When you are presented with the preview of you report, save your new report by selecting Save As from the File menu. Name this report **StdReportWizard1.rpt**.

In Crystal Reports terminology, a *template* can be a copy of a report used as the starting point for creating a new report, or it can be a report whose formatting and functionality is applied to a new report created in the Standard Report Creation Wizard. As it relates to this exercise, you are using a report template to apply one of several professionally designed styles to your report for formatting purposes only. Regardless of which method is used, when acting as a template, the original report remains unchanged.

4

FIGURE 4.15

The Template dialog permits you to select predefined styles to be applied to your report.

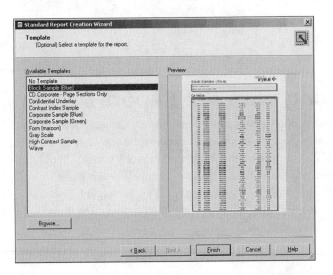

After you select Finish at the end of the Standard Report Creation Wizard process, you will be presented with the executed resultset and a preview of your newly created report. As Figure 4.16 shows, creating a useful and professional looking report is extremely simple when using the Standard Report Creation Wizard. In the preceding exercises, you have connected to a database, identified the tables and fields you wanted to include in your report, linked the tables together, grouped and summarized the data, sorted the data, applied filtering criteria, included a chart object for enhanced visualization of the report results, and applied a report template for quick and easy formatting—all in just a few clicks of your mouse! This process speaks both to the ease of use and power of the Crystal Reports design application.

FIGURE 4.16

The executed result-set and preview of the report you have just created using the Standard Report Creation Wizard.

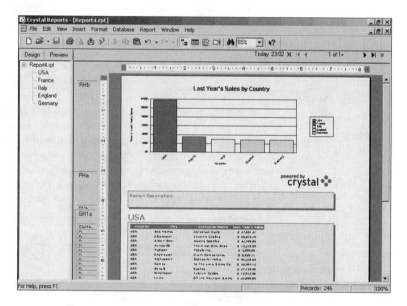

Working with the Report Design Explorers

In addition to the report creation wizards, Crystal Reports 9 includes several report design explorers intended to streamline the report design process. The design explorers are not directly related to the report creation wizards, though they are complementary application tools that can greatly enhance a report designer's efficiency while working with reports. Report design explorers are included here because they are important application components, and they are design tools you will use in building reports throughout the remainder of the book.

The report design explorers are dialog windows that display various objects relevant to the report in a hierarchical tree view to facilitate quick access to and formatting of each respective object and its properties. The explorers allow report designers to easily locate and navigate to specific report objects, such as the report header or a corporate logo image, in order to customize the object for design purposes. All the objects included in a report (report sections, groups, database fields, formulas, parameters, images, charts, and so on) are organized and displayed within one of the design explorers. The concept of design explorers is new to Crystal Reports 9, and it includes three distinct explorers:

- Report Explorer—Provides a tree view of each report section in the report and each of the report objects contained within each section as seen in Figure 4.17. You can work with each report object directly from the explorer rather than navigating to each object separately in either the Design or Preview tab of the report.

FIGURE 4.17

The Report Explorer window offers quick access to each of the report sections and each object located within each section.

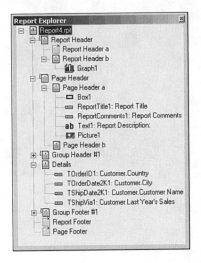

- Field Explorer—Displays a tree view of database fields, formulas, SQL expressions, parameters, running totals, groups, and special fields. You can add any of these field types directly to a report from the Explorer dialog. Fields that have already been added to the report or fields that have been used by other fields (such as formula fields, groups, summaries, and so on) will have a green check mark icon in front of them, as shown in Figure 4.18.

- Repository Explorer—Provides a tree view of each object contained in a report repository. You can work with each report repository object directly from the Repository Explorer rather than locating each object separately for inclusion in to the report during the report design process, as shown in Figure 4.19.

FIGURE 4.18

The Field Explorer window offers quick access to a variety of available report objects.

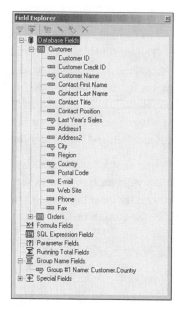

See Hour 18, "Working with the Report Component Repository," for additional details on this topic.

FIGURE 4.19

The Repository Explorer window offers quick access to a variety of available report objects contained in any number of report repositories.

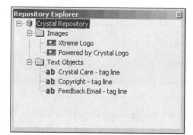

Locating and Using the Report Design Explorers

Each of the explorer dialogs can be *docked* in place or used in a free-floating state. By default, each of the explorers will appear docked on the left side of the report design environment. However, you can manually dock each of them in other locations if you prefer, such as on the right side or the bottom of the report designer screen. The explorers can also be used in free-floating mode: in which case, each of the explorer dialog

windows can be dragged to any location within the report design environment and will
float in place until you either close or reposition them.

1. To view each of the Report Design Explorers, click the View menu and select each
   desired explorer individually, as shown in Figure 4.20.

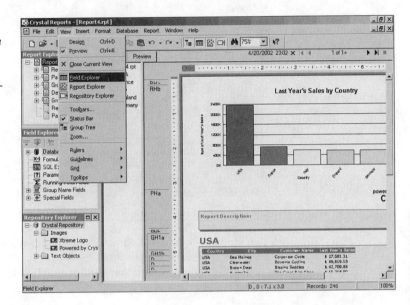

2. From the Field Explorer dialog window, you can add Special Fields objects, such
   as File Author, Modification Date and Print Date, to your reports to provide the
   report consumers with additional information about the report and its data. At this
   point, you can close the Report Explorer and Repository Explorer dialog windows
   if they are still present on the screen, while leaving the Field Explorer dialog window visible. Locate and highlight the Print Date object in the list of Special Fields.
   After the object is highlighted, drag it onto the Preview of the report and drop it
   just above the Report Description field located in the Page Header section, as
   shown in Figure 4.21.

FIGURE 4.21

You can quickly construct meaningful reports by dragging and dropping objects from the report design explorers on to your reports.

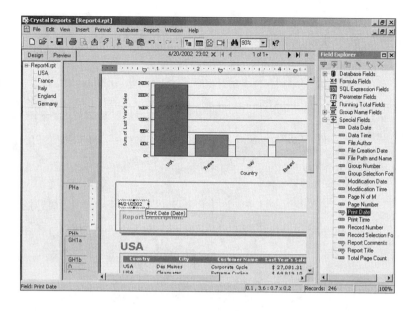

Within the Field Explorer dialog window, you can add, edit, and delete all types of fields listed before you insert them onto your report, with the exception of Database, Group Name and Special Fields.

The Report Design Explorers create a very intuitive way for report designers to quickly add and format report objects while constructing reports. As you progress through the remainder of the book, you will be using these explorers on a regular basis, so it's important that you understand the basics of using these application features.

Summary

In this hour, you have begun working with the Crystal Reports 9 application and constructed a simple report that effectively shows last year's sales by country for the top five performing countries. The exercises in this hour introduced you to several important components of the application—report creation wizards, report templates, and report design explorers—and should help you effectively use these design features you as you continue to learn the Crystal Reports 9 application in greater detail.

Creating a report in Crystal Reports 9 is a very straightforward and uncomplicated process. By taking advantage of the Standard Report Creation Wizard, accessing the Crystal Reports sample database, and using the Field Explorer dialog box feature, you have been able to create your first actual report file using Crystal Report 9.

Workshop

Here's a brief quiz to help you review this hour's terminology, as well as activities for you to try on your own.

Quiz

1. From what dialog screen do you access the various report creation wizards?
2. What are the three distinct report design explorers new for Crystal Reports version 9?
3. Which of the design explorers is used to interact with and add objects to your reports that are stored in a universal object library?

Quiz Answers

1. The Crystal Reports Gallery dialog.
2. The Report Explorer, Field Explorer, and Repository Explorer.
3. The Repository Explorer—Allows report designers to access and interact with a central object library of available report objects.

Activities

You might want to repeat the exercises to rehearse the design features that we have covered in this hour. As an alternative to using the Standard Report Creation Wizard, you can also use the other report creation wizards to quickly construct a variety of different reports. If you'd like, go ahead and take a few minutes to explore the other report wizards, such as the Cross-Tab or Mail Label wizards. The Cross-Tab Report Creation Wizard is also covered in greater detail in Hour 14.

4

PART II
Fundamentals of the Crystal Reports Design Environment

Hour

HOUR 5

Creating and Designing Basic Reports

Because the previous hours have focused on using wizards as much as possible to create reports, this hour focuses on creating reports without the extra help.

The logic of designing a report from the beginning of the thought process will be the key difference for this hour from any of the previous hours. Wizards are great because they are speedy, but let's de-mystify reporting as much as possible.

This hour covers the following:

- Planning a report
- Creating a report storyboard
- Designing a Crystal Report
- Creating a report

Planning a Report

Using the Report Wizard makes the process of creating a report incredibly easy. Now we're going to build a similar report without the wizard. We'll have more control over the look and feel of the finished report and learn a lot of new Crystal Reports features along the way.

Because very few corporate data sources resemble the simple structure of a sample data source in Crystal Reports, this hour will analyze a complex database schema and help you determine how to use it. For example, we'll create a Crystal Report from the database schema shown in Figure 5.1.

FIGURE 5.1

A complex database schema can be challenging for report developers to decipher.

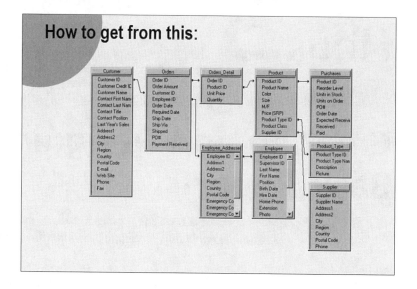

Of course, the reports created in this lesson will not use all these tables in the figure. Using Crystal Reports will allow us to provide a highly formatted report that is easy to understand, as shown in Figure 5.2.

Although the data structures and schemas in Figure 5.1 can be quite a challenge to understand, it is still required that some level of understanding of a data source you need access to for report creation is present. Otherwise, report design can seem chaotic. As a Crystal Report designer, business end users will often ask you to help them make sense of corporate data.

Figure 5.2

A highly formatted report providing relevant information for report viewers.

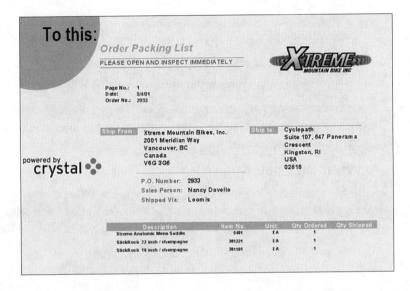

Although understanding the various corporate data sources you'll need to access is a critical success factor in creating Crystal Reports, another key factor is effective report design.

Effective Report Design Considerations

The most common mistake made by report designers is forgetting to plan the creation of a report. Some of the issues to consider might seem quite basic, but it's good practice to walk through the process of validating some key report design considerations before starting.

The basic questions to ask before starting your report are Why? What? How? When?

They might seem simple, but there's nothing worse than finishing a report only to find out that it isn't what the person who requested it wanted. We'll now walk through each of these questions in detail.

Why Do They Need This Report?

As a report designer, you'll never run out of unique requests from end users and report *consumers*. Some requirements will undoubtedly be

- Including summary Numbers (Quarterly reports—enough said).
- Making a collection of numbers make sense. Business users are rarely familiar with the nuances of the database environment.

5

- Needing key business metrics *yesterday.* (There is no time like overdue to ask someone to create a report, right?)
- Converting old legacy reports to a new system.
- Providing consumers with information on the Web.

Of course, the person requesting the reports might not really know *what* he wants, but the common thread throughout each and every report request is the need to bring "people and information together."

What Do They Need?

Perhaps a more appropriate title for this section is "What do they *tell you* they need?" Ever notice that when someone requests a new report, he starts telling you what he wants, but not what he needs? Those types of requests usually consist of statements like

- Just a final number (I don't care how you get it)
- A map
- A pretty chart
- An Executive Summary
- The Quarter End Summary
- The ROI

It's ultimately the job of the report designer to find out what the real business requirements are for *any* report that must be created. It's not enough to just prioritize which reports are created first, second, third, and so on. The design requests within the reports themselves are ultimately what drive the complexity and, hence, design longevity.

How Will We Judge the Successful Completion of This Report?

Experience has shown that to get good answers, it works best to make the business user requesting the report feel useful and needed through interaction during the report planning phase. Starting with simple questions, such as

- What features are required for this report?

  Most reports require some graphical representation of the data within, which means charts or a geographic map potentially.

- Are there other reports I can work from?

  If there are sample or existing reports (maybe it's a older, *legacy* report you need to recreate, such as a mainframe report), it's always faster to work with something than nothing, especially if you're trying to duplicate the look or functionality of an existing report.

- Where is the data coming from?

  This is an important step. If you can't connect to the data that you need to see, you're stuck. Start with a successful database connection, and you'll be off on the right foot. We will be focusing more on this in a future hour. Another follow-up question would be, "Who can I ask to help me get connected to this data source?" Chances are, it's someone in IT.

- What level of detail do you want to see?

  Focus of vision and what level of detail the final results should be are key. If the end result is just a final number, don't spend a lot of time on making the details look pretty. Take the same perspective as the person asking for your help.

- What help or resources can I work with?

  No one is an island in life or in work. Ask colleagues for help and ask a lot of questions. Don't assume anything. Remember, there are no such things as dumb questions.

When Is This Due?

As previously mentioned, make sure to discern the *want* from the *need*. Try to get the requesting business user to understand your perspective, abilities, and the features of Crystal Reports available to them. After all, time is precious. Find out what the key drivers are for the business user and the priority placed on each requirement. Meeting somewhere in the middle is usually a good idea.

Now that we've covered some of the typical and most resourceful questions to get you started in writing a report, let's look the physical process of report design.

Mapping Out a Report

A report can be considered a book. It tells a story in words as well as pictures. The complete story needs to be told to get everyone reading it to understand the message it is delivering. The person who has the ultimate idea of how the story should end is the person requesting the report—the requestor. He has in his mind that the report should have certain information on it and should look a certain way. He might even come to you with a drawing or picture. To organize your thoughts, be prepared to take notes.

As you begin to write down your thoughts, you may notice that you are writing out the story that the requestor is asking for. So, if the requestor is the illustrator in our example here, you could be considered the author. As an author, you can follow the general rules of writing that you learned in school. Start with an outline and build from there.

5

Write a paragraph or two in your own words to tell the story that the requestor has relayed to you. Don't worry about missing information. It's a work in progress, and you can ask questions later. After you've finished the first draft, you'll notice that editing the story becomes essential. That's when the real facts about the story, or report, will surface.

Creating a Report Storyboard

Before opening the report designer, create a report using the effective report design techniques covered in the previous hours of the book.

Imagine the following end-user requirements, received in an email.

Report Design Request Memo

To: Report Designer

From: Bob, the sales manager

Subject: Sales Report

Hey report designer, here are the requirements...

- Sales managers need an Employee Productivity Report.
- The sales managers want to see the status of all orders for an employee by the account that he or she works on.
- The order status will need to highlight late orders and the size of all orders.
- The managers will need to see what courier company is used for each order.

Thanks

Bob

The previous request seems pretty straightforward. Although the requirements seem sensible, try applying some of the questions from the previous section to them. Clearly, more information is required to complete the report. After leveraging some of our new-found report design questions, the requirements end up looking more like the following:

Response to the Report Design Request Memo

To: Bob, the sales manager

From: The report designer

Subject: Sales Report

Bob,

After speaking with you, I found the following key requirements for your report. Please confirm these to be the case, along with the specified timeline for delivery.

- You need to see the order status for all orders for X employee.
- Each account and its total value that each employee works on must be represented and shown separately.
- Late orders (any order not shipped on the day of order) must be shown in red.
- Courier companies for each order must be seen.

Also, my understanding is that the report needs to be completed one month before the end of this quarter, so you can use it to help wrap up account issues.

Thanks,

Report Designer

Notice that this more personalized and direct list of requirements is much more like a database schema. That's because report designers tend to be "data-type" people and need to be more focused on this to make a report successful.

Now that we have a more polished set of requirements, we can look at dividing up the tasks of creating the report in to its core pieces. This will help identify what information needs to go on the report and then translate this into specific fields and tables in the database. Some of them might seem obvious, but let's look at them in order:

- "all orders" = an Orders table
- "X employee" = an Employee table (with probably some user input to find out which employee to look for)
- "account"= a Customer table
- "must be shown separately" = Indicates a level of grouping that is required
- "its total value" = Indicates a summary will on the account is required
- "red" = Indicates a status level or condition that needs to be applied for bringing the reader's eye to pertinent information

We have a list of basic tasks that need to be done to create the report successfully. Dividing the tasks into logical groupings would help us progress faster.

Now let's categorize our findings:

- Tables—Customer, Orders, Employees
- Groups—Account
- Summaries—Total orders for each Customer

5

- Parameters—Employee's Name
- Condition—Late Status

Now that the tasks for creating this report are laid out, the process of report design can begin.

Designing a Crystal Report

After the requirements for creating a Crystal Report have been determined, the actual report can be designed. This involves mapping the gathered business user requirements to the technologies available within the Crystal Reports design application.

Using the Crystal Reports Design Framework

With years of experience in producing reporting software, Crystal Decisions has built Crystal Reports around a design framework, intended to organize reports in a logical manner. Those framework items include

- Tables/Links
- Grouping
- Summaries
- Formulas
- Parameters
- Text objects
- Special fields
- Special formatting

The above items might look familiar because many of them are options in the Report Design Wizard, covered in Hour 4. An order of precedence can be applied to each of these tasks to get a report up and running as quickly as possible.

Basic Items Used to Create a Report

No two reports look alike, nor are they designed in the same way. However, some basic report features must always be present:

- Tables/Links—This is the foundation for your reports. If you need to report on data that resides in multiple database tables (Orders and Customer), without the links to make them work properly together, you will not be able to successfully complete a report.
- Groups—These will be the logical breaking points to support your story.

- Details—Putting the data on the report that will be needed to calculate and tell the rest of the story. These are the records of the report.

- Summaries—To make the details more useful, summarizing them into the basic facts that the business user is looking for is key. There should be no need to grab a calculator or open up Excel to get the numbers. Subtotals and Summaries in Crystal Reports can handle that for you.

Additional Report Components

Beyond these features, Crystal Reports offers major benefits that will enhance the report viewing experience for the business end user:

- Parameters—These are rich business user-focused features that will allow the report consumer to make the reports act differently depending on the user's input. For more information on parameters, check out Hour 12, where this is explained further.

- Formulas—Selection formulas, data manipulation, and complex calculations can be handled with formulas. We will look more closely at selection formulas in Hour 12.

- Sort Order—Ascending and descending order are the most common for reporting, but they are not the only options. You could sort based on group contents. For more information on sorting, see Hour 7.

- Formatting/Pictures/Hyperlinks/Charts/Maps— These are the items that really make the report grab the business users' attention of the. The cool visualizations make it presentable and flashy!

Now that you know what the requirements are for the sales management report, as well as some high-level features of what Crystal Reports offers, let's begin designing the report.

Creating a Report

As a reminder, no Report Wizard will be used for this example. Instead we're going to create this Sales Report from scratch.

If necessary, refer to the last email sent to Bob for the report requirements.

1. Select a report template. After opening Crystal Reports, click on the New button. Then in the Crystal Reports Gallery dialog box, choose As a Blank Report and click OK, as shown in Figure 5.3.

FIGURE 5.3

The Crystal Reports Gallery with As a Blank Report chosen.

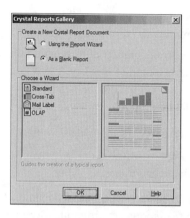

2. Select an appropriate data source. From the Database Expert dialog that comes up, in the Available Datasources list, browse to Create New Connection, ODBC. As soon as you choose ODBC, the ODBC (RDO) dialog will pop up. Scroll until you find the Xtreme Sample Database 9 as in Figure 5.4. Select it and click Finish. (There are no other settings to get this database working, so you can ignore the Next button. We will discuss these additional options in a later hour.)

FIGURE 5.4

The ODBC (RDO) dialog box showing the selected Xtreme Sample Database.

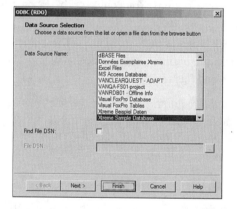

3. Select the appropriate tables. After choosing the appropriate database to connect to, we need to select the tables for this report. Move down in the left list box and expand the Tables item. Choose the Customer, Orders, and Employees tables by using the right-arrow (>) button, as seen in Figure 5.5.

Remember you can choose each table separately and click the arrow button or hold down the Ctrl key to select all tables that you want and then press the arrow button only once. Also, if you want to select several tables in a row, the Shift key will help you with that.

FIGURE 5.5

The Data tab from the Database Expert dialog box—showing three tables added to the report.

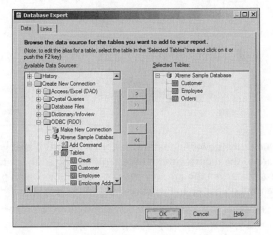

4. Link tables from the database. Move to the next tab in the Database Expert dialog by either clicking the OK button or selecting the Links tab. Notice that all the tables have already been linked. Crystal Reports attempts to link tables using similar field names and sizes whenever possible.

You can enlarge this dialog by using the stretch markers so that you can increase the display area and see more tables at once. The next time you enter this dialog, your adjusted size will be remembered.

We don't need to make any changes at this point, so just press the OK button.

5. Create logical groups of data. Next on our requirements list is to group the records by company name. In order to accomplish this, choose Insert, Group. When the Insert Group dialog appears, scroll down the first list box until Customer Name under the Customer table is available. Select it, as shown in Figure 5.6, and then click OK.

5

Notice that in the Design view of the report, two new sections become available called Group Header #1 and Group Footer #1. Within Group Header #1, the Group Name #1 field is also automatically added.

FIGURE 5.6

The Common tab of the Insert Group dialog box with the Customer Name field selected.

One of the powerful features in Crystal Reports is that you build the structure of the report without necessarily adding all the detail fields first. For example, even though we have not placed any objects on the report yet, we can still go ahead and add a group to the report.

If, however, we were to have some objects on the report already, they would appear in the Report Objects node within the list box, which would appear before the other available fields. This is for ease of use and accessibility.

6. Add summary values to the report. Now that the report information is grouped, add a summary on the orders. Choose Insert, Summary to get the Insert Summary dialog box to appear. In this dialog box, select in the field to summarize the list box to the Order Amount field. The Orders table is pretty far down the list, so keep scrolling. Next, because we plan on finding out how much each customer has ordered, the summary operation in the second list box needs to be changed from Maximum to Sum. Last, because this summary is per customer, we will need to change the location of the summary. Instead of placing it in the Report Footer (where it would summarize all amounts into one grand total), change the Summary Location list box to show Group #1, as shown in Figure 5.7. Click OK.

Notice that in the Design view, in the Group Footer #1, the Sum of Order Amount field has been added.

FIGURE 5.7

The Insert Summary dialog box with Order Amount summed by Customer Name selected.

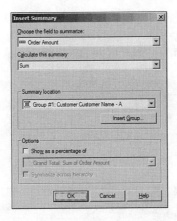

Although we have not formally added the detail records to this report, they are being read in as needed. You don't actually have to spend time on detail information if the request is for the summary numbers.

7. Add detail records to the report. To view the records of concern for this report, let's put the records into the report so we can track them. First, let's bring up the Field Explorer so that we can use it to add the fields to the report. To do this, choose View, Field Explorer. In the Field Explorer that becomes available, open the Database Fields item and then the Orders item to expose our fields that we'd like to add. Select each field separately and drag it to the Design tab using your mouse. Place them side-by-side in the Details Section: Order ID, Order Amount, Order Date, and Ship Date. To leave some space for the status field that we will add later, add the last field (Ship Via) further to the right of Ship Date, as shown in Figure 5.8.

8. Add a parameter to the report. We have been asked to run this report for *X* employee. To insert a parameter field, go to the Field Explorer and choose Parameter Fields. Right-click and choose New. In the Create Parameter Field dialog box, enter the information required. For the name of the parameter, enter **Employee Name**. For the prompting text that the end user will see, ask a question such as, "Which employee would you like to view?" Instead of assuming that the user will type the correct spelling, we can set some defaults for them. To do this, click on the Set Default Values button. In the Set Default Values dialog box that appears, we can choose to select data directly from our database. In this case, we want to get the fist names of our employees. In the Browse Table list box, choose the Employee table and then in the Browse Field list box, choose First Name.

5

Notice that the list of first names appears in the Select or Enter Value to Add list box. By clicking on the double-arrow (>>) button, that list will be brought in as default values as in Figure 5.9. Click OK to this and the previous dialog box.

FIGURE 5.8

The Design Window with all fields added.

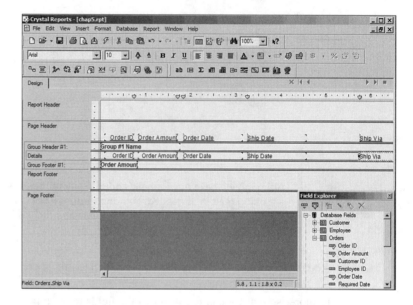

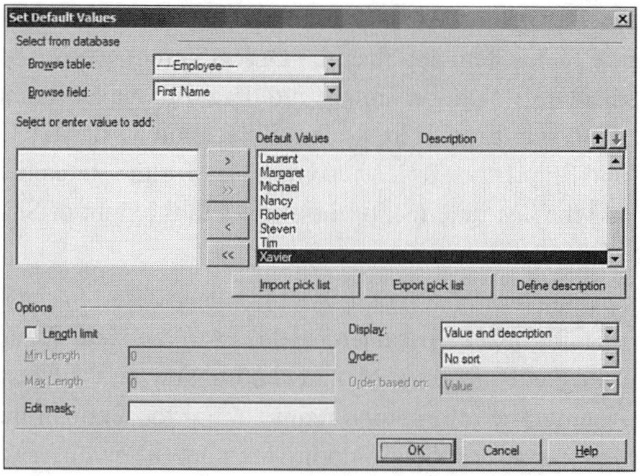

FIGURE 5.9

The Set Default Values dialog box with employees' first names added to the defaults.

9. Connect the parameter to the report's selection criteria (filter). The new parameter field has not been connected to any actual data values yet. This is noted by the lack of a green check mark applied to the parameter item's icon in the Field Explorer. We need to add it to the Selection Criteria within the report to tell the report to

only grab data for a given employee, based on the value that the business user will select in the parameter's prompt. Choose Report, Select Expert to see the Choose Field dialog box. In this dialog box, scroll down and select the Employee's First Name field. Click OK to get to the Select Expert dialog box. In Select Expert, change the list box to Is Equal To. By doing so, notice that another list box opens. From that list box, choose the first item {?Employee Name}, as shown in Figure 5.10. This is the parameter field that we just created. This will allow us to get the information from the user instead of hard-coding it ourselves. Click OK to continue.

FIGURE 5.10

The Select Expert dialog box with the Employee Name parameter field connected to the database.

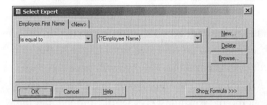

10. View the report. Before going any further, take a look at the report as it stands so far with some data. By Choosing Report, Refresh Report Data, we can access the parameter's prompting dialog to choose an employee. Choose Anne and click OK. A report with meaningful data is returned in the Preview tab like Figure 5.11.

FIGURE 5.11

The resulting report based on steps 1 through 11 in the Preview tab.

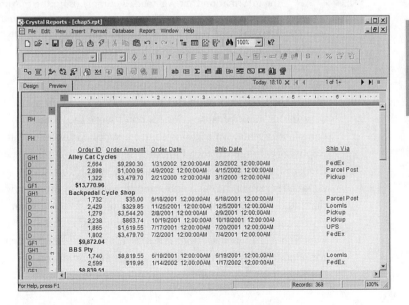

11. Save the report. File, Save will bring up the Save dialog. Provide a suitable name for the report, such as Chap5.rpt.

> If you are concerned about losing work between conscious saves of a report, Crystal Reports has an autosave feature that you can enable. You can set this option by navigating to File, Options, and then selecting the Reporting tab. The Autosave Reports After option can be set and the length of time in minutes between saves can be specified in the edit box to the right of this option.

12. Implement the requested logic flow for the report. In order to check whether the order has been shipped on time, we must compare the ship date with the order date for each order. To accomplish this, we will need to create a formula. In the Field Explorer, right-click on Formula Fields and choose New. In the Formula Name dialog box, name the formula Days Until Shipped and then choose the Use Expert button. This open the Formula Workshop's Formula Expert dialog box.

> If this is your first time seeing the Formula Workshop dialog box, you will undoubtedly notice that the dialog box is not quite large enough to hold all the information that we need. By simply using the maximize button at the top, you can resize this dialog's window to its maximum height and width. The next time you come back to it, your settings will be remembered.

13. Add a formula. Because we need to perform some math on the date fields, we will review the requirement. In this case, we don't want to include weekends or holidays in our math because couriers don't work those days. Instead of writing a complex formula, we're going to use a supplied function that is available in the Repository. In the Custom Function Supplying Logic list, open the Repository Custom Functions item and navigate to Crystal Repository, Crystal, Date, cdDateDiffSkipHolidays and select the object by single-clicking on it. Notice that the dialog fills out nicely with a lot of information regarding this custom function. The only values that you need to enter are in the Value list boxes under the Function Arguments section. For startDateTime, choose Orders.Order Date; and for endDateTime, choose Orders.Ship Date, as shown in Figure 5.12. Click on the Save and Close button in the top left of the dialog.

FIGURE 5.12

The Formula Workshop's Formula Expert with all arguments filled in.

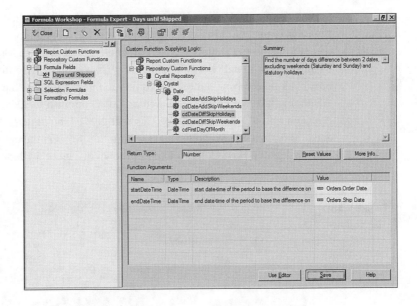

We will examine and explain the Crystal Repository in a later hour. We are only introducing the idea of sharing complex logic at this point.

14. Close and save the formula. Closing and saving this formula in one step allows Crystal Reports to automate some processes for you. It will now ask if you want to save this report. Choose Yes for this and all subsequent messages. Then, place the formula field that appears in the Field Explorer on to the report between the Ship Date and the Ship Via field in the Details section.

15. Left Justify the formula field by choosing the Align Left button in the Formatting toolbar so that the numbers don't overwrite the courier info to the right.

The automation of error checking, as well as insertion of the Custom Function in to the report, is what those messages are about. The real beneficial feature here is that the `cdDateDiffSkipHolidays` function actually requires the use of other custom functions but we're not burdened with having know the details of this. Crystal Reports will ask if you want them all at once. We do, so we just select Yes. All the functions are brought into the report.

16. Format the report. Use the Report Explorer to accomplish this. Select View, Report Explorer to turn on this viewer. In the Report Explorer dialog box, navigate the listing to get to the Details section and choose the DaysUntilShippped1 object. Right-click on it and choose Highlighting Expert. In the Highlighting Expert dialog box, click on the New button. By editing the item values in the Item Editor side of this dialog box, we can add a red color. To accomplish this, change the second list box item to say Is Not Equal To. This will give us the logic of "If this field is not equal to 0, then." Now we must set what to do if this is the case. To accomplish this, change the Font Color to Red, as shown in Figure 5.13, and click OK to continue.

FIGURE 5.13

The Highlight Expert with the late condition applied.

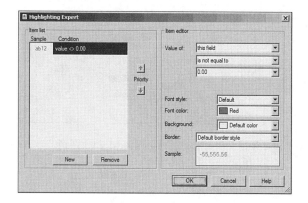

17. View and Save the final report. Review what your report looks like in the Preview tab and save it again as Chap5.RPT so that we can use it in later hours.

Summary

This hour explains how to create a presentation quality report without the use of the first level Report Creation Wizards. You are well on your way to becoming a more advanced Report Design Expert. In this lesson, you've learned good design practices for getting your reports mapped out prior to using the Crystal Reports designer, as well as how to use some of the common features of the designer to accomplish the *basics* of report design. In subsequent hours, we will build on these basic concepts to help you further refine your report design skills.

Workshop

Here's a brief quiz to help you review this hour's terminology, as well as an activity for you to try on your own.

Quiz

1. What are the four basic questions to keep in mind when trying to understand a new report request?

2. What is the suggested Order of Precedence for breaking down and designing a report within Crystal Reports?

3. What expert would you call to change the color of a field based on its value?

Quiz Answers

1. What? When? How? and Why?

2. Order of Precedence:

   - Tables/Links
   - Groups
   - Details
   - Summaries
   - Parameters
   - Formulas
   - Sort Order
   - Formatting/Pictures/Hyperlinks/Charts/Maps

3. The Highlighting Expert

Activities

Now that you know how to effectively design and create a report without using the Report Wizards, try using this new design method on some of your future reports.

5

HOUR 6

Selecting and Grouping Data

As introduced in the previous hour, the Field Explorer provides a quick and easy way to select and display fields on your report and then easily drag and drop them onto the Report Design area. In addition to choosing existing fields from your selected data sources, the Field Explorer enables you to create calculated (formula) fields, parameter fields, running total fields, group summary fields, as well as choose from a predefined set of default special fields. These additional objects enable a great deal of flexibility and power in the information you will deliver through the reports you will create.

In addition to selecting the fields that will make up the raw content for a report, it is often beneficial to group base-level data by country, region, or product line. Grouping the data facilitates relevant business user analysis and enables meaningful summarizations in your reports. Crystal Reports provides easy-to-use grouping functionality that enables nested groups, hierarchical grouping, and drill-down analysis into the different levels of grouping selected.

In this hour, the following will be covered:

- Understanding the different types of field objects
- How to add grouping to your reports
- How to add multiple groups to your report and re-order them
- Hierarchical Grouping
- Creating and using drill-down in your reports
- Hiding and suppressing detail records in your reports

Understanding Field Objects

As described in a previous hour, the Field Explorer displays a tree view of data fields in your report. It shows database fields, formula fields, SQL expression fields, parameter fields, running total fields, group name fields, and special system fields that you have defined for use in your report. In this hour, you will be introduced to all the standard field types available in Crystal Reports.

To activate the Field Explorer, either select it from the View menu or click on the Field Explorer button in the Crystal Reports Standard toolbar. Figure 6.1 shows the sample Crystal Report created in the last hour with the Field Explorer activated and docked on the left side of the screen. As previously mentioned, this can be docked on either side of the designer or at the bottom the screen. Alternatively the Field Explorer can freely float over any part of the design window by simply dragging and dropping it.

The next seven sections introduce the different types of fields accessible from the Field Explorer and provide some introductory ideas on where they might be used in a report. Subsequent hours in the book will cover some advanced uses of these types of fields. Before moving on to explore these different types of fields, here are some common traits shared by all field types:

- Fields that are being used in the report or fields that have been used by other fields (for example, formulas) being used in the report will be highlighted with a green check mark in front of them.
- The buttons along the top of the Field Explorer (Insert, Browse, New, Edit, Rename, and Delete) will be enabled or disabled based on the availability of the selected Field type.
- Detailed report field formatting, positioning, and resizing will be covered in Hour 8, "Fundamentals of Report Formatting."

FIGURE **6.1**

*Crystal Reports
Designer with the
Field Explorer
docked on the left
side.*

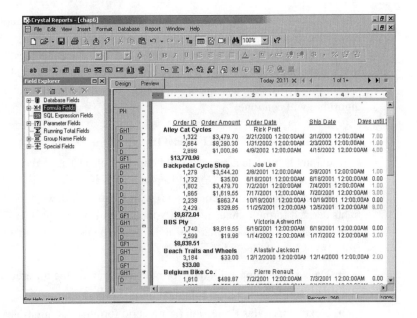

Accessing Database Fields

The database fields branch of the Field Explorer tree is used to add database fields to your report. The fields that can be added to your report are those from standard database tables, views, stored procedures, and so on that you previously selected as data sources for this report (discussed in Hours 3–5). To add additional tables or other data sources to your report, you would use the Database Expert under the Database menu.

To insert the database fields that are available from the Field Explorer into your report, either click and drag them in to the desired location on the report or select them, click the Insert to Report button (or Insert to Report action from the right-click menu), and then select the desired location on the report for the highlighted fields.

If you are uncertain of exactly which fields to add to your report because of ambiguous (for example, WERKS, MENGE, WONKY) or similar (for example, District, Region, Locale, Division) field names, you might be able to determine the appropriate field by selecting the respective field and using the Browse button (or the Browse action from the right-click menu) to view the data type and sample values of data from the table.

Multiple fields can be highlighted simultaneously in the Field Explorer and placed in the report designer window at once. Crystal Reports will drop the first of the multiple chosen fields in the selected location on the report and will place the subsequent fields in order to the right of the initial field. If the report's layout runs out of real estate on the right side of the report, the subsequent fields will be placed one line down and the placement algorithm will continue.

Accessing Formula Fields

Formula fields provide a means to add derived fields (that is, those not directly available in your database) into your Crystal Reports, such as a calculation. They also provide your business users (report consumers) with additional views of data. Crystal Reports treats derived formula fields in exactly the same manner as it does original database fields. Some examples of where formulas might be used on the sample report (Chap5.rpt) from Hour 5 would include

- Days Until Shipped (A date formula determining the difference between the two database fields—Order Date and Ship Date)
- Next Years Sales Projection (A numeric formula that multiples the database field Last Years Sales by 110%)
- Custom Name Field to include the first letter of a customer contact's First Name (a database field) concatenated with a space and the contact's last name (another database field)

The formula fields branch of the Field Explorer tree is used to add existing or new formula fields to a report. A listing of previously created formulas (for example, DaysUntilShipped from the Hour 5 sample report) will appear in this part of the Field Explorer tree. Once created, existing formulas are added to the report by either clicking and dragging and dropping or by selecting the formula and using the Insert functionality—available through the right-click menu or Field Explorer action button—and then selecting the location.

> Both simple and complex formulas can be created on any type of field including numeric, date, string, Boolean, or memo fields. This is explored in Hours 10, "Understanding and Implementing Formulas," and 17, "Using Formulas and Custom Functions to Implement Complex Business Logic."

If a new formula is required, it can be created directly from the Field Explorer by using the New toolbar button. You will be prompted to name the new formula and then select the method of creation. This dialog is displayed in Figure 6.2.

FIGURE 6.2

The Formula Name dialog.

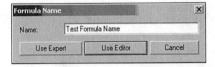

Using the Xtreme Sample Database and the sample report created in Hour 5 (chap5.rpt), one simple formula we might want to add is a Full Name field that comprises both the first and last name of the customer's contact person (Contact First Name and Contact Last Name in the Customer sample table) .

To perform this task, implement the following steps:

1. Highlight the Formula Fields branch of the Field Explorer tree.

2. Select New using either the New button or by right-clicking and selecting New from the fly-out menu.

3. Enter the Formula Name **Full Name** in the Formula Creation dialog and select the Formula Editor using the Use Editor button.

4. Scroll down in the Report Fields window (the top left window in the main frame) to locate and open the Customer table. Select the Contact First Name field by double-clicking on it. The field will be displayed in the main Formula Editing window.

5. Add a space after the Contact First Name field and then type in + " " +. This will act to concatenate the two fields together and also add a space between the first name and the last name.

6. Scroll down in the Report Fields window (the top left window in the main frame) to locate and open the Customer table. Select the Contact Last Name field by double-clicking on it. The field will be displayed in the main Formula Editing window.

7. When you have confirmed that the main formula window looks exactly like that shown in Figure 6.3, save the Full Name formula by clicking the Save button and then closing the main Formula Editor window.

By selecting Save in the Formula Editor, we return to the Field Explorer and the new formula, Full Name, is now available to be placed on the report. Finish this section by placing the Full Name Formula Field on to the report beside the Customer Name.

6

FIGURE 6.3

The Formula Editor with a String concatenation formula created.

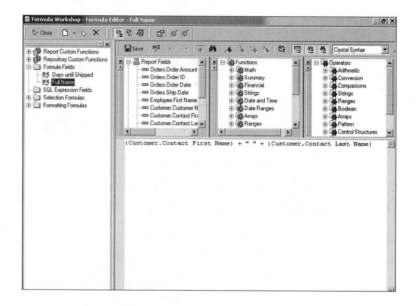

Accessing SQL Expression Fields

The SQL Expression fields branch of the Field Explorer tree is used to add existing or new SQL Expression fields to a report. A listing of previously created SQL Expressions will appear in this part of the Field Explorer tree. Once created, existing SQL Expressions are added to the report by either clicking and dragging and dropping or by selecting the SQL Expression—using the Insert into Report button or action on the right-click menu—and selecting the location.

SQL Expressions are created in the same Formula Editor as formulas but use *Structured Query Language (SQL)* statements (see Hour 22 for more information) rather than the formula syntax. SQL Expressions are used in cases where report-processing efficiency is critical. Using SQL expressions can give report designers greater control over report processing, such as pushing data processing to the database server instead of the Crystal Reports engine because this is often most efficient.

The SQL syntax created in SQL Expressions must be appropriate to the source database. Different databases support various syntactical versions of SQL and even diverse degrees of functionality. This is explored in Hour 22, "Optimizing SQL Queries."

Accessing Parameter Fields

Parameter fields provide a means to create dynamic reports and provide your business users with an interactive method of driving the report content or layout they view. When a Crystal Report contains parameters, it requests certain pieces of information from the business user before processing. The involved Crystal Report can then use those inputted parameters to filter the data that is presented or even suppress entire report sections. Some examples of where parameters might be used include

- A region parameter on a sales report
- A profit center on a financial report
- Beginning and ending dates on a transactional report
- A department on an HR salary listing report
- A salesperson name on a customer order listing report, as in the sample report from Hour 5

The parameter fields branch of the Field Explorer tree is used to add existing or new parameter fields to your report. A listing of previously created parameters (for example, Employee Name in Hour 5's sample report) will appear in this part of the Field Explorer tree. Once created, Parameter fields are added to the report by either clicking and dragging and dropping or by selecting the Parameter Field—using the Insert into Report button or action on the right-click menu—and selecting the location.

If a new parameter is required, it can also be created directly from the Field Explorer by using the New toolbar button. You will be prompted to name the new parameter and enter some supporting information. This dialog is displayed in Figure 6.4.

FIGURE 6.4

The Create Parameter Field dialog.

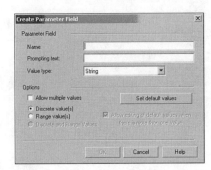

6

Detailed information on parameter creation and utilization as a means to filter report information is covered in Hour 12, "Implementing Parameters for Dynamic Reporting." At this point, it is only important to note the location of this field type.

Running Total Fields

Running total fields provide a means to incrementally calculate a total on a report as the records are processed. In contrast to the summary fields you will learn about later in the book, running total fields enable you to control how a total is calculated, when it is reset, and when it is displayed. Some examples in which running total fields might be used include

- Running Total of Web Site Hits over Multiple Days/Weeks/Months/etc
- Running Total of Sales Expenses over Weeks in a Quarter or Fiscal Year
- Running Total of Average Order Amount over Time
- Running Total of Employee Count over Time

The running total fields branch of the Field Explorer tree is used to add existing or new running total fields to your report. A listing of previously created running totals will appear in this part of the Field Explorer tree. Once created, existing running total fields are added to the report by either clicking and dragging and dropping or by selecting the Running Total Field—using the Insert into Report button or action on the right-click menu—and selecting the location.

If a new running total is required, it can be created directly from the Field Explorer by using the New toolbar button. You will be prompted to name the new running total. Select the field to calculate the running total on, the type of running total (for example, sum, average, variance, and so on), and some other supporting information about when the running total is to be evaluated and reset as shown in Figure 6.5.

FIGURE 6.5

The Create Running Total Field dialog.

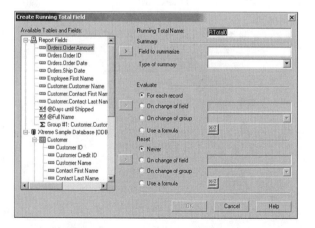

In our sample Customer Order Listing report from Hour 5, an interesting running total to add would be one on the average order amount over time for each sales rep. This running total will tell senior sales management if the average order size for each sales rep is increasing or decreasing over time. To create this running total:

1. Prepare the sample report from Hour 5 for this new field by deleting the Ship Via title and associated database field to clear some room. Select these two fields in either the Design or Preview tab of Crystal Reports and press the Delete key. Also, sort the data by ascending date by accessing the Record Sorting Expert from either the Report menu or the Record Sort icon on the Expert Tools toolbar, and then selecting Order Date as a secondary sort order after Customer Name.

2. Highlight the Running Total Fields branch of the Field Explorer tree.

3. Select New using either the New toolbar button or by right-clicking and selecting New from the pop-up menu. This will bring up the dialog shown in Figure 6.5.

4. Enter the name **Avg Order Size** for the Running Total Name.

5. Select the Order Amount field from the Order Table as the Field to summarize by highlighting it in the field selection window and clicking on the Select button (>).

6. Because we desire an average, select this from the Type of Summary drop-down box.

7. We want to calculate the average order amount for each order, so select the For Each Record option in the Evaluate section.

8. Because we want to calculate this for each salesperson, select the Reset On Change of Group option and select the Customer Name group in the Reset section and click OK to finish.

The completed Running Total dialog is shown in Figure 6.6.

FIGURE 6.6

The Edit Running Total Field dialog.

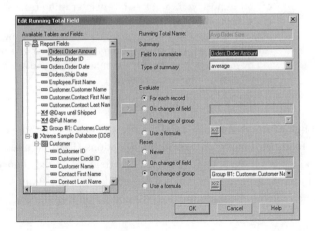

6

After the running total has been created, it only needs to be dragged on to the report in the appropriate section. In this example, the appropriate section is the Detail section to show a changing average order size for every order. The Updated Sample Customer Order report is shown in Figure 6.7. Notice the changing average order size being calculated for each record. This type of report can now provide increasing value to senior sales management.

FIGURE 6.7

A sample Orders report with Running Average Total on Order Size for each sales rep.

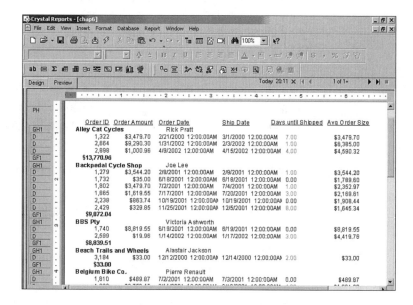

It's not necessary to place running total fields exclusively in the Details Section of your reports. By placing running total fields in different sections of your report, you can receive very interesting results. For example, if you place a running total in a Group Footer section, the running total will display the selected running total up to and including the current group. This can be very useful when analyzing average order size over time and grouping by month or quarter (for example, where you are only interested in some form of aggregated running total).

As highlighted in the Running Total dialog, it is possible to both evaluate and reset the running total fields based on four different options. The first three are self-explanatory— for each record, on the change of a specified field, or on the change of a specified group. The last option, using a Formula, is a powerful and flexible option that should be more fully explored after completing Hours 10 and 17 on formula creation. In its simplest description however, this option enables the creation of a conditional running total or the reset of that running total based on the results of a formula you have created. A good use of this conditional summing is the creation of a running total that calculates the sum of all orders, but only evaluates (or sums in this case) the running total when the total order amount on a given record is greater than a certain amount (for example, 1,000). This running total, in effect, would provide a running total of only large orders so that business analysts can determine the percentage of revenue derived from large orders.

Group Name Fields

Group Name fields will only exist in a report after you have specified one or more groups to add to your report. We will cover that functionality later in this hour. Group Name fields are created at the same time you add a Grouping to a report. Once created, existing Group Name fields are added to the report by either clicking and dragging and dropping or by selecting the Group Name—using the Insert into Report button or action on the right-click menu—and selecting the location.

Special Fields

The special fields provided in the Field Explorer are a number of system fields that Crystal Reports provides. These system fields and a brief description are provided in Table 6.1.

TABLE 6.1 Special Fields Available in Crystal Reports V9

Field	Description	Valid Locations on Report
Data Date	The date the data in your report was last retrieved.	Anywhere
Data Time	The time the data in your report was last retrieved.	Anywhere
File Author	The author of the report. This is set in Document Properties (File\Summary Info in the menu).	Anywhere
File Creation Date	The date the report was created.	Anywhere
File Path and Name	The file path and name for the report.	Anywhere
Group Number	An automatically created group numbering field.	Group Header or Group Footer sections only
Group Selection Formula	The current report's group selection formula. This is created by using the Select Expert covered in Hour 7.	Anywhere
Modification Date	Date that the report was last modified (in any way).	Anywhere

6

TABLE 6.1   continued

Field	Description	Valid Locations on Report
Modification Time	Time that the report was last modified (in any way) .	Anywhere
Page N of M	Indicates Current Page on report relative to total number of pages.	Anywhere
Page Number	The Current Page number.	Anywhere
Print Date	Either the current date or a date specified in the Set Print Date and Time dialog under the Reports\Set Print and Date Time option.	Anywhere
Print Time	Either the current time or a time specified in the Set Print Date and Time dialog under the Reports\Set Print and Date Time option.	Anywhere
Record Number	An automatically created number that counts the records in the detail section of your report.	Details Section
Record Selection Formula	The current report's record selection formula. This is created by using the Select Expert covered in Hour 7.	Anywhere
Report Comments	Comments summarizing the report. This is set in Document Properties (File\Summary Info in the menu).	Anywhere— but only the first 256 characters will be printed.
Report Title	The title of the report set in the Document Properties dialog (File\Summary Info in the menu).	Anywhere
Total Page Count	The total number of pages for this report.	Anywhere

These special fields are added to the report by either clicking and dragging and dropping or by selecting the Special Field—using the Insert into Report button or action on the right-click menu—and selecting the location.

Working with Groups

To this point, your exposure to grouping report data has been limited to using the Report Wizard(s) introduced in Hour 4, "Using the Default Report Wizards," and a brief introduction to manual grouping in Hour 5. Grouping data in a report facilitates business user analysis and enables meaningful summarizations. Examples of common and useful groupings in reports include

- Sales Reports that group by Sales Rep, Product Line, Sales District, or Quarter
- HR Reports that group by Department, Management Level, or Tenure with the company
- Financial Reports that group by Company Division, Product Line, or Quarter
- Inventory Reports that group by Part Number, Supplier, or Manufacturing Plant

Crystal Reports provides easy-to-use grouping functionality that enables multiple types of powerful and flexible data grouping.

Inserting Groups

Taking either the sample report from this or the previous hour, the flexibility and power of grouping can be realized in a few short steps. Let's assume that senior sales management in a hypothetical company is interested in viewing customer order information by country, in addition to the existing grouping by employee/sales rep.

1. Select the Group option from the Insert menu or click on the Insert Group button located on the Insert toolbar. This will bring up the Insert Group dialog as shown in Figure 6.8.

FIGURE 6.8

The Insert Group dialog.

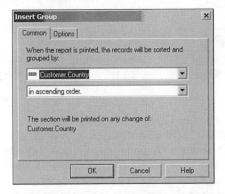

2. The Insert Group dialog prompts for the Data field that the group will be based on. The field you select can be an existing database field already on the report, a database field included in your data sources (perhaps not yet on the report), a formula field, or a SQL Expression. For this exercise select the Country field from the Customer Table for the Grouping field.
3. Select Ascending Order for the Sort Order.
4. Click OK, and the report will be changed to reflect a new grouping on country.

6

The results of this new grouping are shown in Figure 6.9. Note that the country grouping is automatically selected to be the lowest-level grouping. This is the standard and expected behavior when inserting new groups, but based on the sales management's request, we will need to edit the grouping order so that country becomes the highest level. We will do that in the next section.

FIGURE 6.9

A sample report with Country and Customer Name groupings.

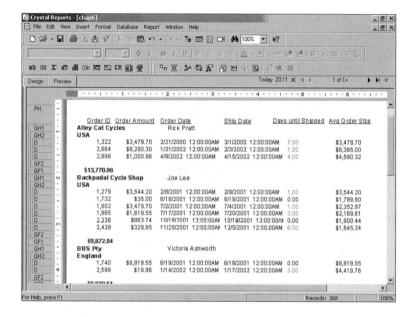

The specified order selection of the Insert Group dialog is particularly interesting because of the great flexibility it provides. With this option, you can dynamically create both groups and a custom order of appearance on the report. A related geographic example would be the creation of a Continent grouping based on the country field in the database with the groupings and order of appearance specified in the Insert Group dialog. You will notice that when you select specified order, two more tabs will appear in the Insert Group dialog (see Figure 6.10). These tabs enable you to specify or create dynamic groupings and also to select a method of handling the other elements that do not fit into your dynamically created groups.

A last note on the Insert Group dialog is that options around group naming are available for customization. These options are accessed through the Options tab and facilitate the process of making your reports most presentable. For example, in another situation you might want to group on a country code instead of a country name for report processing efficiency (that is, numeric fields are sorted faster than string fields), but you still want to present the actual Country Name in the report. You could perform this customization through the Options tab in the Insert Group dialog as highlighted in Figure 6.11.

FIGURE 6.10

The Insert Group dialog with the Specified Ordering tabs displayed.

FIGURE 6.11

The Options tab of the Insert Group dialog.

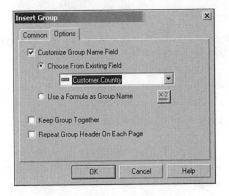

Re-ordering Groups

As you can certainly imagine, it is quite common to want to group data by different fields within a single report. It is also quite common to receive multiple reporting requests for different views of data by various levels of grouping—some examples might be

- View sales numbers grouped by product, region, and by sales rep
- View sales numbers grouped by region, product, and by sales rep
- View sales numbers grouped by sales rep, product, and by region

During report design, one of these different grouping orders could be created initially as we did in the last section with the groups Customer Name and Country. If the other grouping orders were required, these could be quickly accomplished through either the Crystal Reports Design window or the Group Expert. Working in the left-most report section area of the Design tab of Crystal Reports (not the Preview tab), the different

6

groups (sections) can be dragged and dropped before or after each other, quickly rear-ranging the grouping order. To complete the sales management's reporting request from the last section (to group by Country at the highest level and Customer below that), follow the following quick steps:

1. Click on the Design tab of the Crystal Reports Designer if you are not already on that tab.

2. After double-clicking and holding the last click on either the Country Group Header or Footer, drag that group to the outside of the Customer Name Grouping to dynamically re-sort the order of grouping. A hand will replace the normal cursor image when you have grabbed a group, and blue lines will highlight the intended drop location before you release your click and re-sort the grouping order.

> To facilitate identification of groups while in the Design tab, hover over a group header or footer section and a descriptive rollover tip will temporarily appear.

3. Click on the Preview tab, and you will see the benefits of your work—the same report with the groupings instantly rearranged. Figure 6.12 highlights your intended results.

FIGURE 6.12

A sample Customer Orders report re-grouped by country and then customer name.

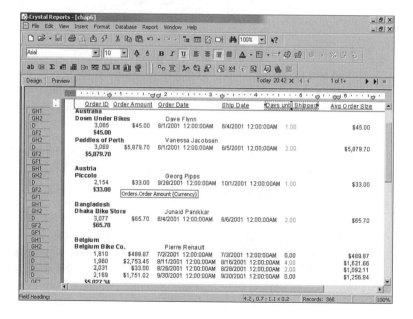

An alternative and powerful method for reordering groups is provided with the Group Expert. It is accessed from the Report menu, and the different groups can be re-ordered through the up and down buttons within the Grouping dialog. This quick re-ordering can present your data in completely different ways, serving multiple analysis requirements with very little report development effort. The next section explores the power of the Group Expert.

Using the Group Expert

Crystal Reports provides an easy method to add multiple groups simultaneously and a central location for accessing all your current groups—the Group Expert dialog. Accessed from the Report menu, the Group Expert dialog, displayed in Figure 6.13, enables the addition of multiple groups at one time and the quick re-ordering of any specified groups.

FIGURE 6.13
The Group Expert dialog.

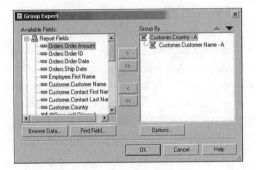

This dialog enables the selection of multiple groups in one location and provides access to the same functionality as the Insert Group dialog through the Options button. The groups can also be easily re-ordered from within this dialog through use of the up and down arrow buttons, located on the upper right of the dialog area.

Grouping on Date/Time Fields

One type of grouping that is common across most organizations is date-and-time related grouping. Analysts from all industries want to see how numbers (for example, sales revenue, units shipped, units produced, employees hired, and so on) change over various periods of time. To facilitate this type of analysis, Crystal Reports provides some built-in flexibility around date-and-time grouping. When you are creating a group that is based on a Date or Time field, an extra drop-down box will appear in the Insert Group dialog (see Figure 6.14). This extra Print by Section box enables the user to have the detail records in the report automatically grouped by any number of time-related criteria. Examples include By Day, By Hour, By Quarter, or even By Second. These automatic grouping options enable quick time-oriented analysis.

6

FIGURE 6.14

The Insert Group dialog with the Date/Time grouping drop-down box expanded.

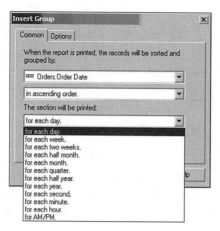

Hierarchical Grouping

Another type of special grouping that is available in Crystal Reports is hierarchical grouping. This special type of grouping enables your report data to be dynamically grouped on a hierarchy kept within a single table of your database. To enable hierarchical grouping, a group of the base-level data should be created through the standard Group Creation dialogs described previously. The Hierarchical Group option dialog can then be selected from the Report menu. To walk through a quick example, try the following steps:

1. Create a new blank Crystal Report and connect to the Xtreme Sample Database(hint: use the ODBC listing).

2. Select the Employee table for the report and Click on the OK button in the Database Expert.

3. Call up the Field Explorer, select the First Name, Last Name, Extension, and Position fields from the Employee table, and drop them into the detail section of the report.

4. Insert a Group on Employee Last Name using the Insert Group dialog (accessed from the Insert menu). Select ascending sort order and click OK in the Insert Group dialog.

5. Select Hierarchical Grouping Options from the Report menu. You will be presented with the dialog displayed in Figure 6.15. Click on the Sort Data Hierarchically option and select either Employee Supervisor or Employee Reports To as the parent field with an indent of 0.33 of an inch.

FIGURE 6.15

The Hierarchical Options dialog.

FIGURE 6.15

The Hierarchical Options dialog.

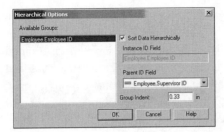

6. Click OK and view your new report. Figure 6.16 displays a report that should be similar and highlights the power of hierarchical grouping.

FIGURE 6.16

A sample hierarchical report.

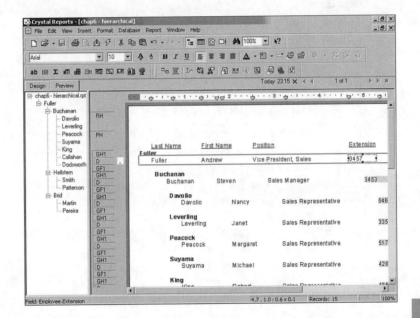

When creating a hierarchical group, the potential Parent fields are selected from the fields in the selected data source that have the same field type (for example, number, string, date) as the Grouped On field.

Understanding Drill-down Reports

As we have highlighted, grouping data facilitates data analysis for business users and enables meaningful summarizations in your reports. Having both the group level and the detail level data available in a view of a report enables the simultaneous analysis of both

6

group level summaries and the supporting detail records (for example, database fields, formulas, and so on). There are situations, however, in which a report consumer or analyst will want to view only aggregated group level information initially and then selectively drill-down into detail records where relevant (that is, drill-down only where the aggregated group level information is interesting, appealing, or stands out). This is easily and quickly accomplished in Crystal Reports through the use of the built-in drill-down capabilities in the product.

When the term *drill-down* is used, it implies that a business user has the ability to move from an aggregated or grouped view of the data (for example, sales revenue for each sales district) to a more detailed level of the data (for example, sales revenue for each salesperson in a selected sales district). In Crystal Reports, this is as easy as double-clicking on the involved group data or aggregated graphic.

Creating a Drill-down Report

By default, whenever a group is created within Crystal Reports, an automatic drill-down path is created from the respective group headers into the child groups and Detail records. The drill-down icon, when the cursor icon turns into a magnifying glass, will appear in your Crystal Reports preview tab as you hover over a group header with drill-down enabled like those depicted in Figure 6.17.

FIGURE 6.17

A sample report with drill-down groups.

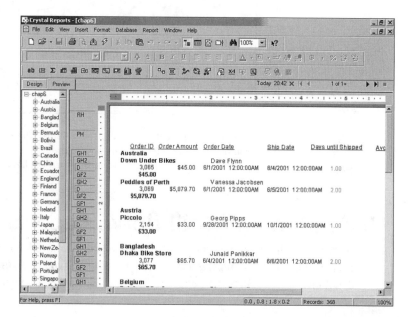

By double-clicking on the involved group header, a new viewing tab is opened with only the relevant group header's supporting information. Figure 6.18 highlights one of these views.

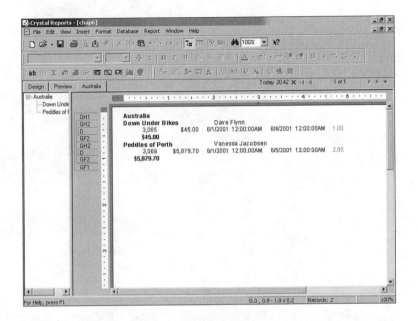

FIGURE 6.18

The Drill-down Viewing tab in Crystal Reports Preview mode.

An alternative method of navigating through report data is to use the Group Navigation tree that is exposed through all Crystal Report Viewers. The advantage of this is that it does not initiate new viewing tabs like those seen in Figure 6.18. If your report does not have a navigation tree displayed, click on the Toggle Group Tree button located on the main toolbar. The Group Navigation tree enables report viewers to quickly jump to any point in the report by highlighting the group level that they are interested in viewing.

Hiding Details on a Drill-down Report

To accomplish the task of only displaying the aggregated group level information in our sample report and not the details, right-click on the Details section—either in the Design or Preview window. Figure 6.19 highlights the resulting right-click menu.

FIGURE 6.19

Detail Section right-click menu.

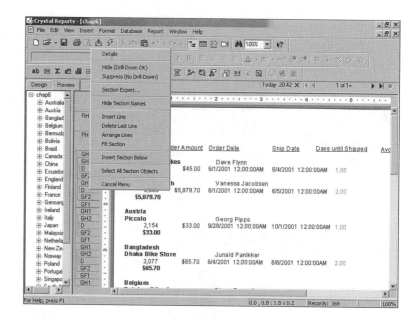

By selecting the Hide (Drill-Down OK) option in this right-click menu, our report will now only show the details within the aggregated groups when a business user drills down into them. Figure 6.20 highlights what the report now looks like in Preview mode. From here, the business user can drill-down to the drill-down viewing tabs (see Figure 6.18) by double-clicking on any of the group header rows or data.

FIGURE 6.20

A sample report with detail sections hidden, but available in drill-down.

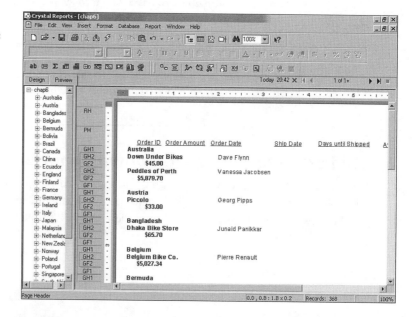

> The Suppress option from the same right-click menu, shown in Figure 6.19, can provide another viewing option to report designers and essentially turn off drill-down in your report. If the aggregated group level section data is to be viewed by business users but they will not be allowed to view detail section data, this can be accomplished by suppressing the detail section.

Summary

In this hour, you explored the different types of fields that are accessible from the Field Explorer and some of their powerful capabilities. You also were introduced to setting up a variety of different types of report groupings and the flexibility that they provide.

You are very likely starting to envision some of the potential report solutions possible using Crystal Reports based on what you've completed so far. Hour 7, "Filtering, Sorting, and Summarizing Data," introduces you to additional functionality that you can combine with your existing reports to further augment their value.

Q&A

Q Will I learn more about creating formulas in Crystal Reports?

A Yes. Hours 10 and 17 will cover formula creation in much greater detail than the cursory introduction in this chapter.

Q Is it possible to hide or suppress sections in a Crystal Report other than the Detail sections?

A Yes. By right-clicking on any of the report sections, a number of options are made available to you—hiding and suppressing among them. Hour 9, "Working with Report Sections," covers formatting sections in much greater detail.

Workshop

The quiz questions and activities are provided for your further understanding of the current hour's topics.

Quiz

1. What is a special field?
2. What is the difference between a formula and a SQL Expression?

6

Quiz Answers

1. The special fields provided in the Field Explorer are a number of system variables that Crystal Reports provides for you to use within your reports (for example, page number, file author, data date, and so on).

2. A SQL Expression must be written in the Structured Query Language of the Database you are using as a data source for the given report. SQL Expressions can increase the efficiency of your reports by passing the entire expression to the database to process. Formulas provide increased flexibility through a powerful library of Crystal and VB syntax, but they slow report processing performance when they must be executed on the server that holds Crystal Reports.

Activities

Now that you have started playing with the Crystal Reports Designer in full Designer mode, try connecting to one of your own local databases and creating a simple listing report with different types of groupings.

HOUR 7

Filtering, Sorting, and Summarizing Data

Up until this point, you have created reports that simply projected the rows of data in your database on to the report surface with little manipulation of that data. Any basic database query tool could achieve this. The value of Crystal Reports is its inherent ability to convert rows of raw data into information. Information will reveal something about the data that cannot be found by simply pouring over pages and pages of records. In the last hour, you began to take advantage of the power of Crystal Reports by applying grouping to a report to organize the data into categorical groups. In this hour, you will build on that by learning how to create reports that perform the following actions:

- Filter data based on a given criteria
- Sort data based on field values
- Summarize and subtotal data

Filtering the Data in Your Report

So far, the reports you have created have returned all the records from your database. Sometimes this is appropriate, but often reports need to filter the data based on a specified criteria. This is most apparent when working with large databases in which there can easily be hundreds of thousands of records returned from a query, especially when joins are applied.

As with many features in Crystal Reports, there are multiple ways to filter data:

- Using the Select Expert—This simple method provides a visual way to specify filtering.

- Using the Record Selection Formula—This more granular, yet powerful, method involves creating a custom formula language expression to determine the filter criteria.

Working with the Select Expert

Let's work through an illustrative example of filtering using the Select Expert. Taking what you have learned so far about creating simple columnar reports, create a new report from the Xtreme Sample Database, adding the Customer Name and Last Year's Sales fields from the Customer table to the details section of the report. The following steps will walk you through adding a filter to this report:

1. To invoke the Select Expert, click its button found on the Experts toolbar or, alternatively, select the Select Expert option from the Report menu.

2. The first step in creating a filter is to choose which field the filter should be created on. Accordingly, the Choose Field dialog is displayed. Both fields that are present in the report and fields from the database are listed. A field does not need to be on the report in order to create a filter using it. At this point, if you forget which values are stored in any of the fields listed, click the Browse button to see a sample list of values. For this example, choose Last Year's Sales field and click OK. The Select Expert dialog appears, as shown in Figure 7.1.

3. The Select Expert has a group of tabs—one for each filter defined inside that report. In the case of your example report, there will only be one tab for the Last Year's Sales field and another called <New>, which is used to define an additional filter. By default, the filter setting on the Last Year's Sales tab is set to Is Any Value. This means that regardless of the value of the Last Year's Sales field, all records will be included in the report. To change the filter in a report, change the value of the drop-down list. For this example, change it to Is Equal To.

FIGURE 7.1

The Select Expert.

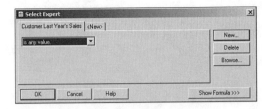

4. When this option is selected, another drop-down list appears. If the exact value to filter the field on is known, it can be typed in to this list box. However, in this case, you might not know exactly what the values of the field are, so you are provided with the ability to browse that field's values by simply pulling down the drop-down list. Choose $300.00 and click OK.

> Often when modifying filters and selections in the report designer, Crystal Reports will display a message asking the user if she wants to use the saved data in the report or refresh the data from the database. Using the saved data in the report is usually a good option because it does not incur a new query to the database. However, especially when modifying filters, it can cause some confusing results because the set of saved data in the report might or might not consist of all the records in the database; that is, a filter might have already been applied. So when modifying filters, it's best to refresh the data whenever Crystal Reports asks you.

5. When returning to the report, you should notice that the report now only displays a single record: the Has Been Bikes company that had sales of $300. A more useful filter would be to show all records that were above or below a threshold. To accomplish this, re-open the Select Expert. This time, change the Is Equal To criteria to Is Greater Than and type **100,000** in to the list box. When closing the Select Expert and returning to the report, a small collection of records should be returned. In just a few seconds, you've created a report showing your top customers.

Let's look at a few more types of filters that can be applied to a report. The following steps will walk you through applying these various types of filters:

1. Open the Select Expert again and change the criteria from Is Greater Than to Is Between.

2. This time, two list boxes are presented, each corresponding to an upper and lower bound. Type in the values **2,000** and **3,000**, respectively (as shown in Figure 7.2), and click OK. The report will display all customers with sales between two and three thousand dollars.

7

FIGURE 7.2

*Modifying the report
to display customers
with sales between two
and three thousand.*

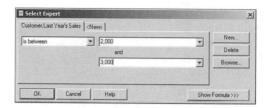

3. So far, only the Last Year's Sales field has been used as a filter. However, any field can be used as a filter, although there are slightly different options for various field types. Go back in to the Select Expert and, while on the Last Year's Sales tab, click the Delete button to remove that filter.

4. Add a new filter on the Customer Name field by clicking the New button and selecting the Customer Name field from the subsequent dialog.

5. To have the report only show a single customer's record, leave the criteria as Is Equal To and choose Alley Cat Cycles from the drop-down list. Applying this filter results in the report only showing a single record.

6. Return to the Select Expert and change the criteria to Is One Of. This option allows you to choose multiple values. Each time a value is selected from the drop-down list, it is added to the bottom of the list box. Select Alley Cat Cycles, Bikes R Us, and Hikers and Bikers and notice how the report now reflects those three records.

7. Next, remove the three values previously selected by highlighting them and clicking the Remove button. Now change the criteria to Is Like and type **Wheel*** in to the drop-down list. Click Add or press Enter to add this item to the list. Applying this filter results in the report showing all customers whose names begin with the word Wheel.

When using the Is Like option, an * acts as a wildcard for any number of characters, whereas a ? acts as a wildcard for only a single character. This can be quite useful when searching through textual fields for a specific text pattern.

The last thing this hour covers with respect to the Select Expert is applying multiple filters. To do so, perform the following steps:

1. Start from scratch and delete any filters you have applied by clicking the Delete button on each tab.

2. Click the New button and add a new filter using the Last Year's Sales field.

3. Change the criteria to Is Less Than and the value to 5,000. This filter would result in showing all customers with sales of less than $5,000, but let's apply another condition.

4. Click the New button and add a new filter based on the Country field. Note that this is slightly different from the previous filters that have been created—not only because more than one filter is being applied at the same time, but also because the filter being created is based on a field that is not present on the report.

5. Change the criteria for the Country filter to Is Equal To and choose Canada from the drop-down list. Clicking Ok will apply this filter will result in a report with multiple conditions: customers from Canada with sales below $5,000. See Figure 7.3 for the output of this report.

FIGURE 7.3

A filter is applied to show all Canadian customers with sales less than 5,000.

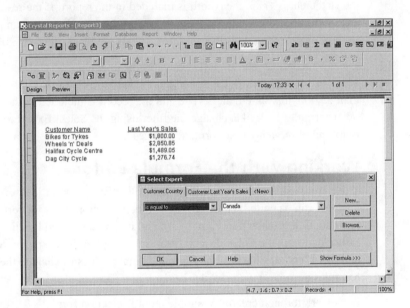

The Record Selection Formula

Although the Select Expert is quite powerful, there are certain situations in which the report developer needs to define a filter that is more complex than the Select Expert allows. Fortunately, Crystal Reports has a built-in formula language that allows custom expressions to be defined as a filter. In fact, this is one of the strengths of the Crystal Reports product: being able to use the formula language to attain a high level of control in various aspects of report creation.

Although you might not have realized it, even when you were using the Select Expert, a formula was being generated in the background that defined the filter. To see this in action, open the Select Expert and click the Show Formula button. This expands the

7

Select Expert dialog to reveal the formula being generated. This formula is called the *record selection formula*. Notice that the formula's value is as follows:

```
{Customer.Last Year's Sales} > $5000.00
```

The formula language is covered in detail in an hour later in this book, but the following are the key points to learn right now. In formulas, braces denote a field. For database fields, the table and field name are included and are separated by a period. The rest of the formula is a statement that tests if the sales value is more than five thousand dollars.

Think of a record selection formula as an expression that evaluates to a true or false result. For each record in the database, Crystal Reports applies the record selection formula, plugging in the current field values in place of the fields in braces. If the result of the statement is True, the record is included in the report. If the result of the statement is False, the record is excluded from the report. Let's look at an example. The first record in the Customer's table is that of City Cyclists who had sales of $20,045.27.

For this record, Crystal Reports evaluates the preceding formula, substituting $20,045.27 in place of {Customer.Last Year's Sales}. Because this value is larger than $5,000, this statement is True and the record is included in the report. To see what other formulas look like, change the filter using the Select Expert to a few different settings and observe how the formula changes.

Working with the Formula Editor

The formula shown at the bottom of the Select Expert is not just for informational purposes: It can be edited. However, a much better editor exists for formulas. It's called the Formula Editor (shown in Figure 7.4), and it can be invoked by clicking the Formula Editor button in the Select Expert or by selecting the Report menu, Selection Formulas, and then Record. Although the formula language doesn't change, the process of creating formulas becomes much simpler because of a focused user interface.

Let's work through creating a simple record selection formula. This formula will attempt to filter out any customers who owe more than $5,000 in tax. Tax owing will be defined as 2% of their sales figure. To implement this, work through the following steps:

1. To begin, launch the Formula Editor as described previously.

2. Next, create an expression that calculates the tax owing. To do this, enter the following expression:

   ```
   {Customer.Last Year's Sales} * 0.02
   ```

3. The previous expression now represents the tax owing. To complete the expression to filter out all customers who owe more than $5,000 in tax, modify the formula to look like this:

   ```
   ({Customer.Last Year's Sales} * 0.02) > 5000
   ```

FIGURE 7.4
The Formula Editor.

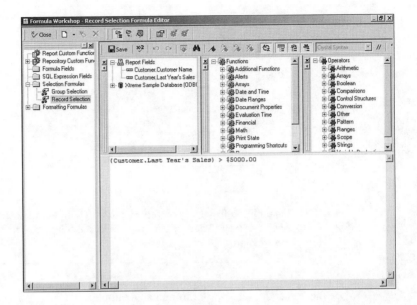

4. To complete the formula and apply the filter, click the Close button at the top left corner of the Formula Editor window, then click OK to close the Select Expert. Focus will return back to the report, and when data is refreshed, only a handful of customers should be listed on the report.

Both the formula language and the Formula Editor are topics unto themselves and will be discussed in more detail in a later hour.

Learning to Sort Records

Although filtering is one of the key components of an effective report, it alone is not enough. Often, to properly see the key pieces of data, a report needs to be sorted. Crystal Reports is quite flexible when it comes to sorting, allowing any field type to be sorted, as well as multiple and ascending or descending sorts. Sorting is applied using the Sort Expert.

Working with the Sort Expert

The Sort Expert is launched from a button on the Experts toolbar, and also via the Record Sort Expert item on the Report menu. Figure 7.5 shows the Sort Expert.

To apply sorting to the report, select a field from the list of available fields on the left side of the dialog area, and click the arrow (>) button to add that field to the sort fields list. Note that like filters, sorts can use fields both on the report and fields not otherwise used in the report.

7

FIGURE 7.5

The Sort Expert.

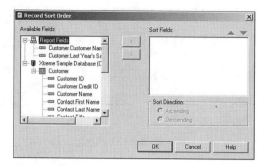

In addition to sorting on report and database fields, you can sort on formula fields as well. Creating a formula field allows you to sort from a custom expression.

To see this in action, let's work through an example:

1. Create a new report using the Employee table of the Xtreme Sample Database and add the First Name, Last Name, and Salary fields to the report.

2. Initially, this report doesn't tell us a lot because the data is in seemingly random order. However, if the report were sorted by last name, it would be more useful. To accomplish this, first launch the Sort Expert.

3. Select the Last Name field from the available fields list and click the arrow (>) button to apply a sort on it. Click OK to return to the report. Notice how the report's records are now sorted in alphabetical order by last name.

The Sort Expert allows sorting on both alphabetic and numeric fields. Let's modify this report to sort on salary instead of last name:

1. Return to the Sort Expert and remove the current sort by selecting the Last Name field from the sort fields list and clicking the < button.

2. Now select the Salary field and add it to the sort fields list.

3. Alphabetic fields are usually sorted in ascending order (from A to Z), but numeric fields are often sorted both ways. In this case, select the Salary field in the Sort Fields list and click Descending for the sort direction. This will list the employees with the top salary first. Click OK to apply the sort and return to the report.

Notice that some employees have the same salary level. If you wanted to perform a secondary sort within duplicates of the primary sort field, you can simply add another sort field. These sort fields can be arranged up and down using the buttons near the top right corner of the Sort Expert.

Creating Effective Summaries

The third key aspect of a good report after filtering and sorting is summarizing. Summarizing creates totals and subtotals that help the viewer of the report understand the data better. The following sections will discuss various types of summarizing.

Grand Totals

The simplest kind of summary is a grand total. This takes a single field and creates a total at the end of the report. To try this out, create a new report from the Orders table and add both the Order ID and the Order Amount fields on to the report.

Initially, this report is more than 30 pages long. A report of this length would make it very difficult to estimate the total amount of all orders, but a summary does that quite easily. Right-click the Order Amount field and select Insert, Summary from the context menu. This brings up the Insert Summary dialog as shown in Figure 7.6. To insert a summary, the first thing that needs to be specified is the field to summarize. Because you right-clicked the Order Amount field, this is already filled in for you. The next piece of information to fill in is the summary operation. The default is Sum, which you'll leave as its default. Finally, Crystal Reports needs to know for which group the summary should be performed. Because there is no grouping in this report, the only option is Grand Total, which is already filled in for you. Click OK to close this dialog.

FIGURE 7.6

Inserting a summary based on the Order Amount field.

When looking at the end of the report, a grand total of the order amount will now be visible in bold text. To edit the summary, right-click on it and select Edit Summary from the context menu. This brings up the Edit Summary dialog. Try changing the calculation from Sum to Average. This will now update the summary to show the average order amount. There are various calculations to choose from including minimum, maximum, variance, count, deviation, and median.

7

Besides the order amount total, it might be helpful to know how many orders there are. To do this, right-click the Order ID field and select Insert, Summary. Change the calculation from Sum to Count and click OK. Now besides the order amount summary, there is a count of all orders.

Group Summaries

Although grand totals are useful, summarizing starts to become really powerful when it is applied at the group level. This enables totaling for each level of a group and tells more about the data than a simple grand total does because it measures the relationships between the various groups. To apply a group summary, a group must first exist in the report.

Using the same report from the last example with the Order ID and Order Amount fields, insert a group on the Ship Via field. This produces a report showing all the orders grouped by the method they were shipped with, for example, FedEx, Loomis, and so on. To compare the different methods of shipment, right-click the Order Amount field and select Insert, Summary. Previously, when you created a grand total, you accepted all the defaults in this dialog. But this time, the summary location needs to be changed. Change Grand Total (Report Footer) to Group #1: Orders.Ship Via, and click OK.

Now a total field is inserted in to the report, which acts much like the grand total except that the total is repeated for each group. By examining these summaries, it can be determined that the largest order amount was shipped via UPS. You could also add a group-level summary to the Order ID field to determine the count of orders for each shipping method. Doing this reveals that the most orders were shipped via Loomis. These conclusions would have been difficult to reach without an effective summary.

When groups have many records inside of them, it sometimes becomes difficult to compare summaries because they aren't all visible on the page at the same time. A good tip for comparing these values is to hide the details section, which contains all the records, and only display the group header and footer that normally contains the group name and its summary. To hide the details section, move to the Design tab, right-click the Details bar on the left side of the screen, and select Hide.

Group Selection and Sorting

On the topic of group summaries comes group selection and sorting. This brings together both filtering and summarizing concepts. Group selection and sorting is to groups what record selection is to records. In other words, defining a group selection or sorting defines which groups will be included in the report and in which order, respectively. A key point to understand is that whereas record selection and sorting work from values of individual fields, group selection and sorting work from summary fields.

In the example from the "Group Summaries" section, you created a report that displayed all orders grouped by the shipment method: But in order to determine which shipment method shipped the highest dollar value of orders, you had to manually browse through the report comparing the numbers. Applying a group sort would provide an easy way to see the rankings. Also, what if you only wanted to show the top three shipment methods? Group selection provides a way to filter out groups in such a manner.

As you might expect, there is an expert for applying group selection and sorting. It's called the Group Sort Expert, and it can be found on the Experts toolbar, as well as from the Group Sort Expert item on the Report menu. When the Group Sort Expert is launched, it displays one tab for each group in the report. In the previous example, there was only a single group on the Ship Via field so that's what you should see. Inside that tab, there is initially only a single list box with a value of No Sort. Changing this list box to All displays a set of options very similar to that of the Record Sort Expert—except instead of having a list of all report fields to choose to sort on, only summaries are listed.

The Group Sort Expert should have initially selected the Sum of Orders.Order Amount summary field and selected Ascending order. In this case, because it's more useful to see the highest dollar value first rather than last, change the sort order to Descending. Clicking OK closes the Group Sort Expert and returns focus to the report, which should have re-ordered the groups from largest to smallest. It's easy to see now that UPS was the method that shipped the highest dollar amount because it is the first group to appear.

There are only six shipment methods, but you can imagine reports that contain many more groups than six. Even if the groups are sorted, sometimes it's just too much data for the consumer of the report to absorb. To solve this problem, you can apply a group selection. To do this, launch the Group Sort Expert and change the All option on the left to Top N. Notice that the options are different from sorting. Applying a Top N selection implies that the groups will be sorted, but allows you to only display a specified number of the top groups in order. The default value is 5: Change this value to **3**.

Another option important to understand is relating to the set of groups that are excluded by the group selection. By default, these groups are all combined under a new group called Others. You might or might not want to include this others group in your report. If you choose not to, uncheck the option labeled Include Others. Clicking OK returns focus to the report that now should only display the top three shipment methods based on the total order amount.

7

Like the record selection, the group selection also has a formula that can be defined to use a custom expression to determine which groups to include in the report. The group selection formula can be found on the Report menu, under Selection Formulas, Group.

Some other options available in the group sort expert include Bottom N, which is the opposite of Top N, and Top and Bottom Percentage, which allow a filtering of the top x percent of groups.

Running Totals

The last kind of summary to be discussed in this hour is a running total. In some older versions of Crystal Reports, to create a running total, a report developer had to create a collection of formula fields, so a feature was added just to handle running totals. To illustrate this, follow the next few steps:

1. Create a new report using the Orders table. Add the Order ID, Order Date, and Order Amount fields to the details section of the report. You can reformat the order date to a more user-friendly format if you prefer by right-clicking the field and selecting Format.

2. Finally, add a sort based on the Order Data field. This report now shows all orders in the order they were placed. This is a perfect scenario for a running total that would show an cumulative total of orders so that the viewer of the report could see what the current order amount was at any given time.

3. To add a running total, right-click the Order Amount field and select Insert, Running Total from the Context menu. The Create Running Total Field dialog is displayed as shown in Figure 7.7.

FIGURE 7.7

Creating a Running Total field.

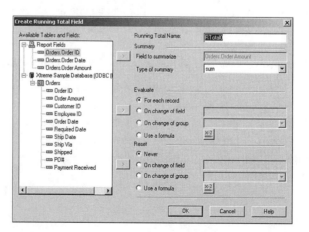

Four pieces of information need to be provided in this dialog, including

- Name of the running total field—The default is somewhat cryptic: It's best to give this a more meaningful name.

- The summary to perform—The Field to Summarize should be pre-populated for you, but you can change the summary type from the default of sum to other standard summary types. Some of the more useful types for a running total are Count and Average.

- When to evaluate the running total—The default and most common setting here is For each record, but this can be modified to only be evaluated when the value of another field is changed or a group value changed, or you can define a custom formula that defines the evaluation criteria.

- When to reset the running total—This setting determines if the running total should reset itself. If no groups are present in the report, you'll likely want to keep the default of Never. But if you have groups, you might want to reset the running total for each group or define a more complex criteria with a formula.

4. For our example, give the running total a name of Cumulative Orders and leave all other settings at their defaults. Completing this running total adds this new field to the report next to the Order Amount field and provides a cumulative total of orders. The output of this report is shown in Figure 7.8.

FIGURE 7.8

A cumulative orders report.

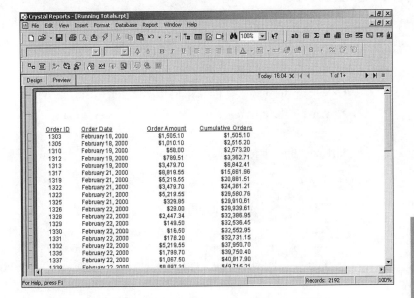

Running totals can also be created from the Field Explorer by selecting the Running Total Field item and clicking the New button or right-clicking and selecting New from the context menu. Creating a field in this way does not automatically add it to the report; you will need to place it on the report in a desired location yourself.

Summary

In this hour, you have learned about three of the key aspects to creating powerful reports—filtering, sorting, and summarizing. Filtering data enables you to focus your audience on a subset of key data by filtering out data that is either not appropriate for a given report or that lies outside of a threshold.

By learning how to sort both records and groups, you've gained an easy way to draw attention to the top or bottom numbers. Finally, you learned how to create summaries to reveal correlations in the data that would otherwise not be apparent by looking at the raw data itself. The mastery of these three features is a step down the road to creating powerful and effective reports.

Workshop

The quiz questions and activities are provided for your further understanding of the current hour's topics.

Quiz

1. What is the name of the expert used to filter data?
2. What is the difference between the record selection formula and the group selection formula?
3. Name three types of summary calculations besides Sum.

Quiz Answers

1. The expert used for filtering data is called the Select Expert.
2. The difference between the record and group selection formulas is on which data they operate. The record selection formula operates on the records and is used to filter out individual values. The group selection formula operates on group summaries and is used to filter out entire groups of data.
3. Some other summary calculations besides Sum are Average, Variance, Maximum, Minimum, Count, and Median.

Activities

To ensure that you are comfortable with the topics discussed in this hour, try to perform the following tasks:

- Create a report on the Customer table that only shows customers from the United States and Canada.
- Modify the preceding report to be sorted first by region and then by city.
- Create a report on the Customer table that shows the top five countries' based on last year's sales value.

7

PART III
Formatting Reports

Hour

Hour 8

Fundamentals of Report Formatting

So far, you have spent the majority of your time reviewing the various functions of the Crystal Reports design application. Equally important, however, is the form (or format) of the report, especially when a report is used as a corporate or industry standard document such as an income statement or balance sheet. This hour focuses on form over function and discusses the mechanisms required to incorporate a myriad of formatting techniques.

You have already reviewed the Crystal Reports 9 report development environment and learned about creating a report from a blank canvas, as well as how to select, group, filter, sort, and summarize your report data—so we will now move on to the more aesthetic report design techniques. Working with report formatting and object properties to create professionally designed reports is very straightforward, but it requires some familiarity with various features of the design application environment. This hour reviews the most commonly used object formatting techniques—fonts, borders, page and margin properties, and object layering—as well as provide a tutorial to apply these techniques to a sample report.

In this hour, we will cover the following topics:

- Positioning and sizing report objects
- Modifying object properties for formatting purposes
- Combining and layering report objects
- Configuring report page and margin properties

Positioning and Sizing Report Objects

After you have completed your functional report design tasks—connecting to the data source, adding report objects, and structuring the report—formatting the various objects on a report is the natural next step in the report design process. As demonstrated in Hour 5, "Creating and Designing Basic Reports," objects can be added to a report via a variety of methods—dragging and dropping objects from the design explorers or selecting objects from toolbar and menu commands and placing them in the desired locations within the report sections—for quick and intuitive report creation. Upon successfully adding objects to your report, each of the respective objects can be positioned, sized, and formatted for display purposes, as demonstrated in the following exercise.

As a visual example of the difference that report formatting efforts can make, compare the presentation value of the report samples shown in Figures 8.1 and 8.2. These two reports accomplish the same functional tasks, but the report in Figure 8.2 is much more visually appealing.

FIGURE 8.1

A customer contact listing report with little to no formatting applied.

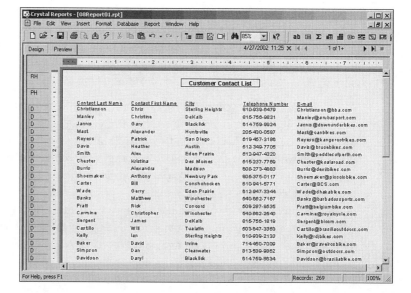

FIGURE 8.2

A customer contact listing report with a moderate amount of formatting applied.

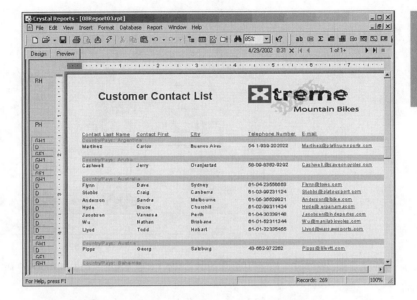

We will spend the remainder of this hour reproducing many of the applied visual elements of the latter report example. By completing the following exercises, you will create your own version of the Customer Contact Listing report using a variety of applied formatting techniques, such as adding a group definition to logically structure customers into their respective countries, formatting the font styles of the report title, column titles, country description, and email address fields to make for a more precise presentation of the report information. By combining the Country database field with a text field, you will also provide for a bilingual display of the country description.

Let's begin the design of our report. The following steps will enable you to create your own Customer Contact Listing report:

1. Open the Crystal Reports application and select to create a new report using the blank report layout from the Report Gallery dialog.

2. From the Database Explorer dialog, expand the Create a New Connection list, and then expand the ODBC (RDO) node to present the ODBC dialog window that lists the available data sources. Select the Xtreme Sample Database from the list of data sources and click Finish to continue to the Database Expert dialog.

3. From the Database Expert dialog, use the arrow (>) button to add the Customer table to the Selected Tables list on the right, as shown in Figure 8.3. Click OK to continue.

FIGURE 8.3

Select the Customer table from the Xtreme Sample Database list.

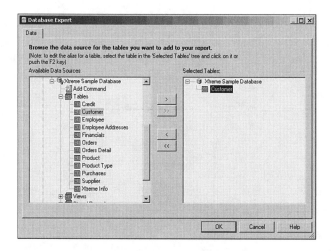

4. From the View menu, select the Field Explorer command to open the Field Explorer dialog.

5. From the Field Explorer, click and drag the Contact Last Name field onto the report's design view and place it to the far left of the Details section area, as shown in Figure 8.4.

FIGURE 8.4

Add the Contact Last Name field on to the Details section of the report.

6. Follow the previous step to add the Contact First Name, City, and Email fields to the Details section of the report, as shown in Figure 8.5.

7. From the Insert menu, select Text Object and drop the object in to the middle of the Report Header section (as shown in Figure 8.5) and type **Customer Contact List** in the text field. Click anywhere outside the text object to remove the cursor focus from the text object.

8

FIGURE 8.5

Position the displayed fields within the respective sections of the report.

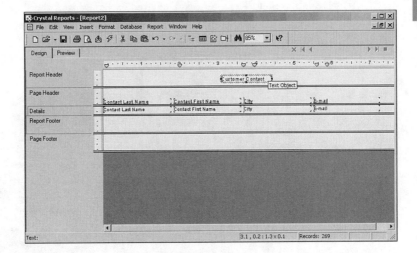

Now that the report includes the field and text objects identified previously, it's time to focus on positioning and resizing these fields for display purposes.

8. As Figure 8.5 shows, you might not be able to see the entire text entered in to the report title text object because it is not wide enough to display your text entry. To resolve this, click once on the report title text object located in the Report Header section so that it becomes highlighted. Using the dark blue handles that encompass the objects perimeters, float over the handle located on the right side of the text object with the mouse pointer; then click and hold the mouse button while dragging the handle farther to the right to widen the text object's display area. Refer to Figure 8.6 to see the result of this action.

Notice that when you float over the perimeter handles of an object with your mouse cursor (or pointer), the cursor icon turns into an alternative shape, such as horizontal or vertical arrows, to illustrate that you can modify the object if you click on the handle.

9. Now that you have widened the display area of your report title object using the concept of object handles, repeat this same step to modify the width of the field objects within the Details report section so that you can insert one additional object into the Details section of your report. Figure 8.6 shows the result of this action.

10. Using the Field Explorer (as discussed earlier), insert the Phone database field from the Customer table into the Details section of your report. Based on the previous steps, practice positioning and sizing the objects in the Details section to accommodate for all the database fields, as shown in Figure 8.6.

FIGURE 8.6

Your report should now display five database field objects in the Details section and one text object in the Report Header section.

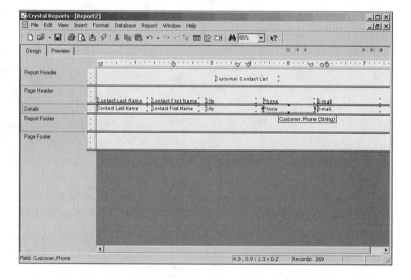

As you might have noticed, the field sizes are often large enough to show the entire field name in the Design view of the report. But from the Preview tab view of the report, you see that fields (such as the Email or Phone fields here) are cut off from the display area. This is not unusual, and it might require you to resize the field objects to ensure that they are appropriate for the report display area. It's best to use the report's Preview tab as a guide to formatting the layout of your reports.

11. Now click the Preview tab to see a preview display of what the report will actually look like, as shown in Figure 8.7.

8

If the Preview tab is not displayed in the application, you have not yet run the report against the database. To run the report, click the Refresh toolbar icon to execute the report to run—the Refresh toolbar icon is represented with a yellow lightening bolt.

FIGURE 8.7

To preview your report, either select the Preview tab or click the Refresh button.

Although it's important to understand the basics of report formatting, you will not necessarily have to go through the often arduous process of formatting reports every time. Report templates can be used to apply predefined and meaningful formatting characteristics in a very quick manner. See Hour 19, "Designing Effective Report Templates," for more details on designing and using report templates.

Modifying Object Properties for Formatting Purposes

Now that the foundation of our report is complete, it is time to focus on how to improve the form of the report—the aesthetic characteristics.

We will concentrate on modifying various object properties to further improve the presentation value of the report. In doing so, we will be using the Format Editor to access a variety of specific properties, such as fonts, borders, colors, and alignment. The Format Editor is a commonly used dialog to quickly and easily modify all your report objects, and its contents are reflective of the specific object type being formatted (text, chart, database field, and so on).

1. From our earlier exercise, return to the Design tab of your report and right-click on the report title text object (located in the Report Header section) and select the Format Text option from the list to bring up the Format Editor dialog, as shown in Figure 8.8.

FIGURE 8.8

The Format Editor dialog is available from the right-click pop-up menu.

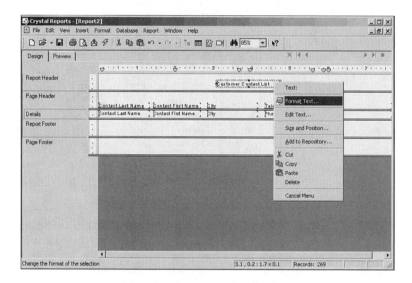

The Format Editor dialog allows you to adjust a variety of properties of the object organized within various tabs.

2. Navigate to the Font tab of the Format Editor and select the Bold font style, a font size of 11, and a font color of Red.

3. Select the Paragraph tab of the Format Editor and choose Centered from the Horizontal Alignment drop-down list, As shown in Figure 8.9.

FIGURE 8.9

The Format Editor dialog provides for quick and easy access to a variety of object properties.

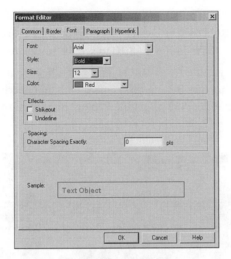

8

4. Now select the Border tab from within the Format Editor and then select Single from each of the four border Line Style drop-down lists (left, right, top, and bottom). Under Color, click the Background check box and select Yellow from the drop-down list as the background color. Based on all of your selected properties in the Format Editor, you should now see a representative example of the text object in the Sample area at the bottom of the dialog box. Click OK to save these settings and return to the Design tab on your report.

5. To improve the effectiveness of your report, you can modify the database field column titles to provide more meaningful descriptions for the business users of your report. Working within the Design tab of your report, double-click on the Phone object in the Page Header section of the report. When the cursor's focus is on this object, you can delete, append, or update the text as you wish. Modify this text to read `Telephone Number` and then click anywhere outside the object to remove the cursor's focus from the object.

As an alternative to the Format Editor, you can also use the toolbar and menu commands to quickly apply common formatting techniques, such as font and alignment characteristics.

6. From the View menu, select Toolbars to present the Toolbar dialog. Make sure that the Standard, Formatting, and Insert toolbar items are all selected and click OK.

7. Click on the Preview tab to see a preview display of what the report will actually look like. Again, if the Preview tab is not displayed in the application, click the Refresh toolbar button to execute the report. From the Preview mode, hold down the Shift key on your keyboard and click each of the five column titles so that they

are all highlighted with a dashed perimeter. With all five columns title fields high-lighted, click the Bold toolbar button, represented with a large bold letter B on the formatting toolbar. Refer to Figure 8.10 to see the results of this action.

8. With the five column title fields still highlighted, click the downward arrow located on the Font Color toolbar button, represented with an underlined letter A on the formatting toolbar. Select the bright blue color from the available list, as shown in Figure 8.10.

FIGURE 8.10

Common formatting properties can be quickly specified via the formatting tool-bar commands, such as font styles and colors.

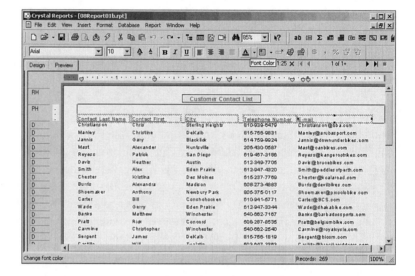

In order to make the Email field appear more meaningful to the business users of the report, let's format the Email database field values to resemble and behave like standard hyperlink text.

9. To remove the cursor focus from the five column titles fields, click anywhere out-side these field areas or press the Esc (escape) key on your keyboard.

10. Click any of the actual Email field values to highlight the Email database field objects and right-click on the same object to present the pop-up menu. From the pop-up menu, shown in Figure 8.11, select the Format Field item.

FIGURE 8.11

Right-clicking on any field object presents you with a list of commands for that particular object.

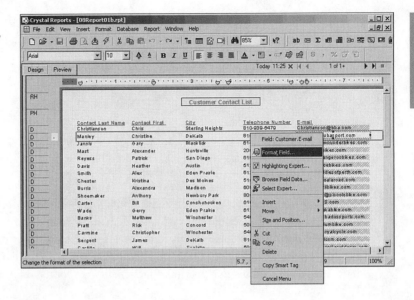

You can use the Hyperlink tab within the Format Editor to create hyperlinks to a Web site, email address, file, or another crystal report. A hyperlink is saved with your report and is available to other users as a way of linking additional information as it relates to your report. Hyperlink definitions can also be defined by formulas, thus making data-driven hyperlinks a very powerful feature of Crystal Reports.

11. Select the Hyperlink tab after you have opened the Format Editor. From the available Hyperlink Types, select Current Email Field Value—this option will automatically create a hyperlink based on the values stored within this field in the data source, and these values must be formatted as proper email addresses in the data source, such as *abc@domain.com*.

12. Now let's make the Email field appear as a standard hyperlink value, commonly known to have a blue underlined font style. Select the Font tab within the Format Editor dialog to apply the blue font color and select the Underline check box. Click OK to return to the report Preview, and then press Esc to remove the cursor focus from all report objects.

13. Based on the completion of the previous step, your mouse pointer should now change into a hand icon as it floats over any of the Email field values on the report. This indicates that upon clicking on any of the Email values, you will initiate an email message to be sent to that address, as shown in Figure 8.12.

FIGURE 8.12

*By applying format-
ting characteristics,
you can enable the
business users to ini-
tiate an email to the
respective customer
contact.*

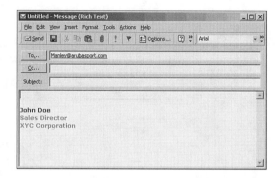

By using the Format Editor, as well as the Toolbar commands, to modify report object
properties, you have very quickly and easily enhanced your report for presentation purposes. Not only did we enhance this report example visually, but we also easily incorporated Hyperlink functionality to add an additional level of interactivity to our report. For
more information on using Hyperlink functionality in reports, refer to Hour 13, "Custom
Formatting Techniques."

Combining and Layering Report Objects

The concepts of combining and layering report objects becomes relevant when you need
to precisely control the relationship between two or more objects when occupying a common space on the report. For example, let's assume that rather than having our country
field read USA, we would like to combine the Country database field with a text object
so that it will read, Country/Pays: USA—displaying the textual description for country in
both English and French. To accomplish this, you can easily combine a text and a database field into one common report object.

We will continue to build on the earlier exercises, and add a more descriptive text object
to our report to produce the desired results. However, we will start by adding a group
definition to our report. The group definition will allow us to logically present each customer within the country in which they are located.

1. From the Insert menu, select Group to present the Insert Group dialog. Select the
   Country field (located under the Customer table) from the uppermost drop-down
   list. Leave the sort order as Ascending and click OK to return to the report.

2. Verify that you are working in the Design view of the report—click on the Design
   tab if necessary. You should now see two new sections listed in the left column
   area of the design environment—Group Header #1 and Group Footer #1. From the
   Insert menu, select Text Object and drop the object to the right of the Group #1

8

Name field in the Group Header section. Type **Country/Pays:** for the textual content of this new object (notice the space after the colon), as shown in Figure 8.13.

FIGURE 8.13

The Insert menu allows you to quickly add a group and text object in to your report.

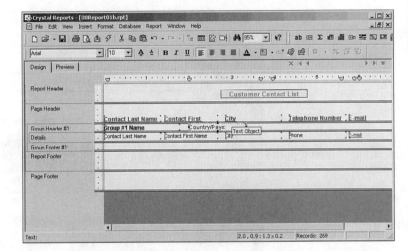

FIGURE 8.13

The Insert menu allows you to quickly add a group and text object in to your report.

3. Highlight the Group #1 Name field object, click and drag it over the new text object field (you can drag the entire object after the mouse pointer has turned into a four-way cross icon), and drop it on to the text object when the flashing vertical cursor indicates that it will fall precisely to the right of the textual description you have entered.

Dragging and dropping objects in order to combine them is a very precise maneuver and might require some practice. If necessary, stop here and rehearse this step until you are comfortable with this technique.

4. After you have successfully combined these objects together, the design application still references the newly combined object as a Text object. We now need to widen the object's display area. Click this object to highlight it and drag the left-side perimeter handle farther to the left until you reach the left margin of the design area, as shown in Figure 8.14.

5. With the combined text object highlighted, use the steps identified earlier in this hour to modify the object's properties to present the field values in a bold red font style, as shown in Figure 8.15. Click the Preview tab to see a how the report results will be displayed. (Use the Refresh toolbar button if the Preview tab is not visible.)

FIGURE 8.14

You have now combined a database field object with a text object to form one common report object.

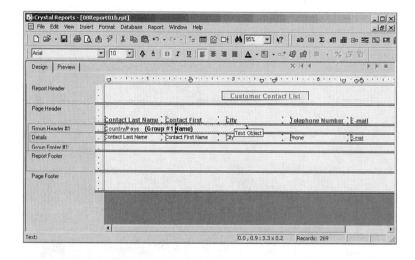

FIGURE 8.15

After combining two or more objects, you can specify formatting properties for the newly combined report object.

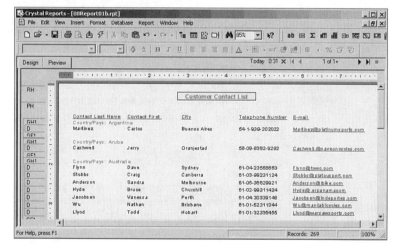

6. We will now add a corporate logo to our report and use this to discuss object layering. Select Repository Explorer from the View menu. When the Repository Explorer dialog is visible, expand the Crystal Repository item and then expand the Images node to reveal two sample images we can use. Highlight the Xtreme Logo image and drag it into the Report Header section. Drop the image into the Report Header section so that its left perimeter will be aligned directly above the left perimeter of the Telephone Number column, as shown in Figure 8.16.

FIGURE 8.16

Drag and drop the Xtreme Logo image object into place in the Report Header section.

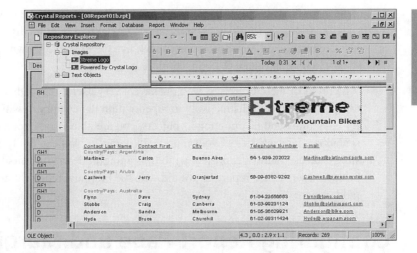

Notice, as illustrated in Figure 8.16, that you have partially covered the report title object with the new logo image. This could have certainly been avoided by placing the image object farther to the right, but in this case we will use the Move property of the report title field to once again make it visible.

7. Right-click the report title text object, select Move, and then select To Front from the additional pop-up options. This will position the report title object on top of the logo image, as you can see in the report preview.

8. To resolve the issue of overlapping objects in the Report Header section, adjust the two objects so that the report title is displayed farther to the left of the logo image, as shown in Figure 8.17. Save your report sample if you wish.

FIGURE 8.17

By adjusting the objects located in the Report Header, you have resolved the need to layer these objects.

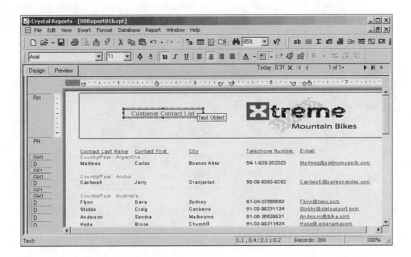

9. As a final step, use the Format Expert dialog to modify the report title text so that it appears in a bold, navy blue, size 20 Arial font with no displayed borders. Your report should now appear very much like the example shown at the beginning of the hour in Figure 8.2.

As a result of these exercises, we now have a very useful report that displays each customer contact record distinctively grouped within the country in which they are located. By combining and layering report objects, you are able to more precisely control the presentation characteristics of your reports. In doing so, you can easily leverage your accessible database fields, yet present a more meaningful descriptive field value to the business users of the report, as we did with the bilingual representation of the country field object.

Configuring Report Page and Margin Properties

As Figure 8.18 illustrates, you can either use specific margin definitions for your reports or select to automatically adjust report margin settings. To set your report margins to meet your exact specifications, follow these steps:

1. From the File menu, click Page Setup, and the Page Setup dialog will appear.

2. Modify the default page margins for your exact requirements.

3. Click OK to save your changes.

Each of the margin settings is calculated from the paper edge. Consequently, a left margin of .25 inches will cause the printing of the report page to start exactly one quarter of an inch in from the left edge of the paper.

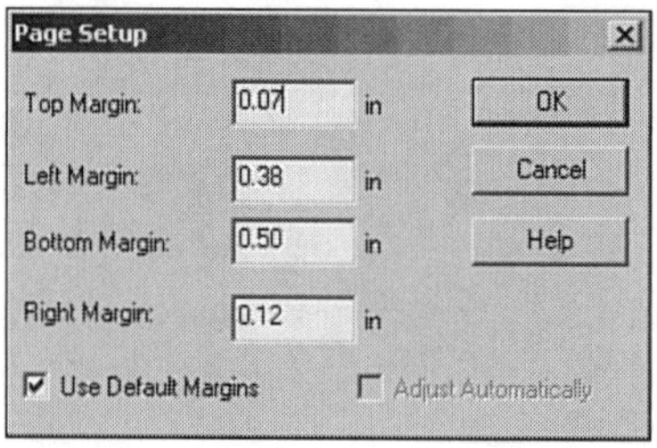

FIGURE 8.18

The Page Setup dialog is used to specify report margin settings.

Page Setup		
Top Margin:	0.07 in	OK
Left Margin:	0.38 in	Cancel
Bottom Margin:	0.50 in	Help
Right Margin:	0.12 in	
☑ Use Default Margins	☐ Adjust Automatically	

8

As an alternative to specifying exact report margins, you can select the Adjust Automatically check box if you want Crystal Reports to adjust the report's margins automatically when the paper size changes. This option maintains the printable area of the report by enlarging or reducing the left/right and top/bottom margins by the same factor. For example, this setting could ensure that a report designed for a printer that can only print within .5 inches of the paper's edge would maintain the same overall size when printed on a printer that could print to within .25 inches of the paper's edge.

If you do decide to select the Use Default Margins options for your reports, there are two common issues to be aware of when printing reports (also described in the Crystal Reports Help files).

- When printing a report in another environment in which the printer's default margins are greater than the report's setting; the report objects on the right side of the report print off the page.

- When printing a report in another environment in which the printer's default margins are smaller (allowing a larger printing area); the entire report moves to the left side of the page.

As a result, it is recommended that you specify your own report margins. It is encouraged that you do **not** select the Use Default Margins option in the Page Setup dialog to avoid these common problems. It is advisable to set your report margins manually using the Page Setup dialog, even if the margins you want to specify are the same as the default margin settings. This issue becomes especially important when you distribute your reports over the Web and have no idea what type of printer the business user will be using.

Summary

In this hour, you have started working with report formatting and object properties to create professionally designed reports. Formatting reports in Crystal Reports 9 is a very straightforward and intuitive process, but requires some familiarity with various features of the design application environment, such as using font, border, object layering, page, and margin settings. You have now reviewed many of the techniques required to apply a variety of formatting specifications to your reports, and you have accomplished this quickly through the use of dialogs, menu commands, and toolbar buttons—all just a few mouse clicks away from having meaningful information in the hands of those who need it.

As a result of following the exercises in this hour, you have constructed a very useful report that displays all the customer contacts, with telephone and email information, for the Xtreme Mountain Bike Company. You have structured this report to group the customers logically into their respective countries and formatted the font styles of the country description, report title, column titles, and email address field to make for a more precise presentation of the report information. By combining the Country database field with a text field, you have also provided for a bilingual display of the country description.

Workshop

The quiz questions and an activity are provided for your further understanding of the current hour's topics.

Quiz

1. What is the name of the wizard that presents various formatting properties that you can apply to a report object?

2. What are the three basic ways to modify the most common formatting properties for any report object, such as font style, borders, and alignment?

3. When specifying margin properties for your reports in the Page Setup dialog, what are the two common printing issues to be aware of?

Quiz Answers

1. Format Editor—The formatting properties accessible within the Format Editor vary according to the type of object selected. These properties include applying borders and colors, changing the font style, suppressing the object so that it does not print, cropping the size of the object, and selecting to maintain the object size or allow it to grow.

2. Format Editor, Formatting Toolbar buttons and the various Menu commands— Each of these permits you to quickly access the most commonly used formatting properties.

3. First, when printing a report in another environment in which the printer's default margins are greater than the report's setting, the report objects on the right side of the report print off the page. Second, when printing a report in another environment in which the printer's default margins are smaller (allowing a larger printing area), the entire report moves to the left side of the page. When specifying Page Setup properties, it is recommended that you manually specify your own report margin settings and do **not** select the Use Default Margins option in the Page Setup dialog.

Activity

As practice, complete the exercises in this hour again to review the various formatting concepts and rehearse the techniques used to apply them. Alternatively, create variances of this particular report example that you can also use to practice your formatting skills on.

8

HOUR 9

Working with Report Sections

At this point in the book, you should now be familiar with some of the more common formatting features within the Crystal Reports 9 designer. Building on the concepts and techniques you have learned for report object formatting, this hour explains how you can format entire sections within your reports. In much the same way that each report object has specific properties that can be modified and used for formatting purposes, report sections also have unique properties.

In this hour, we will take a closer look at these properties and how you can modify and work with them to more effectively create professionally styled reports.

In this hour, we will cover the following topics:

- Formatting report sections
- Modifying report section properties
- Using multiple report sections

Formatting Report Sections

In Hour 2, "Getting Started with Crystal Reports 9," you were introduced to the concept of report sections. Report sections segment reports into logical areas to facilitate more intuitive report design. Report sections are identified by name on the left side of the design environment, and, by default, each report will include a Report Header and Footer, Page Header and Footer, and Details section. If you have inserted any groups into your report, you will also have a Group Header and Footer for each defined group item. As you have been creating reports in the previous hours, you have placed objects such as database fields, text fields, and corporate logo images into the various sections and organized the objects based on your report design requirements.

Each section has unique properties and printing characteristics that you can modify. For example, if a report object, such as an image, is placed in the Report Header section, the image will display and print only once per report, on the first page. If the same image is placed in the Page Header section, the image will then display and print once per page. The same holds true for custom sections, such as Groups. The Detail Section, however, implies that whatever is placed in this section will display, and print, once for each and every row retrieved from the data source.

The Crystal Reports design environment is built upon a *paper metaphor* with *pages* as a concept to facilitate the presentation of information. This page metaphor applies when referring to how reports will print and reviewing various presentation characteristics of report formatting.

As you might have noticed, long names (descriptive names) of each section are provided to the left of the design environment within the Design tab, whereas only the short names (abbreviated names) of sections are presented while viewing reports from the Preview tab. This maximizes the report viewing space while working in the Preview tab, yet it still allows you to access each section's properties by right-clicking on the section name (or label) and selecting from the applicable pop-up menu commands.

We will continue using the report created in the previous hour, Hour 8, "Fundamentals of Report Formatting," to take a closer look at how to format report sections. The following exercises will demonstrate how to format sections such as the Group Header and Group Footer to improve the overall presentation of your report. In addition to modifying display properties, we will also apply conditional logic that modifies the behavior of the Page Header section based on the result of the defined condition (format formula). As you will see, the Section Expert is the central location to work with the most common report section properties, and we will use it to view and modify the properties of each report section throughout the following exercises.

> There are three distinct ways to access the Section Expert; these include
> - Right-click on the name of the section you want to work with and select Section Expert from the pop-up menu.
> - Click on the Select Expert toolbar button located on the Expert Tools toolbar.
> - From the Format menu item, select the Section Expert command from the Report menu.

9

1. Open the report you created in Hour 8. Alternatively, open the report entitled 09Report01.rpt (available from the Sams Publishing Web site when you search by book title—www.samspublishing.com).

2. Open the Section Expert. From either the Design or Preview mode, right-click on the Group Header #1 section and select Section Expert from the pop-up menu. This will present the Section Expert dialog.

We will now apply a background color to our Group Header #1 report section so that the report consumers can quickly distinguish between each country and determine which customer contacts belong to each country.

3. Using the Section Expert, select the Group Header #1 item from the Sections list on the left, and then click on the Color tab on the right. Click on the Background Color box so that it is activated and select Navy from the drop-down list of color options. Click OK to continue.

> From within the Section Expert, you can easily navigate from modifying the properties of one report section to another without closing this dialog window. Regardless of how you open the Section Expert dialog window, you can quickly toggle to other report sections, providing a central location to access and modify the properties of all report sections.

4. Select the Preview tab to view your report display.

5. The Red font used for the object in the Group Header #1 does not look good against the Navy background color. To resolve this, highlight the text object—actually a combined object consisting of a text object and a database field object—and change its font color to White, as shown in Figure 9.1.

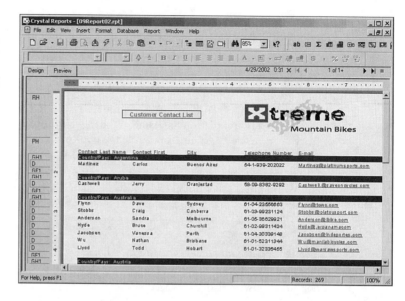

6. To complement the report structure and how you have grouped on the Country field, let's add a summary count of the contacts for each country in the Group Footer #1 section. To do this, select Summary from the Insert menu to present the Insert Summary dialog and select the following items:

   • Customer.Contact Last Name field from the Choose the Field to Summarize drop-down list

   • Count from the Calculate This Summary drop-down list

   • Group #1: Customer.Country from the Summary Location drop-down list

> To access the Insert Summary dialog so that you can add a summary field on to your report, you can either use the Summary command from the Insert menu or the Insert Summary button located on the Insert toolbar.

7. After you have made these selections from the Insert Summary dialog, click OK to continue.

8. You should now see the Count Summary field listed in the Group Footer #1 section of your report. To align the field values to the left and make them noticeable, use the Align Left and Font buttons located on the Formatting toolbar to apply the desired alignment and a Red font color.

9. We will now add additional report section formatting to the Group Footer #1 section. From the Report menu, select the Section Expert command to present the Section Expert dialog. From the Sections list on the left, select Group Footer #1 and then select the Color tab on the right. Specify a Silver background color for this section and click OK to return to the report preview, as shown in Figure 9.2.

10. As a final step, we will change the font color of the database field column titles. From either the Design or Preview view, right-click on the Page Header section title and choose Select All Section Objects from the pop-up menu. After all the column title objects are highlighted, select Teal from the formatting toolbar Font Color button.

9

FIGURE 9.2

Section formatting can be applied specifically to the various sections of your report for a more meaningful report presentation.

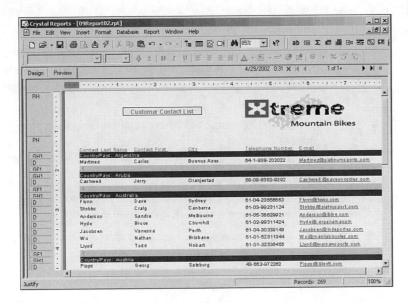

As you have seen, formatting the various sections of your report is very straightforward. Each section has unique and specific properties that can be modified and used collectively to enhance the presentation quality of the entire report.

To quickly remove blank space within report sections and tighten up the alignment of the objects positioned within the sections, you can use the Fit Section command. The Fit Section command is available from the right-click menu of each report section. This will raise the bottom boundary line and reduce unnecessary space within the section.

Modifying Report Section Properties

In addition to formatting properties, each of the various sections has a variety of general properties that you can use to manipulate the behavior of each section within the overall report. For example, if you would like to suppress a particular section from the report display or just hide a section from the initial display but allow business users to still navigate to the underlying details, you can use the Section Expert to accomplish this.

Using the report we created in the previous exercise, we will re-locate the Count summary field into the Group Header and hide the Details section to allow the viewer of the report to access this section only if he double-clicks on the Group Header summary values—commonly known as drilling-down on report data. Let's take a closer look at how we can manipulate the behavior of report sections.

1. First, we will re-position a couple of the report objects. Highlight the Text object in Group Header #1 (the combined Text and Country database field) and move it to the right so that its left margin is aligned under the left margin of the Contact First Name column title.

2. Highlight the Summary field currently located in the Group Footer #1 section (Count of Contact Last Name) and drag it up in the Group Header #1 section so that it is positioned to the left margin of the Group Header #1 section (left justified), as shown in Figure 9.3.

3. While the Summary count field is still highlighted, modify the font properties so that it is underlined and in a bold yellow color.

4. Using what you have learned from the previous exercises, remove the background color of the Group Footer #1 section—the background color property can be located on the Color tab of the Section Expert. Figure 9.3 displays what your report should now look like.

5. To display the listing of customer contacts for each country on a separate and unique page, open the Section Expert and select Group Footer #1 from the section list on the left. As Figure 9.4 shows, the Common tab within the Section Expert provides access to a variety of properties unique to the section that you have selected from the list on the left. In this case, check the box next to the New Page After item and click OK to continue.

FIGURE 9.3

Report objects can be re-positioned into the various report sections to change the presentation of the report.

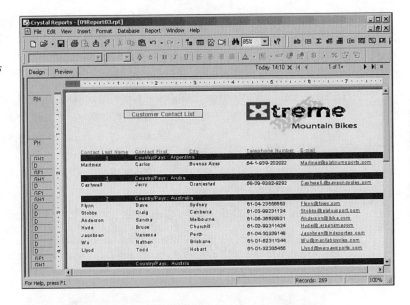

FIGURE 9.4

The Section Expert provides access to a variety of section formatting properties, as well as specifying what happens before and after each section.

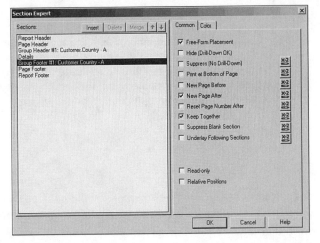

6. Looking at the preview of your report, you will now see each country's list of contacts on a separate page. Although this might be desirable for those countries with a considerable number of contacts, such as Canada, France, and the United States in this report, it is not necessarily the most visually pleasing presentation for the countries that have only one or two customer contacts.

Perhaps the majority of the business users for this report are more interested in the total number of contacts for each country rather than the actual list itself. However, a few of the business users also want to be able to access the contact list on occasion. To accommodate both groups of users, we can manipulate the properties of the Details section.

7. To accomplish this, first disable the New Page After property that was set for the Group Footer #1 section. The Section Expert can be used to remove this setting. Click OK to continue.

8. From either the Design or Preview view of your report, right-click on the Details section title to the far left of the application area and select Hide (Drill-Down OK) from the pop-up menu.

Drill-down functionality is designed to make report viewing easier. You can hide the details of your report and only have the group headers and summaries visible, and, when necessary, the business users of the report can then click on the group header or summary fields to view the report details.

Common report section commands—such as Hide, Suppress, Delete, Hide Section Names, and Select All Section Objects—are accessible via the pop-up menu when you right-click on the applicable section's name. Some of these commands are also available within the Section Expert dialog, although unlike the Section Expert, the right-click pop-up menu pertains only to the specific section you have selected and does not allow you to quickly navigate from one section to another.

As shown in Figure 9.5, you should now see a list of each country with only the total number of contacts displayed. However, upon double-clicking the count of contacts (displayed with the underlined, yellow number) the business user of the report can quickly drill-down into the Details section that presents the actual customer contact specifications.

To indicate to the business user of the report that more detailed information is available behind the summary group level, the mouse pointer will turn into a magnifying glass icon when it floats over the yellow count field of customer contacts, located in the Group Header #1 section.

FIGURE 9.5

A manager can now see a summary list of customer contacts by country, but yet also access the customer contact details if desired.

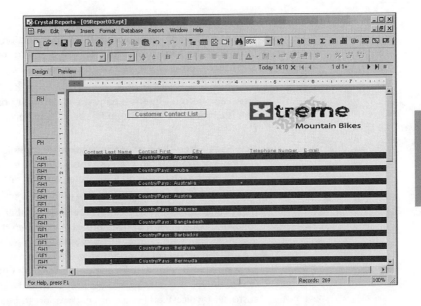

9

As you can see in Figure 9.6, after the business user chooses to drill-down into a particular group's detail listing (France in this example), that group listing is cached in the Crystal Reports application so that it can be easily accessed for future reference. This cached view of the group detail is presented via an additional tab within the application environment. However, when the business user of the report selects to refresh the report, all cached tabs are removed because the data being retrieved from the database might have changed since the previous cached page was last generated.

In addition to the Section Expert options that you have already used, the following Coffee Break provides an overview of the available settings presented on the Common tab of the Section Expert.

Reviewing the Common Tab Settings of the Section Expert

- Free-Form Placement—Places objects anywhere within a section, ignoring all program alignment grids and guidelines. When this option is not selected, objects are placed at fixed points using an underlying grid.

- Hide (Drill-Down OK)—Hides the respective section from the report's initial visual display, but still allows report users to access the section's content upon drill-down.

- Suppress (No Drill-Down)—Hides the respective section from the report's visual display and disables any drill-down capabilities such that the section's content is *not* available to report users.

- Print at Bottom of Page—Causes the current section to print at the bottom of the page. This setting is most useful for printing invoices and other reports where you want summary values to appear toward the bottom of the page.
- New Page Before—Inserts a page break before it prints the section. This is applicable to the Group Header, Group Footer, and Details sections.
- New Page After—Inserts a page break after it displays and prints the section. For example, you can use this setting in the Group Footer section to print each group on a separate page. By default, the Page Header and Page Footer sections will appear on each page.
- Reset Page Number After—Resets the page number to one (1) for the following page after it prints a group total. When this option is used in conjunction with Print at Bottom of Page, a single group prints on a page, the group value is printed at the bottom of the page, and the page number is reset to 1 for the next page. This option is useful whenever you are printing multiple reports from a single file (such as customer invoices), and you want each report to be numbered beginning with Page 1.
- Keep Together—Keeps a particular section together on one page without splitting the section between multiple pages. For example, in a customer list, data on a single customer might extend over several lines. If the standard page break falls within the data for a customer, the data will be split—part on one page and the remainder on the next. You can use the Keep Together setting to insert the page break before the record begins so that all the data will be printed together on the following page.
- Suppress Blank Section—Hides the report section if it is blank, and will only print it if it is not blank.
- Underlay Following Sections—Permits the selected section to underlay the following section(s) when it prints, making the current section transparent.
- Format with Multiple Columns (Details section only)—Presents the Layout tab (otherwise hidden from view) within the Section Expert and allows you to use multiple columns to display report data.
- Reserve Minimum Page Footer (Page Footer section only)—Reserves space at the bottom of each page for your Page Footer sections (a default setting). This allows you to minimize the space reserved for your Page Footer sections, thus maximizing the space available for other report information on each page. This option only affects a Page Footer area with multiple sections.

- Read-only—Locks the formatting and position of all report objects within the section so that they can't be formatted or re-positioned. The Read-only setting uses password protection to allow the report designer to return to the report to make future changes.

- Relative Positions—Locks the relative position of a report object next to a grid object within a section. For example, if you place a text object one inch to the right of a database field object, during report generation the program will push the text object to the right so that the one inch of space is maintained regardless of the width of the database field object.

FIGURE 9.6

The detailed list of customer contacts for France.

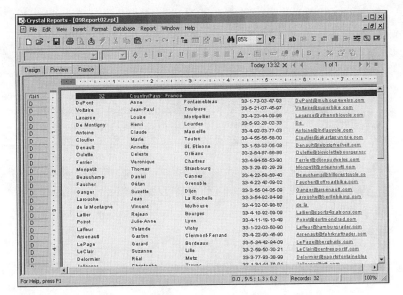

Using Multiple Report Sections

Including multiple sections within each section area of your report provides for an extremely flexible presentation of your report data. Chances are good that you will not need to create more than one occurrence of any of the existing report sections for basic reporting needs. However, Crystal Reports allows you to define multiple report sections within any given section area and to identify section-specific properties for challenging formatting requirements within more complex reports. Certain reporting tasks are performed most efficiently by creating multiple sections within an area.

A *Section Area* is the space in which one or more of the same Report Section types are defined. For example, it is possible to define two or more Page Header sections in a report to satisfy complex formatting requirements (covered later in this hour), and the area in which these Report Header sections are displayed is referred to as the Section Area.

For example, multiple report sections would be very useful if you want to create a form letter for your customers and you need to display only one of two possible return addresses on the letter—an American address for customers based in the United States and a Canadian address for the remainder of your North American customers. To accomplish this, you will need to insert two report header sections in to your report and use Conditional Formatting to dynamically apply the appropriate return address based on where the customer is located.

Conditional Highlighting allows you to define a formula that causes a specific action (formatting in this case) to occur if the formula's results are true. This is also referred to as a *format formula*.

In order to demonstrate how to implement and use multiple report sections, we first need to review the basic operations of resizing, inserting, removing, and merging report sections.

Resizing Report Sections

Report sections might require resizing to accommodate for various sized report objects, such as large database fields, lengthy text objects, or corporate logo images, but they cannot exceed the size of the report page itself. From the Design tab of the report environment, you can drag the bottom boundary of the various sections up and down with the mouse to resize each section. Using the mouse, float the pointer over the horizontal boundary lines of the different sections. When the mouse pointer changes into a double-headed arrow icon, click and hold the left mouse button while dragging the boundary line to the desired position.

Inserting New Report Sections

To display only one of two possible return addresses on a form letter (based on the location of the customer), we need to insert a second page header on to the report. To begin this exercise, either open report 09Report04, as shown in Figure 9.7, or construct the report using the Customer table from the Xtreme Sample Database. By following a few easy steps, you can quickly create the form letter report:

1. Using the Xtreme Sample database, choose not to add any database fields to the report.

2. Create a Group based on the Customer Name field, but do not display the Customer Name field in the Details section. The Group field should automatically appear in the Group Header section.

3. Select the New Page After property for the Group Footer #1 section.

4. Suppress the Report Header section.

5. Insert text objects in the appropriate report sections, as shown in Figure 9.7.

FIGURE 9.7

An example of a simple form letter report.

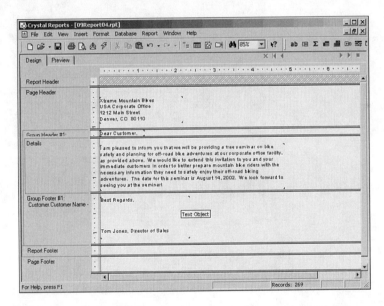

 Notice that in this sample form letter report, each report object displayed on the report is just a text object inserted in to the appropriate section. You do not yet need to include any database fields in the report.

1. To insert a new Page Header section, locate the existing Page Header section, right-click on the section name (on the left of the design environment), and select Insert Section Below from the pop-up menu.

You added a new section entitled "Page Header b" and renamed the original section to "Page Header a" so that you now have two Report Header sections within your report. The application follows this naming convention whenever you choose to add multiple report sections within any section area, appending each section name with a, b, c, and so on.

2. After you have inserted a new Page Header section (labeled "Page Header b"), insert a text object to display a Canadian return address to be used for the non-USA recipients of the form letter, as shown in Figure 9.8.

FIGURE 9.8

A form letter report with two Page Header sections.

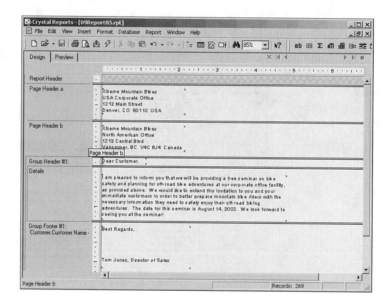

Now that we have the two different return addresses and report sections created, we need to identify the necessary logic within the report to implement the appropriate Page Header section based on each customer's location—whether they are based in the United States or Canada. We only need to evaluate each customer's mailing address—the Country field from the Customer table, to be exact. We're only concerned with North American customers, and if this field is equal to USA, we will use Page Header a to display the return address. If it is equal to Canada, we will use Page Header b.

3. To isolate our report for only North American customers, choose the Select Expert option from the Report menu. From the list of available fields, select the Country field from the Customer table listing and click OK to continue.

4. You should now see the Select Expert dialog. From the drop-down list on the left, select Is One Of and include Canada and USA in the list box on the right as shown in Figure 9.9.

FIGURE 9.9

Use the Select Expert dialog to quickly filter a report to include only the data you want to retrieve.

5. To add additional personalization to the form letter, use the Field Explorer to insert the Customer Name field into the Text Object—located in the Group Header #1 that reads "Dear Customer," —so that it will appear as "Dear {Customer Name}," in the Design tab of your report. To do this, you'll need to modify the text portion of this combined object to read "Dear"—that's the word Dear followed by a space, and then followed by the database field object. The result of this action can be seen later in the exercise in Figure 9.10.

Finally, we need to apply the logic to display the appropriate return address on the form letter. To do this, we will apply a conditional formatting statement (format formula) to each of the two Page Header sections.

6. Using the Section Expert for Page Header a, click on the x-2 button (with the pencil symbol) located directly to the right of the Suppress (No Drill-Down) option on the Common tab. After clicking this icon, you should be presented with the Format Formula Editor dialog window. Within the Format Formula dialog, shown in Figure 9.10, you can use the Field, Function, and Operator windows (located in the upper area of the dialog) to insert the necessary format formula within this dialog, or you can just type in the statement in the lower area of the Editor dialog so that it reads `{Customer.Country}` = `"Canada"`. After you have inserted this statement, click Save and Close to return to the Section Expert.

7. We now need to implement a very similar formatting condition for the Page Header b section. Following the same procedure used for the first section, use the Section Expert to insert a statement that reads **{Customer.Country} = "USA"**.

The report section will be suppressed only if the conditional statement defined in the Format Formula Editor is true.

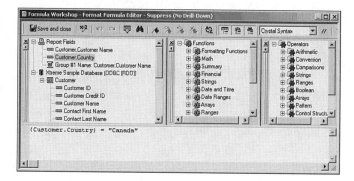

To quickly verify that your formulas are behaving as desired, you can add the customer address database fields on to the form letter as well. This will allow you to check if a customer is in the United States or Canada. We will do this later in the exercise by adding the Country database field to the report.

If you are not familiar with the Format Formula Editor, also known as the Formula Workshop dialog, do not feel intimidated. Although it might first appear as rather complex, it is a helpful and straightforward environment for creating formulas. In this case, we are using it only to create a conditional formatting formula that, in turn, will populate our report with one of two possible Page Header sections—because only one of the two defined conditional formulas will hold true for any given customer. See Hour 10, "Understanding and Implementing Formulas," for additional exercises and details on creating formulas.

It is important to note that formulas are covered in greater detail in Hour 10, and they are only included here for completeness of the exercise on formatting report sections.

8. After you have inserted the format formulas within the Section Expert dialog, the small icon to the right of the Suppress (No Drill-Down) option should now change to red rather than its earlier blue color, indicating that now a conditional formatting formula is defined to suppress this section.

You do not need to check the Suppress (No Drill-Down) check box in the Section Expert dialog for either report Page Header section. By inserting a format formula, you have effectively applied conditional formatting that will suppress the section if the format formula is found to be true. In this case, one of the two format formulas should also be true because the customers are either located in the United States or Canada. Likewise, almost any property of a section can be conditionally formatted using formulas.

9. Close the Section Expert dialog by clicking OK. As shown in Figure 9.11, your report should now display only one of the two possible return addresses on the form letter.

To verify that the appropriate return address is being populated on the form letter report for each customer, you can easily add the Country field from the Customer table into the Group Header #1 section, as shown in Figure 9.11.

FIGURE 9.11

A simple form letter report is now dynamically formatted with the appropriate return address based on the customer's location.

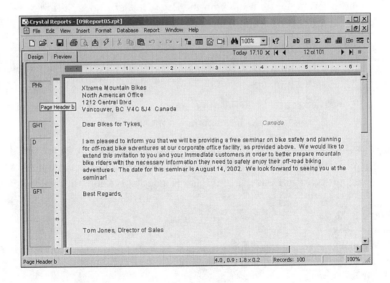

Deleting Report Sections

In much the same manner as inserting new sections, unused report sections can be quickly removed from reports by right-clicking on the section name and selecting Delete Section from the pop-up menu. Be aware, however, that any report objects positioned within the section will also be deleted from the report. If you want to keep any of the objects within a section that you will be removing, you will need to first relocate the objects into alternative report sections before deleting the current section.

> Crystal Reports requires at least one section to be present for certain section types in every report, such that you will be unable to remove the Report Header and Footer, Page Header and Footer, and Details sections. These report sections are generated by default when creating new reports. Also, if Group objects exist within a report, you will be unable to remove the Group Header and Footer sections unless you first remove the Group object itself from the report. However, if you're unable to actually delete them, you can always suppress these sections for display purposes and achieve much the same effect.

Merging Report Sections

When designing reports, you might periodically want to merge two report sections in order to simplify the layout of a report. To merge the two Page Header sections from our earlier example, right-click on the Page Header a section title and select Merge Section Below from the pop-up menu. The Merge Section Below command is available from the right-click menu of any report section that meets two criteria:

- There are more than one of the given section type (Page Headers) within the Section Area.
- The section is not last in a series of sections (Page Headers) consisting of the same section types within a common area.

For example, if three Page Header sections are present on a report (as shown in Figure 9.12), the Merge Section Below command would be accessible from the right-click menus of Page Header a and Page Header b, but not from Page Header c.

FIGURE 9.12

The Merge Section Below command is available from the right-click menu of certain report sections.

Summary

In this hour, you have completed various tasks related to report sections and configuring section properties to create dynamic and highly functional reports. Having experience working with formatting, positioning, inserting, hiding, and suppressing report sections—together with using the Section Expert—will dramatically increase your ability to effectively design and create powerful reports.

Workshop

The quiz questions and activities are provided for your further understanding of the current hour's topics.

Quiz

1. What are the three distinct ways in which you can access the Section Expert?
2. What are the basic steps to apply a background color to a report section?
3. What does the Read-Only section setting do?
4. What is the difference in Hiding versus Suppressing a report section?

Quiz Answers

1. 1) Right-click on the name of the section you want to work with and select Section Expert from the pop-up menu, 2) Click on the Section Expert toolbar button, and 3) From the Report menu item, select the Section Expert command.

2. Open the Section Expert dialog, go to the Color tab, select the Background Color check box, and then select the desired background color from the chosen section.

3. The Read-Only setting locks the formatting and positioning of all report objects within the section so that they can't be formatted or re-positioned. When you select this option, all other choices in the Section Expert become disabled. The Read-only setting is password protected to allow only the appropriate report designer(s) to make future changes.

4. Hiding a report section, via the Hide (Drill-Down OK) option, hides the respective section from the report's initial visual display, but it still allows report users to access the section's content upon drill-down. Suppressing a report section, via the Suppress (No Drill-Down) option, hides the respective section from the report's visual display, and does *not* make the section's content available to report users via drill-down.

HOUR 10

Understanding and Implementing Formulas

In Hour 6, "Selecting and Grouping Data," we briefly introduced formulas—the ability to create them and subsequently drop them into a report from the Field Explorer. In this hour, we'll explore the Formula Editor in more detail.

Formulas provide great flexibility and power when creating Crystal Reports by enabling the creation of *derived* fields not directly stored in available data sources. Formulas also enable the creation of advanced conditional object formatting and the use of flexible selection formulas in a report.

Crystal Reports has a number of built-in tools that facilitate the formula creation and formula reuse processes, the Formula Editor being a good example. With version 9, a powerful new tool called the Formula Workshop has been added to Crystal Reports. The Formula Workshop provides a single convenient access point to almost all of your formula fields within a given report. SQL Expression fields, Record and Group Selection formulas, Formatting formulas and Custom Report and Repository based functions can all be accessed from the new Formula Workshop.

In this hour, the following topics are covered:

- An introduction to the Formula Workshop
- A review of the Formula Workshop Tree Elements
- Formula Editor
- Arithmetic, Date, and String formulas
- Type conversion
- Variables in formulas
- Formula Expert
- Formula Extractor

Using the Formula Workshop

You have already been introduced to a few different areas of Crystal Reports that leverage the formula capabilities of the product for enhanced functionality. As you create more advanced reports, you will come across more of these functional areas. Figure 10.1 displays the familiar Formula Editor within the new Formula Workshop interface.

FIGURE 10.1

The Formula Editor within the new Formula Workshop.

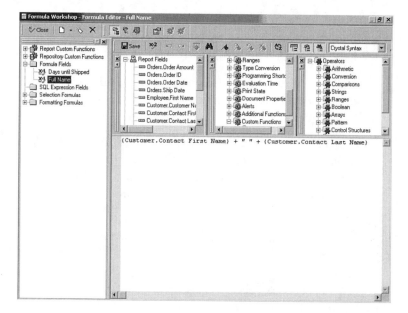

Examples of places where the Formula Editor will be used when creating reports include

- Creation of derived fields (Formulas, SQL Expressions)
- Report Section formatting
- Report Object formatting
- Record Selection formulas
- Group Selection formulas
- Running Total conditions
- Formula-based hyperlinks (covered in Hour 13, "Custom Formatting Techniques")
- Alert conditions (covered in Hour 15, "Using Record Selections and Alerts for Interactive Reporting")
- Use of Report Variables (covered later in this hour)

10

Although the independently accessed Formula Editors for each of these reporting areas provide powerful capabilities, a great new productivity feature in Crystal Reports 9 is the ability to access almost all the formulas held in a report in a single interface called the Formula Workshop—essentially a one-stop shop for all formulas. At the time of writing, the only exceptions to the rule were Running Total and Alert Condition formulas.

The Formula Workshop consists of a toolbar, a tree that lists the types of formulas you can create or modify, and an area for defining the formula itself.

Workshop Tree

Figure 10.2 highlights some of the new Formula Workshop features by expanding the Formula Workshop Tree found in the Formula Editor.

The Workshop Tree is a container for Report and Repository functions, Formula fields, SQL Expression fields, Selection formulas and Formatting formulas—all of which are explained in more detail in the following sections.

Report Functions

Report Functions are Custom functions created by Crystal Report Designers that are stored within the current report file. Although Custom functions are covered in detail in Hour 17, "Using Formulas and Custom Functions to Implement Complex Business Logic," it is important to note that they are accessed from the Formula Workshop along with other types of formulas and functions. New Custom Report functions are created through the Formula Editor by right-clicking on any part of the Report Function section of the Formula Workshop or by Selecting Custom Function from the New menu drop-down list.

FIGURE 10.2

The Formula Workshop with expanded Formula Workshop Tree.

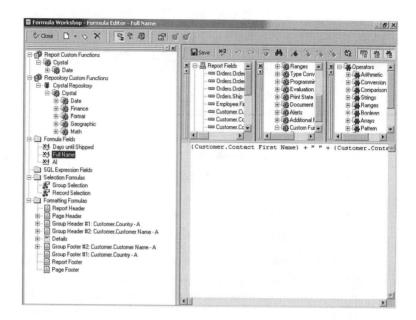

Repository Functions

Repository functions are Custom functions created by Crystal Report Designers and then stored centrally within the Crystal Reports Repository. The repository acts as a central library for these Custom functions among multiple other reusable objects. Although Repository functions are covered in detail in Hour 18, "Working with the Report Component Repository," note that they are accessed from the Formula Workshop along with the other types of formulas and functions. New Repository functions are uploaded by creating a Report function and subsequently adding it to the Repository through the Add Repository option accessed by right-clicking Custom Report Function.

Remember that when trying to add a custom function to the central repository for other report developers to use, it must first be created locally as a Report function and only then can it be added to the central repository. Custom functions cannot be directly added into the central repository. See Hours 17 and 18 for more details on Report and Repository functions.

Formula Fields

As has been mentioned already in previous hours, formula fields provide a means to add derived fields (that is, those not directly available in your database), such as a calculation into your Crystal Reports, as well as provide your business users (report consumers) with additional views of data. Once created, Crystal Report treats derived formula fields in exactly the same manner as it does original database fields. The majority of this hour is dedicated to introducing the different methods of creating formulas through two interfaces—the Formula Editor and the Formula Expert. Both of these will be discussed next, and Hour 17 will explore some advanced features of formula creation and use.

SQL Expression Fields

SQL Expressions provide a means to add derived fields (that is, those not directly available in your database), such as a calculation in to your Crystal Reports that are based exclusively on *Structured Query Language (SQL)* statements rather than standard Crystal formula syntax. As a reminder, SQL Expressions are used in cases where report-processing efficiency is critical.

Using SQL expressions facilitates pushing data processing to the database server instead of the Crystal Reports Server, and this is usually most efficient. Like Formulas, SQL Expressions are created in the Formula Editor but provide only a subset of the functionality because of the dependency on the SQL supported by the report's attached data source. Hour 22, "Optimizing SQL Queries in Crystal Reports," provides a good introduction to SQL.

Selection Formulas

As discussed in Hour 7, "Filtering, Sorting, and Summarizing Data," Selection formulas come in two varieties in Crystal Reports—Group and Record. A Record Selection formula provides a filtering mechanism on records to be included in the final report. Likewise, a Group Selection formula provides a filtering mechanism on the groups to be included in the final report. Each of these selection formulas can be accessed and edited through the Formula Workshop using the familiar Formula Editor component. The Formula Editor will be described in detail soon and in extended detail with respect to Selection Formulas in Hour 15.

Formatting Formulas

Formatting formulas provide flexibility in the presentation of a Crystal Report's report sections and all of the report objects contained within report sections. Examples of object and section formatting options include Background Color, Suppression, ToolTip, Border Color/Style, Section Underlay, and so on. All the formatting capabilities available in the Format Editor dialog (see Figure 10.3) and the Report Section Expert (see Figure 10.4) accessed by the x+2 icon can be set—and be set conditionally through these Formatting Formulas. Advanced Formatting is covered in Hour 13 but it should be noted that this is accessed and set through the Formula Workshop's Formula Editor.

10

FIGURE 10.3

The Format Editor dialog.

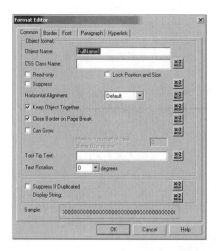

FIGURE 10.4

The Section Expert.

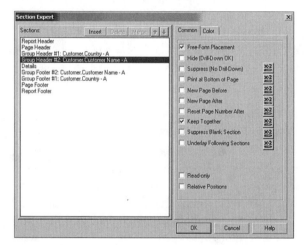

Workshop Formula Editor

The Formula Editor, as shown in Figure 10.5, is a common tool used across all the different types of formulas accessible through the Formula Workshop. The Formula Editor is composed of five distinct areas:

- The Fields area (top left frame of the Formula Editor) includes all the available report, formula, summarization, and database fields that can be added to the current formula.

- The Functions area (top center frame of the Formula Editor) includes the pre-built Crystal Reports functions and Custom functions that are available to be added to the currently edited formula.

- The Operators area (top right frame of the Formula Editor) includes a number of operators that can be used in the currently edited formula. Examples of operators include +, *, IF/THEN/ELSE, CASE, AND/OR, and so on.

- The Editing area (large bottom frame of the Formula Editor) is the free-form text editing area where formulas are formed through either direct typing or double-clicking selections from the other three Formula Editor frames.

- The toolbar area contains a number of Formula Editor options including toggles on the different frames, some book-marking options, an important formula syntax checking button (x+2), and the Crystal versus Basic Syntax drop-down box.

Crystal Reports provides two different formula languages for use in creating formulas. Basic Syntax is very similar to the Visual Basic programming structure and provides a natural fit for report designers with a Visual Basic programming background. The other more commonly used syntax—Crystal Syntax—has no programming language affiliation, but is highly-evolved and easy to use for non-programmers. For the rest of this hour, the examples will be created using the more commonly used Crystal syntax.

10

Formula Syntax Checking button

Fields area   Functions area   Toolbar area

FIGURE 10.5

The Formula Editor within the Formula Workshop.

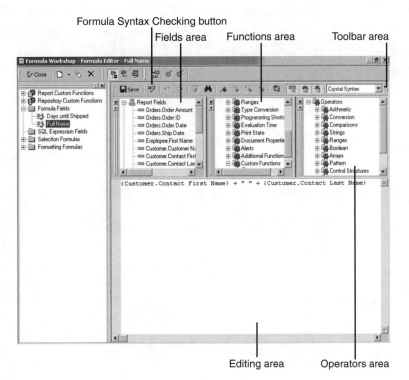

Editing area   Operators area

The available elements in each of the top three areas of the Formula Editor will vary depending on what type of formula you are creating. For example, when creating a Formatting formula, the Functions frame will present a Formatting section not available while editing or creating other types of formulas. Another familiar example is the limited set of fields, functions, and operators presented when creating SQL Expressions. This is, of course, dependent on the supported SQL for the current report's data source.

To facilitate your understanding of the Formula Editor, the following hypothetical business problem provides a hands-on experience with creating formulas within reports. The CEO of Maple Leaf Bikes is planning an *Initial Public Offering (IPO)* of his stock to the marketplace. Having recently acquired another company called Xtreme Cycles (sound familiar?), he wants to fairly share the success of the overall company with these new employees. As such, he wants to allocate stock options to them based on tenure with Xtreme Cycles (a metric of loyalty) and their current salary (a metric of expected contribution). Therefore, the CEO has determined that a fair allocation would be 100 shares for each year of tenure and 100 shares per $10,000 in salary, and he wants a report outlining these allocations so that he can present this proposal at the next board of directors meeting. The following steps will walk through a solution for this problem:

1. Create a new report based on the Xtreme Sample Database ODBC Connection using either the Standard Report Wizard or through the main Report Design menus.
2. Select the Employees and Employee_Addresses tables to be used in the report.
3. Add the Employee ID, Salary, and Hire Date fields into the detail section of the report.

At this point, the design frame (from the Design tab) for the report should resemble Figure 10.6.

The basic building blocks to the requested report have now been added to the sample report, but there is clearly work to be done to capture the CEO's intent. This report will be flushed out through the next few sections as different Formula functions are systematically introduced.

Arithmetic Formulas

Arithmetic formulas are those derived from existing numeric fields (or fields converted into numbers—type conversion information is discussed later in this chapter). These formulas can be simple multiplication or addition operations, or they can be as complex as standard deviations, sums, or correlations. Arithmetic formulas are created within the Formula Editor by selecting any combination of numeric fields, numeric operators and/or numeric-oriented functions. Figure 10.7 displays the Formula Editor re-sized to highlight some common Arithmetic functions and operators.

FIGURE **10.6**

The Crystal Reports Design window with a sample report.

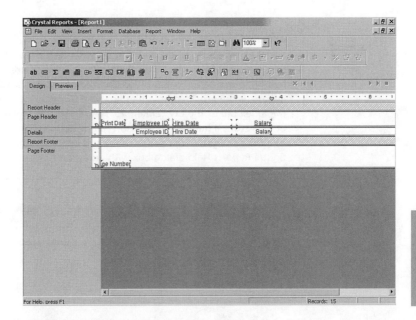

FIGURE **10.7**

The Formula Editor highlighting some Arithmetic functions and operators.

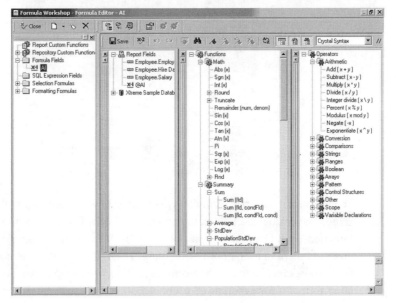

10

With hundreds of formula functions and operators built into Crystal Reports and the new ability to expand that set with Custom functions, it's easy to become overwhelmed with all the available formula possibilities. One very helpful source for information on the many built-in formulas in Crystal Reports is the provided help files accessed through the F1 key. By clicking on the Index tab of the Crystal Reports Help Screen and searching on functions or operators, a detailed description can be accessed on each of the hundreds of different Crystal Reports functions and operators. Figure 10.8 displays the Crystal Reports Help dialog box with an Aging function highlighted.

FIGURE 10.8
Crystal Reports functions Help.

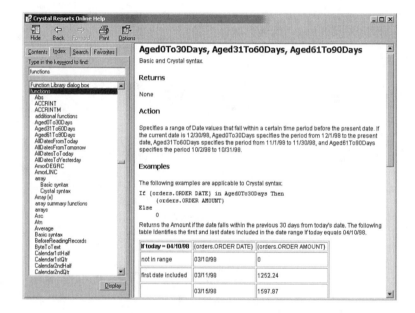

To create an Arithmetic formula (as any other kind of formula) within the Formula Editor, either double-click on the appropriate elements from each of the Fields, Functions, and Operators frames or select them by single-clicking and dragging and dropping them in to the Formula Editing frame. Using either method, a formula will begin to be constructed in the Formula Editing Area/Frame. An alternative means to creating formulas for experienced users is to directly type the formula in to the Formula Editing Area and periodically check the formula's syntax with the x+2 toolbar button, which provides error-checking functionality.

Revisiting the Maple Leaf Bikes reporting scenario, the CEO has designated two criteria for stock option allocation to the Xtreme Sports employees—Tenure and Salary. The Salary component is based on a derivation from a numeric field (salary) and lends itself to the creation of an Arithmetic formula based on the requirements that each $10,000 of salary will contribute to 100 stock options. The following steps, continued from the last section, will move toward a reporting solution for the CEO and provide exposure to the Formula Creation process in the Formula Editor:

1. If the Field Explorer is not already open in your Crystal Reports Design window, open that now by either clicking on the Field Explorer icon or by toggling to the Field Explorer option under the View menu. Figure 10.9 displays the Crystal Reports Design window with the Field Explorer displayed.

FIGURE 10.9

Sample report with Field Explorer displayed.

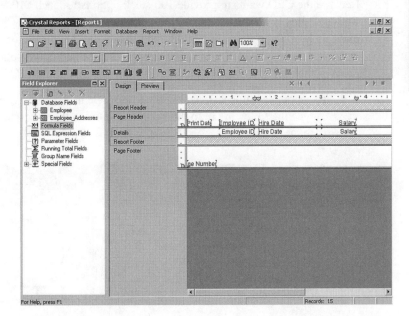

2. Create a new Formula by clicking on the Formula Fields field and either accessing the New option on the right-click menu or clicking the New button in the Field Explorer toolbar. You will be prompted for a Formula Name—so call this formula **Salary Driven Options** and select the Use Editor button to create the formula. If you accidentally click the Use Expert button, have no fear; simply click the Use Editor button that appears in the bottom of that screen. The Formula Expert will be explored later in this hour, but for now, the Formula Editor will be our primary focus. The familiar Formula Workshop (as you saw in Figures 10.2 and 10.5) will appear.

3. Logically stepping through the CEO's request, the first database field we need to access to determine the Salary Driven Component of stock option allocation is Salary, so find the Salary field in the Fields frame and double-click on it.

> More than just providing access to those fields already selected for viewing in the report, the Formula Editor Fields frame provides access to all available database fields for those tables selected as report data sources. Additionally, existing formulas, sums, running totals, and so on can be accessed here, which can be included in other formulas.

Because the CEO wants to provide 100 stock options for each $10,000 in existing salary, we will logically need to divide each employee's current salary by $10,000 and then multiply by 100. To do so, we could either access the Arithmetic operators (/ for division and * for multiplication) in the Operators Frame and double-click on those or simply type them in.

4. To accomplish this task, you will need to type in the numeric constants regardless, so type the following in to the Formula Editor so that it resembles Figure 10.10:
   `/ 10000 * 100`.

FIGURE 10.10

Salary driven options formula creation example.

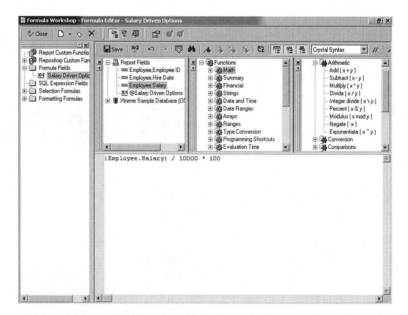

5. Perform Error Checking on your report by clicking the x+2 icon. After you confirm that no errors are found and your formula is identical to that in Figure 10.10, save the formula with the Save button and exit the Formula Workshop by clicking Close.

6. Add the new formula into the report beside Salary and format it to display zero decimals and no currency symbol (hint—right-click on the object and select the Format option). The preview tab of the CEO's report should resemble that shown in Figure 10.11.

FIGURE 10.11

The interim version of the CEO's sample report.

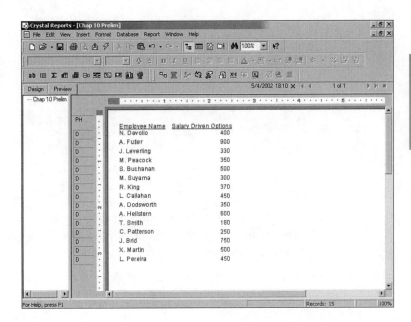

The current version of the report takes the content of the report to about half complete. The tenure driven component of the CEO's request will need to be taken care of with some date calculations.

Date and Time Formulas

Date and Time formulas are those derived from existing date or time fields (or fields converted into dates—see later for type conversion information). These types of formulas can be as simple as extracting a month name from a date field or as complex as determining shipping times in business days (difference between two dates not including weekends and holidays). Date and Time formulas are created within the Formula Editor by selecting any combination of date and time fields, Date operators and/or date-oriented Functions. Figure 10.12 displays the Formula Editor re-sized to highlight some common date functions.

FIGURE 10.12

The Formula Editor highlighting some Date and Time functions.

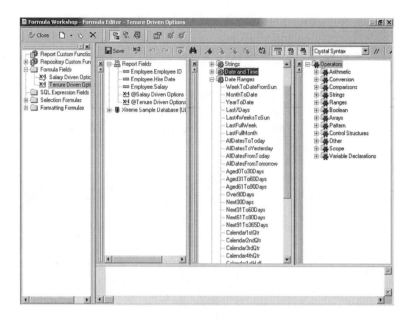

To create a Date/Time formula (as with Arithmetic formulas) within the Formula Editor, either double-click on the appropriate elements from each of the fields, functions, and operators frames or select them with a single-click and drag and drop them in to the Formula Editing frame. Using either method, a formula will begin to be constructed in the Formula Editing Area/Frame.

Some operators that are commonly used with dates include + and -. Those are displayed in Table 10.1 with some quick examples and their effect. These operators work equally well on time fields and date fields.

TABLE 10.1 Common Date Operators, Their Functions, and Examples

Common Date Operator or Function	Formula Usage Example	Effect
+ operator	{Employee.Hire Date} + 365	Returns the one year anniversary date of the given employee in a date format.
- operator	{Orders.Ship Date} - {Orders.Order Date}	Returns a numeric field representing the days taken to ship after receiving an order.

TABLE 10.1 continued

Common Date Operator or Function	Formula Usage Example	Effect
- operator	`{Orders.Warranty Expiration Date} - 365`	Returns a date representing the purchase date of the given item.

Common functions that are used with dates include the use of the pre-built date ranges and date type conversion formulas in Crystal Reports.

- Conversion functions are found under the Date and Time section in the Functions frame of the Formula Editor.
- Range functions are found in the Date Ranges section of the same Functions frame and provide a number of built-in date ranges that can be automatically created in Crystal Reports and used in comparisons. Range examples include `Aged61To90Days`, `Next30Days`, or `AllDatesFromTomorrow`. These ranges can be used with the control structures introduced later in this hour (for example, IF statements) to determine if dates fall within certain predefined ranges.

Revisiting the Maple Leaf Bikes reporting scenario, the Tenure component of option allocation still needs to be created in the report. It is based on a derivation from two date fields (hire date and the current date) and lends itself to the creation of a date formula based on the requirements that each 365 days of tenure will contribute to 100 stock options.

The following steps will move toward a final reporting solution for the CEO and provide exposure to date focused formula creation in the Formula Editor:

1. Create a New Formula in the Field Explorer called **Tenure Driven Options**.

Because the CEO wants to provide 100 stock options for each year (365 days) of tenure, we will logically need to determine each employee's tenure in days by finding the difference (with the - operator) between the current date (with a built-in Crystal Reports function) and the hire date (with a provided database field). This tenure in days measure will then need to be divided by 365 to find the tenure in years before being multiplied by 100 to determine the number of tenure-driven options.

2. To accomplish this, add the Current Date function (`CurrentDate`) to the formula by accessing it under the Date and Time section of the Functions frame in the Formula Editor. Add the - operator (found under the Arithmetic section in the Operators frame) after that, and then add the database field Hire Date to the formula by

10

double-clicking on it. Finally, add the / 365 and * 100 formula pieces by typing them in and, more importantly, wrap two curly brackets around the CurrentDate— {Employee.Hire Date} section of the formula—to ensure the proper order of calculation.

> The Crystal Reports Formula Editor respects the standard mathematical order of operations. In order this would be brackets, exponents, division and multiplication, and, finally, addition and subtraction.

3. Ensure that your formula resembles what is displayed in Figure 10.13 and save it before closing the Formula Workshop.

FIGURE 10.13

A Tenure Driven Options sample formula.

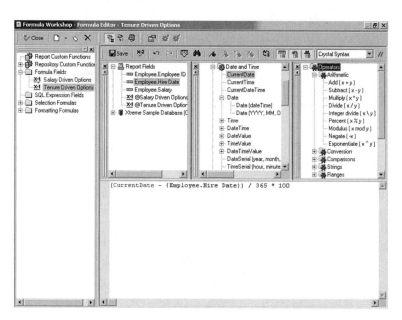

4. Place the new formula on the report beside the Salary Driven Options field and format it to have no decimal places and no currency symbol.

It has likely struck you that most CEOs would not appreciate having to take the two options numbers we have created and add them themselves. It seems like a good opportunity for another formula to sum up those two numbers.

5. Create a new formula called **Total Options** and make that formula be the sum of the two previously created formulas. (Hint: The previously created formulas will appear in the Fields frame, and you can use the addition operator.)

6. Add this new field to the report, remove the hire date and salary fields, and re-format it to make your sample resemble that displayed in Figure 10.14.

FIGURE **10.14**

Sample Crystal Report with multiple formulas.

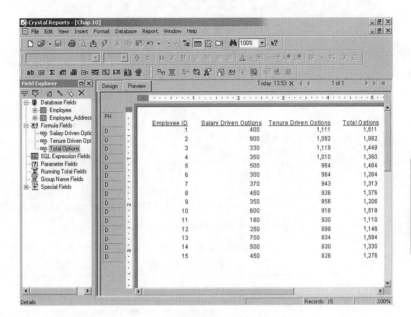

The CEO of Maple Leaf Bikes should be quite happy with the turnaround time on this report. Having created the results so quickly, it might be a good move in career management to spend a little time on the presentation and readability of this report. The next sections and hours will introduce some additional capabilities provided in Crystal Reports and the Formula Editor that will increase the presentation quality of this report.

String Formulas

String formulas are created from existing string fields (or fields converted into strings—see later for type conversion information). These formulas can be as simple as concatenating two string fields or as complex as extracting some specific piece of information from a string field. String formulas are created within the Formula Editor by selecting any combination of string fields, string operators or string-oriented functions. Figure 10.15 displays the Formula Editor resized to highlight some common string functions.

The most commonly created String based formulas involve the concatenation of multiple existing fields from a data source. This is accomplished through the Formula Editor with either the formal Concatenate function from within the Strings section of the Operators frame or by using the much easier + and & concatenate operators. These last two operators enable the dynamic linking of one or more string fields into one large string field.

FIGURE 10.15
The Formula Editor with string-oriented functions expanded.

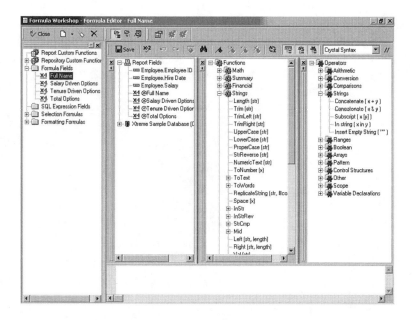

Although the + operator requires all of its arguments to be of the same string type when concatenating, the & operator will perform dynamic conversion to text on any non-string fields included in the operation—a nice timesaving feature.

When creating a string formula that is meant to join two existing strings (for example, First Name and Last Name, or Address 1 and Address 2), the concatenation features of Crystal Reports will dynamically resize the resultant formula to exclude any redundant spaces between the end of the first joined field and the beginning of the next. This is an important presentation feature that prevents the requirement to trim all fields before joining them together.

Revisiting the Maple Leaf Bikes reporting scenario and focusing on increasing the readability of the report, Employee ID can be replaced with Employee First Initial and Last Name. The following instructions will use the string capabilities of the Formula Editor and enhance the report in the described manner:

1. Create a new formula in the sample report called **Employee Name**.

2. Because we only want to present the first letter of the employee's first name, we will need to use the Left function under the Strings section of the Functions frame. Add this to your formula and note that the cursor is automatically placed in the expected location for the first parameter to this function—a string.

3. Without moving the cursor in the Editing area, find the First Name field of the Employee table and double-click on it (you will likely need to expand the Xtreme Sample Database section because this field is not currently added to the report)—thus adding it as the first argument to the Left function.

4. Move the cursor in the editing area to the location of the second expected parameter for the Left function—after the comma—and type **1** (the number of characters to extract). This will create the entry Left ({Employee.First Name}, 1) in the Formula Editor and will instruct the Formula Engine to take the left most single character from the First Name field.

5. To concatenate this with the Last Name in a nice-looking manner, type in + ". " + into the Editing area and then double-click on the Last Name field of the Employee table. Your new formula should resemble that shown in Figure 10.16.

10

FIGURE 10.16

String formula sample in the Formula Editor.

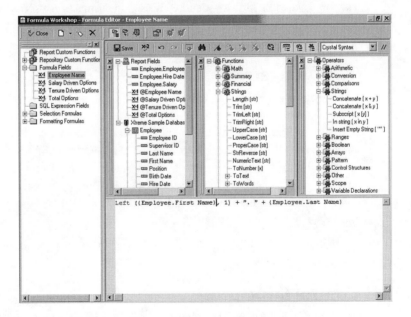

6. Replace the Employee ID field in the CEO's sample report with the new Employee Name formula just created and re-arrange your report to resemble Figure 10.17.

FIGURE 10.17

Maple Leaf Bikes CEO report with String formula.

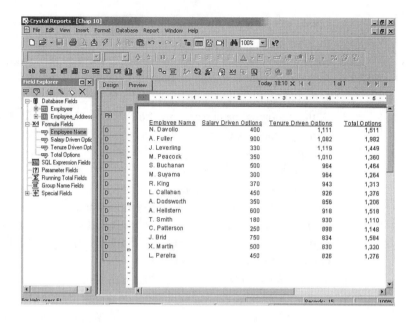

Having covered the primary data types used in strings, it is useful for operating in the real world to know how to move between those data types. The next section discusses data type conversion.

Type Conversion

Often, data is not accessible in the format that is required for a particular operation. The most common example is when numeric fields are stored in a database as string fields and they are required in an Arithmetic formula. For any number of additional reasons, it often happens that data needs to be converted to and from different data types. The Formula Editor provides numerous built-in functions that facilitate this conversion process. These functions are accessible from the Type Conversion section under the Functions frame of the Formula Editor. Figure 10.18 displays the Formula Editor with the Type Conversion section expanded.

A great deal of flexibility is provided with the numerous type conversion functions built into Crystal Reports.

Control Structures

The Formula Editor provides additional power in formula creation through a set of control structures made available in the Operators and Functions Frames. Figure 10.19 displays the involved sections of those respective frames that include the provided control structures.

FIGURE 10.18
The Formula Editor with Type Conversion functions.

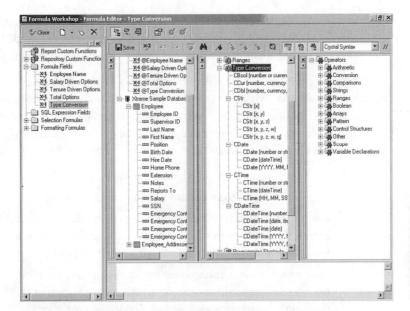

FIGURE 10.19
The Formula Editor with Control Structure functions and operators.

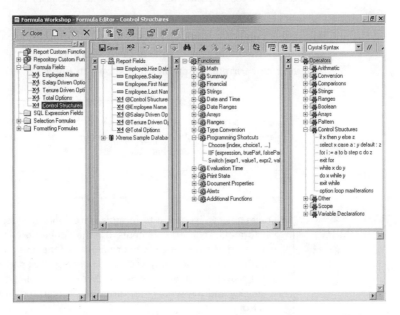

One of the most useful control structures is the If/Then/Else construct. This structure enables the inclusion of conditional logic in Crystal Reports formulas. The If/Then/Else works particularly well when a condition leads to either one of two settings. Although this construct can handle multiple potential settings through nested If statements, creating this type of complicated formula can be avoided with the Select Case operator that allows for multiple settings and multiple potential results.

Revisiting the Maple Leaf Bikes example, lets assume that the CEO has provided a new requirement specifying that employees with a recommended stock allocation of greater than 1500 stock options need to be highlighted for his personal review. Of course, with Crystal Reports, there are multiple methods of providing this highlighting, but using the If/Then/Else control structure, the following steps can accomplish this:

1. Create a new formula called High Option Review.
2. Add the If/Then/Else control structure to the formula.
3. Add the condition that the Total Options Formula (the @Total Options field) is greater than 1500 between the If and Then components so that the beginning of the formula text is IF {@Total Options} > 1500 THEN.
4. Now when this condition is met for any employee, we need to highlight that record for the CEO's special review. To do this, add text similar to "** Review **" (with the double quotes surrounding the text) to the area after the Then part of the If statement construct.
5. When that condition is not met, we can simply print a space or dash. Do this by adding "-" (including the double quotes) after the Else part of the If statement so that your new formula resembles that shown in Figure 10.20.

Carriage returns (via the Enter key) can be inserted into the construction area of the formula, such as between lines and logical breaking points, to make formulas more readable.

Comments can be added to formula statements in order to better document the formula. To insert comments, use the double forward slash (//) at the beginning of a line of code to comment out the entire line. Thus, any text on this commented line would not be processed as part of the formula. There is also a toolbar command within the Formula Editor that allows you to quickly add this syntax into formulas, as indicated with the double slash (//) icon.

6. Add the new formula to the CEO's report so that it resembles the sample report displayed in Figure 10.21.

FIGURE 10.20

A sample formula with an If control structure.

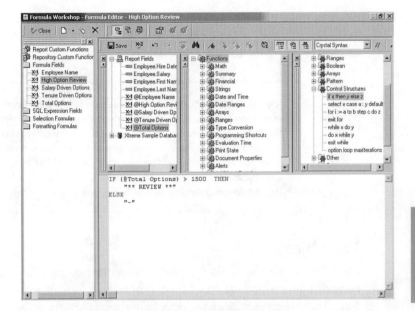

FIGURE 10.21

Revised sample report with a High Option Review indicator.

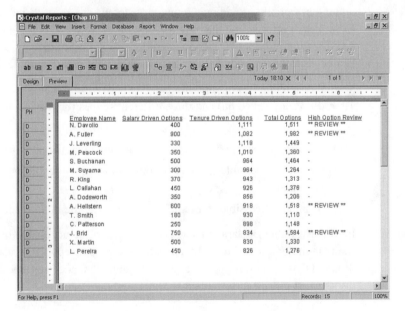

The conditional logic inherent in the If/Then/Else and Select/Case statements provide clear flexibility in formula creation. Another valuable formula capability that programmers will appreciate immediately is the looping functionality. The Formula

Editor provides three different looping constructs (For/Step/Do, Do/While, and While/Do), and each of these enable the evaluation of formula logic multiple times for each evaluation of the formula.

> The Crystal Reports engine has a built-in safety mechanism that displays an error message and stops processing any formula if it includes more than 100,000 loop iterations. This is important to consider when including any of the loop constructs in a formula. It is also important to note that this built-in governor works on a per formula basis and not per loop. This means that if any one formula contains any number of loop constructs that tally over 100,000 looping iterations, the formula will stop processing with an error.

Variables

Crystal Reports has included yet another programming construct—variables—in the Formula Editor to provide even further flexibility in formula creation. Variables provide a powerful means to store and retrieve information throughout the processing life of any report—essentially providing a temporary storage space for valuable information. Examples of information that might be useful to store and retrieve later are previous detail section information, previous group section information, or a one-time calculation that needs to be incorporated into many subsequent report formulas.

Several different types of variables can be declared (for example, String, Number, Date, Time, Boolean, and so on) and three different scopes for each of these variables are as follows:

- Local—Accessible only in the same formula that they are declared within.
- Global—Accessible from all formulas in the main report, but not accessible from subreports.
- Shared—Accessible from all formulas in both the main report and all subreports.

Both the Variable Declaration and Scope operators are accessible from the Operators frame in the Formula Editor. To use variables in your report formulas, they must be declared first—and this applies to every formula that accesses any given variable—not just the first processed formula.

Another important function to remember when using multiple variables in multiple formulas with calculation dependencies is the EvaluateAfter() function. This formula function can force certain formulas (and their variable logic) to be processed after another formula (and its variable logic). This can be very useful when the order of formula calculation is important because of variable and formula dependencies.

Although a detailed discussion on variables is beyond the scope of this book, it is worth noting the power that they provide to maintain some persistent information outside the regular processing path of the report. A practical hands-on use of variables is explored in Hour 16, "Using Sub-Reports for Increased Flexibility."

Formula Expert

The Formula Expert is used to create formulas based on existing custom functions— either from the current report or the Crystal repository. The expert appears when you click the Use Expert button in the Formula Name dialog during the formula creation process. The Formula Expert leverages the power of the new custom functions and repository functionality of version 9. Figure 10.22 displays the Formula Expert dialog.

FIGURE 10.22
The Formula Expert dialog box.

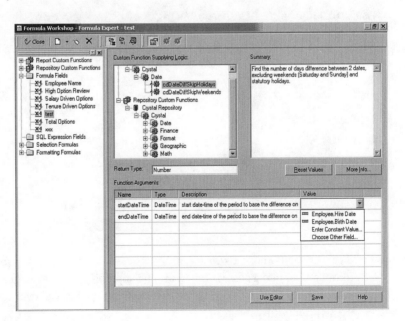

Using the Formula Expert is a simple three-step process:

1. Find the custom function that meets your formula requirements by searching through the Report and Repository Custom Function libraries. The supporting Help description and More Info button can aid in this search.

2. For each parameter of the selected function, select a field from your report data source or enter a constant.

3. Save the new formula using the Save button.

The created formula will now be accessible through the Formula Editor and can be enhanced or edited with the power that that tool provides.

Formula Extractor

The Formula Expert enables the creation of formulas from existing custom functions. The Formula Extractor enables the exact opposite—the creation of custom functions from previously created formulas. This functionality is accessible by creating a new Custom Report Function and selecting the Use Extractor button. Figure 10.23 displays the Extract Custom Function from Formula dialog box accessed when creating custom report functions.

FIGURE 10.23

The Extract Custom Function from Formula dialog.

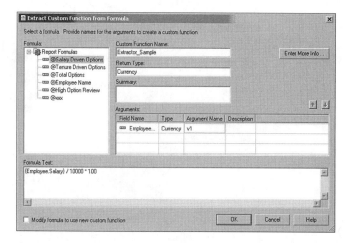

By using the Formula Extractor, it is possible to migrate existing formula logic from a formula field into a custom function. The appropriate part of the migrated formulas can subsequently be replaced with the new custom function and eventually be added to the Crystal Repository.

To create a custom function from an existing formula using the Formula Extractor dialog, follow these steps:

1. In the Formula Workshop, create a new Custom Report Function. Select the Formula Extractor by clicking on the Use Extractor button after you have ensured that the custom function name you have selected follows your personal or organization's standard naming convention.

2. Edit the default argument names (v1, v2, and so on) and descriptions that represent the required parameters for the new function. These argument names and descriptions should communicate the expected information to future users of the custom function. The importance of meaningful information here cannot be underestimated with respect to the future usefulness of the newly created custom function.

3. Add an appropriate summary description to the Summary window so that future report designers using this custom function will understand its proper use.

4. Click on the Modify Formula to Use New Function check box (lower left area of the Extract Custom Function dialog) to place the new custom function into the formula you are basing it on. This is not a mandatory step, but it is a nice feature that quickly enables you to start to take advantage of the reusability of your new custom function.

5. Click the Enter More Info button to add additional support information for the custom function. Figure 10.24 displays the More Info dialog.

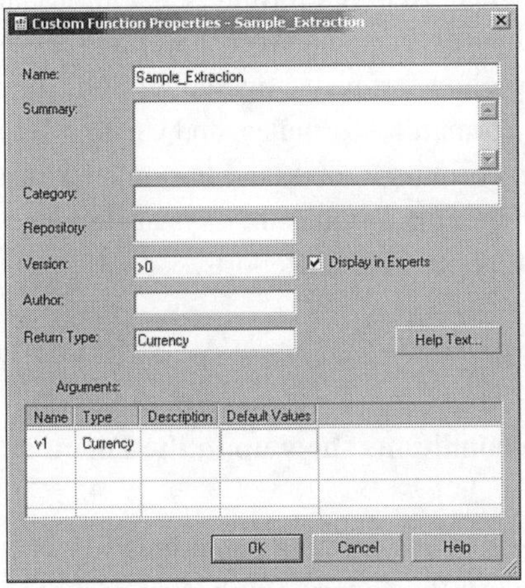

FIGURE 10.24

The Custom Function Enter More Info dialog box.

6. Enter the custom function author (likely yourself) and custom function category information in their respective text boxes.

When entering a custom function category, it is possible to create it at more than one level of subfolder depth by using forward slashes in the Category text box. For example, by entering `MapleLeafs/HR`, the newly created formula will be added to the Custom Function library under the Maple Leafs category and the HR subfolder. By adding and maintaining your custom functions in a logical hierarchy, future users will find accessing them much easier.

7. Optionally set default values for your custom functions arguments by clicking on the default value cells and filling in the Default Values dialog box.

8. Add Help text describing the custom function by clicking on the Help Text button. Again, it is important to consider future report designers using this custom function when deciding on the detail that you should include in this description.

Summary

Formulas provide additional flexibility and power in creating reports through the ability to create derived fields not directly stored in available data sources. Formulas also enable the creation of advanced conditional formatting and selection formulas in a report and its objects.

In this hour, we explored Crystal Report's formula capabilities and the different access points to these formulas. The new Formula Workshop provides a focal point for accessing the majority of your reporting formulas—including SQL Expressions, Record and Group Selection formulas, Formatting formulas, and Custom Report and Repository formulas. The Formula Editor, Formula Expert, and Formula Extractor all provide different capabilities and facilitate the use of formulas in Crystal Reports to enable the creation of increasingly powerful and flexible Crystal Reports.

Q&A

Q Do alerting formula conditions show up in the Formula Workshop or Crystal Repository?

A At the time of writing, alerting formula conditions were not yet part of the Formula Workshop nor the Crystal Repository. But because the product is always evolving these may well be added in a future release.

Q **Is there more information about SQL Expressions, Record and Group selections, and custom functions?**

A Yes—more information on record and group selections can be found in Hour 15, on custom functions in Hour 17, on the Crystal Repository in Hour 18, and on SQL Expressions in Hour 22.

Workshop

The quiz questions and activities are provided for your further understanding of the current hour's topics.

Quiz

1. Can custom functions be added directly into the Crystal Repository?

2. Which tool can create custom functions from existing formulas?

Quiz Answers

1. No—custom functions must be added to a local Report Custom Function library before they can be transferred to the Crystal Repository.

2. The Formula Extractor enables the creation of a custom functions from existing formulas and facilitates the migration of the logic in those formulas into a central library—the Crystal Repository.

Activities

Now that you have had some exposure to the powerful formula capabilities in Crystal Reports, think about how these capabilities can expand the flexibility with which you can deliver professionally formatted reports to your business user community.

10

HOUR 11

Visualizing Your Data with Charts and Maps

Hour 6, "Selecting and Grouping Data," and Hour 7, "Filtering, Sorting, and Summarizing Data," introduced the importance of grouping and summarization in report generation. When grouping and summarizing data in a report for business users, it is also often effective to present this information using various visualization techniques. The charting and mapping features in Crystal Reports provide a very effective way to communicate relevant information using powerful visualization techniques.

Charts and maps with Crystal Reports provide an extensive array of data visualization options to report designers. In addition to potentially familiar chart types including bar charts, pie charts, scatter charts, line charts, and bubble charts, new chart types in version 9 include

- Gantt charts
- Speedometer type Gauges
- Numeric Axis charts

Geographic Mapping with color coding and integrated charting options provides yet another effective method of conveying macro-level information to report consumers.

This hour provides an introduction to various charting and mapping techniques, including

- Enhancing the sample reports from previous Hours with charts and maps
- A review of the Crystal Reports charting expert
- An introduction to the new chart types—Gantt, Gauge, and Numeric Axis charts
- A review of the Crystal Reports mapping expert
- Manual chart and map formatting

A good place to begin with adding visualizations to your reports is with the chart expert.

Using the Chart Expert

Reflecting back on the sample reports used in Hours 5 and 7, you might find that there are opportunities for enhancement through the addition of meaningful charts. As reviewed in Hour 6 with groupings, it is quite easy to summarize the data we collect for a report into meaningful categories or groups. Hour 6 reviews some examples of grouping based on fields such as country and customer name. By hiding or suppressing the detail sections of reports, you learned how to bring the meaningful summarizations around these types of groups to the forefront. (Do you remember how to hide/suppress the detail sections? Hint: use the right-click menu.) To further bring this aggregated data to the business user's attention, you can create a chart on this grouped data using the Chart Expert.

To open the Chart Expert, either click on the Chart icon located on the Insert Toolbar or select the Insert Chart option under the main Insert menu. Figure 11.1 displays the Chart Expert.

After you've accessed the Chart Expert, several steps are required to actually complete the chart. These are reviewed in the next five sections.

Chart Type Tab

The Chart Expert consists of five different tabs. The initial display tab on the Chart Expert is the Chart Type tab, as seen in Figure 11.1. On this tab, the type of graphic or chart is selected. In Crystal Reports version 9, there are more than 40 different basic chart types to select from.

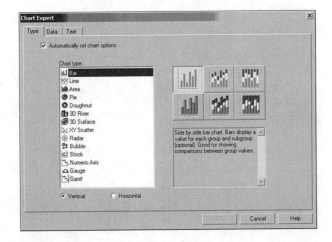

FIGURE 11.1

Chart Expert dialog.

In addition to the classic bar, line, pie, and area charts, new chart types in version 9 are listed in Table 11.1.

TABLE 11.1 New Chart Types in Crystal Reports Version 9

New Chart Type	Chart Type Description
Gantt Chart	A Gantt chart is a project-focused horizontal bar chart used to provide a graphical illustration of a project schedule. The horizontal axis shows a time span, whereas the vertical axis lists project tasks or events. Horizontal bars on the chart represent event sequences and time spans for each task on the vertical axis.
Gauge(s)	A Gauge chart presents data using a speedometer visual and is often used to measure percentage completed against target type metrics.
Numeric Axis	A Numeric Axis chart is a bar, line, or area chart that uses a numeric field or a date/time field as its On change Of field. Numeric Axis charts provide a way of creating a true numeric X-axis or a true date/time X-axis.

These charts have been added to further expand the visualization capabilities of Crystal Reports and enrich the presentation of your reports. Let's explore enhancing the Sample Customer Order Listing (Chap5.rpt) report from Hour 5 by adding a chart to it that highlights the Company's Top 10 Customers in the following steps:

1. Either open the Sample Order Listing (Chap5.rpt) Report created in Hour 5 in the Crystal Reports Designer or quickly re-create the basics of it by selecting the Customer Name, Order ID, and Order Amount fields from the Xtreme Sample

Database, Group by Customer Name, and Summarize Order Amount by the Customer Name group.

2. To restrict the data to the Top 10 Customers, access the Group Sort Expert from the Report menu option. Select a Top 10 Sort based on the Sum of Order Amount and do not include Others.

3. Insert a Chart onto the report using the Chart icon or the Chart option from the Insert menu.

4. Select a bar chart as the main chart type in the list box by clicking on it. Also, click on the Horizontal radio button that is present at the bottom of the dialog box.

5. Select the two-dimensional side-by-side bar chart sub-chart type (top left option) by clicking on the associated graphical icon to the right of the main list box area.

   The last option to set in the Chart Type tab is whether you want Crystal Reports to automatically use the default legend, data-point, color, and axes options for your chart. The automatic option is enabled by default, but it can be turned off by clicking on the check box near the top of the dialog box.

6. At this point, de-select the automatic check box.

Notice that the Axes and Options tabs appear when this check box is not clicked and disappear when it is selected. These tabs are discussed later in this section. Figure 11.2 displays the result of these six steps. We will continue creating this chart in the next four sections.

FIGURE 11.2

The Chart Type tab on the Chart Selection dialog for the Sample Customer Order Listing report.

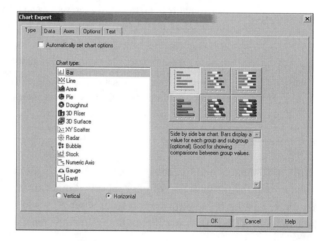

Table 11.2 highlights some common reports, their contained graphics, and the benefit that is realized by using them.

TABLE 11.2   Common Reports with Corresponding Chart Types

Report	Chart Type	Report and Chart Benefit
Company Sales Report	Pie or Donut Chart	Highlights the regional breakdown of product sales across continents or countries facilitating analysis of revenue contribution.
Product Profitability Report	Horizontal or Vertical Bar Chart	Highlights the profit margin per product that a company sells, facilitating comparative analysis of profitability.
Actual versus Target Report	Gauges	Highlights the progress being made against specified targets through the use of a speedometer visual. When used across projects or divisions, it isrelatively easy to compare how they are performing against certain initiatives.

Chart Data Tab

After a chart type has been selected in the Chart Type tab, click on the Chart Data tab. The Chart Data tab enables the selection of the specific data that the chart will be based on and the chart's location on the report. Figure 11.3 displays one view of the second tab of the Chart Expert. This view might vary depending on the different Chart Type options you have selected. The Chart Data tab is comprised of three different sections: Placement, Layout, and Data. These sections and corresponding options are discussed next.

FIGURE **11.3**

The Chart Data tab of the Chart Expert.

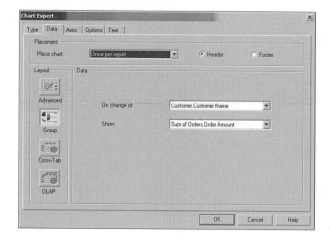

Chart Placement

The Chart Placement section is used to select the location of the chart on the report and, subsequently, the recurrence of the chart throughout the report. Using the drop-down box, the section of the report that the chart is to be located is selected (for example, Group 1, Group 2, and so on). The options available in this drop-down box are limited to the groups previously created in the report in addition to the option to create the graphic only once for the entire report. Using the radio buttons located beside the drop-down box, the header or footer of the selected report section can be selected. By making these selections, you also specify the chart's recurrence in the report because the chart will repeatedly appear in every section you have specified. For example, if a chart was placed on a report for each country group, a separate chart would appear on the report for each country in the report.)

To continue with the addition of a bar chart to the sample report, you will need to

1. Select the Once Per Report option in the Place Chart drop-down box. This should be the only option and already selected by default.

2. Select the Header button to specify placement in the report header.

When you select the Group Layout button (second button from top in Layout section—see the next section for more details), you are presented with the options in the Chart Placement drop-down box based on what groups and summaries are already created in your report. Alternatively, if you select the Advanced Grouping Layout button, you will not be as restricted and can dynamically create summaries across groups not yet in your report.

Chart Layout

The Chart Layout section specifies the data selection options that the selected chart will provide to the report designer. The actual data is selected in the Chart Data section. Note that the options presented in that section are dependent on the specific Chart Layout button you have selected. Table 11.3 lists the different layout buttons and their typical use.

TABLE 11.3   Layout Buttons and Typical Use

Layout Button	Description and Typical Use
Advanced	Description: This layout button provides complete flexibility in chart creation through the provision of controlling all charting options.
	Typical Use: Creation of charts based on summaries not already created in the report or charts to be created for every detail record.
Grouping	Description: Although this button is presented second, it is the default layout. This layout limits the Chart Data Selection options (see next section) to two drop-down boxes specifying the On change Of and Show values and expedites the creation of a chart at the cost of some of the flexibility provided by the Advanced layout button.
	Typical Use: Quick Creation of charts based on summarized fields already in the report and to be displayed at the Report or existing Group level.
Cross-Tab	Description: This layout button only appears as an option when your current report is a Cross-Tab report.
	Typical Use: Creation of a chart based on an existing Cross-Tab in the report.
OLAP	Description: This layout button only appears as an option when your current report is based on an OLAP data source.
	Typical Use: Creation of a chart based on an existing OLAP grid in the report.

The Cross-Tab and OLAP layout buttons, and their related chart creation options, are explored in Hours 14, "Using Cross-Tabs for Summarized Reporting," and 20, "Multidimensional Reporting against OLAP Data," because they relate to very specific report types. The next section explores the detailed data options that the Advanced and Grouping Layouts buttons enable.

Chart Data

Figure 11.3 displays the Chart Data section with the Group layout button selected. As previously described, this layout option is designed to facilitate the quick creation of a chart with a minimal amount of effort. To accomplish this rapid chart creation, two pieces of information are requested through two drop-down boxes— On Change Of

(Grouping item) and Show (field to be shown in the chart) selections. The On Change Of field is used to determine where the selected chart will break the report data to be displayed. The Show field specifies the summary field to be displayed for each break of the data.

Continuing with the addition of a bar chart to the sample report, you will need to follow these steps:

1. Ensure that the Group layout button from the Layout section is selected.

2. Select Customer Name in the On Change Of field. This indicates that the chart will break for every different customer.

3. Select Sum of Order Amount for the Show field. This indicates that the chart will reflect this Sum for each customer. Figure 11.3 should reflect the results of these steps in the Chart Data tab. We will continue this chart creation in the next section.

> When leveraging the Rapid Chart Creation functionality of the Group layout option, it's important to note that you will be limited to chart creation based on existing summary fields already created in your reports and inserted into existing group sections. For more flexible chart creation, you can use the Advanced layout option described later.

Figure 11.4 displays the Chart tab with the Advanced Layout button selected. The additional options presented here enable greatly improved flexibility in the charts that can be created.

FIGURE 11.4

The Chart Data tab with the Advanced Layout button selected.

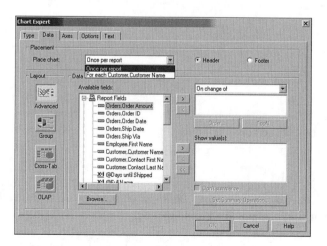

The On Change Of and Show fields should be recognizable in this new window although they are selected in a much more flexible manner (see the right side of the Chart Data section beside the Available fields listing).

The On Change Of field is now only one selection option (among three) in its own drop-down box. If you need to create a chart based on changing a specific field (as we did with the standard group layout), select the On Change Of charting option and then specify the field or fields to break the chart sections on by selecting any of the fields in the available fields listing. Unlike the drop-down box under the Group layout, you can select any of the available report fields in this interface, dynamically order them with the Order button or restrict their display on the report to a specified Top or Bottom N with the Top N button. You can also dynamically select multiple fields for the chart to break on, and none of the selected fields need already be on the report or have summary fields previously existing on the report for them.

The remaining two options in the On Change Of drop-down box are For Each Record and For All Records. These two options enable charts to be created either against all data in a report or for each detailed record in a report.

11

> When using the For All Records charting option, you can select the field to be displayed for each break by selecting a field from the available fields list into the list box beneath the For All Records drop-down box.

When selecting any of these options, you subsequently need to select a Show Value(s) field to enable the chart's creation. This selection specifies the summary field to be displayed for each break of the data and can come from any field (database, report, formula, and so on) that is listed in the available field's list. To select the Show Value fields, highlight the intended field and use the selection arrow buttons adjacent to the Show Value(s) list box.

> As mentioned previously, you do **not** need to have an existing summary on your report to use it for a graph in the Advanced Charting layout options. You can add any field to the Show Value(s) list and then dynamically create a summary by clicking on the Set Summary Operation button. These dynamically created summaries will be automatically created and used by the chart. This is one of the unique features of Crystal Reports and provides report designers with additional charting flexibility.

Chart Text Tab

Once a chart type and data have been specified, select the Chart Text tab. This tab on the Chart Expert enables the specification of titles and title formatting that the chart will use when it is placed on the report. Figure 11.5 displays the Chart Text tab of the Chart Expert.

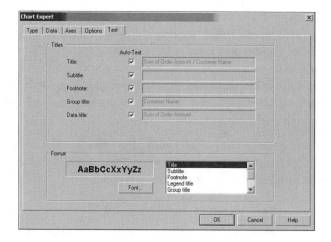

Continuing with the bar chart addition to the sample report, follow these steps:

1. De-select the Autotext check box beside the Title entry. The text box for the title should now become available for you to modify. Change the title to **CR24 - Hour 11 Test Chart**.

2. De-select the Autotext check box beside the Data Title entry. Change the Data Title entry to **Order Amounts**. We will continue with this chart's creation in the next section.

Chart Axes Tab

The fourth tab in the chart expert, the Chart Axes tab, only appears if the Automatically Select Chart Options check box has been de-selected on the Chart Type tab. It can then be selected by clicking on it. The Axes Tab enables you to customize chart gridlines, data value scales, data value ranges, and data value divisions. Figure 11.6 displays the Chart Axes tab of the Chart Expert for a bar chart.

FIGURE **11.6**

The Chart Axes tab of the Chart Expert.

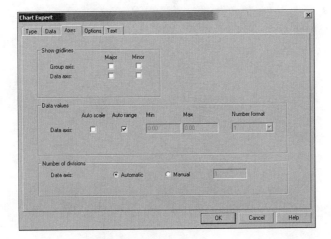

This tab will only appear when the selected chart type has axes within it (for example, bar chart or line chart) and does not display for other chart types (for example, pie chart).

11

Continuing with the addition of a bar chart to the sample report, try the following step: Select the Major Gridlines check box for the data axis. This will facilitate the reading of the bar charts. We will finish off this bar chart creation in the next section.

By manually setting both the Min/Max Data Ranges and the Number of Data Value Divisions, you will be able to set your data axis gridline display labels in a customized manner.

Chart Options Tab

The Chart Options tab in the Chart Expert only appears if the Automatically Select Chart Options check box has been de-selected on the Chart Type tab. The Chart Options tab enables you to customize chart coloring, data-point labeling, legend placement, legend format options, and several other chart type specific formatting options. Figure 11.7 displays the Chart Options tab of the Chart Expert for a bar chart.

FIGURE **11.7**

The Chart Options tab of the Chart Expert.

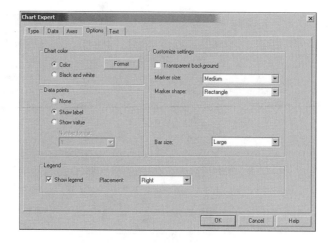

To complete the last customizations on the bar chart being added to your working sample report, follow these steps:

1. Select the Show Value button in the Data Points section.

2. Select the 1K format from the formatting drop-down box.

3. Click the OK button, and you will find a bar chart representing the summarized sales of this company's top 10 customers presented. Figure 11.8 provides a snapshot of this report.

FIGURE **11.8**

A Sample Customer Orders report with a bar chart.

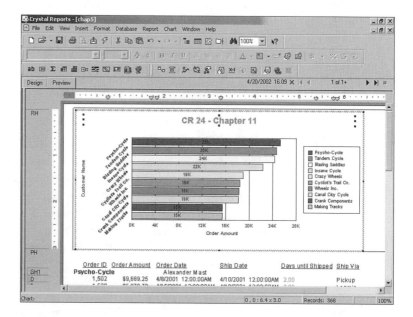

If you find your chart is slightly different in appearance or imperfect, that is okay. You have plenty of powerful fine-tuning tools at your disposal, and they will be partially explored at the end of this hour.

Using the Map Expert

As you explore the charting capabilities, you will discover numerous data visualizations that will enhance the productivity of your reports and business users. Another valuable form of data presentation available in Crystal Reports is geographic mapping. This form of visualization enables the creation of reports that are logically grouped on geographically related information and can communicate meaningful information in a familiar mapping paradigm. When working with geographic data, you can quickly create a map or a map/chart combination on this data using the Map Expert.

> The maps and mapping functionality provided within Crystal Reports are bundled from a third-party company—MapInfo. Additional map layers and types can be purchased directly from MapInfo and can be made accessible from Crystal Reports by adding them to the mapping folders under \Program Files\Map Info X. You can order additional mapping information from MapInfo at www.mapinfo.com.

To open the Map Expert, either click on the Map Globe icon located on the Insert toolbar or access the Insert Map option under the Insert menu. Figure 11.9 displays the Map Expert.

FIGURE 11.9

The Map Expert dialog.

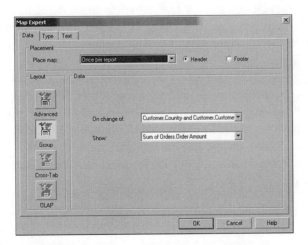

11

In the next three sections, you will be introduced to the functionality of the Map Expert and also be escorted through a brief tutorial on the addition of a map to the sample Order Listing report (Chap6.rpt) discussed in Hour 6. (Note that this report is different from the one we have been working on up to this point.) If you have jumped directly to this hour without reading through Hour 6, you can still follow this guided tutorial by quickly creating a new report based on the Xtreme sample data, adding a few columns of data in the detail section, including Order Amount, and grouping the report by Customer Country and then Customer Name.

Map Data Tab

The Map Data tab on the Map Expert enables you to select the specific data that the map will be based on and where it will be placed on the report. Figure 11.9 displays this tab of the Map Expert. The Map Data tab is comprised of three different sections: Placement, Layout, and Data. These sections, and corresponding options, are discussed next.

Map Placement

The Map Placement section is used in an identical manner as the Chart Placement section for charts. It enables the selection of the location of the map on the report and consequently the recurrence of the map throughout the report.

Using the drop-down box, the section of the report that the map is to be located is selected (for example, Group 1, Group 2, and so on). The options available in this drop-down box are limited to the groups previously created in the report in addition to the option to create the graphic only once for the entire report. Using the buttons located beside the drop-down box, the header or footer of the selected report section is selected. By making these selections, you have also determined the chart's recurrence in the report because the chart will repeatedly appear in every section you have specified (for example, for each country in the group based on country).

To begin with a walk through of an example, perform the following steps:

1. Either open the sample Customer Order Listing Report (Chap6.rpt) from Hour 6— this is the one with groupings on Country and Customer Name—or open the report you have just created based on the specifications given earlier (a new report based on the Xtreme sample data—a few columns of data in the detail section, including Order Amount, and grouping the report by Customer Country and then Customer Name).

2. Open the Map Expert.

3. Select Once Per Report in the Placement drop-down box and select the header as the map's intended location. We will continue with further steps in the next sections.

Map Layout

The Map Layout section specifies the data that the map will use. The actual data is selected in the Map Data section (described next), but the options presented in that section are dependent on the Map Layout button you have selected. Table 11.4 lists the different layout buttons and their typical use.

TABLE 11.4 Map Expert Layout Buttons and Typical Use

Layout Button	Description and Typical Use
Advanced	Description: This layout button provides complete flexibility in map creation through the provision of control of all mapping options.
	Typical Use: Creation of Maps based on summaries not already created in the report or maps based on geographic fields not contained in predefined report groups.
Group	Description: Although this button is presented second, it is the default layout if the involved report has predefined groups and summary fields already created. This layout limits the Map Data Selection options (see next section) to two drop-down boxes specifying the On change Of and Show values and expedites the creation of a map at the cost of some of the flexibility provided by the advanced layout button.
	Typical Use: Quick Creation of Maps based on summarized fields already in the report and to be displayed at the Report or existing Group level.
Cross-Tab	Description: This layout button only appears as an option when your current report is a Cross-Tab report.
	Typical Use: Creation of a Map based on an existing Cross-Tab in the report.
OLAP	Description: This layout button only appears as an option when your current report is based on an OLAP data source.
	Typical Use: Creation of a Map based on an existing OLAP grid in the report.

The Cross-Tab and OLAP layout buttons and their related map creation options are explored in Hours 14 and 20. The next section explores the detailed data options that the Advanced and Group Layout buttons enable.

If you attempt to create a geographic map based on a non-geographic field, the Map Expert will accept your request and then display a blank map when it cannot resolve the selected field values to geographic entities. Therefore, make sure to select a valid geographic field in the Geographic Field item of the Advanced layout section or the On Change Of field in the Group layout section.

Map Data

As you saw earlier, Figure 11.9 displays the Map Data section with the Group layout button selected. As described in Table 11.4, this layout option is designed to facilitate the quick creation of a map with a minimal amount of user interaction. To accomplish this rapid map creation, two pieces of information are requested through two drop-down boxes.

The first drop-down requests you to select the On Change Of field and the second the Show field. The On Change Of field is used to determine where the selected map will break the report data to be displayed (for example, Country, State, or Province). The Show field specifies the summary field to be displayed for each break of the data.

When leveraging the Rapid Map Creation functionality of the Group layout option, it is important to note that you are limited to map creation based on existing summary fields already created in your reports and inserted into existing group sections. For more flexible map creation, use the Advanced layout option described later.

Figure 11.10 displays the Map Data tab with the Advanced layout button selected. The additional options presented here enable greatly improved flexibility in the maps that can be created.

The familiar On Change Of field should be recognizable in this new window although it is selected in a more flexible manner using the selection button in the interface. It is selected in exactly the same manner as the Geographic field selection in this interface by selecting any of the fields in the available fields listing and clicking on the selection button.

FIGURE 11.10

The Map Data tab with the Advanced layout button selected.

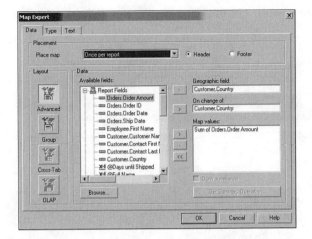

It is important to note that the Geographic and On Change Of fields are often the same, but can be set to be different. These are set to different field values when you want to present pie or bar charts on top of the involved map and for each of the different values in the selected Geographic field. An example of this would be presenting a pie chart for each country that highlights the different order amounts by company—indicated in the On Change Of field.

After selecting your Geographic and On Change Of fields, a Map Values field must be selected to enable the map's creation. This selection specifies the summary field to be displayed for each break of the data and can come from any field (database, report, formula, and so on) that is listed in the available field's list. To select the Show Value fields, highlight the intended field and use the selection arrow buttons adjacent to the Map Value(s) list box.

As mentioned previously, you do **not** need to have had an existing summary on a report to summarize on it using the Advanced Mapping layout options. You can add any field to the Map Values list and then dynamically create a summary by clicking on the Set Summary Operation button. These dynamically created summaries will be automatically created and used by the map.

11

Continuing with the addition of a map to your sample report, follow these steps:

1. Ensure that the Advanced layout button from the Layout section is selected.

2. Select Country for the Geographic field. This indicates that the map will break for every different country. Leave the On Change Of field as Country when this gets populated automatically.

3. Select Order Amount for the Show field and leave the default Sum as the summary operation. This indicates that the map will reflect this Sum of Orders for each country. Figure 11.10 should reflect the results of these steps in the Map Data tab. We will finish this map creation in the next two sections.

Map Type Tab

The Map Type tab allows you to select from the five different types of maps that are available for presentation. The five map types can be logically broken in to two distinct and separate categories—maps that present a summarization based on one or two variables. The Map Type tab with these five map types is depicted in Figure 11.11. All five of the map types are also described in Table 11.5.

FIGURE 11.11

*The Map Expert
Map Type tab.*

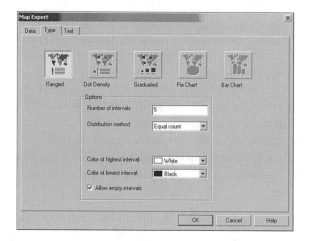

The first three map types listed base their maps on the summary of the selected Show Value field and for each Geographic field—the single fluctuating variable. The last two map types base their maps not only on the changing Geographic field, but also on a second fluctuating variable selected in the On Change Of field. Based on this second variable changing, either bar or pie charts are displayed on top of each of the involved Geographic fields.

Table 11.5 highlights the different map types, as well as a description and an example scenario for each.

TABLE 11.5   Map Types with Corresponding Sample Reporting Scenario

Map Type	Description	Example Scenario
Ranged	A Ranged map breaks data into specified ranges and displays geographic areas on the map in different colors.	A U.S.-based firm looking for a Sales Map that highlights the states that fall into a specified number of sales/revenue ranges.
Dot Density	A Dot Density map displays a dot for each occurrence of a specified item.	A growing wireless company in Eastern Canada wants to view the density and point location of new customers and map that to ongoing marketing campaigns.
Graduated	A Graduated map displays data that is linked to points rather than precise geographical areas.	An Irish beverage company wants a report on geographically dispersed distributors that proportionately highlights the amount of product being distributed.
Pie Chart	A Pie Chart map displays a pie chart over each geographic area. Each slice of the pie represents an individual summarization relative to the whole for the given geographic area.	An employee head-count report for the United States with a pie chart over each state that highlights the breakdown of the employees by status including salaried, hourly, or temporary.
Bar Chart	A Bar Chart map displays a bar chart over each geographic area. Each bar represents an individual summarization relative to the other summarizations for the given geographic area.	A Marketing Media report for a U.S.-based company with a bar chart that highlights the amount of advertising and marketing dollars spent in different media in each region: TV, Internet, newspaper, magazine, and so on.

11

Each Map Type has a small number of associated options that can be set to customize the appearance of that particular map. You are encouraged to explore these options to help you find the maps most useful for your specific design goals.

Map Text Tab

After a map's type and data have been selected, select the Map Text tab. This tab on the Map Expert enables you to specify titles and legend formatting that the map will use when it is placed on the report.

To finish with the addition of a map to your sample report, follow these steps:

1. On the Map Type tab, select the Ranged Map Type.
2. On the Map Type tab, select Yellow and Blue as the respective low and high range colors.
3. Click on the Map Text tab and give your map a title such as `CR24 - Hour 11 Map`.
4. Click OK, and you will find a geographic map added to your report that should look similar to Figure 11.12.

FIGURE 11.12

A sample Customer Orders Report with a geographic map.

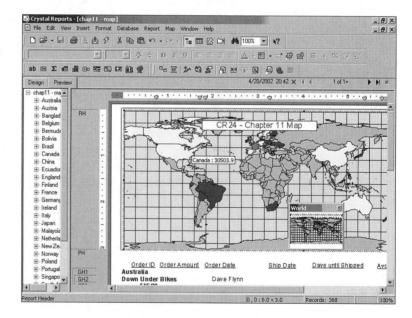

Modifying Chart and Map Properties

After you have successfully created a chart or map and placed it on your report, you have a number of post-creation editing options at your disposal within the Crystal Reports Designer. Both charts and maps provide a number of easy-to-use methods to re-visit and edit your charts or maps. Several of the most common editing methods are listed in the following sections.

Modifying Chart Properties

After a chart has been created and placed on your report, you can perform numerous post-creation edits by right-clicking on the chart object while in the Preview mode. From the Chart menu that appears, you have both the ability to revisit the Chart Expert and use a number of more finely tuned post-creation editing tools, including the powerful and flexible Chart Option functions.

With version 9 of Crystal Reports, increased capabilities to perform numerous in-place edits to chart objects have been added. In the past, this functionality was mostly accessible from a separate tab called the Chart Analyzer. This tab is no longer available. An example is that you can grab a chart title (or other object) and move its location or change its font directly in-place in version 9.

11

Chart Options

The Chart Option menu choice enables you to fine-tune the look of your charts at a very granular level not available in the standard Chart Expert. Although a detailed examination of these charting options is outside the scope of this text, you are encouraged to explore the variety of chart customizations and formatting options exposed through this functionality if the standard chart creation process does not meet your exact requirements.

You will find separate and advanced charting help instructions for these granular options available through the help button present on all the dialog boxes accessed from the Chart Options menu. This advanced help is provided by 3D Graphics—the third party responsible for the charting in Crystal Reports.

Size and Position

This option enables you to identify very specific x and y coordinates in addition to height and width measurements for the involved chart. Charts can also be dynamically resized and repositioned by grabbing any of the sizing handles that appear on the frame of the chart after it is selected.

Modifying Map Properties

After a map has been created and placed on your report, you can perform numerous post-creation edits by right-clicking on the map object while in the Preview mode. From the Map menu that appears when you have right-clicked, you have both the ability to either re-visit the Map Expert or use a number of more finely tuned post-creation editing tools such as Zooming, Layer Control, Map Navigation, and Data Mismatch Resolution.

Layer Control

By clicking on the Layers menu option, you are able to specify the different layers that will display on your map. Examples of this include World Capital Cities and the Mapping Grid. Crystal Reports version 9 is distributed with a number of built-in layers that are accessed through this Layer Control dialog box. These layers can be added and removed from Crystal Reports using this dialog box and more detail oriented layers. Additional maps can be purchased separately from MapInfo (3rd party company) and integrated into Crystal Reports.

Resolve Mismatch

The Resolve Mismatch dialog provides two very useful functions for maps. First, the Resolve Mismatch dialog allows you to select a specific map to use for your report. Several maps are provided out of the box with Crystal Reports and others can be purchased separately. Additionally, you can match the field names stored in the Geographic field you are basing the map onto the names that the involved map is expecting. This powerful feature enables you to take raw, untransformed data and dynamically match it to a geographical map value that the mapping engine can understand. For example, on a map of Canada, you might have multiple inconsistent data entries in your database for the province of Ontario (for example, ON, Ont, Ontario, and so on). Using this dialog box, you can match each of these to the expected value of Ontario, and the mapping engine will successfully interpret all of them.

Size and Position

This option enables you to specify very specific x and y coordinates in addition to height and width measurements for the involved map. Maps can also be dynamically resized and repositioned by grabbing any of the sizing handles that appear on the frame of the map after it is selected.

Zooming and Panning

The Zoom In and Zoom Out options enable you to focus on a particularly relevant part of the involved map. The Panning option enables you to horizontally pan the view of the map to what is most interesting to you and your business users. When any of these options have been selected from the Map Menu, you then are placed in to an interactive mode with the map and your mouse/touchpad. Clicking will zoom you in and out and double-clicking and dragging will facilitate panning.

> When selecting from the Map menu, the Map Navigator provides a thumbnail of the entire map you are currently working with. As you saw earlier, Figure 11.12 highlights this Map Navigator in your report sample. The Map Navigator also provides a dotted outline of the area that is currently selected for display. You can fine-tune the area that will be displayed by grabbing this dotted line, double-clicking on any of its corners, and subsequently dragging or expanding them out or collapsing them in while holding down your second click.

Summary

In this hour, you explored two effective visualization techniques for presenting your data. Charts and maps in Crystal Reports provide an effective way to communicate a great deal of relevant summarized information to your end users. Crystal Reports provides extensive charting and mapping capabilities through the integration of third-party tools from MapInfo and 3D Graphics.

Both the Chart Expert and the Map Expert provide rapid and easy access to the flexibility of the visualization features of Crystal Reports. Additional chart control is available through the Chart Options menu enabling granular level control of the chart visuals you can provide. Additional maps, map layers, and map types are available for purchase from MapInfo and can be seamlessly integrated in to your Crystal Reports.

The next few hours begin to introduce you to some of the increasingly advanced features of Crystal Reports so that you can create increasingly enhanced and powerful reports for business users.

Q&A

Q Where can I learn about Cross-Tab and OLAP Charts and Maps?

A Cross-Tab and OLAP Charts and Maps are covered in hours specifically dedicated to Cross-Tabs and OLAP—Hours 14 and 20.

11

Q What happened to the separate Chart Analyzer tab of Crystal Reports version 8.5 and earlier?

A The functionality previously accessed through the Chart Analyzer tab of Crystal Reports earlier than version 9 is now entirely accessible online and through the five different Chart Option menu sub-options (Template, General, Titles, Grid, and Selected Item).

Workshop

The quiz questions and activities are provided for your further understanding of the current hour's topics.

Quiz

1. When creating Charts with the Chart Expert, which layout option must be used if you want to base the chart on a summary not already created in the report?

2. If you want to perform granular level formatting on an existing chart, what Charting menu selection should you use?

3. If there are inconsistencies in the data you need to use to base a geographic map on, which Mapping Menu option could you use to rectify that situation?

Quiz Answers

1. The advanced layout option enables you to create charts based on summaries dynamically created within the Chart Expert.

2. The Chart Option menu option (accessed by right-clicking on an existing chart) enables you to perform granular level formatting and advanced customizations on your report charts.

3. The Resolve Mismatch menu option (accessed by right-clicking on an existing map) enables you to match non-standard geographic database fields to those expected by the geographic mapping engine.

Activity

Now that you have been introduced to the mapping and charting functionality of the Crystal Reports Designer, try taking the existing sample reports from any of the book's hourly activities and adding a chart or map in both the Report Header and Group Header.

Hour **12**

Implementing Parameters for Dynamic Reporting

A common goal of report design is to provide a single report that can service very specific reporting requirements, yet also accommodate a large audience of business users. Parameter fields allow you to satisfy this requirement and provide three primary benefits:

- Additional level of interactivity for business users when viewing reports—a sales report can prompt the business user for her specific district or territory.

- Ability to segment reports in many different ways to reduce the number of reports necessary to service the demands of the business users—a sales report can be segmented by district to service the needs all district-level business users with one report.

- Greater control over the report query for administrators by filtering the report results to include only the selected parameter value(s)—a sales report can be filtered to include only data for the appropriate district. This also includes the ability to constraint the report query to avoid including excess or sensitive data.

In this hour, we will take a closer look at the value of using parameters in your reports, as well as how parameter fields can be created and implemented. Like many of the Crystal Reports application features, working with report parameters is very logical but requires some working knowledge of the mechanics necessary to apply these items to create effective reports.

In this hour, we will cover the following topics:

- Understanding the value of parameters
- Creating and implementing parameter fields
- Using parameters with Record Selections

Understanding the Value of Parameters

By using parameter fields that allow business users to select from a list of one or more parameter field values (such as district, country, or account type), you can make reports more valuable for the business users while limiting the volume of data that the report retrieves. For example, a sales report is likely to be more valuable for the sales professionals if it allows them to select their specific territory or district, while the report runs more efficiently because it retrieves only the desired data and not an unnecessarily large data set. Parameter fields can prompt users for a variety of information to be used in a number of ways within reports, such as controlling the sort order, grouping order, record selection (filter), report title and descriptions, and other object values.

Parameter fields prompt the business user of a report to enter information—presenting a question that the user must answer before the report is executed. The information that a business user enters then determines what appears in the resulting report.

Parameter fields offer distinct advantages in allowing business users of the reports to select (or enter) values that, in turn, populate report objects. These values can be used to define the report sort order or to update some type of textual content within the report, such as the report title, description, author name, or otherwise. In this way, the parameter value is having only cosmetic implications on the appearance of the report and not directly impacting the actual data set within the report.

Perhaps the greatest benefit of parameter fields for report designers is the opportunity to have one single report service a very large audience, while empowering the business users of reports to personalize information they are requesting within the report. In this way, parameter fields can be used in coordination with record selections so that a single report can be segmented many different ways. Parameter values that business users enter can be used within record selection formulas to determine what data is retrieved from the database.

For example, consider a Worldwide Sales Report for a large organization. This report could potentially include a tremendous amount of data. Not only is the report itself large, but also many of the business users are not concerned with the entire worldwide scope of the sales data. Rather than allow each salesperson to generate the report to include worldwide data, a parameter dialog can be used to ask the salesperson to select from a list of available countries—as shown in Figure 12.1. The report would then return the results for only these specific countries. Thus, by using a parameter field to allow the salespeople to select from a list of countries, the report becomes more valuable for the business users while also limiting the scope of the query—by using the selected parameter value(s) to filter the report and reduce the volume of data retrieved.

FIGURE **12.1**

Prompts allow business users to select values to populate the parameter field.

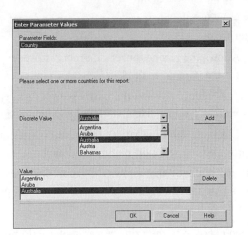

Creating and Implementing Parameters Fields

The process of using parameter fields in reports includes two distinct steps:

1. Creation of the parameter field
2. Implementation of the parameter field into the report

We will use the example mentioned earlier, the World Sales Report, throughout the remainder of this hour to create and implement parameter fields into a report. The World Sales Report is one of the many sample reports that are provided by the Crystal Reports 9 installation.

12

Reviewing Parameter Field Properties

Before we discuss how to create and implement parameter fields, it is useful to understand a few common properties associated with creating parameter fields. Each of the following properties is presented within the CreateParameter Field dialog, as shown in Figure 12.2:

- Name—A logical name for the parameter field.

- Prompting Text—A statement or question that will be presented to the business user within the report prompt dialog for the parameter field.

- Value Type—A list of available field types that correspond to how you want to use the parameter field within the report, including String (the default option), Boolean, Currency, Date, Date Time, Number, and Time.

- Allow Multiple Values—Allows the business user of a report to enter more than a single value for the parameter field.

- Discrete Values—Allows the business user of a report to enter only a single value for the parameter field.

- Range Values—Allows the business user of a report to specify a range, using start and end values, for the parameter field.

- Discrete and Range Values—Allows the business user of a report to enter specific single values as well as a range, using start and end values, for the parameter field.

- Allow Editing of Default Values—Allows the business user of a report to edit any default values provided in the report parameter dialog.

- Set Default Values—A dialog that allows the report designer to specify default parameters values based on either a database field, external pick list, or manual entries.

Now that you have been exposed to the primary parameter field properties, we will use these items while creating parameters for a World Sales Report, as referenced earlier in the hour.

Creating Parameter Fields

The first step in using parameters within a report is to create the actual parameter field and define the primary properties associated with it. In the following exercise, we will use the Field Explorer dialog to create two new parameter fields for the World Sales Report:

- A manual text entry field to use as the report's title

- A database field that prompts the business user to select one or more countries and use this selection to filter the data returned for the report

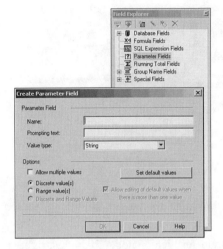

FIGURE 12.2

The primary parameter field properties are presented within the Create Parameter Field dialog.

To begin our exercise, open the World Sales Report within the Crystal Reports designer. This sample report should be installed in the following directory, unless you have chosen an alternative location for the sample reports during the Crystal Reports 9 installation process:

```
C:\Program Files\Crystal Decisions\Crystal Reports
9\Samples\En\Reports\General Business
```

After you have opened this sample report, we can begin the steps necessary to create the parameter field objects:

1. Remove the existing report title text object. After you have opened the World Sales Report, navigate to the Design tab view, highlight and delete the text object currently used as the report's title that reads, World Sales Report, located in the Report Header A section. We will be using our parameter field to populate the report title.

2. Remove the current Top N sort order because it is not needed for our exercises. From the Report menu, select Group Sort Expert, and within the presented dialog modify the For This Group Sort: drop-down setting to display All as shown in Figure 12.3. Click OK to continue.

12

FIGURE **12.3**

Use the Group Sort Expert dialog to remove the Top N sort order from the report.

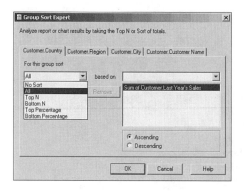

3. Open the Field Explorer dialog via either the appropriate toolbar button or using the View menu.

4. Open the Create Parameter Field dialog. To do this, right-click on Parameter Fields within the Field Explorer and select New from the pop-up menu.

In addition to using the right-click menu to create a new parameter field, you can also use the Field Explorer's toolbar commands to create, edit, rename, and delete parameter fields. The operations available on this toolbar depend on what you have selected in the Field Explorer dialog.

We will first create a manual text-entry parameter field to allow the business user to define a title to display on the report.

5. Define the key properties for the parameter object. Within the Create Parameter Field, enter `Title` in the Name property and provide a meaningful prompting text so that the business user will understand how the entered value will be used, such as, `Enter a title to be used for this report`.

6. Select Discrete Values under the Options area and click OK to return to the Field Explorer.

7. You should now see the `Title` parameter field listed under Parameter Fields in the Field Explorer, as shown in Figure 12.4.

We will now create a second parameter field to use later in the hour when discussing how to user parameter fields in coordination with record selections. In this way, you can filter the report data according to the selected parameter values.

8. Open the Create Parameter Field dialog. To do this, highlight the Parameter Fields item and click the New toolbar button inside the Field Explorer dialog.

Figure 12.4

The Field Explorer is used to access, edit, and create parameter fields.

9. Define the key properties for the parameter object. Within the Create Parameter Field dialog, enter **Country** in the Name property and provide a meaningful prompting text so that the business user will understand how the entered value will be used, such as, **Please select one or more countries for this report**.

10. Select both the Allow Multiple Values and Discrete Value(s) items under the Options area, as shown in Figure 12.5.

Figure 12.5

The Create Parameter Field dialog is used to create and edit parameter fields.

Setting Default Values for Parameter Fields

We now want to define the Country parameter field to include all database values within the Country field of the Customer table. We will map the parameter field to this database field and quickly import these values, allowing the business user of the report to select one or more country values from the available list.

When setting default parameter values, a list of default values can be read from the database or entered manually to provide the business user with a list of available values to choose from. The Crystal Reports application allows you to define the default values list only when you are designing reports, and no direct database connection exists to populate the prompting parameter field list when the business users run the report. The following is an overview of various options available within the Set Default Values dialog to make data entry easier for the business users:

- Browse Table—The database table that contains the default values for the parameter field.

- Browse Field—The database field that contains the default values for the parameter field.

- Select or Enter Value to Add—Used to enter values in the Default Values list. You can type new values in the entry box and then press the Add button (>), or select a value from the list and then press the Add button (>).

- Add, Add All—Used to move one (>) or all (>>) values from the Select or Enter Value to Add list (on the left) to the Default Values list (on the right).

- Delete, Delete All—Used to move one (<) or all (<<) values from the Default Values list (on the right) back to the Select or Enter Value to Add list (on the left).

- Import/Export Pick List—Used to import and/or export a text file containing a pick list of parameter values to be used as the default values. (Note: These two buttons are not available when creating or editing parameters in the OLAP Report Creation Wizard.)

- Default Values and Description—The list of values displayed when business users are prompted to populate the parameter field, and a description for each value (optional). The optional description for each default value is set by using the Define Description button, and corresponding dialog, located just below the Default Values list. The value is used in the DB and what is sent back to it. The description can be used to create a more user-friendly label for the business users. For example, the country field can be stored as a number in the database, but it is more intuitive for the user to select it by name.

- Display—Controls whether the prompt to business user displays either the Value and Description, or just the Description for each default value. In either case, only the Value will be used within any database interaction, such as with record selection definitions.

- Order—The order that the default values are displayed in the prompt to the business users of the report.

- Order Based On—The order of the default values can be based on either the Value or Description property of these values.

- Length Limit—The minimum and maximum length limits for the parameter field.

- Edit Mask—Used to enter an Edit Mask for string data types rather than specifying a range of values. The Edit Mask can be any of a set of *masking characters* used to restrict the values you can enter as parameter values. (The edit mask also limits the values you can enter as default prompting values.) Refer to the Crystal Reports

Help files for a complete list of masking characters and detailed instructions on how to use them.

We will now define the default values for our parameter fields (if necessary, refer to the list of options within the Set Default Values dialog while completing these steps):

1. Open the Set Default Values dialog by clicking on the Set Default Values button, as shown in Figure 12.6.

2. Choose the database table and field from which to set the defaults. Under the Select from Database area of the Set Default Values dialog, select Customer from the Browse Table list, and then select Country from the Browse Field list.

3. Add the actual database values to the default value list. With all the country values listed under the Select or Enter Value to Add area on the left, use the Add All (>>) button to move all these values to the Default Values list on the right, as shown in Figure 12.6.

FIGURE 12.6

The Set Default Values dialog allows you to define the default values for parameter fields.

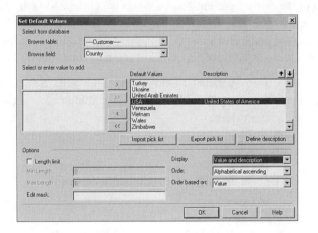

We will now add descriptions to the default values that we have added to the parameter field:

4. Locate and highlight the USA value in the Default Values list. Click on the Define Description button located just below the Default Values list to present the Define Description dialog.

5. Add **United States of America** as the description for USA, as shown in Figure 12.7, and click OK to close the Define Description dialog. If desired, repeat this step for any additional default values.

FIGURE 12.7

The Define Description dialog.

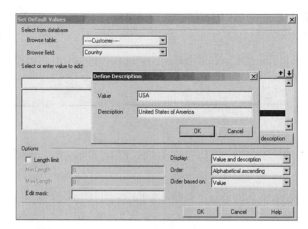

To make the default values friendlier to the business users of the report, you can sort the contents of the display prompt lists based on the Order and Order Based On option settings. Seven distinct options are available to sort the parameter field values that are reflective of the parameter value type, including both ascending and descending for the three data types—alphanumeric, numeric, and date/time—as well as No Sort.

6. Sort the Country parameter field in alphabetic order. Select Alphabetical Ascending from the Order drop-down list, and choose Value from the Order Based On list, as shown in Figure 12.6.

If you select a sort type from the Order list that does not match the parameter field value type, no sorting will be applied.

7. For our purposes here, you can leave the remaining options within the Set Default Values dialog to their default state and click OK to return to the Create Parameter Field dialog. If desired, peruse the overview of default setting options and use these to modify the desired options for your parameter field.

8. Click OK to return to the Field Explorer.

9. You should now see the Country parameter field listed under Parameter Fields in the Field Explorer.

There are a few considerations to keep in mind when working with parameter fields, such as

- Any parameter field prompting text more than one line in length will automatically word wrap.
- You can create a pick list for the business user to choose the parameter field value rather than having them enter it manually.
- A parameter field does not have to be placed in a report in order to be used in a record or group selection formula. You can create the parameter field and then enter it in your formula as you would any other field.

Implementing Parameter Fields

You have now completed the first task necessary to use parameter fields within a report—creating the actual parameter field objects. This section, and the exercises included here, will discuss how to apply these parameter fields and make use of them to provide the business user of the report with more dynamic and interactive reporting experience.

First, we will implement the parameter field created earlier, called Title, to serve as the title to the report. This example demonstrates how a manual text entry field can be used to add useful commentary or descriptive information to a report. We will continue working with the same report, the World Sales Report.

1. Position the Title parameter object onto the report. Open the Field Explorer dialog and expand the Parameter Fields list. Click on the Title parameter field, drag it onto the report, and drop it into the upper-left corner of the Report Header A section, shown in Figure 12.8 in a size 20 Arial font.

2. Preview the report. To view how this parameter is now used within the generation of the report, run the report by clicking on the Refresh toolbar button (represented by the lightening bolt icon). As shown in Figure 12.9, the report will now prompt the business user to enter a value that will be used as the report's title.

If you have already run the report at least once and then select to refresh the report, you will also see the Refresh Report Data dialog that asks you to select from the following two options:

- Use current parameter values
- Prompt for new parameter values

To enter or select new values for any existing parameter fields, you will need to select the second option—Prompt for New Parameter Values.

12

FIGURE 12.8

*Drag and drop the
Title parameter field
into the upper-left cor-
ner of the Report
Header A section.*

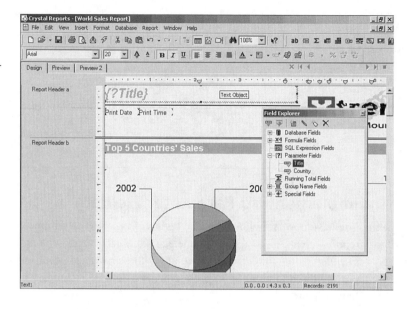

FIGURE 12.9

*Parameter fields offer
a means to add addi-
tional interactivity for
the business users
within the report.*

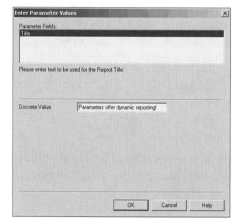

Using Parameters with Record Selections

Now that you have completed the task of implementing a parameter field within a report, such as the report title, we will discuss how a parameter field can also be used to filter the data retrieved by a report. Parameter values that business users enter can be used within record selection formulas to determine what data is retrieved from the database.

In the following exercises, we will use the World Sales Report to implement the Country parameter field (created earlier in the hour) to filter the report results by including the parameter field within a record selection definition (using the Select Expert dialog). In this case, we will allow the business user of the report to select one or more country values to be included in the record selection, thus filtering the report results to include only the desired data. This example demonstrates how a single report can be segmented many different ways:

1. Verify that the Country parameter field is listed below the Parameter Fields group within the Field Explorer.

2. Open the Select Expert dialog. The Select Expert dialog can be accessed from the Report menu by selecting the Select Expert command.

3. Create a new record selection definition. Within the Select Expert dialog, click on the <New> tab to create a new record selection definition. This should present the Choose Field dialog. Choose Customer.Country from the Report Fields list and then click OK to return to the Select Expert dialog.

4. Define the selection formula. Select Is Equal To from the drop-down list on the left, and then choose the {?Country} option from the drop-down list on the right, as shown in Figure 12.10.

Parameter Field objects are denoted with the question mark, ?, and enclosed in brackets, {}. This convention is used within various application dialogs, including the formula workshop and record selections, to signify that these objects are parameter fields.

12

FIGURE 12.10

Parameter fields can quickly be added to record selection formulas via the Select Expert dialog.

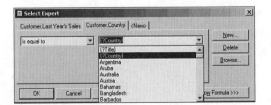

5. Preview the report. To view how this parameter is now used within the generation of the report, run the report by clicking on the Refresh toolbar button (represented by the lightening bolt icon). As shown in Figures 12.11 and 12.12, the report will now prompt the business user to select from a list of country values that will be used to filter the data retrieved by the report and present only the requested values in the report.

FIGURE 12.11

Business users can now select one or more countries to be included in the report results.

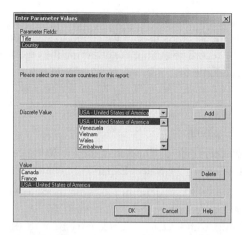

FIGURE 12.12

Based on the selected parameter field values, the report results will display only the desired data.

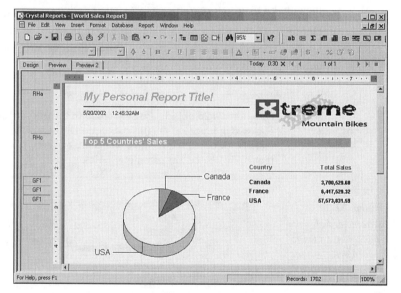

After the parameters have been created and implemented into a report, no extra effort is required for parameters to also work within the Crystal Enterprise solution. See Hour 23, Distributing Crystal Reports for more details on Crystal Enterprise.

Summary

This hour has guided you through creating and implementing parameter fields to construct a dynamic and highly functional report, which is capable of segmenting the worldwide sales data into country specific queries based on the sub-set of information sought by the business user. Using parameter fields can dramatically decrease the number of reports necessary to support the overall business user community. At the same time, parameter field prompts provide the business users with additional interactivity that allows them to selectively execute the report to include only the desired data. Parameter fields can prompt users for a variety of information that can be used in a number of ways within reports—we have introduced you to the more common uses of such parameter fields.

Workshop

The quiz questions and an activity are provided for your further understanding of the current hour's topics.

Quiz

1. What are the two distinct steps necessary to apply parameter fields to a report?

2. What are three different ways to populate the default values for a parameter field?

3. Assuming that a parameter field has already been created, what dialog is used to add that parameter field to the report's record selection?

Quiz Answers

1. The two steps are (1) Create the parameter field via the Field Explorer dialog, and (2) Implement the parameter field by placing the object within the report, such as a particular section, within another object or a selection formula.

2. By adding database field values, manually entering values, and importing a pick list of values.

3. The Select Expert dialog, located under the Report menu list.

Activities

To better understand how parameter fields can add value to reporting requirements, try to identify which reports of your own can benefit from them. A couple of things to look for when deciding which reports might be good candidates for parameters are

- Multiple versions of a particular report that you maintain just to service different business users

- Reports that return large data sets
- Reports that include a natural hierarchy of data, such as geographical locations, product categories, or corporate departments
- Reports that display data between specific time frames, such as a begin date and end date
- Any report that business users can more easily navigate by identifying a more precise data set for their query

PART IV

Enhancing Crystal Reports

Hour

Hour 13

Custom Formatting Techniques

This hour focuses on more complex formatting to make reports look like high-quality information portals rather than simply paper reports:

- Making Presentation-Quality Reports
- Common Formatting Features
- Conditional Formatting—Using Data to Drive the Look of a Report

Making Presentation-Quality Reports

Up to this point in the book, the focus of the hours has been on making sure that the retrieved and presented data is manipulated and appears as required. That is the most important step for report development. However, the next step, formatting, will keep the users coming back to the reports time and time again.

By making reports that are friendly to the business users and easy to read, users will have a good experience with the reports and will come back often for updates and to share the reports with others.

Presentation quality reporting is accomplished using formatting in Crystal Reports. Formatting can take many different forms, from basic font coloring to hyperlinks to conditional formatting (based on the data coming back from the database). This hour examines a cross-section of all these types of formatting to give the report developer a good basis for report formatting.

Because formatting is a visual element of the report, this hour will be a series of tutorials to allow you to actually add formatting to a report started in an earlier hour. Lets assume that the Xtreme Mountain Bike Company would like the report that was started in Hour 5, "Fundamentals of Report Creation and Design," to be improved upon by adding some formatting.

Common Formatting Features

The most common formatting feature is to simply change font color or font face. This can be done by choosing the features directly on the Formatting toolbar, as seen in Figure 13.1.

FIGURE 13.1

Formatting toolbar for all your standard formatting needs.

In Hour 5, the Highlighting Expert was introduced. Because it is an expert and quite self-explanatory, we will assume that you have already learned the fundamentals of the highlighting expert. For more information, refer back to Hour 5.

Because this lesson is considered a more advanced topic, it will focus on the more advanced formatting features. For more information on standard formatting functionality, see Hour 8, Fundamentals of Report Formatting.

ToolTips

All report objects can have rollover text or ToolTips available when the report is viewed. For example, if the report developer would like to use descriptive text to explain why a certain formula was created, this could be done with a ToolTip.

In this example, Xtreme Mountain Bike's first requirement is to let the business user know more about the formula that was created to show the number of days late for each order. Xtreme's management has asked for the following text to appear whenever a user mouses over the Days Until Shipped fields on the report: "Since our corporate standard for quality shipping is same-day service, anything not shipped on the day it was ordered is considered late—in red."

1. Open Chap5.RPT, or the report created earlier in Hour 5. Select File, Open and browse to find Chap5.rpt and open it.

2. Format the field. Right-click on the Days Until Shipped Field in the Details Section of the report and choose Format Field.

3. Add the ToolTip text. In the Format Editor dialog, select the Common tab. In the ToolTip Text box, enter the following text: **Since our corporate standard for quality shipping is same-day service, anything not shipped on the day it was ordered is considered late – in red.** (see Figure 13.2).

FIGURE 13.2
Format Editor, Common tab with ToolTip text added.

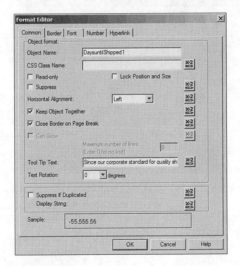

4. Test the ToolTip text. Press OK to finish the formatting. In Preview, scroll the mouse over the same field and see that the rollover text now appears as Xtreme's management requested. Before proceeding, save the report as **Chap13_1.rpt** by choosing File, Save As.

Lines and Boxes

Adding lines and boxes to a report makes it easier to read as well as visually shows grouping for business users of reports.

Xtreme's management would like to expand formatting on Chap13_1.rpt. They would like lines under each Detail section as well as a box around each group to show more

13

actively where the groups begin and end (and to indicate that the subtotals belong to the records above the subtotal instead of below).

1. Use Chap13_1.rpt in Design mode. If the report is not already open, open it using Ctrl+O. Make sure that the report is in Design Mode by choosing Ctrl+D.

2. Insert the line by Choosing Insert, Line. The mouse will change to a pencil. Move the mouse to the left-bottom of the fields in the Details Section. Hold down the left mouse button to begin drawing the line. Scroll the mouse to the right until the end of the Details Section. Once reached, release the mouse button.

3. View the result in Preview mode. Select F5 to refresh the report to see the line with the data as shown in Figure 13.3.

FIGURE **13.3**

Preview of report to show a line under each detail record.

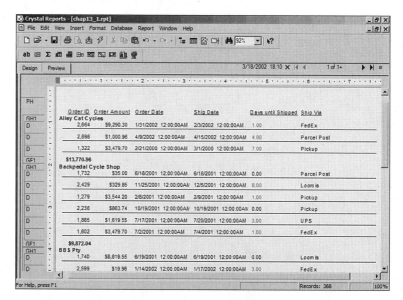

4. Add the box by choosing Insert, Box. The mouse will change to a pencil. Move the mouse to the top-left of the Alley Cats data in the Group Header. Hold down the left mouse button to begin drawing the box. Scroll the mouse down to the bottom left of the Summary amount in the Group Footer and then scroll to the right until the end of the Group Footer section. Once reached, release the mouse button. The resulting box should appear similar to Figure 13.4.

FIGURE **13.4**

Preview of report to show lines and boxes.

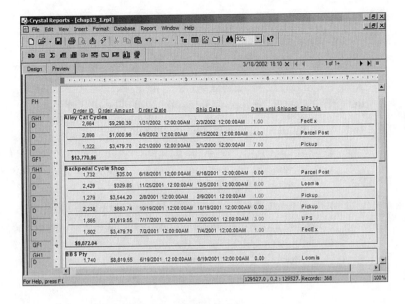

5. Save the report as **Chap13_2.rpt** using File, Save As.

A feature of boxes is that they can be rounded. By right-clicking on a box, choosing Format Box, and selecting the Rounding option, the rounding factor can be changed by the slide or the percentage buttons. Figure 13.5 shows how Xtreme's report would look with rounded boxes.

FIGURE **13.5**

Preview of report showing rounded boxes.

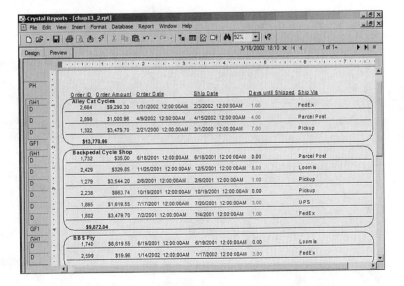

13

Vertical Text

Another visually pleasing feature is the ability to rotate text. This can be very effective when used in conjunction with the Underlay Section property for sections.

Xtreme's management would like the Group Header (Customer Name) to appear down the left side of all the records (rotated by 90 degrees).

1. Start by using Chap13_2.rpt in Design Mode.

2. Format the Group Name Field. In the Group Header section, right-click on the Group Name Field and choose Format Field. Select the Common Tab. Change the Text rotation to 90 degrees and click OK.

3. Resize the field. Because the field needs to go down the page, it needs to be resized to be narrow and long. Select the field and choose the right-most square on the field. By holding down the left-mouse button, resize the object to about 1/4". Now choose the bottom square on the field and stretch the height to 1". Figure 13.6 shows how it should look.

FIGURE 13.6

Design tab with text rotation applied to group name field.

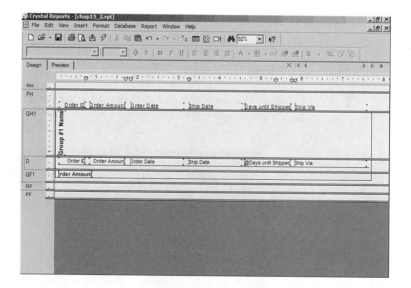

4. Refresh the report to see your progress by pressing F5. It will show the text rotated, although it is not running down beside the records as seen in Figure 13.7

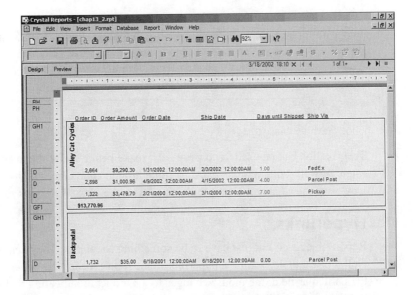

FIGURE 13.7

Preview of report with text rotation.

5. Set the Group Header to Underlay. Because the text does not yet flow to the record level, it must be underlayed. This is a section property. Right-click in the Group Header #1 section located on the left side of the report design area, choose Section Expert, select Underlay Following Sections, and click OK. The desired results should appear similar to Figure 13.8.

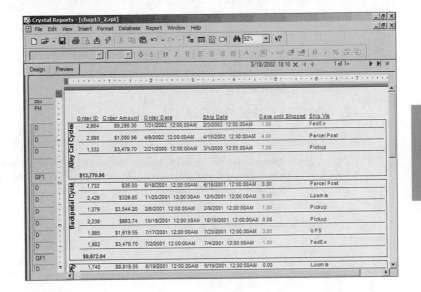

FIGURE 13.8

Preview of report with rotated text flowing beside detail records.

13

Realize that when rotating text, the justification rules might be opposite of what would normally be expected. In the case of 90 degrees, the text must be right-justified in order to have the company name appear to be top-justified as shown in Figure 13.8.

6. Save as `Chap13_3.rpt`.

Text rotation can be used to conserve and make better use of the available report real estate as well. For example, extra wording around charts and graphs could be used in this way—see the Chart.rpt example included with the Crystal Reports sample reports.

Hyperlinks

Report objects do not just have to be something to look at. They can be actionable as well. For example, adding a hyperlink to the report means that when the user scrolls over the particular field, the mouse changes to a hand icon, indicating that if the user selects the field the hyperlink will be executed.

Xtreme's management wants the group name field to link to the Crystal Decisions Web site.

1. Start by using Chap13_3.rpt in Preview mode.

2. Right-click on the rotated text group name field and select Format Field. In the Hyperlink tab, select Website on the Internet and type the following into the edit box. `http://www.crystaldecisions.com`. Click OK.

3. Refresh the data by pressing F5. Scroll the mouse over the group name field. Notice that the mouse changes to a hyperlink hand. If selected, it will take the user to Crystal Decisions' Web site.

4. Save the report as `chap13_4.rpt`.

Remember that ToolTips can be created to change the text that appears when the mouse rolls over an object. A ToolTip with the same text as the hyperlink could be used so that the user can see where the link will take him.

Conditional Formatting—Using Data to Drive the Look of a Report

Up to now, the focus has been on static, non-changing formatting. The next step in making reports as presentable as possible is to apply formatting based on the data that is being returned from a field or even applying formatting on one field based on the value of another.

Conditional formatting relies on the formula language to be used. This is advantageous because the formula language is very extensive. Very complex statements can be made within the formula language to make very complex formatting formulas for use in reports. For this hour, the tutorials will stick with relatively simple examples. For more tips and tricks on using the formula language, see Hour 17, "Using Formulas and Custom Functions to Implement Complex Business Logic."

The simplest way to do this is to use the Highlighting Expert. This feature allows you to quickly and easily apply font face and font color changes to database fields based on their values. For more information on this feature, see Hour 5.

> Almost every formatting option is conditional. To determine which ones are conditional look for the x+2 button next to the option in the Formatting Editor dialogs.
>
> If a formatting option has already been set to a conditional format, the button will appear with red text. Otherwise, it will appear as blue text.

Apply Formatting from Another Field

One of the simplest examples of using one field to format another is to apply an email or hyperlink to a non-Internet field. In the Xtreme example, management would like to replace the Crystal Decisions hyperlink with the customer's email contact field.

1. Use Chap 13_4.rpt as a starting point. Right-click on the Group Name field and choose Format Field. Select the Hyperlink tab. Change the hyperlink type to Email Address.

2. Create the Conditional Formatting Formula. Click the x+2 button to bring up the Format Formula Editor dialog. Because this is an email address, the `Mailto:` Internet keyword will need to be added to the email address. Input the following into the Editor dialog `'mailto:' + {Customer.E-mail}`. Then choose the Save and Close button. Notice that the button on the Hyperlinks tab has changed to red. Click OK.

13

3. Test the email link. Select the field again and notice that the email dialog appears instead of the Web browser and that the email address is different for each company.

4. Save the report as `chap13_5.rpt`.

> The Formula Workshop can be used with Formatting Formulas as well. In fact, it can do something quite amazing. Dragging and dropping formatting formulas from one object to another in the workshop group tree automatically applies the dragged formulas to the new report object. This should increase the productivity of formatting as well.

Summary

This was a very brief taste of what can be done with some advanced formatting features in Crystal Reports. Throughout the rest of the hours, formatting will often come up, whereas the most common features have now been covered. There are so many combinations and uses for formatting that giving just a brief tutorial should spark many ideas on how formatting could be used in existing reports and in reports to come.

This is one section of Crystal Reports that has received much attention in terms of documentation over the years. For more ideas on formatting, see the sample reports that ship with Crystal Reports, the online Crystal Reports Help files, and the Crystal Care Web site for more ideas on making presentation-quality reports through formatting.

Workshop

Now it's time to set your new skills to the test.

Quiz

1. Can bubble text be shown over fields in Crystal Reports?
2. Can text be rotated to 45 degrees?
3. Can formatting be applied based on a value being returned from somewhere else?

Quiz Answers

1. Yes—Using ToolTip text.
2. No—Only 90 and 180.
3. Yes—This is called conditional formatting.

Activities

Apply as much formatting as needed to existing reports. Don't forget that formatting can be conditional as well as static. (Maybe even try using Custom Functions—see Hour 17 for more details.)

13

HOUR 14

Using Cross-Tabs for Summarized Reporting

Cross-tabs are highly formatted and densely populated reports that look a lot like a spreadsheet. This hour will give you an understanding of how and when to use cross-tabs for your reporting needs.

- Fundamentals in Cross-Tab Reports
- Using the Cross-Tab Wizard
- Using Top N with Cross-Tab Reports
- New Features in Crystal Reports version 9

What Is a Cross-Tab?

Before getting into how to use cross-tabs in Crystal Reports, it would be beneficial to know what they actually are and when they are useful in reporting.

A *cross-tab* is a fully summarized set of cells in a grid format. It summarizes values both across as well as down. It is a compact representation of information that is grouped on two different *axes*. There can be more than one level of grouping on either axis (row or column).

A *row* goes across the page, whereas a *column* runs down the page. The intersections between the rows and columns are called *cells*. Cells are places where a value to be summarized will be seen. Totals in the cells are summarized for each row and column as well as the break points for the different levels of groupings.

Benefits of Using Cross-Tabs

Cross-tabs are actually one of the most common types of reports created with Crystal Reports. There are a number of reasons why cross-tab reports are created, but most often it's because they deliver data in a format we are all familiar with: a spreadsheet. They also summarize both vertically and horizontally, have a grid format, and can change size depending on the data.

Several of the most compelling reasons for using cross-tabs will be the focus for this hour:

- Making better use of space
- Leveraging experience with the spreadsheet format
- Horizontal expansion
- Custom formatting

Making Better Use of Space

Because cross-tabs are grouped and summarized both vertically **and** horizontally, they are incredibly efficient on saving space as compared to a typical grouping report. They are very good at showing key information if the information required has at least two levels of grouping.

Let's look at an example: a report that most of us can relate to in some way—school grades for the end of the year. These need to be grouped by course, student, and term. If the report were shown in a standard grouping layout like we've been working with previously, it could be several pages long. Figure 14.1 shows a typical Crystal Reports in which three pages display one course with only 10 students in one class—hardly the most efficient use of the world's number one reporting tool!

FIGURE **14.1**

Standard grouping style used on a typical school grades report.

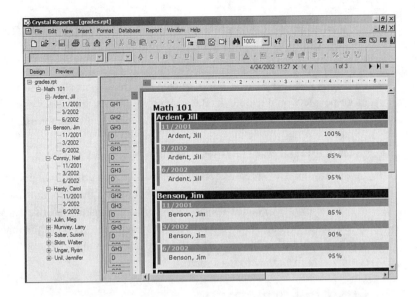

But what if there were a way to replicate the information contained in a teacher's grade book? This commonly looks a lot like a spreadsheet. Also, teachers get a one-stop glance at all the students and all their grades. Figure 14.2 shows how the information is more efficiently presented when a cross-tab is used to display the same information. Now the teacher can view all the student grades information at a glance.

FIGURE **14.2**

Student grades shown in a cross-tab.

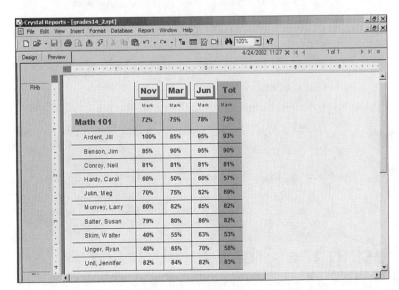

14

Leveraging Experience with the Spreadsheet Format

Another benefit of the cross-tab format is its familiarity to many users of spreadsheet applications. Many people use spreadsheets in their daily routines and are accustom to their look and feel. If we could replicate this in a report style or format, chances are, more people would use them. Because cross-tabs do appear very much like spreadsheets, Crystal Reports offers a familiar format and reporting style for many users.

Horizontal Expansion

Cross-tabs, as with spreadsheets, can expand both vertically and horizontally. In Crystal Reports, cross-tabs are one of only two object types that account for expansion across horizontal pages. Crystal Reports handles this expansion automatically, so the designer of the report doesn't have to worry about this feature. This means that if there is more data to display than the original size of the cross tab allows for, it doesn't cut off any critical data from the cross-tab area.

Custom Formatting

As with other objects in Crystal Reports, cross-tab objects are also highly customizable in terms of formatting. Everyone has different needs from their data, so Crystal Reports allows for a great deal of changes to the formatting of these objects. Some of the most highly useful formatting features that are used in cross-tabs are

- Customizable Styles (colors, grid lines, and so on)
- Vertical and horizontal placement of summaries
- Formatted grid lines
- Toggle for summary totals (rows/columns)
- Cell margins
- Indented row labels
- Location of totals (beginning or end for both rows/columns)
- Repeatable row labels

The preceding list is just a glimpse at how powerful the customization of cross-tabs can be. Chances are, some ideas of how your reports could benefit from cross-tabs have already come to mind, so let's get started with learning how to create them.

Using the Cross-Tab Wizard

Let's work through an example for the Xtreme Mountain Bike Company—the fictitious company that corresponds to the sample database provided with Crystal Reports.

Xtreme management needs a summary report to provide a quick glance of its shipped orders. They want to know how much has been spent by country for every six month period, but they only want to see the top 10 countries.

1. Create a new report by choosing File, New and when the Report Gallery appears, choose As a Blank Report and then click OK.

2. The Database Expert appears. In the Available Data Sources list, expand the following nodes: Repository, Crystal Repository, Commands, CustomerOrdersShipped, CustomerOrdersShipped. After the last object (CustomerOrdersShipped) is chosen, click the arrow (>) button.

> We are not focusing on learning the specifics of the repository or commands at this point. If you want more information on these, see Hour 18, "Working with the Report Component Repository."

3. The Enter Parameters dialog now appears. The prompt asks whether you want shipped orders or not. Because the requirements for this report is for shipped orders, choose True from the Discrete Values list box and then click OK.

4. The Database Expert dialog appears again. The command will now be added to the Selected Tables list box. Click Ok.

5. Insert a Cross-Tab by choosing Cross-Tab from the Insert menu, or click the Insert Cross-Tab button on the Insert toolbar (the fourth item from the left). This should present the Cross-Tab Expert dialog.

6. Set up the initial cross-tab. In the Cross-Tab tab of the Cross-Tab Expert, we need to enter the grouping and summarizing fields for the Xtreme report. The rows of the report will be the countries, so select Country from the Available Fields and then click the arrow (>) button under Rows. The column grouping is going to be by order data, so choose Order Date from Available Fields and then click the arrow (>) button under Columns. Because the OrderDate is supposed to be by quarter, click on the Group Options button under Columns and change the third list box from Each Day to For Half Year and then press OK to close the Group Options dialog. Finally, choose Order Amount from Available Fields and click the arrow (>) button under Summarized Fields so that the cell's summary is also selected. See Figure 14.3 for an example of the Cross-Tab Expert.

14

FIGURE 14.3

Cross-Tab Expert—
Cross-Tab tab.

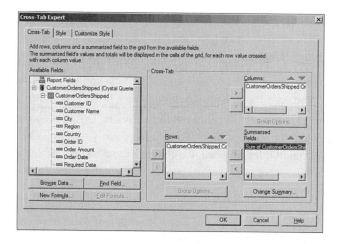

7. Data input is practically done. Now that we've specified the necessary items to get the needed data, click the OK button to close the Cross-Tab Expert. Then place the object connected to your mouse in the top left corner of the Report Header section. Press F5 to refresh the report and see the result in the report Preview as shown in Figure 14.4.

FIGURE 14.4

Cross-tab in Preview.

	1/2000	7/2000	1/2001	7/2001	1/2002	Total
Argentina	$0.00	$0.00	$1,664.70	$0.00	$0.00	$1,664.70
Aruba	$0.00	$0.00	$5,879.70	$0.00	$0.00	$5,879.70
Australia	$0.00	$0.00	$9,899.99	$0.00	$0.00	$9,899.99
Austria	$5,895.20	$10,285.08	$6,223.17	$4,081.46	$2,232.50	$28,717.41
Bahamas	$0.00	$0.00	$659.70	$0.00	$0.00	$659.70
Bangladesh	$0.00	$0.00	$65.70	$0.00	$0.00	$65.70
Barbados	$0.00	$0.00	$329.85	$0.00	$0.00	$329.85
Belgium	$789.51	$2,792.86	$8,514.10	$33,223.52	$2,960.10	$48,280.09
Bermuda	$0.00	$0.00	$5,879.70	$0.00	$0.00	$5,879.70
Bolivia	$0.00	$0.00	$97.02	$0.00	$0.00	$97.02
Brazil	$0.00	$0.00	$1,885.10	$0.00	$0.00	$1,885.10
British Virgin	$0.00	$0.00	$33.90	$0.00	$0.00	$33.90
Canada	$2,920.78	$9,144.31	$95,750.88	$93,232.99	$58,223.80	$259,272.76

8. Before we continue, let's save our work. Choose File, Save As. Let's call this **cross-tab1.rpt** and then click OK.

Using Top N with Cross-Tabs Reports

Group sorts can be done on a report level so that the records are sorted and removed as necessary. However, there are times when the records will be needed in the overall report but not in a cross-tab. Why not just do a group sort or Top N on the cross-tab? Remember that Xtreme only wants to see its top 10 countries in this report, so let's complete this last step.

1. The only missing piece, in terms of the data requirements, is that Xtreme management only wants to know its top 10 countries. Right-click in the top-left corner of the cross-tab where there is no data or words and choose Group Sort Expert. Choose Top N for the primary list box and change 5 to 10 in the Where N Is field. In this example, let's assume that the management at Xtreme does not want the remaining countries on the report, so make sure that the Others option is not selected.

2. Click OK in the Group Sort Expert to view the final result, as shown in Figure 14.5.

FIGURE 14.5

Cross-tab with a Group Sort applied.

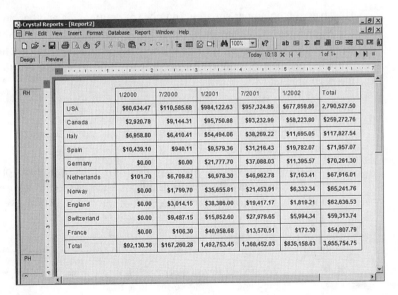

3. Save your work by choosing File, Save As. Let's call this **cross-tab2.rpt** and then click OK.

Xtreme Mountain Bikes now has a report that answers the original request—a summary report to provide a quick glance of its shipped orders.

14

Using Advanced Cross-Tab Features

Crystal Reports version 9 includes significant cross-tab improvements in that they are even more customizable and easy to work with. The advanced features give cross-tabs improved flexibility and functionality to satisfy even more reporting requirements.

We'll continue to improve the Xtreme Mountain Bikes report (crosstab2.rpt) that we've already started to further demonstrate these new features.

Relative Position

When it comes to planning the width or length of cross-tabs, they can be thought of as an accordion. With the addition of new information or data, the number of rows or columns can grow or shrink. This makes putting objects at the end of a cross-tab very difficult because it's unclear when the object will be overwritten (if new data comes along).

The bottom of a cross-tab has an easy solution. Just put the new object in the next report section—even if it means adding a new section. By default, objects in Crystal Reports will not overwrite a section, so the solution is a simple one.

However, the columnar situation (number of columns) is another problem altogether. In the Xtreme report, management wants the Xtreme logo to be displayed to the right of the cross-tab. But, in Design, the size of the cross-tab doesn't match what we see in Preview. We will need to use a section format property called Relative Position to get the image in the desired place.

Let's work through an example to see the result:

1. Open crosstab2.rpt. Let's start with our last saved document by choosing it from the File list at File, Open.

2. Insert the logo image from the Repository. In Design mode, open the Repository by choosing View, Repository Explorer. Navigate to the Images folder and select the Xtreme Logo. Drag it to the right of the cross-tab and drop it there, as shown in Figure 14.6.

 We are not focusing on the Repository in this hour. For more information on the Repository, please see Hour 18.

3. Preview the report. Click F5 to see the result. It's not exactly as we intended.

4. Set the Relative Position property. Right-click on the Report Header label (on the left where it says Report Header, or RH, in the gray area). Choose Section Expert. Toggle the Relative Positions check box and click OK. To see the resulting report is what Xtreme management wanted, as shown in Figure 14.7.

FIGURE 14.6

Design with Cross-tab and image side by side.

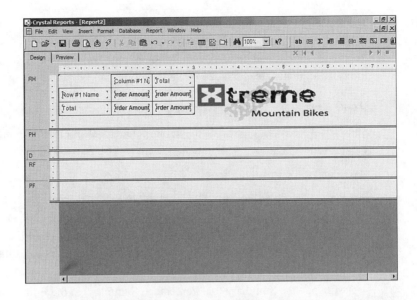

FIGURE 14.7

Preview of the cross-tab and image as requested.

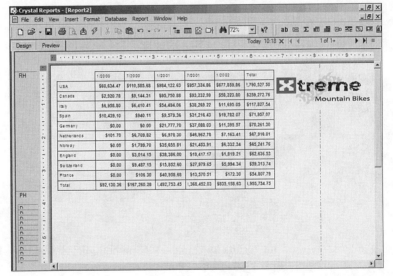

Notice that Crystal Reports creates a second horizontal page to handle the need in this report. If a cross-tab needs a second page, it's created automatically.

14

The Relative Position property works on the left, top, and right borders of the cross-tab. Remember that the bottom border of the cross-tab is handled by the end of a section. Relative Positions can be used in many situations. For example, showing a chart on the information in the cross-tab can be very useful.

Percentage of Summary

Summary values can also be displayed as percentages of either the total rows or total columns. Let's assume that the management at Xtreme needs this in their report as well.

Let's continue on with our report:

1. Add another summary. Right-click in the top left of the cross-tab where no data appears and choose Cross-Tab Expert. In the Cross-Tab step, choose to add the CustomerOrdersShipped.Order Amount to the Summarized Fields list box by clicking the arrow (>) button. Notice that it looks like it duplicates the summary above it, so choose the Change Summary button.

2. Change the Summary to a Percentage Summary. In the Edit Summary dialog, select Show As Percentage Summary. Notice that it has an option for Row or Column. In Xtreme's case, management wants to know by country (row) where the percentage split is, so keep Row selected as shown in Figure 14.8.

FIGURE 14.8

The Edit Summary dialog.

3. Preview the results by clicking OK on both dialog windows. It should look like Figure 14.9.

Notice that the USA is consistently the largest percentage of Xtreme's orders. It's very easy to see this when percentages are added to the cross-tab.

Of course, the look of the cross-tab is not yet ideal. More advanced formatting will help in this matter.

FIGURE **14.9**

Percentages by country.

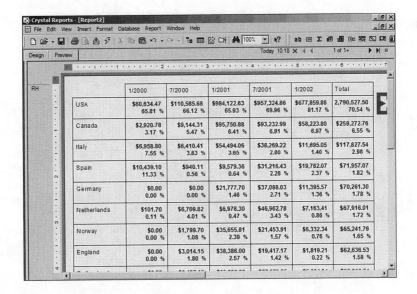

Horizontal and Vertical Placement

Because the percentages add up to 100% down the page, it would be easier to understand if the summaries could be displayed side by side instead of one on top of the other. That way, the numbers down the page could be added up easily.

Crystal Reports allows the toggle between horizontal and vertical placement of summaries, so let's make this update to the Xtreme report.

1. Launch the Cross-Tab Expert. Right-click in the top-left of the cross-tab again and choose Cross-Tab Expert. Select the Customize Style tab. Under Summarized Fields, choose Horizontal as well as selecting the Show Labels option.

2. View the report. Click the OK button and see the changes made to the cross-tab. Figure 14.10 shows an example.

It's been a while since a Save has been done. Save reports often or use the Autosave option, located from the File menu at Options, Reporting. To be on the safe side, save at the end of each set of steps.

14

FIGURE 14.10

Horizontal placement of summaries.

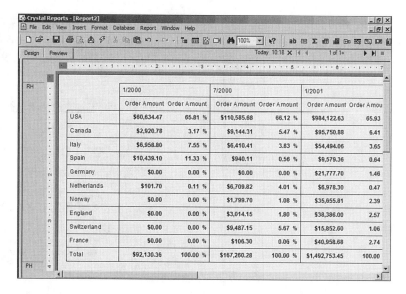

Summary Labels

Notice that on the report in Figure 14.10, both titles for the percentage and the summary are exactly the same (Order Amount). This is because Crystal Reports is showing the field that a summary is acting on. In this case, where the field is being acted on twice, it's not a good choice.

Crystal Reports allows you to edit these labels right on the cross-tab in both Design and Preview modes.

1. Edit the Summary's Title. Right-click on the first Order Amount field in the cross-tab and choose Edit Text. Delete the Order Amount Text and add Sum instead. Click off the object and see the result.

2. Edit the Percentage Title. Repeat the previous step for the second Order Amount field, but instead of changing the text to sum, change it to %, as shown in Figure 14.11.

The formatting of this cross-tab is coming along, and Xtreme is very happy with its progress. There is one more requirement before the report can be submitted as complete.

Adding a Display String

Cross-tabs are based on the need for numbers or currency to be summarized, but there are times when the numbers don't need to be seen to get the point across. Instead of seeing the numbers, why not show something more *inventive*?

FIGURE 14.11

Cross-tab with both labels changed.

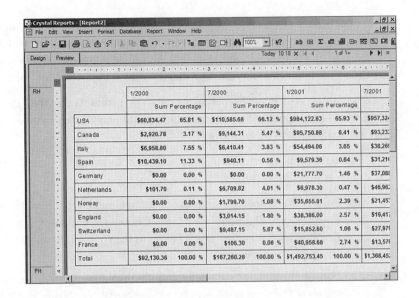

Crystal Reports has a feature for all fields called Display String. This formatting feature allows a different representation for a field than its underlying value. For example, what if a teacher wanted to see a grade letter beside a percentage mark, as shown in Figure 14.12?

FIGURE 14.12

Math 101 marks with letter grades as display strings.

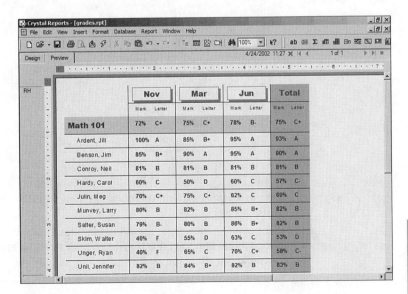

14

As previously mentioned, cross-tab cells are always an intersection of rows and columns with a summary because the strings are the visual representation of the underlying summary being computed in the cross-tab. We can affect this string using the advanced Cross-Tab features of Crystal Reports.

Crystal Reports can now separate the data value from its display. This is a powerful feature and is *not* limited to cross-tabs; although it plays a major role in cross-tabs because of the requirement of summaries.

To complete this report, Xtreme's management team requires that all $0.00 amounts be shown as NONE on the report.

1. Format the Order Amount Summary. Right-click on one of the $0.00 amounts on the report and choose Format Field. Choose the Common Tab and then choose the Conditional Formatting (x+2) button to the right of Display String. The Formula Workshop will appear.

2. Format Formula for strings. Use an If-Then-Else formula structure to accomplish the task. The final result will be If CurrentFieldValue = 0 Then "NONE" Else ToText(CurrentFieldvalue) (see Figure 14.13).

FIGURE **14.13**
Display String for-
matting formula.

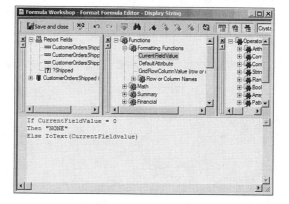

Try to avoid using explicit field names in these formulas so that they can be reused in other places.

Also, remember that these are string formulas. That's why the ToText is needed around the CurrentFieldValue. Both Then and Else clauses must contain similar data type results.

3. Close the dialog windows. Choose the Save and Close button on the Formula Workshop and then the OK button on the Formatting dialog. See the result as shown in Figure 14.14.

FIGURE 14.14

$0 changed to NONE by using the Display String feature.

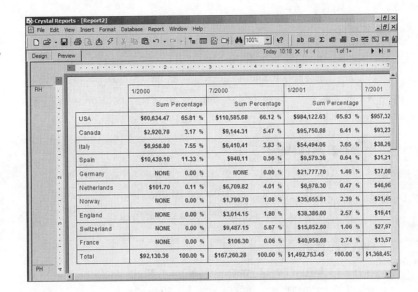

4. Save the report as **Crosstab3.rpt** by choosing File, Save As.

Summary

This hour has guided you through creating a cross-tab report and implementing various report design features necessary to construct it. This hour has provided you with an understanding of how and when to use cross-tabs for your reporting needs. Cross-tabs can provide a concise representation of your data, and many users related them to spreadsheets because they are most often highly formatted and densely populated reports.

You've learned how to reduce reports effectively by providing a concise cross-tab to show the most important data in a quick view. Also, you've learned how to format these cross-tabs to be even more user-friendly.

Take this knowledge and apply it to your existing cross-tabs.

14

Workshop

The quiz questions and an activity are provided for your further understanding of the current hour's topics.

Quiz

1. Can cross-tabs contain more than one summary?
2. Can labels for summaries be changed? If so, how?
3. Does the Relative Position section format feature work for the bottom of a cross-tab?

Quiz Answers

1. Yes. And they don't even need to be on the same field.
2. Yes. By right-clicking on the label and choosing Edit Text.
3. No. Use a new section for that requirement.

Activity

Create a cross-tab on your own data and apply the tasks you've learned in this hour to improve the look and feel of your report.

Hour **15**

Using Record Selections and Alerts for Interactive Reporting

One of the things you've probably learned so far is that it's quite easy to create a report with a whole bunch of data. The challenge in creating an effective report is to highlight the subset of report data that is important. Think of a report as just a smaller haystack. You still have to look for the needle, but helping the reader find the needle is the real art. Key information is often *outliers*: data that falls above or below the average or a specified threshold. This usually indicates either a good or bad trend. Bad trends need attention so that they can be corrected, and good trends need attention so that they can be repeated.

This hour focuses on drawing attention to key data by building up your proficiency on record selections and introducing SQL Expressions, as well as an introduction to adding alerting to your reports.

Creating Advanced Record Selection Formulas

Although many filters are simple enough to be defined using the Select Expert, most real-world reports require editing the record selection formula itself. Being able to create advanced record selection formulas is one of the key skills you'll need to acquire to create effective reports. Before diving into the best practices for creating these formulas, let's do a quick review of what you've learned so far about record selections.

Record Selection Review

Record selections, or filters, are defined by a record selection formula built using the Crystal syntax of the Crystal Reports formula language. You can build a record selection formula using the Formula Editor by selecting the Report menu, Selection Formulas, Record. Another more simpler way to build record selections is to use the Select Expert accessed via the Experts toolbar. The Select Expert builds a record selection formula behind the scenes for you.

A record selection formula is a formula that returns a Boolean value indicating whether a given record should be included in the report. It is evaluated for each record in the database. Any time a database field is used in the formula, it is replaced by the actual field value.

Now that you've been reminded about what you've learned thus far about record selection formulas, let's build up your knowledge by arming you with some of the best weapons for conquering tough record selections.

Dealing with Dates

One of the most common record selection formulas is `{field}` = `value`, where `{field}` is a database field and `value` is a corresponding value of the same data type. An example of this would be

```
{Customer.Country} = "Canada"
```

This kind of formula is very easy to create, but it gets a bit more complicated when the data types of the values to be compared are not the same. This tends to manifest itself with new report developers who first attempt to filter data based on dates. A common attempt would be to use a formula like this:

```
{Orders.Order Date} > "2/25/2000"
```

When clicking the Check button to check the formula's syntax, Crystal Reports pops up a message saying A date-time is required here and when closing the message box, "1/29/1998" is highlighted. The problem here is that because the Order Date field has a data type of date-time, the formula is attempting to compare a date-time to a string, which is not implicitly allowed. Comparisons must always be performed on objects of the same data type. To rectify this, instead of using a string literal to describe a date, the formula could use the DateTime function to return a date-time value. Here is an example of the corrected formula:

```
{Orders.Order Date} > DateTime(2000, 2, 25, 0, 0, 0)
```

You'll notice that when the DateTime function is used, it takes arguments for not only year, month, and day, but also for hour, minute, and second. This is because in order to compare this value to the Order Date field, it needed to be a date-time value. In this case, you might not care about the time part of the date-time value. The best way to solve this would be to first convert the Order Date field into a date from a date-time, and then use the Date function instead of DateTime. The improved formula follows:

```
Date({Orders.Order Date}) > Date(2000, 2, 25)
```

To make this even simpler, the Crystal Reports formula language also supports dates specified in the following format:

```
#YYYY/MM/DD HH:MM AM/PM#
```

Using this syntax, the following formula is also valid:

```
{Orders.Order Date} > #2000/2/25 12:00 AM#
```

Another nice feature of this syntax is the ability to omit the time portion. When this done, a default of 12:00 AM is used.

Various functions are available for converting between strings, dates, and date-times. These can be found in the Function Tree window of the Formula Editor, under the Date and Time folder.

Another issue that comes up often is filtering on a field in the database that contains dates but is defined as a string field. The following fictitious formula, although it will not return any errors when checking the syntax, does not do what you might expect:

```
{Shipments.Ship Date} > "1/1/2001"
```

This will not perform a date comparison because both fields are of type string. To correct this formula, you could use one of the functions provided by the DTS (date time string) user function library called DTSToDate.

A user function library is a library of functions that can be used from the Crystal Reports formula language. Crystal Decisions provides several of these with the product, and others are available from third-party vendors. If you are proficient with Visual Basic or C++, you could even create a user function library yourself. The user function library can be found under the Additional Functions folder in the Function Tree of the Formula Editor.

The DTSToDate function takes a string that is in the proper date format and converts it to a date value. The correct formula is shown here:

```
DTSToDate({Shipments.Ship Date}) > Date(2001, 1, 1)
```

Where the Ship Date field contains a date in *DD/MM/YYYY* format.

Working with Strings

As with dates, simple string comparisons are easy to achieve using the record selection formula. Slightly more complex comparisons can easily become tedious unless you are armed with knowledge for effectively dealing with strings. A simple example is a listing of customer data for a set of countries. Creating a record selection formula like the following can become quite tedious:

```
{Customer.Country} = "England" or
{Customer.Country} = "France" or
{Customer.Country} = "Germany" or
{Customer.Country} = "Denmark"
```

Rather than using multiple comparisons, this can be accomplished with a single comparison using a string array.

An array in the context of the Crystal Reports formula language is a set of values that can be referenced as a single object.

The previous record selection formula can be rewritten to look like this:

```
{Customer.Country} in ["England", "France", "Germany", "Denmark"]
```

Notice that there are several differences. First, instead of using multiple comparisons, only a single comparison is used. This is both simpler to read and easier to maintain. The four country values are combined into a string array. Arrays are indicated by square brackets with values separated by commas. Finally, instead of an = operator, the in operator is used. This operator, as its name implies, is used to determine if the value on its left is present inside the array on its right.

> Although string arrays are being described here, arrays can be made holding other data types, such as integers and currency values.

In this example, the countries are hard-coded into the selection formula. Although this makes it easy to read, the report would need to be modified if the country list were to ever change. A better way to handle this would be to create a multiple value parameter and use it in place of the country list. If you did that, the formula would look like this:

```
{Customer.Country} in {?CountriesParam}
```

During the parameter prompting, the user will be allowed to enter multiple values, and you can even provide a list of default values to choose from.

Pushing Record Selections to the Database

When dealing with large sets of records, performance will become important. The record selection you use can make a huge difference in the performance of a report. Crystal Reports does have the capability to perform database-like operations on the data such as grouping, filtering, summarizing, and sorting. However, in general, asking the database to perform those kind of operations will result in a faster overall transaction. Because of this principal, Crystal Reports will attempt to ask the database to perform these operations if possible.

In the context of record selections, this means that when Crystal Reports queries the database, it will attempt to incorporate as much of the logic of the record selection formula as possible into the query. Ideally, all the logic can be incorporated into the query, which means that the database will perform all the filtering and only return the records that met the criteria. However, because the SQL language doesn't support all of what the Crystal Reports formula language does, there could be certain situations in which some or all the logic of the record selection formula cannot be converted to SQL. In this case, Crystal Reports needs to pull some or all the records from the database and perform filtering itself.

When working with a desktop database like Access or FoxPro, the performance difference between the database engine or the Crystal Reports engine doing the filtering would be minimal because it really comes down to which filtering algorithm is faster. Because databases are made for just this purpose and are customized for their own data structures, they will generally perform this kind of operation faster. However, when dealing with client/server databases in which the database resides on a backend server and Crystal Reports resides in your desktop machine, the difference becomes much more apparent. This is mostly because of network traffic. There's a big difference between sending 50 records back over the network than there is in sending 100,000. This performance hit gets even worse when using a slow connection such as a dial-up modem.

To determine whether the logic you've used in the record selection formula or select expert is being incorporated into the query sent to the database, it's helpful to have a basic understanding of the SQL language. You need not be an expert at SQL, but being able to recognize if the query is performing a filter on a certain field makes record selection formula tuning much more effective. For more information on SQL, see Hour 22, "Optimizing SQL Queries in Crystal Reports."

Although there are some guidelines for creating record selection formulas that will be fully passed down to the server, often the best approach is to simply check the SQL statement manually and determine if the record selection logic is present. To view the SQL statement that Crystal Reports has generated, select Show SQL Query from the Database menu. The resulting dialog is shown in Figure 15.1.

FIGURE 15.1

The Show SQL Query dialog.

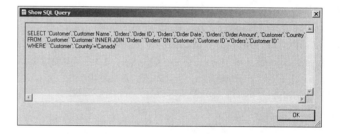

You can infer from the preceding SQL query that this report is based on the Customer table, is using the Customer Name, Web Site, and Last Year's Sales fields, and has a record selection of

```
{Customer.Last Year's Sales} > $20000
```

All the logic of the record selection formula has now been passed down to the database in the SQL query. However, let's say that this report had a formula field that calculated the tax. That formula might consist of the following:

```
{Customer.Last Year's Sales} * 1.07
```

This formula field might be placed on the report to indicate the tax for each customer. The problem occurs when this formula is used in the record selection formula. Although the following formula seems logical, it is inefficient:

```
{@Tax} > $10000
```

If you were to look at the SQL query being generated for this report, you would see that there is no WHERE clause present. In other words, the report is asking the database for all the records and doing the filtering locally, which, depending on the size of the database, could result in poor performance. A better record selection to use—which would produce the same results, but perform the filter on the database server—would be

```
{Customer.Last Year's Sales} > $142857
```

This works out because at a tax rate of 7%, $142,857 is the minimum a customer would need to sell in order to have tax of more than $10,000. Using the previous record selection would result in a SQL query with the following WHERE clause:

```
WHERE `Customer`.`Last Year's Sales` > 142857
```

Although this approach returns the correct data, a slightly less cryptic approach would be to use a SQL Expression.

An Introduction to SQL Expressions

Crystal Reports formulas are useful because they allow you to use the full Crystal Reports formula language as well as a suite of built-in functions. However, as you've learned in this hour, they can be a factor in report processing performance. SQL Expressions are often the answer to this.

A SQL Expression, as the name implies, is an expression written in the SQL language. Instead of consisting of a whole formula, a SQL Expression consists of an expression that defines a single field just like a formula field does. The difference between a formula field and a SQL Expression is based on where it is evaluated. Formula fields are evaluated locally by Crystal Reports, whereas SQL Expressions are evaluated by the database server and thus produce better performance when used in a record selection formula.

To better understand this, let's look at the example discussed in the previous section. The example had a report with a Crystal Reports formula that calculated tax based on the Last Year's Sales field. Although there certainly are situations in which formula fields need to be used, this is not one of them because the logic being used in the formula is simple enough that the database server is able to perform it. Instead of creating a formula field, a SQL Expression could have been created. SQL Expressions are created via the Field Explorer, which was introduced in Hour 4. Right-clicking on the SQL Expressions item and selecting New will begin the process of creating a SQL Expression. When choosing to create a new SQL Expression, the SQL Expression Editor is launched (see Figure 15.2).

FIGURE 15.2

The SQL Expression Editor.

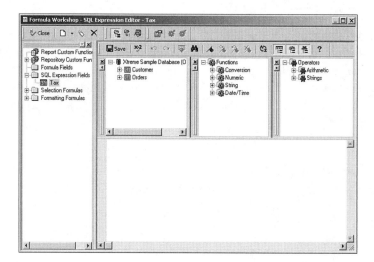

This editor is, in fact, the same editor used to create Crystal Reports formulas, but with a few small changes. First you'll notice that in the field tree, only database fields are present to be used in the expression. Because SQL Expressions are evaluated on the database servers, Crystal Reports constructs, such as parameter fields and formula fields, do not exist and thus cannot be used in the expression.

To create a SQL Expression that calculates the tax, the following expression can be used:

```
`Customer`.`Last Year's Sales` * 0.07
```

Notice that instead of using the {Table.Field} syntax for fields, the `Table`.`Field` syntax is used. This is because the quoted syntax is how you define fields in the SQL language.

When dropping this SQL Expression on the report and checking the SQL Query, you will find Crystal Reports has generated SQL similar to this:

```
SELECT `Customer`.`Customer Name`, (`Customer`.`Last Year's Sales` * 0.07)
FROM `Customer` `Customer`
```

Basically, the SQL Expression that was defined into the report is plugged into the main SQL statement that Crystal Reports generates. This means that you can use any database specific syntax or function inside a SQL Expression.

Getting back to the topic of performance, you'll remember that using the tax calculation formula field in the record selection formula resulted in all the records being returned and Crystal Reports having to locally perform the filtering. Fortunately, any SQL Expressions used in the record selection are always passed down to the database server. Therefore, a better record selection for filtering out customers who pay less than $10,000 in tax would be the following:

```
{%Tax} > 10000
```

In this record selection formula, {%Tax} is the SQL Expression discussed previously. This record selection formula would result in Crystal Reports generating the following SQL query:

```
SELECT `Customer`.`Customer Name`, (`Customer`.`Last Year's Sales` * 0.07)
FROM `Customer` `Customer`
WHERE (`Customer`.`Last Year's Sales` * 0.07)>10000
```

Adding Alerting to Your Reports

Now that you've learned how to effectively filter the data in your report to show relevant information and ensure peak report performance, let's move on to how to clearly identify the key pieces of information in your report to your end user. Although this can be accomplished by using conditional formatting, there is an alerting feature inside Crystal Reports that allows for more interactive identification of the key data.

A report *alert* is a custom notification created within Crystal Reports that is triggered when a predetermined condition is met. An alert is comprised of three integral parts:

- An alert name
- An alert trigger (condition or threshold)
- An alert message

Alerts serve the dual functions of bringing end-user attention to a certain condition being met and focusing end-user attention on specifically relevant data in a report—thereby increasing user efficiency. Some examples of reports in which alerts could provide a benefit are outlined in Table 15.1.

TABLE 15.1   Reports with Potentially Useful Alerts

Report	Alert	Alert Trigger and Result
Product Sales Report	Product Profitability Warning	Trigger: Specific product profitability below 10%
		Result: A listing of the least successfully selling products
Customer Churn Report	Regional Customer Churn Warnings	Trigger: Specific regions where Customer Churn Rate is higher than 3% in a quarter
		Result: A listing of regions to increase competitive analysis or to review regional management practice
Income Statement	Company Divisions with net losses	Trigger: Company division with net income < 0
		Result: A listing of divisions where deeper business analysis is required

Report alerts are triggered when the report is processed and the associated condition has been met. Once this condition is true, the alert message will be displayed. Figure 15.3 displays a triggered alert from within the Crystal Reports Designer.

FIGURE 15.3

A report alert being triggered.

Creating, Editing, and Using Alerts

To create or edit alerts in Crystal Reports, select the Report, Alerts, Create or Modify Alerts menu items. This dialog (shown in Figure 15.4) allows you create a new alert, edit existing alerts, and remove existing alerts.

FIGURE 15.4

The Create Alerts dialog.

After you have clicked the New Alerts button, the Create Alert dialog pictured in Figure 15.5 is displayed.

FIGURE 15.5

Creating a new alert.

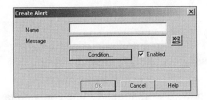

Use the following steps to create the alert:

1. Give the alert a name. This name should be meaningful and will be displayed to the user when the alert is triggered.

2. Specify a condition for which to trigger the alert. An example of this would be: {Customer.Last Year's Sales} < $10000. The condition is simply a formula using either Crystal or Basic syntax that evaluates to a true or false result. True means the alert should be triggered; false means that it should not. (Note: You can use other formulas and parameters inside this condition.) Using a parameter to determine the threshold on your alert is useful because the report could then be viewed by different audiences with different thresholds, and they could still see the alert triggered for their respective numbers.

3. Give a alert a message to display when the alert has been triggered. This can be a hard-coded string, or can be a formula such as

```
"Sales are over $" + ToText({Customer.Last Year's Sales})
```

To see your alert in action, refresh the report with data that meets your alert condition, and triggered alerts will be displayed.

Finally, not only are you notified that the alerts have been triggered, you can click the View Records button on the Report Alerts pop-up dialog to filter the report to show only those records that triggered the alert. This is a good way to draw attention to the key outliers in the data.

Using Alerts in Crystal Enterprise

The Report Alerts dialog displayed in Figure 15.3 is only available from within the Crystal Reports Designer. If you are delivering your reports via another mechanism such as the Web, alerts are handled differently. To have your end users take advantage of Crystal Reports alerting, you will need to either use Crystal Enterprise for report distribution or exploit the built-in alert functions (`IsAlertEnabled()`, `IsAlertTriggered()`, and `AlertMessage()`) within formulas you create in your report. For more information on Crystal Enterprise, see Hour 23.

Summary

In this hour, you have increased your skills in creating reports that identify key pieces of data by both filtering out unwanted data and drawing attention to outlier data using alerts. You have also learned how to work around some common tasks in record selection formulas, as well as have been provided with an understanding and tips to tweak your selection formula for maximum performance.

Workshop

The quiz questions and activities are provided for your further understanding of the current hour's topics.

Quiz

1. What's wrong with the following record selection formula, and how would you fix it?

   `{Orders.Order Date} > "2/25/2000"`

2. What is the purpose of a SQL Expression?

3. How are triggered alerts displayed to the user?

Quiz Answers

1. This record selection formula is comparing a date to a string literal. The string on the right would need to be converted to a date-time value before making this comparison. One of the possible solutions is

   ```
   {Orders.Order Data} > #2/25/2000#
   ```

2. The purpose of a SQL Expression is to create a formula that is processed on the database server to either use a database-specific function, or to ensure maximum performance when using that formula in the record selection formula.

3. When an alert is triggered, it is displayed to the user in the form of a pop-up dialog, as shown in Figure 15.3.

Activities

To ensure that you are comfortable with the topics discussed in this hour, try to perform the following tasks:

- Create a report on the Orders table with a parameter that allows the user to select which date he wants to see orders for. Perform the appropriate filtering in the record selection formula.

- Create a report on the Employee table that uses a SQL Expression to calculate the employee's age based on the Birth Date field.

- Create a report on the Orders table with an alert for any order of more than five thousand dollars.

HOUR 16

Using Subreports

The first 15 hours of this book introduced you to the design of individual reports using single aggregated datasets. Crystal Reports provides further flexibility and reporting capabilities through the use of additional reports embedded directly within an original main report. These embedded reports, referred to as Subreports, provide enhanced value that extends your reporting solutions to an expanded domain that we will explore in this hour.

In this hour, the following topics are covered:

- A description of Subreports
- The usefulness and value of Subreports
- Linked versus Unlinked Subreports
- In-Place versus On-Demand Subreports
- Passing data between the main report and Subreports

Understanding Subreports

The next two sections will provide you with

- an introduction to Subreports
- an idea of when you might use them
- a lesson on how to use Subreports

Crystal Reports provides the ability to embed multiple Crystal Reports within a single existing main report to facilitate increased flexibility in reporting solutions. These Subreports can be thought of as reports within reports, and can contain their own data sources, formatting, and record selections. The embedded Subreports can be existing Crystal Reports or can be dynamically created at report design time using the insert Subreport functionality. When presenting a report that contains one or more Subreports to business users, the Subreports can be displayed either in-place, providing a seamless integration, or on-demand, minimizing the amount of required up-front report processing.

Common Subreport Usage

A few particular reporting problems are difficult to solve without the use of Subreports. Some of the most common problems and a specific example of each are listed in Table 16.1.

TABLE 16.1 Common Reporting Problems Solved by Subreports

Generic Reporting Problem	Specific Example
1. The presentation of data from two (or more) completely unrelated data sources on a single report.	On a Manufacturing Plant Efficiency report sourced from your internal SAP system, you want to display industry average information sourced from a completely different and unrelated industry or trade database.
2. A report that needs to combine data from different tables with only derived (and not direct) database field links.	On a Customer Profile report, you want to combine Order Information from your ERP (for example, SAP, Baan, Peoplesoft) system with call-center information from your call-center application (for example, Peregrine) and your CRM system (for example, Siebel), but the employee ID field is stored slightly different in each system. The Subreports enable the linking of the different employee IDs by allowing linking on formulas or derived fields.

Generic Reporting Problem	Specific Example
3. The presentation of the same data in two (or more) different ways in a single report.	On a Sales Summary Report, senior management wants to present a high-level summary of sales by region but also wants to present a separate and personalized summary of sales by product for each salesperson who will be viewing the report.
4. The inclusion of a summary field in the report that is unrelated to the established grouping in the main report.	On an employee HR report, HR managers want to see employee salary information grouped by Business Unit, Division, and Department. Additionally, they want to view a count of the different departments that this employee worked for in the previous year. The main report groups employees by department (and by division and business unit), whereas the Subreport groups departments by employee to determine a department count.
5. The inclusion of a reusable component (example: standard reporting header or footer) in numerous reports across an organization that can be dynamically updated for all reports in a single location.	A firm wants to deploy all reports in its organization with a standard header including standard logos and titles. In addition to using the new Report Templates and Repository, Subreports can be used within all the reports as a header and provide a single location for updating the header across all the reports.

Data presented in Subreports is often related to the data presented in the associated main report, but it does not have to be. Subreport data can be a twist on the main report's information or sourced from a completely different database.

Using Subreports

Adding a Subreport to your main report is as easy as adding any other Crystal Reports object. After selecting the Subreport option from the Insert Menu, you will be presented with the Insert Subreport dialog, that is presented in Figure 16.1.

FIGURE 16.1

Insert Subreport dialog.

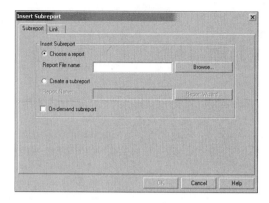

To explore one of the number of challenges solved by using Subreports, let's solve the hypothetical reporting problem faced by the Chief Operating Officer (COO) of Maple Leaf Bikes Corporation. This COO wants a single report that highlights the company's top-selling products in one bar chart and additionally highlights the company's top selling sales reps in a corresponding pie chart. The two charts are sourced from the same sales information but have no direct relation or links to each other. To resolve this request, complete the following:

1. Create a New Report and point this report at the Xtreme Sample Database.

2. Select the Orders, Order Detail, and Product Tables and then select the Product Name and Order Amount Fields to Display on the report.

3. Group the report by Product Name and Add a Summary to the report that sums Order Amount for each Product Name group. Also limit the report to display only the top five groups based on the Summarized Field. (Reminder: You can use the Group Sort Expert under the Report menu option to accomplish this last task and remember to explicitly not include an "Others" group by selecting that check box.)

4. Add a bar chart in the Page Header to represent the top five selling products, and you should have a report similar to that depicted in Figure 16.2.

5. Make room for the COO's requested second visual by resizing the bar chart to only take up half of the page header's width.

6. Select the Insert Subreport option by either accessing that option from the Insert menu or clicking on the Insert Subreport icon. The Insert Subreport dialog in Figure 16.1 will appear.

7. Select the Create a Subreport option by clicking on the associated radio button.

8. Enter a Name similar to Top Sales Reps and click on the Report Wizard button.

9. As you step through the familiar Report Wizard to create this Subreport, select the Xtreme Sample Database and the Employee and Orders tables. From the list of available tables, select the First Name and Order Amount.

FIGURE **16.2**

Preliminary Sample Report to Solve COO problem.

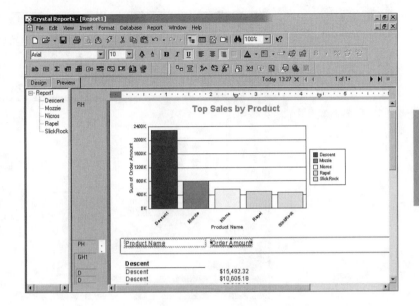

16

10. Group the Subreport on Employee First Name and create a Summary on the Sum of Order Amounts for each Employee Group. Limit the report to display the top five employees based on this sum, add a pie chart to this report, and click the Finish button.

11. Ensure that the On-Demand Subreport check box is unchecked, click OK on the Insert Subreport dialog. Drop the Subreport on the right side of the main report so that it does not overlap the existing bar chart. The details of On-Demand reports are described later in this chapter.

12. To clean up the final presentation of our main report and included Subreport, edit the Subreport by right-clicking on it and then hiding all the sections of the report except the report header. As a reminder, hiding sections is accomplished by right-clicking on the name of the involved sections in the Design or Preview tab and selecting the Hide option. Figure 16.3 shows the final result of this quick report.

As mentioned in the previous sections, Subreports *are* Crystal Reports in their own right, and as such they have their own Design tab in the Crystal Reports Designer. To format the details of a Subreport, it is necessary to open the Design tab for that Subreport from within the Designer of the main report. This can be accomplished by right-clicking on a Subreport and selecting the Edit Subreport option. Figure 16.3 displays the tabs for both the sample's main report and the Subreport.

FIGURE 16.3

*Sample Report with
Subreport to solve
COO problem.*

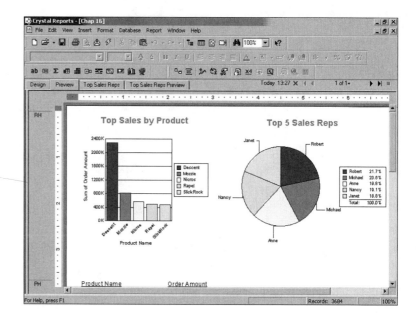

With that introduction to Subreports, you should begin to see some of the flexibility and power that they offer in solving difficult reporting problems. The next few sections explore this in more detail.

Understanding Linked Versus Unlinked Subreports

The hypothetical COO scenario just explored highlights an example of an unlinked Subreport. In Crystal Reports terminology, this means that the parent, or *main*, report did not have any specific data connections (or links) to its related child report (the Subreport). Unlinked Subreports are completely independent from their main reports and do not rely on the main report for any data. Many reporting problems in which multiple views of the same or different data sources are required in a single presentation can be resolved with unlinked Subreports. If a requirement exists to share data between the parent/main report and its Subreport, linked reports provide the answer.

Contrary to unlinked Subreports, linked Subreports are bound (or linked) to the data in their associated main report. The links are defined in the second tab of the Insert Subreport dialog as highlighted in Figure 16.4.

FIGURE 16.4

Link tab of the Insert Subreport dialog.

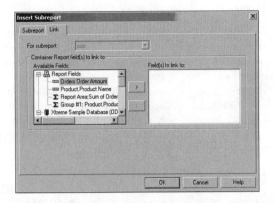

The Link tab enables the linking of report, database, or formula fields in the main report to fields in the Subreport and enables filtering of the Subreport based on the data passed in from the main report.

The Available Fields section of the Links dialog enables the selection of the field from the main report to be linked on. More than one field can be selected for linking. After at least one field has been selected, a separate Field Links section will appear at the bottom of the Links tab. For each linked field, a parameter in the involved Subreport must be selected to receive and hold that information. These parameters can be existing parameters predefined in the Subreport, or they can be a parameter that is automatically created for each field you have selected to link. (These will be automatically created in the Subreport with the prefix '?Pm-'.)

Finally, for each linked field from the main report, a data filter can be created in the Subreport based on that parameter. This is accomplished by checking the Select Data in Subreport Based on Field check box and selecting the report field, database field, or formula field in the Subreport that you want to have filtered based on the linked parameter from the provided drop-down box. In effect, checking this box will create a selection filter in your Subreport that is based on the selected filter field and the selected parameter field.

The capability to link Subreports and main reports with formulas provides a flexible method of presenting data from different database tables that is not possible otherwise. The Crystal Reports Database Linking Expert only allows joining of fields from different tables and does not permit joining formulas to fields. By using formulas and Subreports, a derived formula can now be linked to another database field in a Subreport.

An example of where this would be beneficial is if a firm's Order Processing system (for example, SAP) stored a customer ID as a nine-digit number (for example, 999123888), but that same company's *Customer Relationship Management (CRM)* system (for example, Siebel) stored the same customer ID as a nine-digit number prefixed with a regional code (for example, ONT999123888). These fields could not be joined in the Crystal Reports Database Linking Expert, but they could be linked using a Formula that extracts the nine-digit number from the CRM/Siebel Customer ID and links to the SAP Customer ID in a Subreport.

To explore a reporting solution with linked Subreports, let's solve the hypothetical reporting problem faced by the same COO of Maple Leaf Bikes Corporation. The COO now wants a single report that highlights the company's top-selling products in one bar chart (as before), but now wants a list of suppliers for those top-selling products to be available for review—essentially, a Subreport linked to the main report based on the Supplier ID of the top-selling products. To accomplish this, follow these steps:

1. Open the previous sample report from this hour and delete the previous Subreport containing the Top 5 Sales Rep pie chart.

2. Bring up the Insert Subreport Dialog and create another new Subreport called Supplier Info using the provided Subreport Report Wizard. Connect this new Subreport to the Xtreme sample database, select the Supplier table, and add the Supplier Name, City, and Phone Number fields to the report. Finally, click on the Report Wizard Finish button, but do not exit the Insert Subreport dialog.

3. Click on the Link tab in the Insert Subreport dialog. Now, select the Supplier ID field from the Available Fields list as the Field to link on (It can be selected from the Product Table). This will initiate the Supplier ID Link section at the bottom of the dialog. Use the default (and automatically generated) parameter `'?Pm-Product. Supplier ID'` for the link on the Subreport.

4. Ensure that the Select Data in Subreport Field Based On check box is selected and that the Supplier.Supplier ID field is selected in the drop-down box. Click OK to add the Subreport and place it in the Group Header (based on product) on the right side of the report.

5. Edit the Subreport to remove the default provided date and re-size the bar chart graphic on the main report. You will have a new sample report for the COO resembling the report depicted in Figure 16.5. Congratulations!

FIGURE 16.5

Sample Report with Linked Suppliers Subreport.

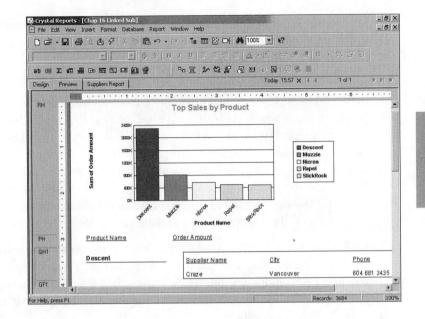

The COO can now make an informed analysis on whether his firm has too much reliance on a small number of suppliers or not, and you have learned some of the benefits of a linked Subreport.

You should notice that unlike the initial sample report presented in this hour where we placed the Top Sales Rep Subreport in the Report Header and it ran once for the entire main report, the Product Suppliers Subreport is run multiple times—in fact, once for every product. This is the case because the Subreport was placed in the Group Header of the main report, and it will therefore be executed for every different group in the main report. This is important to note with respect to performance and specifically when your databases and reports become large.

Considering Subreport Execution Time and Performance

There are two types of Subreports—In-Place and On-Demand. Both of the sample reports have been what are called In-Place Subreports. An *In-Place* Subreport is one that is virtually indistinguishable from the main report components when viewed because it is run at the same time as the main report. In-Place Subreports are displayed as components of the main report like any other report object and require no special business user interaction to view them. *On-Demand* Subreports, on the contrary, are not executed at the same time as the main report and require user interaction to be viewed.

All In-Place Subreports on a main report are run at the execution time of the main report. In the two examples presented in this hour, this has clearly not caused any performance problems, but as you might imagine, it could on larger databases. Imagine running the last sample report (with the Product Suppliers Subreport in every Group Header) for a large conglomerate with thousands of products. The Product Suppliers Subreport would need to run thousands of times to complete the presentation of the main report. Moreover, the thousands of supplier Subreports would be unlikely to be used by any given business user and would therefore have run extraneously. An elegant solution to that problem is the use of On-Demand Subreports.

Unlike In-Place Subreports, On-Demand Subreports only execute when a user requests them. They lie dormant until that time. The performance benefits to On-Demand reports are clear; however, it does come at the expense of a less seamless integration than In-Place Subreports and a small delay in viewing because the Subreport executes dynamically after being requested.

Taking the last example, follow these quick steps to make the Product Suppliers Subreport an On-Demand Subreport:

1. Open the most recent sample report if you have closed it.
2. Right-click on the Product Suppliers Subreport and select the Format Subreport option. Many familiar formatting options will be available here (see Figure 16.6), but click immediately on the Subreport tab.

FIGURE **16.6**

Format Subreport dialog.

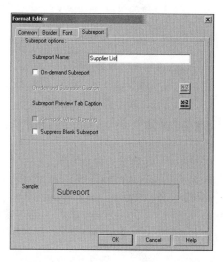

3. Click the On-Demand Subreport check box to turn on that option. You will notice that the On-Demand Caption section will become un-grayed.

4. Click on the On-Demand Caption button (x-2) and type '**Supplier List**' (include the apostrophes) in the Text Editing area. Click on the Save and Close button, and you should now have a main report that resembles Figure 16.7.

FIGURE 16.7

Sample Report with Linked and On-Demand Suppliers Subreport.

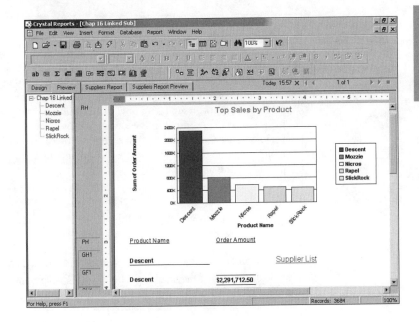

16

Careful consideration should be given to report design when deciding between In-Place and On-Demand Subreports. There is a trade-off between the seamless integration of In-Place Subreports and the performance benefits of On-Demand Subreports that must be considered in addition, of course, to the specific requirements of the business users' overall experience.

Using Variables to Pass Data Between Reports

The examples up to this point in the hour that involve passing data between a main report and a Subreport have worked exclusively through the Subreport Linking tab or Dialog. Although the functionality provided there is certainly powerful, circumstances might require more flexible passing of data between the main report and the Subreport or the passing of data the other way—from a Subreport to a main report.

With the use of variables, it becomes possible to pass data between the main report and any of the Subreports or even among different Subreports in the same main report. By declaring the same shared variable in formulas in both the main report and at least one Subreport, data can be exchanged back and forth fluidly, and each report can leverage information from the other in a very flexible manner.

> Using Subreports and variables to pass data back to a main report from a Subreport is an effective way to capture important summarizations or external information in your reports that are not possible otherwise because of the default groupings of the main report. A simple example in this hour's last sample report would be the inclusion of a count on the number of suppliers for each product. Using only the default groupings provided in the main report (By Product), this count would be impossible to calculate. By using a Subreport, however, that count can be calculated external to the main report (in a Subreport), shared using variables, and eventually displayed on the main report.

To explore the power of shared variables, follow these steps in modifying this hour's last sample report:

1. Open the most recent sample report if you have closed it. Turn the Supplier Subreport back to an In-Place Subreport (versus On-Demand).

> When passing shared variables from a Subreport to a main report, the involved Subreport cannot be set to On-Demand. The reason, of course, is that Subreports are not run until specifically requested by the business user. Therefore, their associated variables are not set until that time, making them unusable in the main report.

2. Edit the Supplier's Subreport by right-clicking on the Subreport and selecting the Edit Subreport option.

3. Select the Supplier Name field and insert a summary field that counts the distinct supplier names in this report. This summary will shortly be assigned to the shared variable that will be created and used to pass the information back to the main report.

4. Insert a formula into the Report Footer of this Subreport and call it **'Assign Supplier Count'**. In this formula, declare a shared numeric variable called **SupplierCount** and then assign this variable to equal the Supplier Summary created in the last step. (Reminder: You can access the summary created in step 3 by double clicking on it.) The formula definition should resemble Figure 16.8.

FIGURE 16.8

Formula with a shared variable declaration in the Subreport.

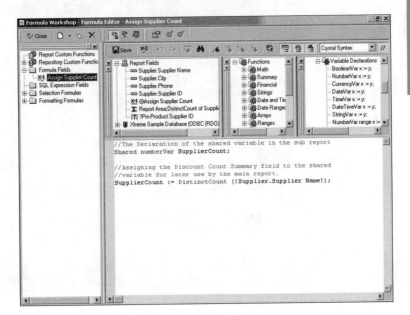

5. Now click on the Preview or Design tab of the Crystal Reports Designer to take you back to the main report, insert a formula into the Product Group Footer section, and call it **"Place Supplier Count"**. In this formula, declare the same shared numeric variable—SupplierCount—and make this variable the output of this formula. Figure 16.9 highlights what this formula should look like.

6. Add a text field to the report to complement the Supplier Count field called **"Supplier Count"**, and your report should resemble that shown in Figure 16.10.

Perhaps not the prettiest report ever designed, this quick example does begin to convey the power and importance of shared variables in report design.

FIGURE 16.9

Formula with a shared variable declaration and output in the main report.

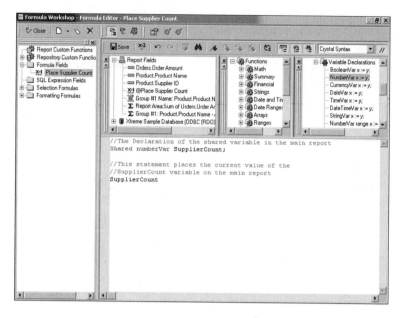

FIGURE 16.10

Sample report with Supplier Count sourced from a shared variable in a Subreport.

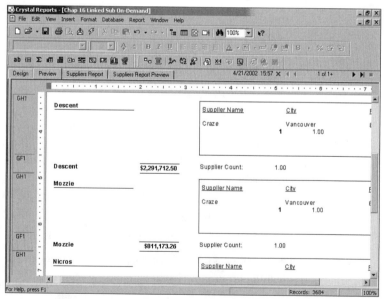

Emulating Nested Subreports

Based on the title of this section, it can de deduced that it is not possible to nest Subreports—why else would you need to emulate that behavior? Crystal Reports does not currently support Subreports within Subreports. Report Hyperlinks and Report Parts do however provide a new and flexible method in advanced navigation between and within reports. This form of flexible navigation can be used to emulate nested Subreports. Report Hyperlinks are introduced in Hour 13, "Custom Formatting Techniques," and the advanced features of Report Parts and their associated navigation is discussed in Hour 24, "Crystal Reports in Applications—A Developer's Perspective."

16

Summary

This hour has introduced the additional flexibility in Crystal Reports provided through the use of embedded Subreports. The use of reports within reports provide an enhanced value that enables an increased breadth of reporting solutions. As discussed, a variety of reporting scenarios exist that are difficult to solve without the use of Subreports.

When implementing Subreports, you have the option of selecting linked or un-linked and On-Demand or In-Place. Each combination of these options provides a different set of advantages (and considerations) that were discussed in this hour and need to be evaluated when creating your reports.

The remaining hours explore the increasing complexity of advanced reporting features and prepare you to create even more powerful Crystal Reports.

Q&A

Q Do Subreports need to be based on the same data source as their associated main report?

A No—Subreports can be based on completely independent data sources than those of their associated main report.

Q Can I save embedded Subreports as standalone Crystal Reports if I have created them within a main report.

A Yes—by opening the Subreport in its own design window, the Save Subreport As option can be accessed from the main File menu.

Workshop

The quiz questions and activity are provided for your further understanding of the current hour's topics.

Quiz

1. How many levels of Subreports can you nest in a Crystal Report?

2. Is it possible to link a Subreport and a main report on a formula field?

3. What Crystal Report feature enables passing information from a Subreport back to a main report?

Quiz Answers

1. Only one level of Subreporting is supported in Crystal Reports. Alternative forms of passing data between reports such as hyper linking can be used to support further report linking requirements.

2. Yes—a distinct advantage that Subreports provide over basic data linking is the capability to join data based on derived formulas.

3. Shared variables enable the sharing of information between the main report and its Subreports, as well as between Subreports on the same main report.

Activity

Now that you have developed a comfort level with Subreports, revisit the reports you created in the previous hours' activities and explore adding Subreports to them to make them more meaningful or powerful reports.

HOUR 17

Using Formulas and Custom Functions to Implement Complex Business Logic

This hour looks at how to use more advanced formulas and functions to accomplish many mundane and repetitive tasks. Also, we will look at how the formulas and functions can help alleviate redundancy:

- Becoming More Productive with Formulas
- Choosing a Formula Language: Crystal Versus Basic Syntax
- Brackets Have Meaning
- Characters also Have Meaning
- New in Crystal Reports Version 9

Becoming More Productive with Formulas

Because an earlier hour focuses on the basics of formulas, this hour focuses on some lesser known facts and tricks to make formula work more productive as well as less repetitive.

Choosing a Formula Language: Crystal Versus Basic Syntax

In previous hours, the Crystal syntax was used for all formulas. However, formulas in Crystal Reports can be created, edited, and modified using one of two *languages*. The Crystal syntax is the most commonly used language, but the Basic syntax is also available.

Both languages are equal in their functionality—meaning that if something was added to Crystal syntax, it was also added to Basic. The reason for having a choice is for the report designer's comfort—a designer can use whichever language he is more comfortable with.

Syntax Differences

The Crystal syntax is most similar to the Pascal or Delphi programming languages. It's not exactly like Pascal, but if you're a Delphi developer or a longtime Crystal Report developer, this syntax is probably your first choice.

The Basic syntax is most similar to Visual Basic as a programming language. If you're a Visual Basic developer, you'll likely find this syntax most beneficial.

Some specific differences between the two languages are as follows:

TABLE 17.1   Differences Between Crystal and Basic Syntax

Description	Crystal	Basic
Variable declarations	StringVar	Dim
Statement endings	;	None required
Comment characters	//	'
Variable assignment	=	=
Formula statement	None required	required
Formula returns	None required	Return statement
Multiline statement indicators	None required	_
If statement ending	None required	End If

Why Was the Basic Syntax Added?

Many functions and operators provided by the Basic language would make Crystal Reports users more productive. By implementing the whole language, the existing Crystal syntax users could benefit from the new operators and functions and at the same time: Newer users who are familiar with the Basic language through other development endeavors could easily make the jump to creating formulas in Crystal Reports.

Some of the functions and operators that were added as a result of the addition of the Basic syntax are

- Date functions such as `DateAdd`, `DateDiff`, and `DateSerial`
- Financial functions such as Present Value (PV)
- Control structures such as `Do While`, `Do Until`, and `For Next` statements

Selecting the Best Syntax for You

Whether you choose Basic or Crystal syntax, they are both equally capable of doing the job and there is no performance implication in making this choice. The decision is entirely based on the comfort level and familiarity of each language for report designers.

> Whichever syntax is your ideal, you can set it up as the default for all new formulas by going to File, Options, Reporting, and choosing the desired syntax in the Formula Language list box.

Brackets Have Meaning

Regardless of which syntax is chosen, some fundamental concepts to formula creation are important.

A bunch of different brackets are used within the formula language, and it can be confusing which one to use at a particular time. To clear up some of the confusion, here is a way to remember them phonetically:

- {}French = Fields ex. `{Table.Field}`—Used to refer to fields, formula fields or parameter fields in the report definition.
- []Square = Selected ex. `{Table.Field}[1]` returns only the first character of a string field—Square: Used for indexes on array types (for example, strings or array data types).

17

- ( )Parenthesis = Parameters ex. Function (`{Table.Field}`) passes the field to the Function—Used to define which parts of a calculation or formula should be performed first (that is, defines order of precedence for mathematical and non-mathematical operations).

Characters Also Have Meaning!

Similar to the section, symbols in the formula language (or in the icons) have specific meaning as well. To shed some light on this, check out the listing of symbols that represent different field types in Crystal Reports:

@ = Formula	`{@Formula}` is a formula field
? = Parameter	`{?Param}` is a parameter field
# = Running Total	`{#RunTtl}` is a running total field
Σ = Summary	`ΣfieldName` is a summary field on the report
% = SQL Expression	`{%SQL}` is a SQL Expression field

New in Crystal Reports Version 9

Although the use of formulas in Crystal Reports is one of the most basic of design functions, ways to improve formula usage always exist. This latest version focuses on productivity and usability improvements.

Much of the usability features around formulas have already been addressed in this book, mostly in Hour 10, "Understanding and Implementing Formulas." Therefore, the focus here will be on the functional and productivity enhancements made around formulas.

Memos in Formulas

In the past, Crystal Reports developers had not been able to access string fields that were longer than 255 characters within the formula language other than to find out whether they were null. This limitation has been completely removed in version 9.

For our purposes here, let's assume that the Xtreme Mountain Bike Company management needs an HR report that shows only the female employees, but there is no gender field in the Xtreme database. That is not a problem! In the Notes field in the Employee table, the word "she" is used for all female employees. However, Xtreme's management has indicated that they might need to search for other words as well, so they want to have a keyword search instead of hard-coding the search values. We will now create such a report to fulfill this reporting requirement.

1. Open the Employee Profile Report. Press Ctrl+O to open a report. Find the Crystal Reports 9 sample report called Employee Profile. Most installations will have it in `c:\program files\crystal decisions\crystal reports 9\samples\en\reports\general business`.

2. Create a parameter field, by selecting View, Field Explorer. Right-click on the Parameter Field item in the Field Explorer and choose New. In the Create Parameter Field dialog, call the parameter **Search-A-Word**. Prompting Text should be **What word would you like to search for?**. The Value Type should be `String`. Click on the Set Default Values button. In the Set Default Values dialog, add `"<none>"`, `"she"`, and `"he"` to the default values. The final result should look like Figure 17.1. Click the OK button. The Create Parameter dialog should look like Figure 17.2. Click OK.

FIGURE 17.1

The default values for a Search-A-Word parameter.

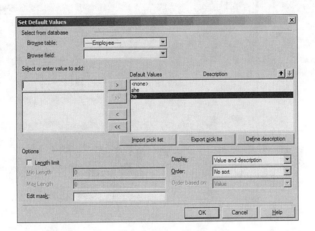

FIGURE 17.2

The parameter settings for Search-A-Word.

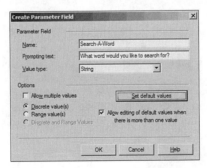

3. Connect the parameter to the Selection Formula. Select the Formula Workshop via Report, Formula Workshop. Then choose Selection Formulas, Record Selection from the Workshop tree. Enter the following selection formula into the editor: `IF {?Search-A-Word} = "<none>" THEN TRUE ELSE ({?Search-a-Word}) IN LowerCase({Employee.Notes})` and press the Save and Close button.

4. Run the report. When prompted, choose she from the Parameter Field prompt and choose to refresh the data. The end result is that only the female employees will appear on the report as shown in Figure 17.3. Save the report as `Chap17_1.rpt`.

FIGURE **17.3**

The Employee Profile showing female employees only.

Notice that we only put the `LowerCase()` function call around the `{Employee.Notes}` field and not the parameter. This is because we put the values into the parameter as lowercase by default. However, because we allow the business users to input their own values into the parameter, it might be a good idea to put the `LowerCase()` function on the parameter as well. This will allow Crystal to compare apples to apples when evaluating these exact values. Alternatively, both could have been set to `UpperCase()` as well.

> Not all databases support the ability to search large string fields, so if this type of keyword search is required, more records than necessary might come across the network. For the preceding example, 15 records were returned from the datasource but only the 6 that were female were shown on the report. This is because the datasource couldn't be passed this selection criteria to handle on the server side.
>
> It is a powerful new feature, but keep in mind that it might bring back more records than would have been originally expected.

A keyword search is just one example of how to use a memo field in a formula. The 255 character limitation for formulas being removed in version 9 of Crystal Reports means that practically all database field types can now be accessed in formulas and manipulated. Remember that memo fields are really just long string fields, so they are treated as strings in the formula language. Wherever a string can be called, now a memo field can be called as well.

Additional Financial Functions

In previous versions of Crystal Reports, the financial functions capability of the formula language was limited to 13 functions. However, in version 9 of Crystal Reports, more than 50 financial functions are now available. With overloads for parameters, these functions count up to about 200 variations.

These functions were implemented in order to give as much functionality as possible to a very highly skilled group of report designers. In the past, they had to hand code the financial functions. By including the standard financial functions that most users have seen in MS Excel, these report developers can now develop their formulas much more quickly.

For more information on the Financial Functions available, refer to the Crystal Reports 9 Help file. In the Index, look up "Financial Functions" for a complete list of what's available.

Custom Functions

Custom Functions are completely new to Crystal Reports 9. Although they have been introduced in Hour 10 already, this section focuses on some more detailed information on what they are and how they could be used in Report Development.

What Are Custom Functions?

Custom functions are packets of business logic that are written in Basic or Crystal syntax. These functions do not have any reference to any database fields at all. Because these functions contain logic that will change values and return a result, the values must be passed in and the results of the logic must be passed out or returned.

Only 10% of a custom function is different from your average formula. As mentioned previously, parameters must be passed in to allow for data manipulation because a custom function is *stateless*. This means that it has no meaning outside the function it's called in. It acts just like all the other formula functions in the formula language. The only difference is that custom functions can be created, edited, and deleted, whereas Crystal Formula Functions are completely unchangeable.

Here is a custom function that is provided within the sample repository that comes with Crystal Reports 9:

```
Function cdExpandRegionAbbreviation (regionAbbreviation _
  As String, Optional country As String = "USA")
  Select Case UCase (country)
   Case "CANADA"
    cdExpandRegionAbbreviation _
      = cdExpandRegionAbbreviationCanada (regionAbbreviation)
   Case "USA", "U.S.A.", "US", "U.S.", "UNITED STATES", _
    "UNITED STATES OF AMERICA"
    cdExpandRegionAbbreviation _
      = cdExpandRegionAbbreviationUSA (regionAbbreviation)
    Case Else
        cdExpandRegionAbbreviation = regionAbbreviation
    End Select
End Function
```

Some of the things you will notice about the preceding code are as follows:

- It's in Basic syntax. This is not a requirement of custom functions. They can be in either Basic or Crystal syntax.

- It does not reference database fields directly. Any information that is needed from a database must be passed in via the parameters in the first statement (regionAbbreviation).

- It has an optional parameter (Optional country As String = "USA"). This means that this parameter is not necessarily needed to be passed in for the function to work. If this parameter is not supplied by the developer in the formula, the value of "USA" is used by default.

- It calls other custom functions. `CdExpandRegionAbbreviationCanada` and `cdExpandRegionAbbreviationUSA` are also custom functions. In fact, they are Crystal syntax custom functions. (This shows that Basic and Crystal syntax can call one another.)

- It has a definite end-point (`End Function`). This allows for the final result (after all the functions return) to be passed back out to the formula making the call.

Creating Custom Functions from Existing Formulas

For many report developers, they might already have fully functional formulas that would make great custom functions. Making the necessary changes to the function format feels like a large task. The good news is that Crystal Reports 9 contains a feature that actually does this for the report developer. It's called the Formula Extractor. To get a better understanding of what the Formula Extractor does, here is a working example:

1. Open the Chap5.RPT. Press Ctrl+O to get the Open dialog and browse until Chap5.RPT is found. Select it and click OK.

2. Extract the formula. Select Report, Formula Workshop and right-click on the Report Custom Functions item in the Workshop group tree. Select New. Call the Custom Function **DaysUntilShipped** and then select Use Extractor.

> Because a Custom Function is similar to a reserved word, there can be no spaces in the name. If a space is required, consider using the underscore instead.

3. Choose the formula created earlier, also called `DaysUntilShipped`. Because the name of the Custom Function has already been entered, it is automatically placed in the Name box.

4. Add the necessary information. Add the following text to the Summary box: **This function takes two dates and determines the number of business days between them.** Also, rename v1 to **Start** and v2 to **End**. Add **Start Date** as the description for the first variable (`Start`) and **End Date** as the description for the second variable (`End`). Finally, make sure that Modify Formula to Use New Custom Function is selected. The end result should look like Figure 17.4.

FIGURE **17.4**

Extract Custom
Function from
Formula dialog.

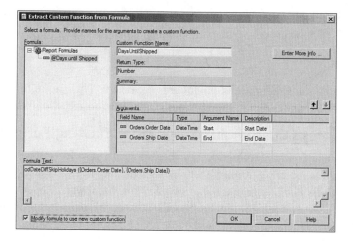

The Enter More Info button takes the report developer to another dialog where she can enter much more descriptive text around the custom function. It also contains fields for categorization and authors. From there, the report developer can also add help text via another dialog. For more information on these dialogs, consult the online help.

5. Save and close the newly formed custom function. By clicking the OK button, Crystal Reports returns to the Formula Workshop with the Editor view of the newly created function. In the workshop tree, navigate to Formula Fields, Days Until Shipped to see the results. The formula now uses the new custom function DaysUntilShipped as indicated in Figure 17.5. Close the Formula Workshop by clicking on the X in the top-right corner of the dialog.

6. Save the report as **Chap17_2.rpt** by choosing File, Save As.

Creating custom functions from existing reports can be handled quickly and easily using the Formula Extractor. If you require creating custom functions from scratch, see more information in the online help.

FIGURE 17.5

Formula converted to use custom function.

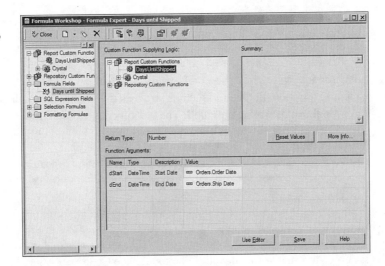

Sharing Custom Functions with Others

Two ways in which you can share custom functions are

- By using them in multiple places in one—Because custom functions are stateless, different parameters can be passed in to allow for instant function reuse.
- By sharing them in the Crystal Repository—Custom functions are one of four report object types that can be shared in the repository.

Custom functions can be used in many ways. Take your existing formulas, convert them, and share their logic with others.

Understanding Runtime Errors

New in Crystal Reports 9 is the ability to get more information about variables within formulas when a runtime error occurs. In the past, when a runtime error (such as a Divide by Zero) occurred, Crystal would simply take the report developer to the line of the formula giving the error. However, this was not altogether helpful, especially if the error was because the data being passed in from the database could have been at fault. So, in version 9 of Crystal Reports, there is a new feature that shows all variables and data field values used in all related formulas when an error occurs. You can think of this as a variable stack.

17

The runtime error stack only appears when a runtime error occurs (when real-time data forces an error). It appears where the workshop group tree normally would in the Formula Workshop.

The runtime error stack shows all variables and all database field data related to the formula in question. If custom functions are called within the formula, their variables will appear above the formula as well. The last function to be called will appear at the top.

> The idea of a stack (reverse order) is useful in that the last function called most likely will be where the error is. But, of course, that might not always be the case.

This concept is best shown as an example. Let's assume that Xtreme Mountain Bike Company's management would like to take the Chap17_1.rpt and find out how much money is not accounted for by days when not shipped (Calculation = Order Amount / Days until shipped).

1. Use the Chap17_1.rpt again. If it's not already open, open it by choosing Ctrl+O.

2. Use the Formula Workshop. Select Report, Formula Workshop. Right-click on the Formula Field branch in the workshop tree and choose New. Name the formula **Unaccounted Amount/Day** and select Use Editor.

3. Add the required logic. In the Editor, enter the following "**{Orders.Order Amount} / {@Days until Shipped}**". Click the Save and Close button in the top-left corner. Choose Yes when prompted to save. If the report is not already in Preview mode, press F5 to refresh the report. If you don't see any data, choose Report, Section Expert and make sure that the Details section isn't suppressed. If it is, toggle the option and click OK.

4. Drag the field onto the report. From the Field Explorer (View, Field Explorer), select the newly created formula and drag it onto the report to the right of the Days Until Shipped field. Notice that the Divide by Zero error comes up right away. Click OK.

5. View the Runtime Error Stack. As shown in Figure 17.6, see the runtime error stack and how it works. In this case, the formula is quite straightforward. The problem is occurring because some of the orders are on time (zero days wait). Xtreme's management would like to show 0 if the orders are on time, so change the formula to the following: "**if {@Days until Shipped} = 0 then 0 else {Orders.Order Amount} / {@Days until Shipped}**". Click the Save button.

FIGURE 17.6

Runtime Error Stack next to the newly updated formula.

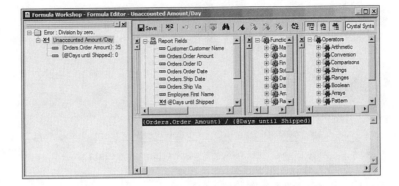

6. Click F5 to refresh the report. See the values of the resulting formula as shown in Figure 17.7 and then save the report as **Chap17_3.rpt**.

FIGURE 17.7

Resulting Report with the latest Xtreme requirements added.

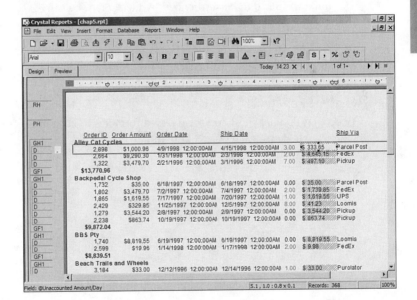

Summary

Using formulas in Crystal Reports makes data in the database more useful information for the report developer as well as the business users viewing the report. There are many ways to create formulas and many tricks to create them effectively. In this hour, tricks, as well as experts in the software, were used to show just some of the power of the Crystal Reports Formulas feature.

Workshop

Now that you've added some new tools to your formulas and functions toolkit, let's test them out.

Quiz

1. What does {} represent in the Formula Language?
2. Can a custom function be created easily from an existing formula?
3. Why doesn't the Stack appear when a formula is being created?

Quiz Answers

1. A field ex. `{Table.Field}`—The French braces always surround a report object when it's referenced in a formula. All report objects that can be referenced in a formula will need to be surrounded by these braces.
2. Yes—Using the Formula Extractor.
3. Because it's only available when data is actually run through the formulas. Hence the name Runtime Error Stack.

Activity

Try converting your most commonly used formulas to custom functions and place them in the repository for easy reuse in the future.

HOUR 18

Working with the Report Component Repository

This hour focuses on how to optimize your efficiency by applying the principals of reuse of objects. The Report Component Repository will help you along this path. The topics covered in this hour are

- Sharing Report Design Components
- Understanding the Crystal Repository
- Improving on Sharing of Report Objects
- Understanding the Repository Explorer
- Understanding How the Repository Works
- Adding Objects to the Repository
- Editing Repository Objects
- Understanding Deletions in the Repository
- Sharing Report Objects with Others
- Sharing Logic

Sharing Report Design Components

Report designers have many tricks up their sleeves to make their report design efforts more productive. In the past, many report designers would maintain basic report *templates* containing the most reused objects and business logic. In many cases, these reports would contain corporate logos, formatted page headers and footers, text objects with typical text (like the company's address), and even some typical formula logic. We could call them warehouse reports.

Report designers would copy and paste these objects between the warehouse report and the newly created reports on a regular basis. This would save the report designer a significant amount of time by not recreating these objects from scratch. Of course, when logic or other objects change, the warehouse report could be updated so that all newer reports would also benefit. The report designer would have to remember which reports could have been affected, open them up, and update them by hand. This process was cumbersome but necessary.

Imagine the ability to reuse and share the most commonly used components of your best Crystal reports with other developers within your organization. What if components such as SQL statements, images, text objects, and common formulas could all be accessed through one common source, rather than dozens, or even hundreds, of individual Crystal Reports? Such a capability would dramatically increase the overall productivity of a single Crystal Reports developer, let alone a team of Crystal Reports developers.

Wouldn't it be great if there were a warehousing utility that could act upon reports without all the report designer's manual labor? A warehouse or database of objects that could be linked to the reports? A repository! This common source for report components is now available via the Crystal Reports 9 Component Repository. These reusable report objects are stored in a central repository, making the process of change management incredibly easy because a single change to an object (such as an image) can be easily propagated across any number of Crystal Reports.

Understanding the Repository

Crystal Reports' Repository feature is the answer to these questions in the prior section. The Crystal Repository is a central library of report objects for report designers to access, update, and share between reports. This feature can be shared among multiple report designers as well.

The Crystal Repository is a database that contains common report objects that can be shared. The types of report objects that can be shared in the repository are

- Text Objects—Reusable text, such as company addresses or confidentiality text, as examples.
- Images—Pictures or logos.
- Custom Functions—Business logic that could be reused by passing in new fields as variables.
- SQL Commands—Encapsulated database commands that produce tables to report from. They might contain complex SQL statements. These commands could even be parameter driven.

Sharing of Report Objects

The Crystal Repository takes into account all the typical sharing techniques that report designers have been leveraging in the past. The difference is that the new repository is **independent** of a given report. It handles logic, formatting, and objects. Fortunately, it also handles the major concern that was lacking in the RPT sharing scenario mentioned previously. By its very nature as a separate library (or database), it is referenced by the report when the report is opened, and, as a result, it can actually update the repository objects automatically for the report designer so that the added work of copying new logic and other objects is eliminated.

Benefits of Using the Repository

Updating a company's name can be used as a real-world example. Before Crystal Decisions, the company that created Crystal Reports was called Seagate Software. All the sample reports that shipped with older versions of Crystal Reports contained contact information in the bottom that mentioned Seagate Software in two text objects—one for copyright information and one for feedback.

To use the repository, the original objects were removed from each of the reports and were replaced with the repository objects. The reports were then saved. Later, the company name changed, and all the sample reports needed updating. The report designer opened one of the sample reports, disconnected the two objects from the repository, updated them from Seagate Software to Crystal Decisions, and then updated the repository objects with the newly updated text. That report was then saved.

The report designer then opened all the other reports at once. Because all the reports were connected to the repository, all their text objects were updated with the same change that the report designer made in the initial report magically. It was handled by Crystal Reports itself. All the report designer had to do was close and save the reports. The entire task of updating took about five minutes by using the repository. The old method would have taken considerably more time to copy and paste all these changes in each report.

18

Understanding the Repository Explorer

The Repository Explorer is the one-stop shop for adding, updating, and reusing repository objects within the design environment of Crystal Reports.

It can be activated by selecting View, Repository Explorer. This floating dialog can be docked to the design environment as well, as covered in Hour 4.

Organizing the Repository

The Repository Explorer represents the repository database as a tree structure made up of folders and objects. The structure is not dictated by the repository itself. It is up to the report designer how he wants to organize it. For example, the sample Crystal Repository that ships with Crystal Reports 9 is sorted by object types. The folders are named to indicate their contents (Images, Text Objects, and Commands). However, the content creator or report designer can use folders to his organizational advantage.

To add new folders to the repository, right-click on the desired folder where the intended sub-folder is to be placed. If the folder is intended to be at the root, right-click on the repository name. Choose New Folder from the context menu.

To rename a folder, simply choose the folder to be renamed, right-click on it, and choose Rename from the context menu. Once the folder name is editable, make the necessary change.

Hosting Objects in the Repository

Within the Repository Explorer, the report designer has access to the Repository Objects that can be placed on the report design surface. Text objects and image objects are visible from the Repository Explorer. To use repository objects in your reports, simply drag and drop these objects on to the report as required.

Also, SQL commands are visible in the Repository Explorer, but they are not usable directly on the report. However, their properties can be viewed from here.

Custom Functions are **not** viewable from the Repository Explorer because they are housed inside of Formulas. To view custom functions available in the Repository, go to Report, Formula Workshop. In the group tree, the Crystal Repository branch can be seen and all custom functions can be viewed from there.

Understanding How the Repository Works

The Crystal Repository that ships with Crystal Reports 9 is a standalone database. It is a Microsoft Access database that Crystal Reports maintains, which means that Crystal Reports internally understands how to create the tables and structures it requires to make the repository work.

If a new repository database is needed, all Crystal needs to know is where the database is located. The database itself need not have any tables or fields in it prior to populating the repository with objects and folders. Crystal Reports will create all the necessary tables and fields to make the repository work successfully. Be aware that a report can only connect to one repository at a time.

Crystal Reports uses ODBC to communicate with the repository database. This design is used so that if the report designer chooses, he can use any data source desired as a back-end database (such as Microsoft SQL Server, IBM DB2, Oracle, and others). You are not limited to Microsoft Access as the repository data store.

> For more information on ODBC, see Hour 3.

18

Some things you can do within the repository include

- Adding objects and folders
- Updating existing objects
- Renaming folders and objects
- Updating properties of objects
- Deleting objects and folders

Adding Objects to the Repository

Depending on the type of object that is going to be saved in the repository, different methods of adding them are required. All repository objects can be added in an intuitive way. Report objects can be dragged and dropped, SQL commands can be added when the commands are written, and custom functions can be added from the Formula Workshop. Let's look at the different processes more closely.

Text Objects and Images

Repository Objects can be added to the repository in folders contained in a tree structure. To add a new object to the repository, a simple drag-and-drop is all that's required:

1. Take the object on the design or preview surface and drag it to its rightful place in the Repository Explorer.

2. If a folder location is warranted, simply drag the object over the folder until the folder opens and then let go. The Repository Properties dialog will appear.

3. Enter the relevant information (such as the name of the object) and click OK.

An alternative way to store an object in the Repository is to right-click on the object in the report design or preview. From the context menu, choose Add to Repository. A more complex properties dialog will appear. Add the name, and so on (as previously mentioned), as well as choose the location for the object as the last step in this dialog. (This step was avoided in the drag and drop scenario because the location was implied in that procedure.)

SQL Commands

Imagine that you have a fairly difficult SQL (Structured Query Language) statement that you want to share with others, but you want to control it in case changes need to be made at a later time. This can be done using SQL Commands and saving them in the Repository.

SQL Commands can be added to the Repository from the Data Explorer or the Data step of the Report Wizard. The steps are the same for both, so let's use the Data Explorer to illustrate.

1. Connect to the database desired in the Available Data Sources list box and choose Add Command from the list of available options. Select Add Command by double-clicking on it. This will bring you to the Add Command to Report dialog.

2. Enter the SQL statement you want into the query box. If parameters are required, you can use this dialog to create them as well. An example would be

```
"SELECT `Employee`.`Last Name`, `Employee`.`First
Name`,`Employee_Addresses`.`Address1`,
`Employee_Addresses`.`Address2`,
`Employee_Addresses`.`City`,
`Employee_Addresses`.`Region`,
`Employee_Addresses`.`Country`,
`Employee_Addresses`.`Postal Code`, FROM `Employee`
`Employee` INNER JOIN `Employee Addresses`
`Employee_Addresses` ON `Employee`.`Employee
ID`=`Employee_Addresses`.`Employee ID` "
```

For more in-depth information on Structured Query Language and using SQL Commands, see Hour 22, "Optimizing SQL Queries in Crystal Reports."

3. Before leaving this dialog, make sure that the Add to Repository option at the bottom of the dialog is selected, and then select OK.

4. The Add Item dialog will appear (similar to the dialog for text objects and images). Select a name for the command and a location in the Repository.

If the name of the command has spaces in it, keep in mind that many of the data access drivers will convert them to underscores _. See Hour 3, "Accessing Your Data," for more information on data access drivers.

Notice that descriptions are not as free form as they were with text objects and images. By default, they contain the SQL statement, but this can be edited, appended to, or simply removed. It is included as a default because most report designers have requested to see the results of the statement.

18

Editing Repository Objects

Regardless of the type of Repository Object, from time to time, objects will likely need to be updated. For example, the company address text object would need to be updated if the company moves to a new location. To successfully update any repository object, two fundamental steps must be taken:

1. Disconnect the object from the repository and then make the change to the object.

2. Update the object in the repository.

Disconnecting a Repository Object

Because the Repository is basically a library to store objects, it has no update functionality in itself. This means that updates to objects must be done directly inside a Crystal Report. All connected repository objects are automatically considered read-only and cannot be changed. To update a specific object, you first need to disconnect it from the repository. This can be done by right-clicking on the object and choosing Disconnect Repository Object in the Design or Preview tabs.

> Remember that there are different places where repository objects can be accessed and acted upon depending on their type. Text objects and images can be accessed from the Repository Explorer and the design application's Design and Preview tabs. SQL Commands can be accessed from the Report Wizard and the Data Expert. Custom functions can be accessed from the Formula Workshop.

After the object is disconnected, the needed changes can be applied to the object. However, the changes do not become global to the repository and all other reports using the object until the object is connected back to the repository.

Reconnecting an Updated Object to the Repository

Now that the object has been updated as desired, only the report where the update has occurred is currently changed. This is because the repository has not been made aware of the change. To make the repository aware, the object must be reconnected to the repository.

To reconnect a text object or image to the repository, simply drag and drop the object from the Design/Preview environment back to its original repository object name/location in the Repository Explorer. A dialog will appear to confirm if you want to update the original object or add a new one. Because Update is already chosen, clicking OK will update the object.

For example, if a logo has been changed and the original object was called `corporate logo`, drag the new logo image directly over the name *corporate logo* in the Repository Explorer. When prompted to update or add, confirm it as an update and click OK. The corporate logo for this report will now be reconnected, and the repository will be updated for all other reports as well.

To reconnect a Custom Function in the Formula Editor, simply right-click on the disconnected and updated custom function's name in the workshop tree and choose Add to Repository. There will be a prompt for which specific repository you want to update. But because there is only one in this case, clicking OK will reconnect the object and update the repository in one step.

> Because Custom Functions are called by name, no two custom functions in the repository can have the same name. Notice that no dialog requesting Add or Update has appeared. This is because the name of the Custom Function hasn't changed, and it will automatically update the existing one.

If the name for a custom function has been changed (perhaps because it's a hybrid of another function), it will be added to the repository under the new name.

To reconnect a SQL Command to the repository, the Add to Repository toggle in the Modify Command dialog (where the changes to the command have been made) will need to be selected. Once the OK button is clicked, the updated command will be reconnected to the repository. This can be done from either the Database Expert dialog or the Data tab in the Report Expert.

When updates occur to objects in the repository, the older versions are not actually gone. They are simply not viewable in the Repository Explorer. Crystal Reports always looks for the latest version of an object to display in the report design application.

During an update action, the repository database increases the version number for the newly updated object automatically so that when the next call to the repository object is made (either by adding it new to a report or during the update action upon opening a report), the latest version number will be used.

Sharing a Repository with Others

The focus of this lesson has been on sharing objects, formatting and logic between reports. This focus has been for one report designer to increase his productivity. However, the idea of a report object repository raises the question, "Can this sharing of information be shared between multiple report designers?"

The answer to this question is *yes*. By creating the repository as a database, the idea was two-fold—to share knowledge between reports as well as to share that same knowledge with other report designers. However, the underlying database type is the key.

Crystal Reports needed to provide the sample Crystal Repository in a small compact database, so Microsoft Access was chosen as the default source. However, this database is not conducive to sharing among many users. Fortunately, the fact that an open data access method (ODBC) is used as a middle tier (or middleman) means that other relational databases could be used as well.

For example, if a report designer has access to Microsoft's SQL Server database, he could publish his repository to this database source (by importing his existing MDB) and give access to the repository to other colleagues. By sharing one repository, all the report designers would more likely be consistent across their reports and more productive with their design efforts.

To inform the Crystal Reports application about the change to the location of the data source, the report designer will have to create an ODBC data source for his new database.

Make sure that Crystal Reports is closed before making this change.

For more information on how to create an ODBC DSN specification, follow the directions located in the Crystal Reports Help files to ensure correct configuration of Data Source Names (DSN).

After the data source is created, edit the ORMap.INI located in `c:\program files\common files\crystal decisions\2.0\bin`. Change the name after the = sign at the end of the file to be the exact data source name that has recently been created. Run Crystal Reports and open the Repository Explorer. Notice that the database has changed to the new data source.

If the new database requires a username or password to connect to it, these credentials will be prompted for upon initially opening the repository. But, opening and closing the repository explorer will not log off the server. Therefore, prompting is kept to a minimum.

Because the repository is now shared with others, it can be updated and maintained by others as well. If there is a need to limit the updating ability, this must be done on the database side by limiting the update rights of a particular user.

For more information on rights, see your database documentation because all databases are different.

Understanding Deletions in the Repository

When an object is deleted from the repository within Crystal Reports, it is not truly deleted from the database itself. It is marked as deleted so that it will not show up in the Repository Explorer, but the object still exists within the physical database. This marking of a deleted object is often called *flagging as dirty*, or *logical deletion*. This allows the report designer to roll back the object to make it visible again if it was accidentally deleted.

Because objects are never truly deleted from the underlying database, the objects still take up space. To save that space, the objects must be physically deleted. To accomplish this, the report designer will have to use a database utility to physically delete the objects. For more information on physical deletion for your database, see your database documentation.

Sharing Report Objects with Others

Reports that have been connected to the repository are still portable. They do not need to be physically connected to a given repository to be viewable by others. Crystal Reports files were designed to save all objects within them so that if the repository is not available to check for updated versions of the objects, the report will load with the last version of the objects that were stored within the RPT file. The is advantageous because it allows report designers to share RPT files while not necessarily sharing the same repository. When the original RPT file is returned (with changes made by the second report designer) and opened, the repository will update the report as necessary.

18

Summary

In this hour, you've learned the concept of object reuse and how the Report Component Repository can help you to design reports more quickly and easily (especially for maintenance purposes).

Workshop

The quiz questions and activity are provided for your further understanding of the repository topics learned in this hour.

Quiz

1. What types of objects can be stored in the repository?

2. What database type is the sample Crystal Repository?

3. Can repositories be shared among multiple report designers? If so, how?

Quiz Answers

1. Text objects, images, SQL Commands, and Custom Functions
2. Microsoft Access MDB
3. Yes, by using a multiuser database via ODBC

Activity

Consider which objects in your existing reports could be more useful in the repository and add them in. Then replace all other objects of the same type in other reports with the repository objects. This will help with future report maintenance tasks.

HOUR 19

Designing Effective Report Templates

To further enhance your reports and to make many reports look as similar as possible, we will use this hour to discuss how to create templates from existing reports as well as new reports. We will look at applying templates to reports that were dealing with getting the required information so that they look presentable as well. This hour's topics are as follows:

- Reuse in reporting
- What is a template?
- Using already existing templates
- How to create an effective template
- Using Template Field Objects
- Maximizing the net effect of templates

Reuse in Reporting

Up to now, you've been creating feature rich reports that are very functional. Most likely, no two of the resulting reports from the previous hours have a consistent look and feel.

One of the most demanding and time-consuming parts of Report Design is giving all of your reports a consistent look and feel. In many situations, report designers are asked to conform to a corporate standard like letterheads (all page numbers in the bottom right corner, and so on) or perhaps even something as demanding as GAAP or SEC.

In a perfect "Report Designer–centric" world, less work would be required if the report designer were allowed to focus her efforts on one report and use it as a guide for all other reports that require visual, presentation-focused (yet time-consuming) features. After one report is completed with the appropriate formatting, why not *apply* its contents and format to other reports? Applying an existing report's layout to other reports is very straightforward with Crystal Reports 9. This is made possible through enhancements to the report templates functionality.

Understanding Report Templates

A report template is nothing more than a regular report (RPT) file. It can be any RPT file. Templates are *applied* to other reports so that their formatting and layout can be used as a basis for the other reports. What is useful about the application of templates to other reports is that formatting is applied to the report as well as the layout. An example of this would be a report that has four fields in a detail section, where all sections are "squished" together before applying a presentation-quality template. After the template is applied, the location of the fields in the template would force the fields in the existing report to span out and possibly even change some font information, depending on the specific template.

Using Report Templates

Think of a template as the form that everyone in a company must comply to. Templates can house many types of objects. These objects can be applied to a report after the data-intensive portion of the report design is completed. Applying an existing template to a report can save hours or potentially days of mundane formatting tasks.

Some types of tasks that can be accomplished by (but are not limited to) applying a template to a report are as follows:

- Corporate logos and other images
- Consistent page numbering formatting

- Font style/color/typeface for data fields
- Field border and background formatting
- Field sizing
- Group headers and footers formatting
- Summary field formatting
- Watermarks
- Tricky formatting
- Lines
- Boxes
- Repository objects
- Report titles
- Website links
- Formatting based on data-field type

How Are Templates Better Than Styles in Previous Versions?

Templates are better than the Styles in prior versions of Crystal Reports in so many ways that it's challenging to explain in a short coffee break topic. However, because not every report designer has used Crystal Reports prior to version 9, it's a worthwhile subject. (For those of you new to Crystal Reports with this version, feel free to skip this coffee break.

The main issue with the old feature of Report Styles in previous versions of Crystal Reports (such as 8.5) was that they were not customizable. The styles that one person created when the feature was initially introduced were the only options available. Even if you just didn't like the color red as the group name field and wanted to change it to blue, you were not able to, which was very limiting. This limitation alone made the Styles feature practically useless outside of learning how to create very simple reports.

These styles were also limited to data and group fields. No images or static text objects were included, and again because the styles could not be modified, they could not be updated in this way. The styles were hard-coded into the Crystal Reports designer so that no external RPT files were used, whereas Templates allow the use of any RPT file.

19

Using Existing Crystal Reports as Templates

Now that we've introduced the major benefits of Report Templates, let's actually apply a template to one of the reports created in an earlier hour. The report in Hour 5 is a good example.

The report as it looked in Hour 5 was pretty plain because the focus was on making sure
that the data requirements were satisfied. There wasn't a lot of time to play with formatting, so now we are going to apply a template that has some nice grayscale formatting
and an underlay applied.

1. Open the report. Choose File, Open to get the Open dialog box, and browse until
   the report is found. (The report is probably named CHAP5.RPT). Choose it and
   click Open to continue.

2. Look at the report prior to applying the template as shown in Figure 19.1. To get a
   good view of the application of the template, make sure that the Preview tab is
   selected. If the Preview tab is not selected or available, choose View, Preview.

FIGURE **19.1**

*The report from
Hour 5 as it appears
in Preview.*

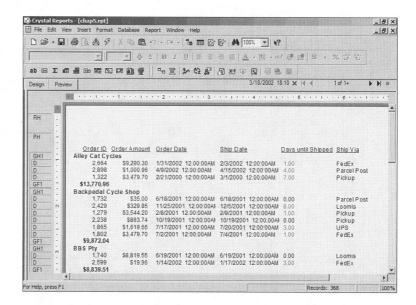

3. Apply the template. To apply some formatting quickly, choose Report, Template
   Expert. In the Template Expert dialog, feel free to choose each file so that you can
   see the associated thumbnail. For this case, let's choose Confidential Underlay, as
   shown in Figure 19.2, and then click OK.

For more information on thumbnails, review the Preview Pictures coffee
break at end of this hour.

FIGURE 19.2

FIGURE 19.2

*The Template Expert
with the Confidential
Underlay template
chosen.*

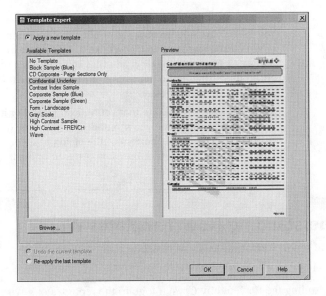

4. Save the report. The report will then open with the formatting from the applied template as shown in Figure 19.3. You can now save the report as `CHAP19.rpt`.

FIGURE 19.3

*The target report
with the Confidential
Underlay template
applied.*

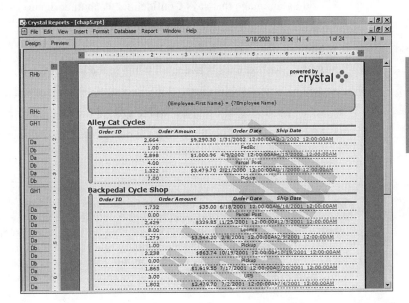

19

You might have noticed that just about anything you do when designing a report can be undone if you don't like it. This is also true when applying templates. However, the mechanism of accomplishing this is slightly different from all other undo operations. It does not appear in the regular undo list on the Standard toolbar.

If you don't like a template that you've just applied or it doesn't accomplish what you had hoped for, you can undo this action by going back in to the Template Expert. At the bottom of the dialog box, you will find a button that says Undo the Current Template. After selecting it and clicking OK, the template is removed.

Understanding How Templates Work

A lot of report formatting tasks were accomplished in the two minutes it took to apply the template in the previous exercise, including

- Adding the Powered by Crystal logo to the report (along with its ToolTip and hyperlink) from the Crystal Repository. The Crystal Repository is discussed in more detail in Hour 18, "Working with the Report Component Repository."
- Adding an image that says Confidential as an underlay to each page of the report.
- Modifying the fonts and positions of all the database fields.
- Showing the Record Selection Formula on the report.
- Adding dashed lines between all items in the Details Section.
- Adding a rounded box around the Record Selection Formula.
- Using a rounded box to show where groups start and end.
- Moving the Field Headings for each data field into the Group Header and formatting them with double lines.

One of the more advantageous features of templates is that even if more fields are in the target report's Details section than the template has, it duplicates the data field formatting for those extra fields. It puts them into a separate Detail Section (usually titled Details B) so that they will all appear together but they won't overwrite each other. The fields can then be moved around without having to worry about applying the same formatting by hand.

Creating Useful Report Templates

If a Crystal Report already exists that has been regularly copied in the past or a report that is viewed as the *perfect report*, consider it to be the beginning of an effective template. Because any report can be the basis for a template, the report designer might just need to refine a few functional or formatting characteristics to make the existing report more robust for use as a formal template.

If the report designer doesn't have any reports to use for creating templates, you don't need to be concerned. Everything you've learned so far (and in the upcoming hours) will help with effective template design. By creating a nice presentation-quality report, you have also created a likely candidate that can then be used as a useful report.

> We are going to make an assumption here that you have some report creation and design skills already under your belt based on your work in the previous hours.
>
> If you don't feel comfortable creating reports and maybe have skipped a few hours to get to this one, it might be a good idea to take a look at Hour 5.

Keep in mind a few key things when using an existing report for a template.

As previously mentioned, templates can be used to accomplish formatting tasks at lightning pace after data collection is done. Because any report can be used as a template, a Crystal Reports designer might already have a library full of ideas.

Applying one report layout as a template to another could cause some minor issues if the databases that are connected to each report are completely different in terms of schema, structure, or content. However, with some minor adjustments, the template report can be applied more effectively.

Formulas, for instance, can be problematic when applying a report as a template to another report. Because most formulas require database fields to function, they are closely tied to the actual database and structure of the data that is coming in to the report. Because formulas are used to act on database fields, using them in templates is not very effective as errors might occur when applying a template report to another report that accesses a different database. However, some tools are available that can minimize this effect. Using Custom Functions instead of prewritten formulas can alleviate some of the data dependencies, as can using the CurrentFieldValue evaluator for formatting formulas.

19

Also, even relatively small things can make a significant difference. Sometimes just focusing on the page headers or footers can go a long way in effective report template design. By reducing the repetitive nature of general page formatting, you will increase your report design productivity.

Using Custom Functions as Replacements for Data-Dependent Business Logic

Because we've already introduced Custom Functions in a previous hour, the focus of this section is how to use custom functions to avoid formula errors when applying templates. For more information on Custom Functions, see Hour 17, "Using Formulas and Custom Functions to Implement Complex Business Logic."

The reason Custom Functions are more useful in templates than straight formulas is that they are *stateless*, which means that they have no direct dependency on the database fields to get their data. Custom Functions see the data only as parameters that are passed in to the report. Instead of searching through an entire formula to find all uses of a given field, by passing it in to a Custom Function once, Crystal Reports will effectively do the search and replace repeatedly on the report designer's behalf.

Another advantage to using Custom Functions in a report template is that within the one report—the template report—it might be possible to use one Custom Function more than once because the logic might be used over and over with the only difference being the data that's used.

If a report that contains many formulas is applied as a template to a report that contains a different table name—for example, template.field and target.field—the formulas would not change over correctly. Therefore, all the formulas will result in compiler errors upon the first run of the report to the preview. Because the report designer would have to go through all the lines of business logic and replace each and every database field occurrence, it could be a very tedious process. If the search-and-replace time could be limited to one line per formula, the report designer would be far more productive.

Of course, current formulas in a pre-existing report are already working and we would not want to break them. Or would we? What if there were some compelling reasons? (Like the advantages previously mentioned?) What if the formulas could be taken—logic and all—and converted into a Custom Function structure in one step? Sounds pretty painless, doesn't it?

By using the Formula Extractor, which is new to Crystal Reports 9, the Crystal Reports designer will actually review the existing formula, break it down, find the data-specific pieces, convert them into parameters, and reformulate the formula to accept those parameters and save it as a Custom Function. It will even rebuild the initial formula that created the Custom Function to apply the new Custom Function so that the report designer doesn't have to go back and perform that step manually.

> For more information on the Formula Extractor, see Hour 10, "Understanding and Implementing Formulas."

Even after formulas are converted, there will still be the need to make adjustments for data-specific fields that would need to be passed in as parameters to those functions. However, because most Custom Functions reduce the lines of code, and pass in the data only once, the search-and-replace tasks are greatly reduced.

> In general, to make formulas even easier to work with, use the new Formula Workshop as much as possible. This virtual all-in-one workspace for formulas means that navigation between formulas is quick and easy without having to open each one up separately or guess at their names.

> Another good idea to keep in mind if there is concern about losing old formula logic when converting the formula, just comment out the old formula code and put the Custom Function in. Of course, commenting each line by hand can be cumbersome. By using the Comment/Uncomment (//) button on the toolbar, you can highlight all the contiguous lines of code you want to comment out, and then click this button. It will comment them all out in one quick step.

19

Using the `CurrentFieldValue` Function

When using formulas to create conditional formatting, they are usually designed to be data dependent—so much so that the database field name is used at every opportunity. However, to make formatting formulas more portable (and reusable), use the `CurrentFieldValue` formatting function instead of the actual field name that would always change depending on where the formula is located.

`CurrentFieldValue` is a special signifier in the formula language that tells the formatting formula to look at the value of the field it is associated with, without actually having to know the name of the field. This is advantageous in two ways:

- For general formatting, this allows for copying of formatting formulas and reusing the formatting formulas within a single report or within multiple reports without having to replace data-specific field names.
- For template formatting, this is especially useful because we can't be sure that the database field is going to be of the same name, let alone of the same data type.

By keeping the reuse factor in mind when creating and maintaining formulas from now on, creating effective templates will become much easier over time.

Using Template Field Objects

During the process of designing a report template, a need might arise to provide some specific formatting for a field not based on its position in the report, but instead based on the type of field it is. For example, a company might require that all date/time fields be displayed in military time regardless of operating system defaults. For example, "6:02 p.m. on March 31, 2002" would have to look like "3/31/02 18:02". Another requirement could be a space as the thousand separator for all numbers (instead of the usual comma).

These requirements could easily be corporate or industry standard requirements, such as the ISO 9000 standard. At the time the template is created, it's unknown where these fields will be located in the report or how many of them there will be. A report designer would have to find another way of handling special formatting requirements. Template Field Objects help in this endeavor.

When designing a report specifically as a template, Template Field Objects take the place of regular database fields in a report. They can be placed anywhere that a database field would normally be placed.

These fields are a special type of formula field that contain no data but allow formats to be applied to them as if they were of any data type. Template Field Objects have a special dialog associated with them that exposes all the Formatting tabs of the Format Editor regardless of type. This provides a one-stop shop for all of your formatting needs regardless of the data type for a given position of a field in a report.

The best way to explain this is by actually performing it, so let's implement the examples given previously in this section:

- Military Time: "6:02 p.m. on March 31, 2002" to appear as "3/31/02 18:02"
- Thousand Separator as a space: 1,000 to appear as 1 000

Starting with a new report, the steps are as follows:

1. Create a new report. After opening Crystal Reports, click the New button. Then within the Crystal Reports Gallery dialog, choose As a Blank Report and click OK.

2. Skip the data source step. Because this report is going to be a template, there is no need to have a data source associated with it. Click the Cancel button in the Database Expert to close this dialog.

3. Insert a Template Field Object. To insert the first Template Field Object, select Template Field Object from the Insert menu. Place the resulting field into the left-most area of the Details section (see Figure 19.4).

FIGURE 19.4

The Design tab with the first template object added to the report.

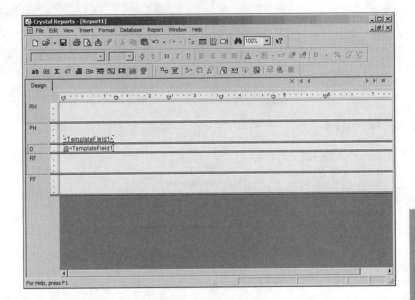

4. Add five more template objects. Repeat the previous step five more times and place each new field to the right of the last one. Once completed, the Design tab will look like Figure 19.5.

5. Select all template objects to format. To select all template objects, hold down the Ctrl Key while single-clicking on each template object in the Details section. After all six objects are selected, right-click on the last object you chose and select Format Template Fields from the pop-up menu.

6. Format Date/Time to military time (3/31/02 18:02). After the Format Editor appears, select the Date and Time tab. Choose the third option in the Style list box that represents date/time as 3/1/99 13:23 because this is the option required, as shown in Figure 19.6.

FIGURE 19.5

The Design tab with six template objects added to the report.

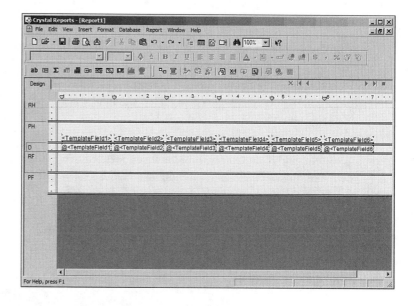

FIGURE 19.6

The Date and Time tab of the Format Editor with Military Date/Time selected.

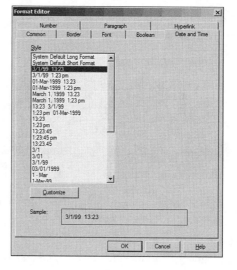

7. Format Number with a space as the thousand separator (1 000). Now select the Number tab in the Format Editor dialog box. Because our style does not appear in the Style list box, select Customize. In the Custom Style dialog box, change the Symbol to ,. Select OK to return to the Format Editor. Select OK again to return to the Design tab with the changes applied (see Figure 19.7).

FIGURE 19.7

*The Custom Style
dialog box with the
space set as the
Thousand Separator
symbol.*

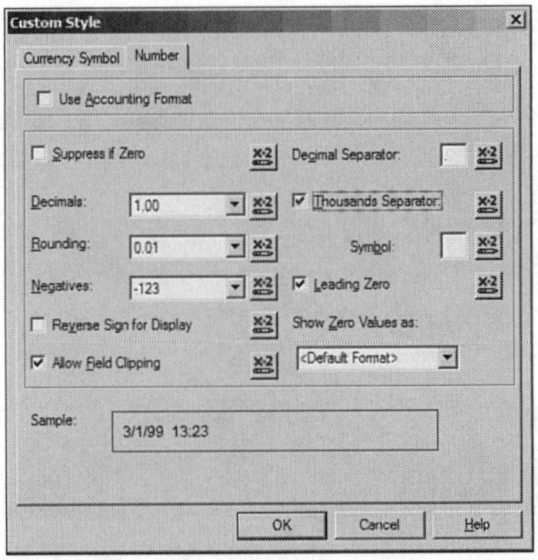

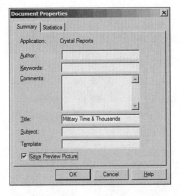

8. Give the template a name and a preview picture. When the report appears in the Template Expert, it will have a name associated with it. The name is saved as the Report Title. To change the Report Title, select File, Summary Info. Input the name **Military Time & Thousands** in to the Title property field and select the Save Preview Picture check box as shown in Figure 19.8. Select OK to continue.

FIGURE 19.8

*The Report Title set
to describe the
Template report.*

19

9. Save the report to the template folder. Choose File, Save As to save the report. Call the report **TemplateObjects.RPT** and place it in the Template folder. The Template folder is usually found at c:\program files\crystal decisions\crystal reports 9\templates. When it is saved, close the report.

10. Open the CHAP5.rpt report. This is the same report we used earlier as our base report. Notice that all the date fields and numbers are in the standard format, as shown in Figure 19.9.

FIGURE **19.9**

FIGURE **19.9**

The Preview tab showing how the report looked when Hour 5's lesson was completed.

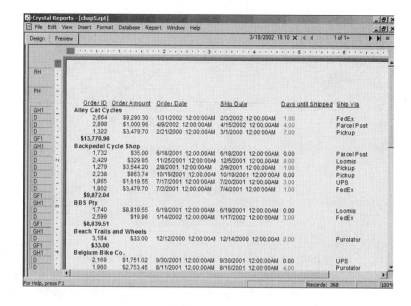

11. Select the template. To select the template that was saved earlier, select Report, Template Expert. Select Military Time & Thousands from the Available Templates list, as shown in Figure 19.10.

FIGURE **19.10**

The Template Expert dialog box with a template selected.

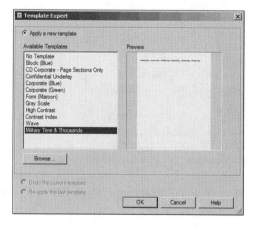

12. To apply the template, simply click the OK button. The report will appear as shown in Figure 19.11.

You will notice that the report appears to close. Do not be alarmed because this is standard behavior. Crystal Reports saves a temporary file with the old look of the report and then applies the template during the new open command.

FIGURE 19.11

The Preview tab showing how the report looked after the template was applied.

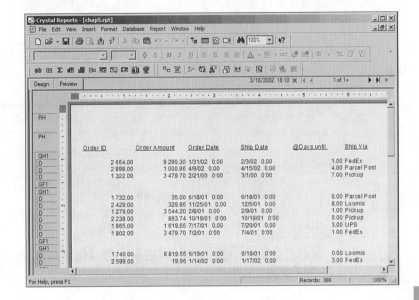

Undoing a template is always an option. If for some reason, you do not like the look that the applied template has given to your report, just return to the Template Expert and choose the Undo command at the bottom of the dialog box. Selecting this option and then clicking OK lets Crystal Reports revert to the original report before the template was applied.

Crystal Reports accomplishes this by opening up the temporary backup RPT that it saved before applying the template file.

13. Save the report. Choose File, Save As, call the report
    CHAP5_templateapplied.rpt, and click OK.

Notice that there was no need to know where the date and numeric fields were located in the report because the Template Field Objects were all formatted to handle the different requirements for the different fields. Using Template Field Objects along with the other template tips mentioned in the hour will make report design quick and easy.

19

Preview Pictures

During the previous exercise, you might have noticed that the intended template did not show a preview picture on the right of the dialog window. This can be caused by one of two situations. The Save Preview Picture option in the Document Properties dialog box was not selected. If that option had been checked and the thumbnail still did not appear, it is because the template report was not saved with a Preview.

In the example that was just completed, the template report was not previewed before the report was saved.

Preview Pictures, or *thumbnails* as they are commonly called, are just that—Pictures of the Preview of the report. If a report has not been previewed, it will not have the thumbnail to save.

Another key point to notice on Preview Pictures is that if changes are made in the design of the template and then a save is done, the changes will not be reflected in the thumbnail because the Preview tab was not updated with the changes.

Preview Pictures are very useful in the Template Expert because these images provide the report designer with a visualization of what the template will do to the existing report. In order to have them saved as a default with all reports, select the Save Preview Picture option in File, Options under the Reporting tab.

Using Report Templates to Reduce Report Creation Effort

So far in this hour, the focus has been on new features and functions that can be used to create templates. Templates can accomplish many of the more intense designer-related tasks, including

- Conditional formatting
- Field highlighting
- Page headers/footers
- Charting standards
- Lines/boxes/borders
- Color standards
- Logos and images
- Web sites/hyperlinks/email addresses
- Standard custom functions
- Repository objects

- Locking size or position of any object
- Special fields

Applying Multiple Templates

Because any report could be used as a template, it is also conceivable that many reports could be applied to any single report as a template.

This can prove quite useful if the templates are doing different things. For example, one template might be applying the standard page headers and footers to all reports within a company, whereas another template could be used to apply department-based colors to the details section. Because both templates are encapsulated separately, they can be applied separately and will not affect each other. The end result is one report with both the corporate style (headers and footers) as well as the specific department's colors (in the Details section) applied.

Templates can be applied repeatedly, even if new fields are added to the report after the initial template was applied.

Simply choose Reapply Template in the Template Expert to have the template address any new fields.

Summary

Report Templates can be used to improve productivity in Report Design by allowing designers to handle formatting once and apply their changes to many reports with the click of a button.

No special knowledge is required to create templates because they are simply report files. However, Template Fields Objects can be used to take template creation to the next level.

Applying templates to existing reports is a straightforward step using the Template Expert, and the Expert also gives a preview of what the end result of the report will look like—taking the guess work out of formatting. By using customizable templates, report designers can now focus their efforts on getting the right information out of the data instead of spending countless hours formatting and reformatting their reports.

19

Workshop

The quiz questions and activities are provided for your further understanding of the current hour's topics.

Quiz

1. What feature can be used to replace more formulas to reduce search-and-replace tasks when creating templates?

2. What file extension does a template have?

3. What two steps must be done in order to have a thumbnail appear in the Template Expert for a given template?

Quiz Answers

1. Custom Functions by way of the Formula Extractor

2. .RPT (A template can be any report file)

3. Save Preview Picture must be selected in Document Properties, and a Preview tab must have been available when the report was saved.

Activities

Look through the templates that come standard with Crystal Reports and change them as you see fit to be more useful to your needs. On a typical installation, the default template directory can be found at `C:\Program Files\Crystal Decisions\Crystal Reports 9\Templates`.

PART V

Advanced Report Design Concepts

Hour

Hour **20**

Multidimensional Reporting Against OLAP Data

Through the first 19 hours, you have been exposed to a wide variety of the reporting capabilities found in Crystal Reports version 9. Up to this point, however, all the reports you have created were based on relational data sources—otherwise known as *Online Transactional Processing (OLTP)* databases—where most organizations generally keep their operational data.

In many organizations and for many people today, data reporting ends with Crystal Reports pointing at existing relational data sources such as Microsoft SQL Server, Oracle, DB2, Sybase, or even Microsoft Access. All these relational databases have been designed for the efficient storage of information. These databases were not designed optimally however for the efficient extraction of data for aggregated analysis across multiple dimensions—that is where OLAP databases excel.

OLAP stands for *Online Analytical Processing* and is designed to allow business users to quickly identify patterns and trends in their data while reporting against multiple dimensions at once. Examples of dimensions for analysis include time, geographic region, product line, financial measure, customer, supplier, salesperson, and so on. Crystal Reports 9 provides exciting new OLAP-based reporting capabilities. These will be introduced in this hour, in addition to a brief introduction to Crystal Report's OLAP-centric sister product—Crystal Analysis.

In this hour, the following will be covered:

- Introduction to OLAP concepts and OLAP Reporting
- New OLAP features in Crystal Reports 9
- Creation of OLAP-based Crystal Reports
- Introduction to Crystal Analysis

Introduction to OLAP Concepts and OLAP Reporting

OLAP is an analysis-oriented technology that enables rapid analysis of large sets of aggregated data. Instead of representing information in the common two-dimensional row and column format of traditional relational databases, OLAP databases store their aggregated data in logical structures called *hypercubes*—more commonly referenced simply as *cubes*. These OLAP cubes are created around specific business areas or problems and contain an appropriate number of dimensions to satisfy analysis in that particular area of interest or for a specific business issue. OLAP is a technology that facilitates data viewing, analysis, and navigation. More than a particular storage technology, OLAP is a conceptual model for viewing and analyzing data. Table 20.1 highlights some common business areas and typical sets of related dimensions.

TABLE 20.1 Business Areas and Commonly Associated OLAP Dimensions

Business Area	Associated Business and Common OLAP Dimensions
Sales	Sales Employees, Products, Regions, Sales Channels, Time, Customers, Measures
Finance	Company Divisions, Regions, Products, Time, Measures
Manufacturing	Suppliers, Product Parts, Plants, Products, Time, Measures

OLAP cubes pre-aggregate data at the intersection points of all of their associated dimension's members. A *member* is a valid field value for a dimension. (For example: Members of a time dimension could be 2000, 2001, Q1, or Q2; and members of a product dimension could be Gadget1, Gizmo2, DooDah1, and so on.) This pre-aggregation facilitates the speed-of-thought analysis associated with OLAP.

Precalculating all the numbers at the intersection points of all of an OLAP cube's associated dimension members enables rapid high-level analysis of large volumes of underlying data that would not be practical with traditional relational databases. Considering the example of analysis on several years of sales data by year, quarter, and month and by region, sales manager, and product, the preaggregated nature of OLAP facilitates quick speed-of-thought analysis on this data that otherwise would not be practical working with the phenomenal amount of storage space required in a traditional relational (OLTP) database system.

When a Crystal Report uses an OLAP cube as a data source, it will present the multidimensional data in a two-dimensional OLAP Grid that resembles a spreadsheet or crosstab. The focus of Crystal Reports when reporting against OLAP cubes is to present professionally formatted two-dimensional (or flat) views of the multidimensional data that will be of particular business use for report consuming end users and not necessarily analysts.

The concepts of OLAP usually become more understandable once they are actually explored. To that end, later sections in this hour will step you through a Crystal Reports report creation example against an OLAP cube.

New OLAP Features in Crystal Reports 9

This section is specifically targeted for users of previous versions of Crystal Reports. Table 20.2 lists the new OLAP oriented features of version 9 and their practical use or benefit. If you are a new user to Crystal Reports or you have not previously used the OLAP reporting features in the product, you might want to skip directly to the next section.

20

TABLE 20.2   New OLAP Features in Crystal Reports 9

NEW OLAP Feature	Feature Benefit and Value
Filter/Page Dimension Parameter links	This Productivity feature enables for the direct linking of report parameters to pages and filters in the OLAP grid.

TABLE 20.2 continued

NEW OLAP Feature	Feature Benefit and Value
	This enables the end user to dynamically specify the values of filters and pages in the OLAP grid. The feature is accessed in either the OLAP Report Creation Wizard or the OLAP Report Settings option under the Report menu.
Interactive OLAP Worksheet (Analyzer) in new Cube tab	The New OLAP Analyzer feature (a Cube tab in Crystal Reports Designer) is accessed by right-clicking on an existing OLAP grid object and selecting the Launch Analyzer option. The Cube tab provides a fully functioning drag-and-drop OLAP worksheet that enables rapid selection of the most appropriate OLAP viewpoint for the Crystal Report. All changes made in the Analyzer worksheet are reflected in the associated Crystal Reports OLAP grid, where advanced formatting can be applied.
Interactive drill-down of OLAP grids in Preview Tab	The OLAP grid presented in the Crystal Reports Preview tab has now been made more fully functional. In addition to having access to advanced OLAP grid functionality from the right-click button including calculations, exception highlighting,

TABLE 20.2 continued

NEW OLAP Feature	Feature Benefit and Value
	sorting, filtering, and member reordering, the OLAP grid now enables the report designer to expand (drill-down) and contract members directly from within the Preview tab.
New and improved data sources	At the time of writing, it was expected that Crystal Reports 9 would have improved and flexible OLAP connectivity to Hyperion Essbase and new connectivity to SAP BW.

The following sections explore the creation of an OLAP report through the OLAP Report Creation Wizard, the added value of the OLAP Expert, and the advanced interactivity features of version 9.

OLAP Report Creation Wizard and OLAP Expert

Crystal Reports 9 provides two easy ways to create reports against OLAP data sources. As introduced in Hour 4, "Using the Default Report Wizards," Crystal provides several report wizards to step you through the creation of some popular types of reports—one of those is OLAP. The OLAP Wizard involves five steps/screens and walks you through the process of creating an OLAP grid and an optional supporting graphic based on an existing data source. The OLAP Wizard is accessible when you are creating a new report.

The second method of creating an OLAP based report is through the OLAP Expert that is accessed from the Insert OLAP Grid on the Insert menu. This expert provides six tabs that step through the creation of an OLAP grid to be placed anywhere on a report.

The two methods of creation offer very similar degrees of functionality, and their respective dialog screens and tabs are almost identical. The OLAP Report Creation Wizard does provide a built-in Charting screen not found in the OLAP Expert, whereas the OLAP Expert provides Style Customization and Label tabs not found in the OLAP Wizard.

20

Although Crystal Reports has been designed to report off of numerous multidimensional\OLAP databases including Hyperion Essbase, Microsoft SQL Server Analysis Services, and SAP BW, for the purposes of demonstration in this hour, examples will be based on the SQL Server sample cube—FoodMart. If a different OLAP Database is available, the general principles should be followed against that native OLAP cube.

Specifying an OLAP Data Source

The OLAP Data tab (or screen in the OLAP Wizard) requests the OLAP data source on which the report is to be based. This wizard and its associated dialog screens are to multidimensional data sources what the data explorer, introduced in Hour 3, "Accessing Your Data," is to relational data. Figure 20.1 shows the OLAP Data screen from the OLAP Wizard.

FIGURE 20.1

The OLAP Data dialog from the OLAP Report Creation Wizard.

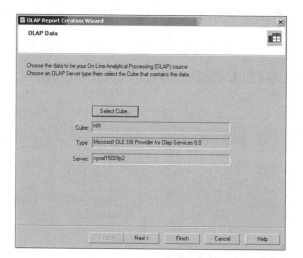

When this tab/screen is first displayed, a cube will need to be selected with the Select Cube button. Clicking on this button brings up the Crystal OLAP Connection Browser, which is displayed in Figure 20.2. From the tree control presented in this dialog, the desired cube is selected.

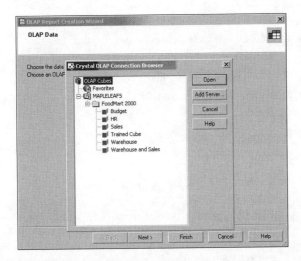

FIGURE 20.2
Crystal OLAP Connection Browser.

To help you learn about the creation of an OLAP based Crystal Report, here are the introductory steps to doing exactly that against SQL Server's sample FoodMart cube. Other steps will follow these initial steps after subsequent tabs/screens have been explained:

1. Create a New Crystal Report and select the OLAP Wizard from the Crystal Reports Gallery dialog.

2. Click the Select Cube button from the OLAP Data dialog.

3. Assuming that the location of the OLAP Server has not already been identified to the Crystal OLAP Connection Browser, Click the Add Server button and identify the location of your SQL Server Analysis Server and the sample HR cube. Figure 20.3 highlights the New Server dialog.

FIGURE 20.3
The New Server dialog is used to connect to new OLAP data sources.

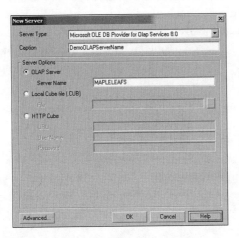

20

4. Enter a caption for the OLAP Server you will be adding. This caption will appear in the Crystal OLAP Connection Browser. Enter the name of the SQL Server Analysis Server for the server name and click OK.

5. Back in the Crystal OLAP Connection Browser, navigate into the presented listing of servers (there will likely only be the one you just added) and double-click on the sample HR cube.

6. Click the Next button to proceed..

On the Data Screen of the OLAP Report Creation Wizard, in addition to the Select Cube button, a Select CAR File button exists. CAR files are *Crystal Analytic Reports (CAR)* and are created with the sister product to Crystal Reports—Crystal Analysis. This product is an OLAP-focused reporting and application tool and will be briefly introduced later in this hour. These CAR files can be treated as multidimensional data sources because they themselves contain connectivity information to an underlying OLAP data source.

At this point, we will review the concept of Rows and Columns in our OLAP report.

Specifying OLAP Rows and Columns

The Rows/Columns dialog screen enables the selection of both the dimensions and fields to be presented along the columns and rows of the OLAP grid. All the available dimensions in the selected cube/data source are listed in the Dimensions list box depicted in Figure 20.4.

To select a dimension for placement in the rows section or the columns section of the OLAP grid, highlight the desired dimension and click either the column or row arrow (>) button. It is possible to select multiple dimensions to be displayed and have these nested in the OLAP Grid by successively selecting multiple dimensions for either the rows or the columns section. It is also possible to remove dimensions from the existing row or column list boxes; however, the column and row dimension list boxes cannot be left empty.

After the desired dimensions are selected, a subset of the fields (also known as *members*) for those dimensions can be selected using the Select Row Field or Select Column Field buttons. Examples of this might be selecting only a certain subset of provinces or states in a region dimension or, alternatively, selecting only a certain year's worth of data in a time dimension. By highlighting a dimension in either of the Rows or Columns list box and then selecting the appropriate Selection button, a subset of the members for the involved dimension can be selected from the Member Selector dialog as depicted in Figure 20.5.

FIGURE 20.4

The Rows/Columns dialog of the OLAP Report Creation Wizard.

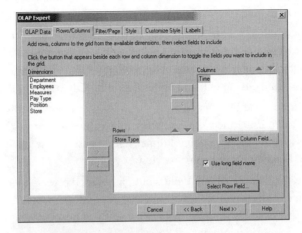

FIGURE 20.5

The Member Selector dialog.

The Member Selector dialog provides some powerful shortcuts for the selection of certain logical groups of members. These selection shortcuts are accessed through either the Select drop-down box or by right-clicking on any part of the Member Selection list box. Example selection shortcuts include the ability to select all base level members or all members at a highlighted level.

20

Continuing with the creation of the sample report started in the last section, the following steps walk through the Rows/Columns Screen part of this report creation example and allow for the refinement of the data to be viewed in the OLAP grid:

1. Select the Store Type Dimension from the available dimensions list as the Row Dimension using the Row Dimension Arrow Button. (Note: It will likely be necessary to remove a default dimension to ensure that this is the only dimension in the Row Dimensions list view.)

2. Using the Select Row Field's button, select all the Store Types (for example, Supermarket, Headquarters, and so on) from the Member Selection dialog, but deselect the aggregated top level All Stores field. This will enable the OLAP grid to present all the different store types down the side of the grid as rows.

3. Select the Time Dimension from the available dimensions list as the Column Dimension using the Column Dimension arrow (>) button. (Note: It will likely be necessary to remove a default dimension to ensure that this is the only dimension in the Column Dimensions list view.)

4. Using the Select Column Field's button, select the years 1997 and 1998 from the Member Selection dialog, but deselect all children members for these members. This will enable the OLAP grid to present a comparison of the two years data in two side-by-side columns.

5. Click the Next button to proceed.

At this point, we will review the concept of OLAP dimension filters and pages in our OLAP report.

Specifying OLAP Dimension Filters and Pages

The Filters/Page dialog, shown in Figure 20.6, of the OLAP Report Creation Wizard enables the selection of values or members for the dimensions that were not selected to be row or column dimensions. In the OLAP world, these dimensions are often called *paged dimensions*.

The Filter list box lists all the paged dimensions and their current member settings. The default setting is usually all members for any given dimension. An example is that for the Store Dimension, the default slice setting is All Stores. To change the member selection (filter) for a particular dimension, that dimension must be selected in the Filter list box and the Select Filter Value button must be used to bring up the familiar Member Selection dialog (see Figure 20.5). This dialog is identical to the Member Selection dialog used previously except that only one member from the selected dimension can be selected. If multiple members from a paged dimension are required in a report, the Page list box should be used.

FIGURE 20.6

The Filter/Page screen of the OLAP Report Creation Wizard.

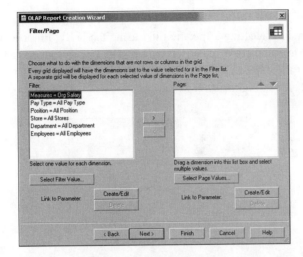

The Page list box is initially empty but can contain any dimensions outside the row and column dimensions that require multiple member selection. An example could involve selecting the three countries of North America as store regions. The selection of multiple values for a paged dimension creates completely separate grids (based on the same preselected rows and columns) for each selected member value. To select multiple members for a dimension, the involved dimension needs to be selected in the Filter list box and moved to the Page list box using the transfer arrow buttons between the list boxes. Once moved to the Page list box, the Select Page Values button enables multiple member selection through the Member Selection dialog.

The last, but perhaps most powerful, feature of the Filter/Page screen is the Link to Parameter functionality provided for each of the Filtered and Paged dimensions. This capability provides the business user or report consumer with the ability to interact with the report and control its content by entering parameters that directly affect the information displayed in the OLAP grid(s) on the report.

Because Hour 12, "Implementing Parameters for Dynamic Reporting," has already covered parameters in detail, you are likely familiar with this topic already. Of significance for this wizard screen is that the parameter creation process is directly accessible here, and this facilitates the rapid development of formatted and interactive OLAP reports. If necessary, review Hour 12 for a refresher on creating and editing parameters.

Continuing with the creation of the sample report, the following steps walk through the Filter/Page dialog part of this report creation example and will enable the business user to select the measure that will be displayed in the OLAP grid:

20

1. Select the Measures dimension from the Filter list box.

2. Instead of selecting a specific filter using the Select Filter Value button, click the Link to Parameter Create/Edit button to enable the business user to dynamically select this filter every time the report is run. The Edit Parameter Field dialog, as displayed in Figure 20.7, will appear.

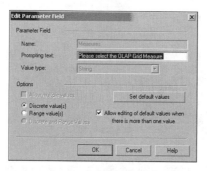

FIGURE 20.7

The Edit Parameter Field dialog called from Filter/Page screen.

3. In the Prompting Text text box, enter the text that you want your user to be prompted with when this report is run. In this case, it could be something similar to Please select the Measure to be used in your report. Also, ensure that the Discrete Value(s) radio button is selected because a range of entries is not required (or allowed) here.

4. To avoid the requirement of the user needing to type in any text, defaults can be set so that selection from a drop-down box is possible. To do this, click the Select Default button and the dialog in Figure 20.8 will appear.

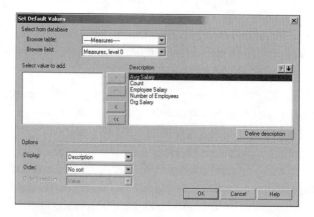

FIGURE 20.8

The Set Default Values dialog.

5. The Measures table will be preselected because the report understands the links that are being made based on your previously highlighted dimension. Select the level 0 field in the table drop-down box. (There will only be one option here because only one level is available in this dimension.)

6. Move all the member values presented to Description list box by clicking on the double arrow (>>) button. Note that the program automatically displays the more meaningful member descriptions instead of the more cryptic long names.

7. Ensure that the Display drop-down box has Description selected and that the Order drop-down box has no order selected. Click OK twice to get back to the Filter/Page dialog of the OLAP Report Creation Wizard.

8. Once back, highlight the Pay Type dimension in the Filter list box and click the arrow transfer/select button to move this to the Page list box. The Member Selection dialog will immediately appear with the Pay Type Dimension Hierarchy presented.

9. Select the Hourly and Monthly pay types (children of All Pay Types) and deselect the All Pay Types field. Page views (individual OLAP Grids) will now be created for each of the monthly paid employees and the hourly paid employees. If this isn't clear now, it should make more sense when we are visualizing the report.

10. Click OK and then Next to proceed.

After Parameters or Multi-Value Paged Dimensions have been set in the OLAP Report Creation Wizard, you must access the OLAP Report Settings option under the main Report menu to edit them. These settings are not configurable in the OLAP Expert.

At this point, we will review the concept of styles in our OLAP report.

Adding Report Styles in the OLAP Report Wizard

20

The Style dialog in the OLAP Report Creation Wizard enables the selection of any one of a predetermined number of styles for OLAP Grids available in Crystal Reports 9. Figure 20.9 displays the Style dialog. The styles are often considered a good starting point for formatting the OLAP Grids on your reports and can be enhanced through both the Customize Style tab of the OLAP Expert (described later in the hour) and using many of the advanced formatting features you have already learned about.

FIGURE 20.9

The Style dialog of the OLAP Report Creation Wizard.

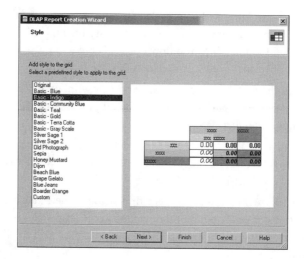

Adding Charts Via the OLAP Report Wizard

The Chart dialog provided in the OLAP Report Creation Wizard allows for the quick addition of a graphic to the OLAP report being created. The graphics available in this wizard, as shown in Figure 20.10, are only a subset of the graphics available (refer back to Hour 11, "Visualizing Your Data with Charts and Maps," for a refresher) in Crystal Reports 9, but they do enable the rapid visualization of your OLAP data without the need for using the Chart Expert.

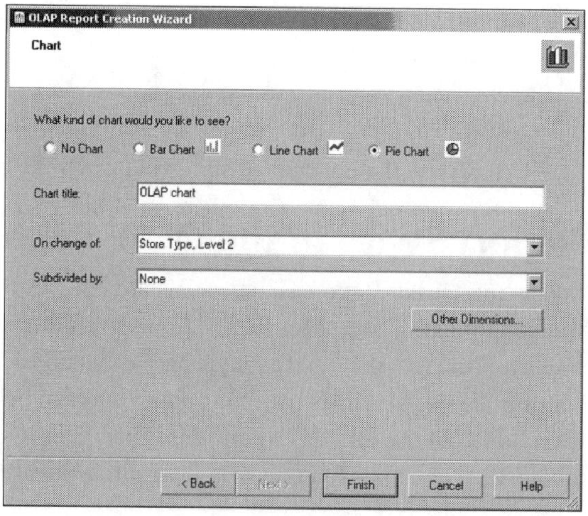

FIGURE 20.10

The Chart dialog of OLAP Report Creation Wizard.

Aside from selecting the type of chart (bar, line, or pie) and specifying a title on this screen, an On Change Of field must be specified with an optional Subdivided By field before this screen is complete. As Hour 11 previously discussed, the On Change Of field is the field in your data source that will provide the breaking point for the involved graphic. Examples could include country, region, year, store, product, and so on. The Subdivided By field can provide a second variable to base your charts on. An example of a two-variable OLAP Chart using the FoodMart sample cube would be a chart showing salary information by store type and then subdivided by year. Using pie charts, Figure 20.11 displays what that might look like.

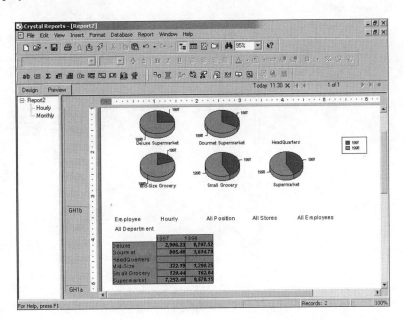

FIGURE 20.11

A two-variable OLAP Chart.

Now, to complete the OLAP report creation process, the following steps will take us through the addition of a style, a chart, and the creation of the finished report:

1. On the Style dialog, select any style that suits your preference and Click the Next button.

2. On the Chart dialog, select Pie Chart as the Chart Type by selecting the radio button associated with that chart type. This will provide a nice way of visualizing comparables across different store types.

3. Provide your chart with a title similar to `Hour 20 Sample OLAP Report` by entering this in to the Chart Title text box.

20

4. Select Store Type as the On Change Of field. This will facilitate the comparison of the six different store types. Leave the Subdivided By drop-down field empty.

5. Click Finish on the OLAP Report Creation Wizard. You will be prompted to select a parameter for the Measure dimension. After selecting Average Salary (or another field if you prefer), a report will be generated that should look similar to Figure 20.12.

FIGURE 20.12

The sample OLAP Report created using the OLAP Wizard.

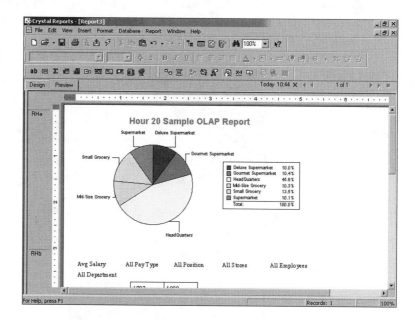

The OLAP Report Creation Wizard provides an efficient and effective method to getting value out of OLAP data in a short timeframe. After an OLAP grid or OLAP Chart has been placed on your report through the wizard, further formatting and analysis can be performed through a variety of built-in Crystal Reports formatting tools. The next two sections explore further customization options and the three subsequent sections discuss the powerful new interactivity available in Crystal Reports 9 OLAP objects.

Customizing Styles in the OLAP Expert

After an OLAP grid has been added to a report, with or without a selected style, Crystal Reports provides the ability to enhance and customize the formatting of that grid through the Customize Style tab accessed on the OLAP Expert. The OLAP Expert dialog is displayed in Figure 20.13 and is accessed by right-clicking on an existing OLAP Grid object or by selecting the Insert OLAP Grid option from the Insert menu.

FIGURE 20.13

The OLAP Expert dialog.

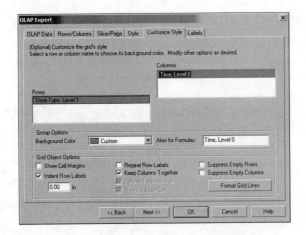

Four of the tabs in the OLAP Expert have identical functionality as presented in the previous Report Wizard sections. The Customize Style tab highlighted in Figure 20.13 however, is unique to the OLAP Expert and provides the ability to fine-tune the formatting of the Row and Column dimensions selected for the involved OLAP grid. By selecting any of the column or row dimensions from the presented list boxes, custom colors can be selected for the backgrounds of the OLAP grid row and column headings. This tab also provides a number of formatting options for the presentation of the grid including indentation, blank column/row suppression, margins, and labels. Also provided is an option to format grid lines, shown in Figure 20.14. This dialog enables granular level formatting and selection of grid lines for display on the OLAP grid's layout.

FIGURE 20.14

The Format Grid Lines dialog.

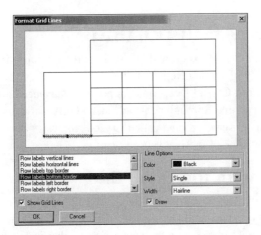

20

Customizing Labels in the OLAP Expert

The Labels tab of the OLAP expert, shown in Figure 20.15, provides the ability to customize the display of the paged-dimension (non row/column dimensions) labels on the OLAP grid.

FIGURE 20.15

*The Labels tab of
OLAP Expert.*

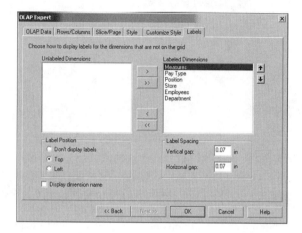

Paged Dimension member values for the display grid can or cannot be displayed by simply moving the selected dimension between the unlabeled dimension and labeled dimension list boxes using the transfer arrow (>, >>, <, <<) buttons. Additional labeling options—such as label location, label spacing, and dimension names—can also be selected in this tab.

Advanced OLAP Reporting

Up to this point, the OLAP Expert and OLAP Report Creation Wizard have demonstrated the capability of Crystal Reports to rapidly create OLAP based reports. More than these capabilities, Crystal Decisions has provided advanced analytic capabilities against OLAP data sources through some advanced OLAP-oriented features in Crystal Reports and through a sister product called Crystal Analysis. The last four sections of this hour introduce some of these advanced features.

Interacting with the OLAP Grid

Crystal Reports provides some powerful interactive OLAP features from directly within the Crystal Reports Preview and Design tabs. Figure 20.16 displays the right-click menu that appears when right-clicking on the year 1998 member in this hour's sample report.

FIGURE 20.16
Advanced OLAP features provided in the right-click menu.

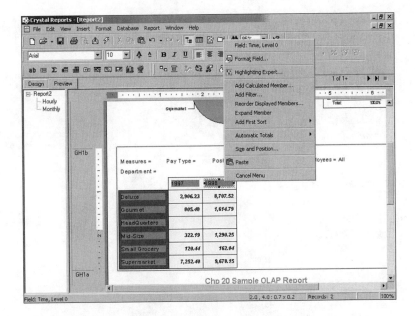

Advanced features made available here include conditional member highlighting, adding calculations, adding filters, reordering members, expanding members, adding sorts, and adding automatic totals to the OLAP grid. Although exploring these features in detail is beyond the scope of this book, it is important to note their availability for enhancing your OLAP grid presentations and reports.

One feature of note is the active nature of the column and row dimensions in the OLAP grid. By double-clicking on any member in either the row or column headings—and assuming that the selected member has lower level members (children)—the OLAP grid will dynamically expand to include that member's children in the grid. In OLAP parlance, this is called *drilling-down*. Figure 20.17 highlights the result of drilling-down on the 1998 Header in this hour's sample report.

A dimension member can subsequently have its children contracted by double-clicking on the parent member. This feature enables the report designer to interactively determine the best static viewpoint to provide to the business user audience for the report.

Pivoting OLAP Grids

After an OLAP grid has been added to a report, as in this hour's sample, Crystal Reports has provided the ability to easily swap the grid's columns and rows. In OLAP parlance, this is referred to as *pivoting* the OLAP grid. Figure 20.18 highlights this hour's sample report after being pivoted with this function. To access this function, right-click on the

20

OLAP grid and select the Pivot OLAP Grid option. Pivoting the OLAP grid will not affect any OLAP charts or maps already on the report.

FIGURE 20.17

Sample OLAP based report with 1998 member's children expanded.

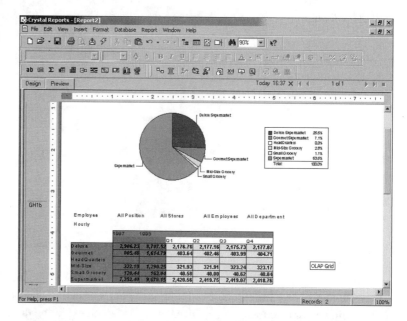

FIGURE 20.18

A preview of the sample report after pivoting the OLAP grid.

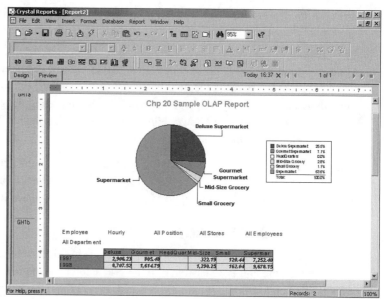

This function is particularly useful when attempting to decide which viewpoint of the involved OLAP grid will be most useful to your business users of the report.

Using the OLAP Analyzer

The OLAP Analyzer is a powerful worksheet analysis tool new to version 9 of Crystal Reports. The OLAP Analyzer is initiated through the Launch Analyzer option on the right-click menu of the OLAP grid (make sure that you don't have any specific grid objects selected) and is exposed through a new tab, titled Cube View, in the Crystal Reports Designer (see Figure 20.19). Report designers and analysts familiar with other OLAP interface tools will be instantly comfortable with the Analyzer because it provides access to the OLAP cube through a traditional OLAP worksheet.

FIGURE 20.19

The Cube View tab launched by the OLAP Analyzer.

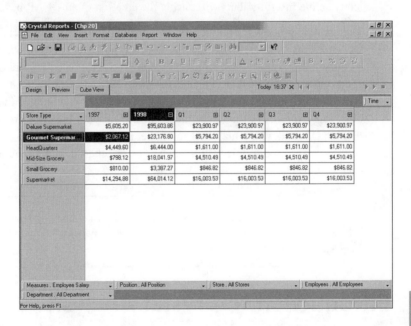

Unlike the OLAP grid presented in the Crystal Reports Preview tab, the Cube View tab's worksheet is designed for rapid analysis of the underlying OLAP data through a rich and interactive interface not available in the OLAP grid. Dimensions can be rapidly shifted, swapped, and nested by double-clicking on them and dragging them into any of the row, column, or paged dimension areas. Dimension members can be quickly expanded and contracted by clicking on their associated + or – icons. Additional calculations, sorts, filters, automatic totaling, exception highlighting, and custom captions can also be accessed through a right-click menu in the OLAP Analyzer view of the cube.

20

This new Cube View in version 9 is a powerful new report design tool because it lets Crystal Reports developers create some very powerful flat views of the underlying multi-dimensional/OLAP data in a very short timeframe and subsequently format the created OLAP grid in the Preview tab.

Using Charts and Maps Based on OLAP Grids

As alluded to in Hour 11 and discussed briefly in the "Adding Charts in the OLAP Report Wizard" section earlier, OLAP grid data can be presented through visually appealing charts and maps. To create either a chart or a map based on OLAP data, an OLAP grid must pre-exist on your report as a data source for the chart/map to be based on. Selecting the Insert Chart or Map command from the Insert menu (or the respective icons on the Insert toolbar) will enable the creation of an OLAP-based visualization.

The creation process for both charts and maps requires the specification of an On Change Of field. This is the field that the chart or map will break its summaries on (for example, country, state, product, sales rep, and so on). An additional optional Sub-divided On field can be specified as well. The results on specifying an extra variable to divide the data on will have different results for various chart types. It is encouraged that these different charts are explored to find those most suitable for your business problem. Using the Sub-divided On field with a map will add either a bar or pie chart to every main region on the selected map. An example of this might be a pie chart depicting the breakup of sales for each country.

It is imperative that the On Change Of field be a geographic based field when creating a map. Otherwise, the mapping component will return an empty map.

Introduction to Crystal Analysis

Crystal Analysis Professional is a new reporting tool from Crystal Decisions that enables organizations to deliver action-based OLAP analysis to business users. It enables better insights to help decision makers affect business performance through interactive analysis. Crystal Analysis Professional takes OLAP reporting to the next level by allowing report designers to create intuitive and highly interactive reports that offer a guided analysis approach to business issues.

Power users implementing Crystal Analysis can create analytical reports, based on OLAP data, using a powerful designer (similar in concept to Crystal Reports). Crystal Analytic Reports can contain many pages, each presenting a different predefined view of the OLAP cube. Data can be presented in tables or visualized through a wide range of charts, exception highlights, data sorts, filters, and/or analytic transition buttons. Business managers can use the resulting analytical reports to drive the business decisions they need to make every day. Figure 20.20 displays a sample analytic report created in Crystal Analysis Professional. These reports, in the same manner as Crystal Reports files, can be published to, secured, managed, and distributed by the Crystal Enterprise solution—also available from Crystal Decisions. For more details on Crystal Enterprise, see Hour 23, "Distributing Crystal Reports."

FIGURE 20.20

A Sample Crystal Analysis report that includes an OLAP grid, chart objects, and several transition buttons for guided analysis.

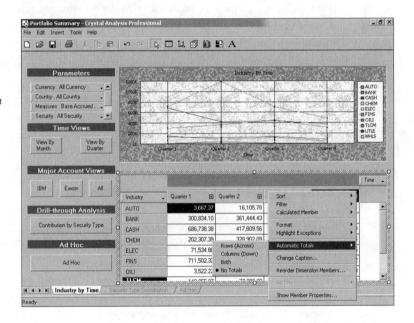

Although the details of Crystal Analysis are beyond the scope of this book, it is a tool worth investigating if highly interactive analytic reports for OLAP data sources are requirements for any given project you are involved in.

20

Summary

In this hour, the difference between *Online Transactional Processing (OLTP)* and *Online Analytical Processing databases (OLAP)* was introduced. Most organizations generally keep their operational data in relational OLTP databases. Increasingly, however, organizations are moving aggregations of their relational data into multidimensional (OLAP) data stores to facilitate high level speed-of-thought analysis of key business issues. The multidimensional nature of OLAP data sources like Microsoft SQL Server Analysis Services or Hyperion Essbase permits this rapid analysis of aggregated data.

Crystal Reports 9 provides exciting new OLAP based reporting capabilities that facilitate the presentation of professionally formatted OLAP sourced reports. The OLAP Report Creation Wizard and OLAP Expert enable quick and flexible OLAP grid creation, and the Crystal Reports charting and mapping tools provide a means to visualize the data in meaningful ways.

Q&A

Q Can a Crystal Report contain an OLAP grid sourced from an OLAP data source and additional data sourced from a separate relational data source in the same report?

A Yes—Crystal Reports can present both OLAP-sourced data and relationally sourced data within the same Crystal Report. To accomplish this, create your original report based on the desired relational database and then subsequently insert an OLAP grid to the desired place in your report.

Q Are the new and advanced OLAP features in Crystal Reports intended to replace the need for a separate OLAP Analysis tool?

A No—Crystal Reports is an advanced and powerful reporting tool that meets the business intelligence requirements of most business users in an organization. Advanced analysis tools, such as Crystal Analysis Professional, are more appropriate for those employees in an organization that require advanced analytics. The advanced OLAP features in Crystal Reports are designed to enable Crystal Report designers to provide meaningful and professionally formatted reports to their business users—not fully interactive analytic tools. Crystal Analysis Professional adds greater interactivity for business users and more flexible integration with market-leading OLAP data sources for report designers.

Workshop

The quiz questions and activity are provided for your further understanding of the current hour's topics.

Quiz

1. What does the OLAP acronym stand for?
2. What advantage do OLAP databases have over OLTP databases?
3. Does Crystal Reports provide the ability to add additional calculations and formulas to OLAP grids?

Quiz Answers

1. OLAP stands for Online Analytical Processing. OLAP databases are aggregations of underlying relational data and facilitate end-user analysis.

2. Because OLAP databases are pre-aggregated along dimensions that have been identified as being useful for analysis, they are designed for end-user analysis. Similar forms of analysis on OLTP databases can be complex and time-consuming because OLTP databases were primarily designed for storing information.

3. Yes—through the Add Calculation option in the right-click menu in both the OLAP Grid (Preview tab) and the Cube tab, additional calculations not stored in the OLAP cube can be added to the Crystal Report's OLAP grid.

Activity

Now that you have been introduced to OLAP reporting and assuming that you have access to a multidimensional cube, practice your report design skills by creating a report that uses both relational data and OLAP data by adding an OLAP grid to an existing relational report.

20

HOUR 21

Additional Data Sources for Crystal Reports

When thinking about data sources for Crystal Reports, most people tend to think about popular databases such as Microsoft SQL Server, Microsoft Access, Oracle, IBM DB2, and so on. However, the extent of Crystal Reports reaches far beyond these traditional relational databases. You've already learned about how Crystal Reports can use OLAP-based data sources in Hour 20, "Multidimensional Reporting Against OLAP Data;" this hour will describe a few more advanced data sources that give you even more flexibility than you already have. The data sources discussed in this hour are as follows:

- COM-based data sources
- Java-based data sources
- XML as a data source
- Solution kits

COM-based Data Sources

Crystal Reports provides direct access or *native* drivers for some databases. These drivers are written specifically for a particular database and are often the best choice. However, because hundreds of types of databases exist, Crystal Decisions can't possibly write direct access drivers for all of them. So often, users turn to using standard data access layers such as ODBC or OLEDB to connect to their databases. Often, the vendor of a database will provide an ODBC driver or OLEDB provider so that other applications can access the vendor's database. Sometimes though, even this is not enough. Customers have data that they would like to report off of that is not accessible by any Crystal Reports data source driver or via ODBC or OLEDB. To this, customers often turn to the COM Data Source driver or the Java Data Source driver. This section describes the COM version of the driver, but much of the theory applies to the Java Data Source driver as well.

> COM, or the *Component Object Model*, is a Microsoft-based technology for software component development. It's the underlying technology that runs things such as Visual Basic and Active Server Pages. A *COM object* is a piece of code that adheres to the COM specification and is easily used by other components, both inside a single application or between disparate applications.

Because COM is a popular technology, Crystal Decisions decided to leverage it to create an extensible data source driver mechanism. This COM Data Source driver doesn't connect to a database—rather it gets data from a COM object written by you. This means that if you are somewhat savvy in the Visual Basic world, you can write your own "mini data source driver" (called a *COM Data Provider*) that enables access to data that would otherwise be unavailable.

To better understand the concept on writing your own COM Data Provider, let's look at a few scenarios in which this can be beneficial.

Legacy Mainframe Data

Although new technologies are surfacing at an alarming rate, many companies still have data held in legacy mainframe systems. Often, the nature of these systems doesn't allow for any kind of relational data access, and thus lowers the value of the system. However, these systems can often output text-based files containing the data held in them. These text-based files are often more complicated than a set of simple comma separated values and thus require a "bridge" between the files and a data access and reporting tool like Crystal Reports. Writing a COM Data Provider can serve just this purpose. The Data Provider would read the text files, parse out the required data, and return it to Crystal Reports for use in numerous reports.

Complex Queries

Often, companies have a database that is accessible via standard Crystal Reports data access methods. However, the process of connecting to the database and performing a query can be quite complex. Sometimes this is because of database servers constantly changing, queries becoming more complex, and other business processes. By writing a COM Data Provider, a clever person can abstract the location and complexity of the database interaction away from the user designing a report. The user simply connects to the Data Provider, and the rest of the logic is done transparently in the background.

Runtime Manipulation of Data

Performing a simple query against a database that returns a set of records is often all that is needed. However, sometimes logic needs to be incorporated into the query that cannot be expressed in the database query language (using SQL). Other times, per-user manipulation of data needs to be performed, such as removing all salaries stored in a database for all other users than the currently logged in user for confidentiality purposes (often called data-level security). This runtime manipulation can be performed by a COM Data Provider.

These three scenarios outline just a few of the reasons why you might want to use the COM Data Source driver and create your own COM Data Provider. The following sections describe the technical details of doing this.

Creating a COM Data Provider

COM Data Providers can be written in any development language or platform with the capability of creating COM objects. Most commonly, they are created in either Visual Basic or Visual C++. The following example uses Visual Basic, but it can easily be translated to other development languages:

1. Open Visual Basic and create a new project. Instead of choosing the standard project type of Standard EXE, choose ActiveX DLL (see Figure 21.1). ActiveX is another name for COM technology. Doing this creates a project that contains a COM object (by default called Class1).

2. The interface between the COM Data Provider that you will create and the Crystal Reports COM Data Source driver is based on *ActiveX Data Objects*, or *ADO*. To use ADO in your project, you must first create a reference to it. From the Project menu inside Visual Basic, select References. From the list on the ensuing dialog, look for Microsoft ActiveX Data Objects. You might have just a single version of this on your machine, or you might have several. It's usually easiest to just select the latest version. Figure 21.2 illustrates this.

21

FIGURE 21.1

Creating a new Active DLL project in Visual Basic.

FIGURE 21.2

Referencing the ADO Library.

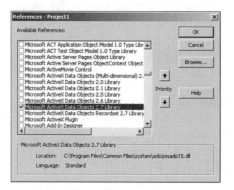

3. After that is done, the only thing left to do is create a function inside your class that returns an ADO recordset. The basic outline for this function is shown here. See the next section for more information on returning an ADO recordset.

```
Public Function GetRecordset() As ADODB.Recordset
    Dim rs As New ADODB.Recordset
    ' Populate the recordset
    Set GetRecordset = rs
End Function
```

4. By default, the class will be named `Class1`. It's best to give this a more meaningful name, such as `DataProvider`. This can be done by selecting the Class1.cls file in the Project Explorer and changing the `(Name)` property from the Property Browser.

5. Also, the project name will be Project1 by default. It's best to give this a more meaningful name such as the company name or type of data name: for example, Xtreme or Sales. This can be done by selecting Project1 Properties from the Project menu and changing the Project Name setting.

6. Build the dll by selecting Make from the the File menu; the name is not important.

7. Open the Crystal Reports designer and create a new report. From the data explorer, choose Create New Connection and then expand the More Data Sources item, then choose COM Connectivity. This will present a dialog asking for you to enter the Program ID. To identify your COM Data Provider, enter the ProjectName.ClassName: for example, Xtreme.DataProvider.

8. You'll receive a table list just like from a traditional database, but the table list is actually a list of methods on your COM object that return ADO recordsets.

Returning an ADO Recordset

There are generally two ways to obtain an ADO recordset: performing a database query and constructing it yourself. The following code example illustrates how to perform a database query and obtain a recordset—in this case using a query against the Xtreme sample database.

```
Public Function CustomerOrders() As ADODB.Recordset
    Dim rs As New ADODB.Recordset
    Dim sql as String
    sql = "SELECT * FROM Customer, Orders WHERE Customer.`Customer ID`"
    sql = sql & " = Orders.`Customer ID`", "DSN=Xtreme Sample Database 9"
    rs.Open sql
    Set CustomerOrders = rs
End Function
```

The question you might be asking yourself is how this query could be parameterized. The COM Data Source driver handles this nicely. It will map any arguments you have defined to your method into report parameters. The following code example illustrates a Data Provider function that has a parameter:

```
Public Function Customers(CountryParam As String) As ADODB.Recordset
    Dim rs As New ADODB.Recordset
    rs.Open "SELECT * FROM Customer WHERE Country = '" & CountryParam & "'", _
            "DSN=Xtreme Sample Database 9"
    Set Customers = rs
End Function
```

When a Data Provider with a parameterized method is used from the report designer, the user will be prompted for a parameter value.

As was mentioned previously, one way to obtain a recordset is to perform a query. Listing 21.1 illustrates how to construct a recordset on-the-fly and read data out of a text file.

21

LISTING 21.1   A COM Data Provider that Parses Data from a CSV File

```
Public Function CSVText(FileName As String) As ADODB.Recordset
    Dim rs As New ADODB.Recordset

    ' Open the text file
    Dim FileSystem As New IWshRuntimeLibrary.FileSystemObject
    Dim fileText As IWshRuntimeLibrary.TextStream
    Set fileText = FileSystem.OpenTextFile(FileName)

    ' Read the first line of text to grab the field names
    Dim buffer As String
    buffer = fileText.ReadLine()
    Dim fields() As String
    fields = Split(buffer, ",")
    Dim i
    For i = LBound(fields) To UBound(fields)
        ' Add a field in the recordset for each field in the csv file
        rs.fields.Append fields(i), adBSTR
    Next

    rs.Open

    ' Read the contents of the file
    While Not fileText.AtEndOfStream
        buffer = fileText.ReadLine()
        rs.AddNew
        For i = LBound(fields) To UBound(fields)
            ' Grab the field values
            fields = Split(buffer, ",")
            rs(i).Value = fields(i)
        Next
        rs.Update
    Wend

    Set CSVText = rs
End Function
```

This code could be used as is or adopted to meet the needs of other kinds of files or data sources. Using the COM Data Source driver gives you complete flexibility and control over the data source.

Java-based Data Sources

The COM Data Source Driver is targeted at Visual Basic and Visual C++ developers. Because Crystal Reports 9 has a full Java SDK, an equivalent Java Data Source driver provides equivalent functionality of the COM driver for developers using the Java platform.

The process of creating a Java Data Source driver is conceptually similar to that of creating a COM Data Source driver. A Java class needs to be created that has a public function with a return type of `java.sql.ResultSet`. Listing 21.2 shows a simple Java Data Provider.

LISTING 21.2   A Java Data Provider that Parses Data from a CSV File

```java
import java.lang.*;
import java.sql.*;

public class XtremeDataProvider
{
    public ResultSet Employee()
    {
    // connect to the database
    Class.forName("sun.jdbc.odbc.JdbcOdbcDriver");
        String url = "jdbc:odbc:Xtreme Sample Database 9";
        Connection con = DriverManager.getConnection(url, "", "");

    // run a SQL query
        Statement stmt = con.createStatement(ResultSet.TYPE_SCROLL_SENSITIVE,
ResultSet.CONCUR_READ_ONLY);
        String query = "SELECT * FROM Employee";
    ResultSet rs = stmt.executeQuery(query);

    // return the results of the query
        return rs;
    }
}
```

To identify a Java class, instead of typing in its name, place the .class file into a given directory, and add that directory's name to the following registry key of your Windows operating system:

```
HKEY_LOCAL_MACHINE\Software\Crystal Decisions\Crystal Reports
9\DatabaseOptions\JavaUserClassPath
```

During the process of creating a report, Crystal Reports will search through all classes contained in the folder(s) specified in the registry key discussed previously. It will then provide a list of methods with return types of `ResultSet`. The same rules about function arguments apply. Any arguments to the Java method will be mapped to report parameter fields. Using Java code, you can control exactly what data comes back.

21

XML as a Data Source

With the emergence of XML as a data interchange format, many customers wanted to create reports on XML documents. So in Crystal Reports 8.5, a new driver was released that allowed just this scenario. This ODBC driver reads certain types of XML documents. A new feature of this driver in version 9 of Crystal Reports is the ability to read multiple XML files, most commonly a folder of XML files that have the same schema. When using this driver, you will specify either a folder name or a file path to an XML file. Once connected, XML elements at the first level will be represented as fields that you can place on a report.

If you require more flexibility around reading XML files, a good approach to take is to write a COM or Java Data Provider to read the XML. This Data Provider can use one of the many readily available XML parsers to read in the XML and choose exactly what fields to return to Crystal Reports. Listing 21.3 is a sample Visual Basic COM Data Provider that reads in a simple XML file.

LISTING 21.3   A COM Data Provider that Reads XML Data

```
' Loads an XML document with the following structure:
' <employees>
'   <employee>
'     <name>X</name>
'     <dept>X</dept>
'     <salary>X</salary>
'   </employee>
' </employees>
Public Function SimpleXML(fileName As String) As ADODB.Recordset
    Dim rs As New ADODB.Recordset

    Dim xmlDoc As New MSXML2.DOMDocument
    xmlDoc.Load (fileName)

    rs.fields.Append "Name", adBSTR
    rs.fields.Append "Dept", adBSTR
    rs.fields.Append "Salary", adCurrency
    rs.Open

    ' Loop through each employee element
    Dim employeeNode As MSXML2.IXMLDOMElement
    Dim childNode As MSXML2.IXMLDOMElement

    For Each employeeNode In xmlDoc.documentElement.childNodes
        rs.AddNew
        For Each childNode In employeeNode.childNodes
            rs(childNode.nodeName).Value = childNode.Text
```

LISTING 21.3 Continued

```
        Next
            rs.Update
      Next

      Set SimpleXML = rs
End Function
```

Solution Kits

Beyond relational databases, Crystal Reports also has the capability to access data held inside major ERP (Enterprise Resource Planning) and CRM (Customer Relationship Management) systems. Crystal Decisions has produced solution kits for SAP, Baan, and Siebel. The Solution Kits are designed to work with large scale ERP and CRM deployments and are therefore based on Crystal Enterprise. These solution kits contain data source drivers for each of these systems, as well as documentation on how to create and edit reports based on these data sources. Also included are packages of pre-built reports that can be used against your real data.

For more information on these solution kits, contact Crystal Decisions, or visit the following site:

```
http://www.crystaldecisions.com/tycr/partners/
```

Summary

During this hour, you've learned about some of the more advanced data sources that are available to you. You've learned how you can control the data access by writing a COM or Java Data Provider. You've also learned how to use XML documents as data sources for reports. If you are a user of SAP, Baan, or Siebel, you know that you can build custom reports off those systems using the solution kits that Crystal Decisions provides.

Workshop

The quiz questions and activities are provided for your further understanding of the current hour's topics.

Quiz

1. What is the difference between the COM Data Source driver and a COM Data Provider?

21

2. What does a function in a COM Data Provider need to return in order to be used inside Crystal Reports?

3. How do you identify your Java class as a Java Data Provider?

Quiz Answers

1. The COM Data Source driver is the Crystal Reports Data Source driver that contains the mechanism for consuming COM Data Providers. A COM Data Provider is a COM Object written by a developer that performs some sort of data access and returns data back to Crystal Reports.

2. A function inside a COM Data Provider needs to return an ADO recordset in order to be used inside Crystal Reports.

3. To identify your class as a Java Data Provider, copy the file into a given directory, and then add an entry into the registry key discussed in this hour that contains the folder where you put the Java class files.

Activities

To ensure that you are comfortable with the topics discussed in this hour, try to perform the following tasks:

1. Create a COM Data Provider in Visual Basic that returns customer data from the Xtreme Sample Database. The Provider should have a parameter that filters the customers by region.

2. Create a Java Data Provider that makes a JDBC connection to an XML file and returns that data to Crystal Reports.

3. Create a COM Data Provider that runs a basic query against the Orders table from the Xtreme Sample Database. Loop through the ADO Recordset and remove the Customer ID value for all orders over $1000.

HOUR 22

Optimizing SQL Queries in Crystal Reports

Earlier in this book, you learned about the new SQL Commands feature introduced with Crystal Reports 9. For those users not familiar with the SQL language, this hour will serve as an introduction and will help you get started with writing your own SQL Commands. For those users who are familiar with *SQL (Structured Query Language)*, this hour will serve as a refresher with some important tips pertaining to the use of SQL with the new SQL Commands feature. This hour provides the following:

- A review of SQL Commands
- An introduction to the SQL Language

Review of SQL Commands

Hour 3, "Accessing Your Data," introduced the new SQL Commands feature of Crystal Reports 9. Let's perform a quick review of what this feature is and what advantages it has.

With reports based on tables, views, or stored procedures, Crystal Reports does the dirty work of generating a query in the background. This query incorporates which fields you have used in the report, any sorting or filtering you've applied, and even some calculations. This is one of the strengths of Crystal Reports—you need not be an expert at writing SQL to use the product. All that complexity is abstracted away from the user designing the report. However, sometimes the person developing the report is familiar with the SQL language, and perhaps is also the database administrator. In situations like this, these people often want to write their own query. This could be because of several reasons, including

- An already defined query, which has the required fields, is in use elsewhere.
- The user wants to optimize her query beyond what Crystal Reports provides "out of the box."
- The user wants to perform a complex query that is beyond what Crystal Reports automatically generates; for example, a union query.

The SQL Commands feature is meant to address these needs. Rather than adding a table or view to a report, you can add a SQL Command. This command represents a SQL query that you will type in. After this SQL Command is created, it is treated just like a table in that it contains fields that can be used in the report and can be linked to other tables or SQL Commands. For more information on the creation of SQL Commands, see Hour 3.

An Introduction to the SQL Language

As its name implies, SQL is used to express a database query. SQL has facilities for defining which fields should be returned from the query, if and how the query should be filtered and sorted, and so on. Although SQL is an industry standard language, various specific versions and editions of the standard are implemented by SQL-based databases. Crystal Reports does not use just a single syntax, but rather is robust enough to handle most major SQL language derivations. The rest of this hour walks you through the SQL Language and points out specific areas that are of concern to Crystal Reports. Although this hour doesn't focus on a specific version of the SQL language, it does point out differences where appropriate.

The SELECT Statement

Even though the name implies that SQL is only about querying databases, most implementations also allow inserting, deleting, and updating of records inside the database. Each of these distinct actions has its own command: SELECT (query), INSERT, UPDATE, and DELETE. Although SQL Commands allow any valid SQL statement that returns records to be used, SELECT statements are generally the only statements to be used.

However, there are situations in which other statements can be used in addition to a SELECT statement. One example of this is running an INSERT statement to create a record to log the fact that the report is being run.

A basic SELECT statement has the following syntax:

```
SELECT field-list
FROM table-list
```

SELECT statements always begin with the word SELECT. The general convention is to cap-italize all SQL keywords used in the query to make it clear which is SQL and which is a table or field name. The list of fields to include is a comma-separated list of field names, such as "Name, Age, Gender." To include all fields in the specified table(s), use an * instead of listing individual field names. If the name of a field contains a space, the field name should be surrounded by a quote character ('field name'). Various SQL imple-mentations allow different quotes, but most of them support ` (single quote) as a quote character. The list of tables follows the same convention: They are separated by commas and are optionally enclosed in a quote. Any extra whitespace or carriage returns are usu-ally ignored by the database. The following is a SQL statement example using the Xtreme Sample Database:

```
SELECT `Customer Name`, City, Country
FROM Customer
```

You'll notice that quotes were only used for the Customer Name field because it was the only field with a space in the name. However, as a general convention, quote all your field and table names to be safe. The same statement could be written like this:

```
SELECT `Customer Name`, `City`, `Country`
FROM `Customer`
```

Depending on the type of database, table names can also be prefixed with the associated database name; for example, MyDatabase.MyTable. When using a qualified name such as this, you need to quote both names separately; that is, `MyDatabase`.`MyTable`.

When using a SQL Command in Crystal Reports, the fields that you specify in the field-list part of the SELECT statement determine which fields will be available to you inside your report. Although it's easy to use a SELECT * ... statement, keep in mind that you could be bringing back fields that aren't used, thus taking up more processing time and bandwidth. It's better to specify individual fields. You can always add or remove a field after the SQL Command is created by bringing up the Database Expert, right-clicking on the Command object, and selecting Edit Command from the context menu.

In the previous examples, data was being returned for each customer. However, if you wanted to return a list of countries, you might use a query such as the following:

```
SELECT `Country`
FROM `Customer`
```

Although this wouldn't return incorrect results, it would return redundant results because there are more than one record that contain the same country name. To work around this, use the DISTINCT keyword, which filters out all duplicate records.

```
SELECT DISTINCT `Country`
FROM `Customer`
```

Filtering Records

By learning a basic SELECT statement, you have the ability to return any or all fields. But so far, the query would return all records stored in that table. This section builds on what you've learned up to now by introducing a new clause in the SQL statement. You might ask, "Why would I want to filter records?" Consider that an "average" corporate data source might contain millions of records of data, and without being more specific in a query, you are putting an undue load on the database server as well as overwhelming the business user with more data than she needs.

The WHERE clause enables you to specify which records should be included in the query. If the WHERE clause is omitted (as it has been in the examples thus far), all records from the table are returned. Specifying a WHERE clause can limit these records to a more relevant subset. The syntax of SQL statement with a WHERE clause is as follows:

```
SELECT field-list
FROM table-list
[WHERE condition]
```

 Any components of the SQL statement enclosed in square brackets indicates that they are optional and need not be included in the SQL statement.

The condition can be any equality expression. Fields from the table can be used in the condition, as well as text literals and numbers. Let's look at a few examples:

```
SELECT `Customer Name`, `City`
FROM `Customer`
WHERE `Country` = 'USA'
```

The preceding SQL statement will return all customers who have a Country of USA. Notice that in this statement a text literal is used ('USA'). Text literals are surrounded by a text delimiter. The most common delimiter is the single quote, as used here.

22

Conditions can be combined together with ANDs and ORs, as shown in the following example:

```
SELECT `Order ID`, `Order Date`
FROM `Orders`
WHERE `Order Amount` > 2000 AND
         `Customer ID` = 123
```

 Sometimes it's appropriate to use a SQL statement that has a hard-coded (static) number or string. However, it's often more common to use parameters in the place of such values. That way, the report can be re-processed with different values showing diverse information without having to modify the SQL Command each time a change is needed. To create a parameter in SQL syntax, click the Create button in the Create SQL Command dialog and substitute the parameter name in place of the hard-coded value.

Sorting Records

Like filtering, sorting can be performed by Crystal Reports on your local workstation. However, it's always faster to have the database itself perform the operation because a typical database server has far more processing power than your desktop PC. This section introduces another clause to the SQL statement that will allow you to specify the order in which the records are returned.

The ORDER BY clause is used to specify sorting. The syntax is as follows:

```
SELECT field-list
FROM table-list
[WHERE condition]
[ORDER BY field-list [ ASC | DESC ] ]
```

The ORDER BY clause comes last in the SQL statement and is followed by a comma-separated list of fields. The records returned from the query will be sorted first by the first field specified, and then by the second, and so on. By default, fields are sorted in ascending order (from smallest to largest, or A to Z); but by adding ASC or DESC after the field name, you can specify either ascending or descending (largest to smallest, or Z to A) sort order.

The following SQL statement sorts the records by country, and then by region:

```
SELECT *
FROM `Customer`
ORDER BY `Country` ASC, `Region` ASC
```

The preceding example is sorting alphabetically. The following example shows where sorting is done on a numeric field. This query returns a list of customers in the order of highest sales first.

```
SELECT `Customer Name`, `Last Year's Sales`
FROM `Customer`
ORDER BY `Last Year's Sales` DESC
```

Joining Multiple Tables

So far, we've only used a single table, but of course multiple tables can be used. You might have already tried a statement like this:

```
SELECT `Customer Name`, `Order ID`
FROM `Customer`, `Orders`
```

Although this might initially seem correct, this query will most likely not return what you are looking for. Although only 2,192 records are in the Orders table, this query will return over 500,000 records and, with a larger database, could actually bring down the database server! This is because for each record in the Customer table, the entire set of records in the Orders table is included. In other words, the database doesn't know how to match up the records between the tables. If more than one table is used, a join should be applied that indicates how to match up the tables. There are various syntaxes for joins, but the simplest is to add a WHERE clause to the SQL statement (shown as follows), which produces an equal join:

how?

```
SELECT field-list
FROM table1, table2
WHERE table1.field = table2.field
```

This type of join applied to the previous example query would look like this:

```
SELECT `Customer Name`, `Order ID`
FROM `Customer`, `Orders`
WHERE `Customer`.`Customer ID` = `Orders`.`Customer ID`
```

Notice that because there is a Customer ID field in both the Customer and Orders tables, when that field is referenced in the WHERE clause, it is prefixed with the table name so as not to be ambiguous.

Aliasing

One beneficial feature of the SQL language is the ability to give fields and tables more meaningful names. Often fields are defined in the database with non-meaningful names such as ACTID instead of Account ID, and it would be useful to rename, or alias, this name.

22

Aliasing is straightforward: After the field that you want to alias, simply append `'AS field-name'`, where *field-name* is the new name for the field. Here's a working example:

```
SELECT `Customer Name`, `Region` AS `State`
FROM `Customer`
WHERE `Country` = 'USA'
```

In this example, because the records are being filtered to only include customers from the USA, it can be inferred that that the Region field will contain the State (where other countries such as Canada might use the Region field for the province). Because of this, the field is aliased to State. Note that the alias name need not be contained in quotes unless it has a space; but as stated earlier, it's good practice to always quote field names.

Calculated Fields

It's often a requirement to display data on the report that doesn't exist directly in the database—that is, data inferred or calculated based on other fields in the database. Although Crystal Reports provides a full formula language for defining these "formulas," when using SQL only, you need to follow its rules and limitations. The SQL language does have the ability to handle basic expressions like this. An expression, or calculated field, is specified in the SELECT part of the SQL statement just like any other field. Consider the following example, which uses an expression to concatenate a first and last name field together:

```
SELECT `Customer Name`, `Contact First Name` + ' ' + `Contact Last Name`
FROM `Customer`
```

If you were to use this SQL statement in a SQL Command, you get the correct field values returned however, the calculated field would be named something slightly cryptic like Expr1001. It's clear to you that this field represents a Contact Name, but the database can't easily infer that. To correct this problem, let's draw on the aliasing concept explained in the previous section. The corrected SQL statement is here:

```
SELECT `Customer Name`,
       `Contact First Name` + ' ' + `Contact Last Name` AS `Contact Name`
FROM `Customer`
```

In addition to textual expressions, you can perform mathematical expressions as well. The following SQL statement uses a calculated field to determine the tax paid based on sales:

```
SELECT `Customer Name`, `Last Year's Sales`,
       `Last Year's Sales` * 0.07 AS `Tax Paid`
FROM `Customer`
```

For more information on what kind of expressions can be used in your SQL command, consult the documentation for your database.

Union Queries

In the Xtreme Sample Database, each table represents a certain type of object, but often multiple tables represent the same type of object. For example, rather than having a single table called Orders, you might have multiple tables called Orders2001, Orders2002, Orders2003, which each contain the orders for a particular year as indicated by the table name. If you only want to report off one of those tables at a time, you need not do anything special. But, if you'd like to consolidate those together into a single query result, you must use a union query.

> The Union queries feature was not inherently supported by Crystal Reports in previous versions. However, the introduction of SQL Commands in Crystal Reports 9 allows this feature to be used fully.

The syntax for a union query is as follows:

```
SELECT statement
[ UNION
SELECT statement ]
```

Here is a SQL statement with a UNION clause combining some fictitious order tables:

```
SELECT * FROM `Orders2001`
UNION
SELECT * FROM `Orders2002`
UNION
SELECT * FROM `Orders2003`
```

These tables can be unioned together because they have the same table structure. You are not able to perform a union on two tables with different fields.

Grouping

The final SQL concept to be discussed is grouping. Grouping allows records to be grouped together based on a specified field, and then summarized using a given summary operation. Note that grouping in a SQL command will not allow a drill-down to the detail records. The syntax for grouping is as follows:

```
SELECT field-list
FROM table-list
[WHERE condition]
[GROUP BY field-list]
[ORDER BY field-list [ ASC | DESC ] ]
```

The following example groups all customers by country and summarizes the sales:

```
SELECT `Country`, SUM(`Last Year's Sales`) AS `Total Sales`
FROM `Customer`
GROUP BY `Country`
```

Two components to grouping exist in a SQL statement. The first is the summary operation—that is, SUM, COUNT, AVG, and so on. This operation determines which field will be summarized and in what way. The second component is the GROUP BY clause, which specifies for which field the data should be summarized—in other words, on which field the data should be grouped.

Summary

In this hour, you have recollected the SQL Commands feature. You then learned the mechanics of a SQL statement, from basic to advanced. Along the way, you picked up tips and notes about how different SQL statements will be treated by Crystal Reports. Although poor database design cannot be corrected by Crystal Reports, a good knowledge of SQL will help you make better, faster performing reports.

Workshop

The quiz questions and activities are provided for your further understanding of the current hour's topics.

Quiz

1. Why would you need to surround a field or table name in quotes?
2. Why would you want to incorporate sorting and filtering into the SQL statement if Crystal Reports already supports those operations?
3. What does aliasing a field do?

Quiz Answers

1. You would need to surround a field or table name in quotes if it contains a space, but it's good practice to always quote both field and table names.
2. By incorporating as much of the sorting and filtering logic into the SQL statement, the report will run faster because the database is always faster on these operations.
3. Aliasing a field gives the field a virtual name that is more user friendly or appropriate for that particular query.

Activities

To ensure that you are comfortable with the topics discussed in this hour, try to perform the following tasks. Using the Xtreme Sample Database, attempt to create the following queries as SQL Commands:

- All customers whose sales are over $5000 from the USA, sorted by customer name
- All products sorted by product type name (Hint: you'll need to use both the Product and Product_Type tables)
- The total salary for employees grouped by city

PART VI
Sharing and Distributing Crystal Reports

Hour

Hour **23**

Distributing Crystal Reports

Prior to this point, you've focused on learning how to *create* Crystal Reports. It's highly likely that you haven't spent all this time learning to create reports exclusively for your own consumption, but rather for other people's benefit as well. The inevitable question to be asked then is, "Once I'm done creating a report, how do I *share* it with others?" Fortunately, Crystal Decisions provides numerous methods of report distribution.

Whether the audience for viewing Crystal Reports is one or many, Crystal Decisions provides an appropriate distribution mechanism.

In this hour, the following will be covered:

- A review of Report Distribution Options
- Report distribution with the Report Application Server
- Unmanaged Crystal Enterprise Report Distribution
- Managed Crystal Enterprise Report Distribution
- Report distribution with the Report Designer Component

Reviewing Report Distribution Options

You might be wondering why an entire chapter would be devoted to report distribution. It seems logical that report files could simply be emailed or even printed and sent to whoever has a need for that particular information. This simplistic viewpoint however would overlook some important considerations when delivering reports to business users:

- Static Data vs Live Data—As soon as a report is printed to paper or exported to an external format like Adobe Acrobat (PDF) or Microsoft Excel (XLS), it becomes static and potentially out of date. Depending on the nature of the data being used in the report, this might be an issue. Even for situations in which having live data isn't important(for example, reports based on historical data), interactive features such as drill-downs are lost when printing or exporting a report.

- IT Maintenance— Because features such as drill-downs and hyperlinks are supported by the Crystal Reports Designer, it might seem logical to install the designer on each person's desktop who might need to view reports. This powerful, distributed report creation capability might be overwhelming to some end users and more importantly can grow into an IT maintenance headache when the audience for reports grows large.

- Report Maintenance— Distributing out reports and their associated files to the desktops of business users makes it cumbersome to make updates and additions to those reports because of the need to manually update each user's machine and associated reports.

- Security—Only certain business users should have access to certain reports, and even within this group of authorized business users, certain levels of restrictions should be in place. The average business user might be given the ability to change the data displayed in a report by entering parameter values, but should not be able to change core aspects of a report. This report design and modification capability should be reserved for a subset of the reporting user base.

- Presentation to a Variety of Formats—Often, reports need to be presented in various formats, whether it is being previewed onscreen using one of the Crystal Reports viewers, embedded into a Web-based portal, or even displayed on a wireless device (for example, PDA, Mobile Phone, and so on).

Although more factors that affect report distribution exist, those listed previously are important ones to initially consider. As stated earlier, there are various methods for distributing Crystal Reports. Each method addresses some or all of the preceding report distribution factors. Often, if one of the factors is not addressed, it can be addressed with some additional work or by using a different method that might cost more in licensing and development time. This build versus buy decision will be a factor in which report distribution system you choose to implement.

The main report distribution scenarios are as follows:

- Building a custom application that delivers reports. Sometimes the entire purpose of the application is to do just this—other times, reporting is just a component of a surrounding application. If the application is a desktop application, the *Report Designer Component (RDC)* should be used. If the application is Web based, the *Report Application Server (RAS)* should be used.

- Using a pre-built report distribution system—Crystal Enterprise. There are two editions of Crystal Enterprise: Standard and Professional. These two editions address different needs outlined later in this hour.

 When distributing your Crystal Reports and depending on the method selected, additional licenses might need to be purchased beyond your copy of Crystal Reports 9. To determine requirements or to purchase additional licenses, a Crystal Decisions sales representative should be contacted through the www.crystaldecisions.com Web site or by calling 1-800-877-2340.

Table 23.1 presents an overview of the different methods of Web report distribution and of each method's distinct advantages and disadvantages.

TABLE 23.1 Web Reporting Distribution Methods

Crystal Reports Web Distribution Method	Advantages	Challenges	Software and Versions Required
Crystal Enterprise Standard— Unmanaged	1. Direct URL access to Crystal Report files in virtual directories. 2. Flexible URL commands supported to control viewers, parameters, filters, exporting, and so on.	1. Unsecured reports. 2. Scalability limitation— single server deployment. 3. No scheduling capabilities.	Crystal Reports v9 Professional, Developer, or Advanced Edition Crystal Enterprise Standard or Professional

TABLE 23.1   continued

Crystal Reports Web Distribution Method	Advantages	Challenges	Software and Versions Required
	3. Five free concurrent user licenses.	4. No personalization. 5. No user-based security.	
Crystal Enterprise Standard—Managed	1. Secured Repository for Crystal Report files directly accessible from Crystal Reports Designer. 2. Provided Crystal Management Console for Web-based administration. 3. Sample e-Portfolio interface or flexible URL commands to access reports in a secured manner. 4. Five free concurrent user licenses.	1. No user-based security. 2. Scalability limitations—single server deployment. 3. No personalization. 4. No extensibility in object management (for example, Crystal Analysis).	Crystal Reports v9 Professional, Developer, or Advanced Edition Crystal Enterprise Standard
Crystal Enterprise Professional	1. User and User Group level security model—Personalization and Publish/Subscribe models. 2. Horizontally and vertically scaleable server architecture. 3. Advanced report scheduling capabilities, including event dependencies.	1. Increased administration commensurate with increased functionality. 2. Increased licensing costs to match increased out of the box functionality	Crystal Reports v9 Professional, Developer, or Advanced Edition Crystal Enterprise Professional

TABLE 23.1   continued

Crystal Reports Web Distribution Method	Advantages	Challenges	Software and Versions Required
	4. Sample ePortfolio interface or flexible URL commands to access reports in a secured manner.		
	5. Secured Repository for Crystal Report files directly accessible from Crystal Reports Designer.		
	6. Extensible architecture to manage third-party objects in addition to Crystal Reports (for example, Crystal Analysis or Excel).		
	7. Open Security model to enable integration with LDAP or NT authentication.		
	8. Fault Tolerant and Seamless Fail-over architecture.		
Report Application Server	1. Ultimately flexible access to report creation, access, and viewing functionality.	1. Requires programming expertise to leverage power of object model.	Crystal Reports v9 Advanced Edition Crystal Enterprise Professional for Delivering to Large User Bases
	2. Multithreaded object model to facilitate scaling on Crystal Enterprise infrastructure.	2. Requires Crystal Enterprise Professional to scale to large numbers of users.	

23

TABLE 23.1   continued

Crystal Reports Web Distribution Method	Advantages	Challenges	Software and Versions Required
	3. Available in both COM and Java object models.	3. Still does not provide 100% of Crystal Reports Design functionality in the object model.	
Report Design Component Advanced	1. Ultimately flexible access to report creation, access, and viewing functionality.	1. DLL is required to be present on Web server—further limiting scalability and introducing Web server contention.	Crystal Reports v9 Developer or Edition
	2. Familiar to Crystal Reports designers who have used previous versions of the RDC.	2. COM object model only—No Java object mode available.	Crystal Reports v9 Report Creation API License for any Report Creation programming
		3. Requires programming expertise to leverage power of object model.	

Each of the distribution methods for Crystal Reports will be explored in more detail in the next three sections. With the exception of the RDC, each of the different methods provides a surprisingly simple migration to the next one up in the functionality ladder. Hour 24, "Crystal Reports in Applications—A Developer's Perspective," explores the advanced developer methods of report distribution in addition to the new Report Parts distribution options in Crystal Reports version 9.

Unmanaged Report Web Access via Crystal Enterprise Standard

The simplest (and perhaps most familiar to existing Crystal Reports users) method of making Crystal Reports available over the Web is through the use of virtual Web directories set up on your Web server. (On Windows IIS, these can be set up through Internet Services Manager accessed through the Control Panel.) To provide Web access in this manner, Crystal Enterprise must be installed on either the Web server or a separate machine: If the latter, the Web Connector component of Crystal Enterprise must be installed on the selected Web Server. The Crystal Enterprise installation guide or online help files distributed with the Crystal Enterprise components should be consulted for help on installing components of Crystal Enterprise.

> At the time of this book's printing, the latest shipping version of Crystal Enterprise was 8.5. This version does not support the Crystal Reports 9 file format and therefore will not work in conjunction with Crystal Reports 9. Soon after the release of Crystal Reports 9, a new release of Crystal Enterprise is expected that will fully support Crystal Reports 9. However, the Report Application Server (RAS) method of Web distribution discussed later in the hour will be available concurrent with the release of Crystal Reports 9.

To "Web-enable" existing Crystal Reports using this method and with Microsoft *Internet Information Server (IIS)* on the same physical server as Crystal Enterprise, the following steps are required:

1. Copy all relevant Crystal Reports into a single physical directory accessible by your IIS Web server.

2. Create a virtual Web directory for that selected physical directory by right-clicking on the folder from within Windows Explorer and selecting the Properties menu option.

3. Click on the Web Sharing tab and select the Share This Folder radio button. Figure 23.1 displays the Web Sharing and Alias dialogs you will be faced with.

FIGURE 23.1
Virtual Directory Setup dialogs.

23

4. Enter an appropriate alias for your virtual directory (for example, Reports or CrystalWebReports).

5. Click OK until you have saved all your changes, and the Crystal Reports in the selected physical directory will now be available over the Web at `http\\web-servername\virtualdirname\reportname.rpt`, where

   - `Webservername` is replaced with your Web server's name

   - `Virtualdirname` is replaced with the Web sharing alias you created in step 4.

   - `Reportname` is any of the reports you have placed in the physical directory in step 1. Also, note that you need to include the .rpt extension.

Figure 23.2 displays one of the Crystal Reports sample reports being accessed through this method in a previous version of Crystal Enterprise.

FIGURE 23.2

A sample of a URL accessed Crystal Report.

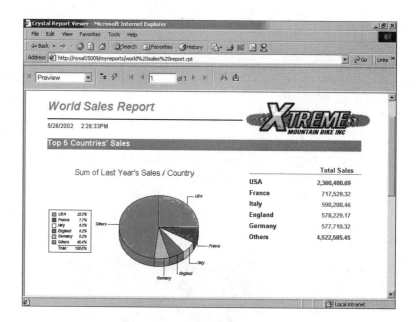

More than just basic and direct access to existing Crystal Reports through this unmanaged method, Crystal Reports and Crystal Enterprise provide numerous methods of controlling the delivery of reports. Table 23.2 lists a number of additional URL-based commands that enable enhanced control of the Web delivery of the Crystal Reports.

TABLE 23.2   Crystal Reports URL Based Commands

URL Suffix	Suffix Description	URL examples
INIT	The INIT command specifies the report viewer that will be used to view the report. If the INIT command is not specified, Crystal Enterprise detects the type of browser requesting a report and provides a default viewer that is most appropriate for that browser. The default viewer for Microsoft Internet Explorer is the ActiveX viewer. The default viewer for Netscape Navigator is the Java viewer. Other options include actx = Active X Viewer java = Java Viewer html_frame = DHTML with frames html_page = HTML java_plugin = Java plug-in nav_plugin = Netscape plug-in	`http://machine/virdir/` `rpt.rpt?init=actx`
CONNECT	The CONNECT command is appended to the INIT command with a colon. It reestablishes a connection to the Crystal Report Processing Server. This allows the business user to reset the report's parameters and logon information, and reprocess the report if necessary without having to begin a new browser session.	`http://machine/virdir/` `rpt.rpt?init=actx:connect`
PROMPTEX	The PROMPTEX command specifies values for parameters on a report or any of the main report's subreports.	Passing the country parameter "Ireland" into the sample report.

23

TABLE 23.2   continued

URL Suffix	Suffix Description	URL examples

	The PROMPTEX command can be used to pass multiple values or a range of values for a single parameter. Multiple single values can be passed into a report by separating them with commas. Ranged values can use square and round brackets in the following flexible manner:
	
	Bounded intervals
	`["<value>"-"<value>"]`
	`("<value>"-"<value>"]`
	`["<value>"-"<value>")`
	`("<value>"-"<value>")`
	
	Unbounded intervals
	`("<value>"-)`
	`["<value>"-)`
	`(-"<value>")`
	`(-"<value>"]`
	
	A square bracket indicates that the interval is closed at that end, and that the specified number is included in the range; a round bracket indicates that the interval is open at that end, and that the specified number is not included in the range.
	
	In order to pass Date or DateTime parameter values over the URL, use the single value or date range methods as specified here:
	
	For single value Date or DateTime parameters, the `promptex-<promptname>` command requires double quotes. For passing date ranges, brackets must be used as shown previously.
		`http://machine/virdir/`
		`rpt.rpt?init=actx&promptex`
		`-country="Ireland"`
		
		Passing the city parameter `"Toronto"` into the sample report's subreport called sub1.
		
		`http://machine/virdir/`
		`rpt.rpt?init=actx&promptex`
		`-city@sub1="Toronto"`
		
		Passing the region parameters `"Asia"` and `"Europe"` into the sample report.
		
		`http://machine/virdir/`
		`rpt.rpt?init=actx&promptex-`
		`regions="Europe","Asia"`
		
		The following URL extensions highlight the flexibility in the parameter range functionality:
		
		Passing April through May into the report:
		`promptex-monthrange=("3"-"6")`
		
		Passing March through May into the report:
		`promptex-monthrange =`
		`["3"-"6")`
		
		Passing July through December into the report:
		`promptex-monthrange =("6"-)`

TABLE 23.2 continued

URL Suffix	Suffix Description	URL examples
		Passing date range parameters through the URL should follow the pattern of the following suffix: promptex-DateRangeParm=["date(2002,07,08)"-"Date(2002,12,10)"]
SF	The SF command allows for the specification of a selection formula for the report. Any selection formula passed via the URL using the SF command will be appended with the logical AND statement to any existing selection formulas already in the report.	http://machine/virdir/rpt.rpt?sf={Customer.Country}='Canada'
GF	The GF command specifies a group selection formula for the report. This command works in an identical manner to the selection formula SF command.	http://machine/virdir/rpt.rpt?gf=Sum({Customer.Sales},{Customer.Country})>1000000
PromptOnRefresh	The PromptOnRefresh command forces the involved report to prompt the business user for parameter field values when refreshed.	http://machine/virdir/rpt.rpt?promptOnRefresh=1
CMD and EXPORT_FMT	The CMD and EXPORT_FMT commandsenable the involved report to be exported to the any number of the different file formats outlined here: Adobe PDF - U2FPDF:0 HTML 3.2 - U2FHTML:2 HTML 4.0 - U2FHTML:3 XML - U2FXML:0 Excel 5.0 (XLS) - U2FXLS:3 Excel 5.0 (XLS) Extended - U2FXLS:4 Crystal Reports (RPT) - U2FCR:0 Rich Text Format (RTF) - U2FRTF:0 Word Document (DOC) – U2FWORDW:0	This URL will bring up the rpt.rpt report file in Adobe Acrobat format within a Web browser. http://machine/virdir/rpt.rpt?cmd=EXPORT&EXPORT_FMT=U2FPDF:0

23

The URL commands outlined in the Table 23.2 highlight the breadth of flexibility available when delivering Crystal Reports over the Web through the unmanaged mode of
Crystal Enterprise. When any report is accessed through this mode, a Crystal Enterprise
guest license is used for the duration of the time the report viewer is active and (by
default) until 20 minutes after the last sign of activity on a report viewer (for example,
Next Page, Last Page, Drilling-down, and so on). It is important to forecast maximal
concurrent usage before Web deploying reports to ensure that no business users are dis-
appointed with a no-access notification message. User license requests above and beyond
what is licensed on the Crystal Enterprise system will be rejected.

Managed Web Report Access via Crystal Enterprise Standard and Professional

Although the unmanaged method of deploying reports provides a quick and easy method
of Web enabling reports, Crystal Enterprise provides additional rich scalability, scheduling, security, and personalization functionality as described in Table 23.2 that can only be
accessed through the managed method of report distribution. Publishing Crystal Reports
over the Web using either version of Crystal Enterprise (Standard or Professional) can be
accomplished in one of three ways:

- Use the File Save As Command in Crystal Reports and select the Enterprise icon.
  This will prompt for Crystal Enterprise Credentials and will require the administrator ID and password for Crystal Enterprise Standard or any valid user ID and password in Crystal Enterprise Professional. Figure 23.3 displays a Crystal Enterprise
  Logon screen.

FIGURE 23.3

*Crystal Enterprise
Publishing Logon
from Crystal Reports
File Save As menu
option.*

- Use the Crystal Management Console provided with Crystal Enterprise. Figure
  23.4 displays a previous version of the console in which reports can be added
  through the Add Objects function. The Crystal Management Console is actually
  the central point of all Web administration for Crystal Enterprise, but its detailed
  description is beyond the scope of this book. See the Crystal Decisions Web site
  for more information on Crystal Enterprise functionality.

FIGURE 23.4

Crystal Management Console for publishing Crystal Reports.

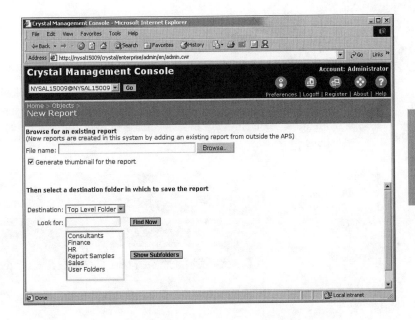

- Use the Publishing Wizard provided with Crystal Enterprise. Figure 23.5 displays a previous version of the Publishing Wizard that is accessed through the Start menu and then the Programs and Crystal Enterprise menu options. The Publishing Wizard will step you through the report publishing process, which is the recommended process for beginners.

FIGURE 23.5

The Crystal Publishing Wizard allows for Crystal Reports files to be quickly published into the Crystal Enterprise system.

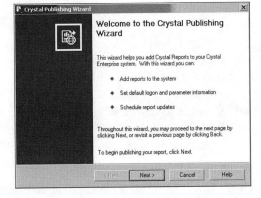

Once published into Crystal Enterprise using any of these methods, a copy of the involved report is transferred into a secure file repository managed by Crystal Enterprise, and a record of the involved file is created in the Crystal Enterprise system database.

The published reports are now stored in a secured reporting system and can only be accessed by authorized Crystal Enterprise users.

Access to these managed stored reports is provided through two methods:

- Using the Crystal Enterprise client interface called ePortfolio, accessed from the Start menu under Programs, Crystal Enterprise and the Crystal Launch-pad. Figure 23.6 displays a previous version of ePortfolio with the default logon ID of guest.

FIGURE 23.6

ePortfolio—Default Crystal Enterprise interface.

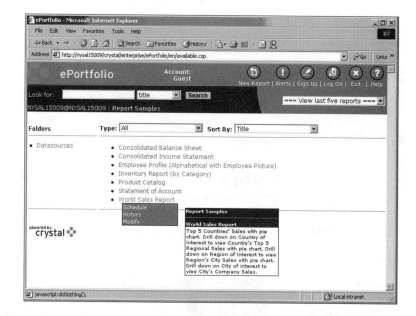

- Using direct URL commands in an almost identical nature to that described for unmanaged report distribution with a slightly modified format. Instead of direct requests to the Crystal Report in a virtual directory, requests are made to the Crystal Enterprise system, and Crystal Reports are referenced through a Crystal Enterprise View Report command (viewrpt.cwr) and an Object ID that can be accessed from the Crystal Management Console. A sample URL could be http\\server\crystal\enterprise\viewrpt.cwr?id=1210.

All the URL suffix commands described in Table 23.2 can be applied to the end of these managed URL requests. The direct URL based report access method described previously is further extended within any managed Crystal Enterprise environment to include additional commands to leverage the additional security functionality that is provided.

These additional commands are described in Table 23.3, but the full descriptions are beyond the scope of this book. For more information on direct URL access to Crystal Reports through Crystal Enterprise, the Crystal Enterprise Manuals should be consulted.

TABLE 23.3 Additional URL Based Commands

URL Suffix	Suffix Description	URL Example
ID	A required suffix for accessing reports in Crystal Enterprise through a URL. The ID is a unique identifier of current report within the Crystal Enterprise system. It can be discovered through the Crystal Management Console.	`http://server/crystal/` `enterprise/` `viewrpt.cwr?id=510`
APSTOKEN	The APSTOKEN provides one of two methods of passing user authentication information to Crystal Enterprise to enable the system to validate the credentials of a selected user. The APSTOKEN is actually a series of numbers and characters created by Crystal Enterprise when a business user logs on and facilitates license management by keeping track of which users are logged on at any given time. The Crystal Enterprise user guide will need to be consulted to fully understand how to access and use the APSTOKEN.	`http://server/crystal/` `enterprise/` `viewrpt.cwr?id=` `510&apstoken=` `APSName:A5I5`
APSUSER, APSPASSWORD, APSAUTHTYPE	The other method that allows Crystal Enterprise to authenticate users is with the APSUSER, APSPASSWORD, and APSAUTHTYPE commands. These commands allow the passing of the necessary values to authenticate the business user against the Crystal Enterprise system database.	`http://server/crystal/` `enterprise/` `viewrpt.cwr?id=` `510&apsuser=` `Administrator&` `apspassword=pwd123&` `apsauthtype=` `secEnterprise`

More than simply providing secure access to Crystal Reports, Crystal Enterprise provides a comprehensive set of enterprise reporting features, including those highlighted in Tables 23.2 and 23.3. Although a detailed description of Crystal Enterprise features is beyond the scope of this book, additional system features and information can be found on the Crystal Decisions Web site. Crystal Enterprise is the Web distribution system that should be used whenever reports are mission critical, used when there is a large business user or report base, or used when security, personalization, or report scheduling are required.

Programmatic Report Distribution Using RDC or RAS

Crystal Decisions provides two software developer kits that enable report sharing via windows and Web-based applications. Both the RDC and RAS object models are available in the Developer or Advanced editions of Crystal Reports v9. RAS is also available in the Professional Edition. Both object models provide access to advanced Crystal Report capabilities for integration into custom developed applications.

The RDC components are fully compatible with the Microsoft *Component Object Model (COM)* and will be familiar to developers acquainted with previous versions of Crystal Reports. The RDC functionality can be accessed from any language that is COM-compatible—Visual Basic, Active Server Pages using VBScript or JavaScript, C++, Delphi, or the Microsoft Web Development Environments (InterDev or FrontPage). Three drawbacks to using the RDC in your Web applications are: (1) it must be present on your Web server to operate, (2) it is single threaded, and (3) it must run in process on your Web server. These three factors lead to challenges when trying to scale an application, and RDC-based applications do not provide a simple migration path to Crystal Enterprise. Because of these reasons, the RDC is targeted toward use in desktop applications only.

The RAS object model was created to address these concerns and has been designed to be multithreaded and server- based. Additionally, the RAS has been designed as a seamless component of the Crystal Enterprise architecture, providing developers with a smooth migration path from this server to large-scale deployment on Crystal Enterprise Professional. The final vote to support using RAS over RDC is that RAS has been designed to be both COM and Java compliant. These parallel versions of the object model access the same Crystal Reports functionality and open up the power of Crystal Reports and Crystal Enterprise to the Java development community. In summation, the arguments for using RAS over RDC in custom application design are

- It is multithreaded.
- RAS is server based (does not need to reside on a Web server).
- It integrates seamlessly into the Crystal Enterprise framework.
- It is scaleable.
- The RAS object model will be available in both COM and Java formats.

The next hour discusses the RDC and RAS components, as well as other Crystal Reports development aspects, in more detail. Whatever approach you select to distribute your Crystal Reports files, it is important to keep these in mind as options for your initial foray into Web distribution of your Crystal Reports.

Summary

After reports have been created using all the inherent power and flexibility of Crystal Reports 9, the intrinsic value of those reports is best realized by sharing those reports with an appropriate audience that could include executives, employees, customers, or suppliers.

Crystal Decisions makes the distribution of Crystal Reports easy by providing numerous methods of Web report distribution to meet the needs of all reporting communities. Whether the report distribution requirements involve the provision of simple Web hyperlinks to reports or include a broad enterprisewide secured environment, Crystal Decisions has the appropriate deployment solution.

The next hour discusses some of the advanced report distribution options in more detail. Crystal Enterprise documentation will also be able to provide the required education on advanced Web reporting projects.

Q&A

Q Can I access version 9 Crystal Reports over the Web through previous versions of Crystal Enterprise (version 8 or version 8.5)?

A No—Version 9 Crystal Reports can only be accessed through Version 9 of Crystal Enterprise. If you need to deploy an enterprise reporting solution before the release of Crystal Enterprise version 9, you have two choices: (1) use Crystal Reports version 8.5 with Crystal Enterprise 8.5 as an interim solution and upgrade upon the release of the complete version 9 Crystal suite, or (2) use the Report Application Server that is targeted for release with Crystal Reports 9 and seamlessly migrate to Crystal Enterprise upon its release. At the time of the writing, it was also understood that Crystal Decisions would provide an advanced registration capability for some number of free licenses of a Crystal Enterprise Standard version to be automatically shipped upon its release.

Q Can I access my version 9 Crystal Reports through a URL command if I do not have Crystal Enterprise installed?

A Out of the box, the answer is no. To directly access Crystal Reports from a URL, Crystal Enterprise must be installed. Using RAS and ASP or JSP Web pages, you could, however, code Web pages that would provide URL based access.

Workshop

The quiz questions and activities are provided for your further understanding of the current hour's topics.

Quiz

1. Can a report receive multiple parameters through a URL request?
2. Can work created using the RAS object model be scaled up with the use of Crystal Enterprise 9?

Quiz Answers

1. Yes, through the use of a flexible `promptex` URL command suffix, multiple parameters can be passed to a Crystal Report through either an enumerated list or a range setting.
2. Yes, Crystal Enterprise is designed as an open architecture and a Report Application Server (RAS) plug-in exists for that infrastructure. Multiple copies of the RAS server can be run simultaneously on Crystal Enterprise, ensuring the ability to scale effectively.

Activities

To better understand the extra benefits provided through Crystal Enterprise, visit the Crystal Decisions Web site and then consider which method of Web distribution is most appropriate for your information delivery situation.

HOUR 24

Crystal Reports in Applications—a Developer's Perspective

In Hour 23, you learned about the various methods for distributing reports. Sometimes, the only requirement is to get the report into a business user's hands, potentially by printing a hard copy. However, this hour focuses on more advanced requirements, which involve delivering reports electronically to business users in the form of a custom application. Sometimes, the entire purpose of the application is just to display reports, but more commonly, reporting is just a component of the surrounding application, which has another purpose such as a general ledger or inventory management.

In this hour, you will learn about the developer tools available to you in Crystal Reports 9 Developer or Advanced Edition and also the Crystal Enterprise Report Application Server included with Crystal Reports 9. You'll understand the application development scenarios that Crystal Reports 9 targets, which developer tools fit your scenario best, and how to get started developing applications that incorporate Crystal Reports.

Overview of Developer Tools

From the inception of Crystal Reports, Crystal Decisions (then Crystal Services, soon to become Seagate Software) saw that although the Crystal Reports designer and report engine together made a great tool, there was huge value in providing a *software development kit (SDK)* that enabled developer-savvy customers to leverage the power of Crystal Reports inside their applications. They were able to display reports inside the application they were building, including full support for features such as parameters, database credentials, exporting, and formatting. Many of these features—such as exporting reports—could be done interactively just like inside the Crystal Reports designer, or could be performed entirely in the background, hiding the user interface from the customer and just presenting the end result.

The first SDK for Crystal Reports consisted of a C++ header file and a DLL (dynamic link library) that exposed functions to open, modify, process, display, and export reports. Any developer with a C++ compiler could use this SDK (called the CRPE, or Crystal Reports Print Engine) inside of his application. While this was popular, over the following years and versions, the Crystal Reports SDK expanded to support an ever-changing developer tools market. Most of these subsequent SDKs were based on Microsoft's ActiveX/COM technology. Today, Crystal Reports 9 has full SDKs for COM, .NET, and Java developers building both desktop and Web applications.

Although some of these SDKs fell into the "legacy" category over the years and have since been removed from the product, several remain for compatibility reasons. Given the large palette of developer tools available, it could be difficult to decide which one is best for your given scenario. To make this process easier, let's break up applications into the following application architectures/scenarios to best understand which component best fits your requirements:

- Desktop applications—Standalone applications running on a single tier
- Simple Web applications—Web sites that display reports in HTML format
- Advanced Web applications—Web applications that involve the creation, manipulation, and display of reports, as well as delivery in HTML format

The following sections describe each of these application scenarios, as well as which Crystal Reports SDK is recommended for each scenario.

Desktop Applications

Desktop applications, while still popular today, were what started it all. These are standalone applications that run entirely on a single tier and are installed locally on a user's machine. These applications are most commonly built using Visual Basic, but are also sometimes built using Visual C++ or Delphi.

All sample code in this section will use Visual Basic syntax, but can easily be adapted to other languages that support COM. For sample code in other languages, visit Crystal Decisions' support site at http://support.crystaldecisions.com.

All these development environments, and many more, support Microsoft's COM technology. *COM (Component Object Model)* is a standard technology used for exposing SDKs in the Windows world. Much of Microsoft's own SDKs are based on COM. It follows that the recommended Crystal Reports SDK for desktop applications would also be based on COM. Its name is the Report Designer Component, and it consists of the following components:

- A report designer integrated in to the Visual Basic environment
- An object model built around the report engine used for manipulation of the report inside an application
- A report viewer control used for displaying reports inside an application

The following sections describe each of these components in more detail.

The Visual Basic Report Designer

The Visual Basic Report Designer enables developers to create and edit reports from within the comfort of the Visual Basic environment. Figure 24.1 shows the report designer active inside Visual Basic.

FIGURE 24.1

The Visual Basic Report Designer.

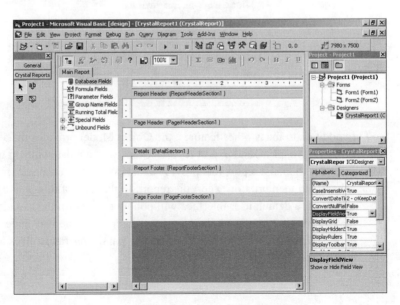

To add a new report to a project, select Add Crystal Reports 9 from the Project menu inside Visual Basic.

The Visual Basic Report Designer supports most of the features of the Crystal Reports designer and can be used to create everything from simple columnar reports to highly formatted, visually appealing reports. The menus that you would normally find in the standalone Crystal Reports designer can be found by right-clicking on an empty spot on the designer surface. The same dialogs and commands are available.

This report designer works only inside Visual Basic, but the viewer and object model work in any COM-compliant development environment. When using a non-Visual Basic environment, or just by personal preference, the regular Crystal Reports designer can be used to create the reports to be used inside the application.

Report Engine Object Model

The Object Model is the main entry point to the Crystal Reports engine for desktop applications. As mentioned earlier, it is based on COM and can be used from any COM-compliant development environment. In Visual Basic, this component shows up in the References dialog as Crystal Reports ActiveX Designer Runtime Library, as shown in Figure 24.2. (The filename is CRAXDRT9.dll.)

FIGURE 24.2

Referencing the Report Designer Component's Object Model.

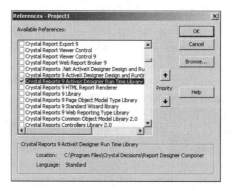

In addition to many other features, the Object Model provides the ability to open, create, modify, save, print, and export reports. Some of the most common uses of the report engine is to load a report file, provide database logon credentials, provide parameter field values, and then print or export the report. In the case of things like parameters and exporting, a default user interface will pop up to perform the associated action, but often developers want to present their own user interface or perhaps hide the user interface entirely. Listing 24.1 illustrates how to pass parameter field values and database logon credential.

LISTING 24.1   Parameter and Logon via the Object Model

```
Dim Application As New CRAXDRT.Application
Dim Report As CRAXDRT.Report

' Open the report from a file
Set Report = Application.OpenReport("C:\MyReport.rpt")

' Provide database logon credentials (in this case
' for an OLEDB connection to a SQL Server database)
Dim tbl as CRAXDRT.DatabaseTable
Set tbl = Report.Database.Tables(1)
tbl.ConnectionInfo("Data Source") = "MyServer"
tbl.ConnectionInfo("Initial Catalog") = "MyDB"
tbl.ConnectionInfo("User ID") = "User1"
tbl.ConnectionInfo("Password") = "abc"

' Provide parameter field values
Report.ParameterFields(1).AddCurrentValue("USA")
Report.ParameterFields(2).AddCurrentValue(10000)

' Export the report to a PDF file
Report.ExportOptions.FormatType = crEFTPortableDocFormat
Report.ExportOptions.DestinationType = crEDTDiskFile
Report.ExportOptions.DiskFileName = "C:\MyReport.pdf"
Report.Export False
```

24

There are two ways to load reports: via a standalone RPT file or via an embedded designer class. In the first situation, you simply call the `Application.OpenReport` method, passing in a file path to an RPT file. The preceding code example uses this method. For the second situation, if you've got the report inside your Visual Basic project (either by creating a new report with the Visual Basic Report Designer, or importing an existing report into the project), a corresponding class will represent that report. For example, if you added a new report to your application, it will have a default name of CrystalReport1 and will have a DSR extension. Let's say that you renamed it as MySalesReport.dsr. You would then be able to declare an object like this:

```
Dim Report As New MySalesReport
```

The `MySalesReport` object is the same as a `CRAXDRT.Report` object, but it is stored inside the resources of the application and doesn't require an external RPT file.

Report Viewer

In the previous section, only printing and exporting was mentioned as options for delivering reports. You might have been wondering how to view reports onscreen. This is where the Report Viewer comes in. This report viewer control is usually referred to as the ActiveX viewer, or the Crystal Reports Viewer Control. It is an ActiveX control,

which means that in addition to being able to be dropped on to any Visual Basic form—
like the other components of the Report Designer Component—it can be used in any
COM-compliant development environment. It's filename is CRViewer9.dll. Figure 24.3
depicts the ActiveX viewer displaying a report from a Visual Basic application.

FIGURE 24.3
*The ActiveX viewer in
action.*

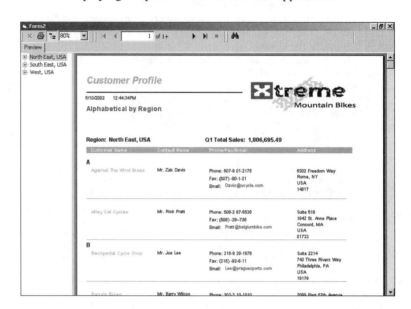

The ActiveX viewer works in conjunction with the Object Model to render the report to
the screen. The Object Model talks to the report engine to process the report, and then
the ActiveX viewer asks the Object Model for each individual page, which it then displays onscreen. The following code snippet illustrates how to view a report with the
Report Viewer control.

```
Dim Application As New CRAXDRT.Application
Dim Report As CRAXDRT.Report

Set Report = Application.OpenReport("C:\MyReport.rpt")
CRViewer.ReportSource = Report
CRViewer.ViewReport
```

The ActiveX control has many properties and methods that enable the developer to customize its look and feel, such as hiding the toolbar or group tree. In addition, the control
has a full event model that allows the developer to be notified when certain actions are
performed, such as a drill-down or a page navigation. For more information on the
Report Designer Component, consult the Crystal Reports 9 developer help file installed
with the product.

These three components, the Visual Basic Report Designer, the Report Engine Object Model, and the ActiveX Report Viewer control (collectively called the Report Designer Component), are the recommended solution for integrating reporting into desktop applications.

Creating Simple Web Applications

While desktop applications are still in wide use today, a large percentage of new applications being developed are Web-based applications. Most of the reasons for this centers around maintenance and central management; it's much easier to maintain and manage an application that resides entirely on a single Web server than an application installed on thousands of business user machines across a company.

You'll notice that this scenario is titled Simple Web Applications, and the next is Advanced Web Applications. The reason for this separation is because of distinct requirements that Crystal Decisions has heard from its customers. This scenario, Simple Web Applications, is really just about getting reports up on the Web. The most common requirements here are HTML-only delivery of reports, basic parameter prompting, and database logon credentials.

Sometimes a Web page is nothing but a empty page with a Crystal Report on it. Other times, the report is integrated into an existing Web page with other HTML elements on it. Sometimes report parameters and database logon information are prompted for on the page: In other situations, one or both of these items are set transparently in the background. The possibilities are really only limited by your own imagination.

Because Crystal Reports is the world leader in reporting, it needs to work well in a variety of customer situations and platforms. For the desktop application space, most developers are using COM technology, but when moving to the Web, developers use a mix of COM (ASP), Java (JSP), and .NET (ASP.NET) technologies. Because of this, Crystal Reports 9 includes report viewers for each of these platforms.

Web Report Viewing in ASP

As you might know, COM is the underlying technology that runs *Active Server Pages (ASP)*. Crystal Reports 9 has a report viewer built just for ASP (although it also works in any other COM-compliant Web platform such as Cold Fusion). This COM Report Viewer is conceptually similar to the ActiveX viewer in that it communicates with the report engine to display a report. However, instead of residing on the business user's machine like the ActiveX viewer, the COM Report Viewer resides on the Web server. When included in an ASP page, it renders any report to HTML. This means that although the business user still receives a rich view of the report, it comes to him in a zero-client environment;

24

that is, no Crystal Decisions software or controls need be downloaded or installed to the business user's machine. This zero-maintenance report delivery architecture is one of the most popular uses of Crystal Reports today.

To use the COM Report Viewer to display a report in an ASP page, use the following code:

```
<%

' Create the COM Report Viewer
Dim Viewer
Set Viewer = CreateObject("CrystalReports.CrystalReportViewer")

' Set the COM viewer's report source to a path to an RPT file
Viewer.ReportSource = "RAS://C:\MyReport.rpt"

' Call the ProcessHttpRequest method to write the HTML output of
' the report into the response stream
Viewer.ProcessHttpRequest Request, Response, Session

%>
```

Figure 24.4 shows the result of this page.

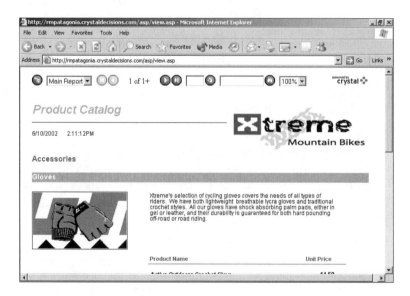

Like the ActiveX viewer, the COM Report Viewer has a ReportSource property that is used to identify which report to display. You'll notice that in the case of the COM Report Viewer, a file path to an RPT file is set, prefixed with "RAS://". This prefix is used to indicate that the viewer should use the *Report Application Server (RAS)* to process the report. The `ProcessHttpRequest` method does the actual HTML rendering and writes the output of the report into the response stream. In the following example, there is no other HTML or ASP code in the page, but other code and HTML can coexist.

Like the ActiveX viewer, the COM Report Viewer has properties and methods that allow the business user to customize the viewer and the output it creates. Some of the common tasks, such as passing parameter field values and database logon information, can also be accomplished. The following code provides an example of this:

```
<%

Dim Viewer
Set Viewer = CreateObject("CrystalReports.CrystalReportViewer")
Viewer.ReportSource = "RAS://C:\SecuredReportWithParam.rpt"

' Set the database logon credentials, in this case for the first
' table in the report, which then propagates across any
' subsequent tables in the report
Viewer.DatabaseLogonInfos(0).UserName = "user id"
Viewer.DatabaseLogonInfos(0).Password = "password"

' Set the value of the first parameter field to a string. Other
' data types such as numbers and boolean values can be set
' here as well.
Viewer.ParameterFields(0).CurrentValues.Add "USA"

%>
```

To learn more about the specific properties and methods available, consult the COM Report Viewers help file installed with Crystal Reports 9, as well as the sample report wizard application that uses the COM Report Viewer.

Web Reporting in Java

Crystal Decisions has always had a huge market share in the Microsoft developer community. With Crystal Reports 9, it extends this market leadership to the Java community. For the first time, Java developers can building reporting into their Web applications with a 100% pure Java SDK.

As you've probably guessed, delivering reports on the web in Java is very similar to COM. Crystal Reports 9 comes with a server-side report viewer control written in Java which can be used inside JSP-based applications. It is functionally the same as the COM Report Viewer, but is a native Java component, which means that it is targeted toward use in J2EE applications. The following code listing illustrates a JSP page with a report hosted inside it:

24

```
<%@ page import="com.crystaldecisions.report.web.viewer.*" session="true" %>
<%

// create the viewer object
CrystalReportViewer viewer = new CrystalReportViewer();

// set the report source to the path to an RPT file
viewer.setReportSource("RAS://C:\\MyReport.rpt");

// call the processHttpRequest function to  render the report into
// HTML, then write to the response stream
viewer.processHttpRequest(request, response,
                          getServletConfig().getServletContext(), null);

%>
```

As with the COM Report Viewer, the Java Report Viewer has a `setReportSource` function for identifying the report to display. Also similarly, the `processHttpRequest` function is called to render the report.

Like the other report viewers, common tasks such as passing database logon credentials and parameter field values can be accomplished via the Java Report Viewer. An example of this is seen in Listing 24.2.

LISTING 24.2   Parametersand Logon with the Java Viewer

```
<%@ page import="com.crystaldecisions.report.web.viewer.*,
➥ com.crystaldecisions.sdk.occa.report.data.*"
        session="true" %>
<%

// Create a viewer object and pass it a report
CrystalReportViewer viewer = new CrystalReportViewer();
viewer.setReportSource("RAS://C:\\SecuredReportwithParam.rpt");

// Set the database logon credentials, in this case for the first
// table in the report, which then propagates across any
// subsequent tables in the report
viewer.getDatabaseLogonInfos().getConnectionInfo(0).setUserName("user id");
viewer.getDatabaseLogonInfos().getConnectionInfo(0).setPassword("password");

// Set the value of the first parameter field
Fields params = new Fields();
ParameterField param = new ParameterField();
Values paramValues = new Values();
ParameterFieldDiscreteValue paramValue = new ParameterFieldDiscreteValue();

params.add(param);
paramValue.setValue(new String("1389"));
paramValues.add(paramValue);
```

LISTING 24.2   Continued

```
param.setCurrentValues(paramValues);
param.setName("Publisher");
viewer.setParameterFields(params);

%>
```

Web Reporting in .NET

Microsoft's new .NET technology, specifically ASP.NET, is becoming more and more popular each day. More developers are migrating their existing desktop or ASP applications to ASP.NET. Crystal Decisions was at the forefront of Web reporting in .NET. It began working with Microsoft years before the Visual Studio .NET product was released and co-developed Crystal Reports for Visual Studio .NET, which shipped with Visual Studio .NET itself. For more information on this product, see Appendix A. In Crystal Reports 9, Crystal Decisions has upgraded that product and integrated it back in to the mainstream Crystal Reports product.

The .NET Web Form Report Viewer works much the same way as the COM Report Viewer. It is a server-side ASP.NET Web control that resides on a Web server and is used inside aspx pages. It renders reports to HTML for zero-client Web report delivery.

The following is a snippet from an aspx page illustrating how to integrate a report into an ASP.NET page:

```
<h1>My Report</h1>
<cr:CrystalReportViewer ReportSource="RAS://C:\\MyReport.rpt" />
```

You'll notice that unlike the COM and Java report viewers, you don't need to write code to display the report. Instead, you can use a special tag inside of the ASPX page to specify various property values. This is common to all .NET Web form controls such as the data grid and calendar control. The .NET Report Viewer has similar properties, events, and methods that allow for total control over how the report is delivered.

One of the nice things about adding reporting to an ASP.NET application is using the Visual Studio .NET development environment. Many of these properties can be set visually via the Property Browser. Figure 24.5 shows an ASP.NET Web form with the .NET Report Viewer hosted on it inside of the Visual Studio .NET development environment.

FIGURE 24.5

Adding reporting to an ASP.NET application.

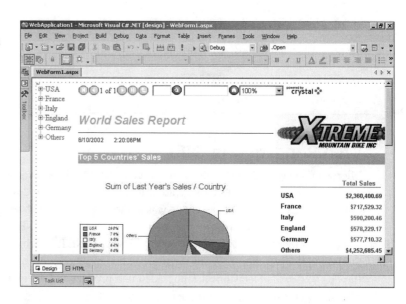

Like the other report viewers, the .NET Report Viewer can accept database logon credentials, parameter field values, selection formula, and so on. The following code listing provides an example of some of these actions in the C# language:

```csharp
// Some objects in the Shared namespace are needed
using CrystalDecisions.Shared;
...
// Set the report source to something
viewer.ReportSource = "C:\\Temp\\SecuredReportWithParam.rpt";

// Create a parameter value object, in this case a discrete value
ParameterDiscreteValue paramValue = new ParameterDiscreteValue();
paramValue.Value = "USA";
// Add the value to the parameter's current values
viewer.ParameterFieldInfo[0].CurrentValues.Add(paramValue);

// Set the database logon credentials
viewer.LogOnInfo[0].ConnectionInfo.UserID = "user id";
viewer.LogOnInfo[0].ConnectionInfo.Password = "password";
```

Both the Crystal Reports for Visual Studio .NET product and Crystal Reports 9
come with a report viewer based on the .NET Windows Forms framework.
This report viewer is functionally similar to the ActiveX report viewer, but is
a native .NET control. It can be used in either desktop applications (called
Windows Applications in Visual Studio .NET), or on the client tier of ASP.NET
applications.

For more information on both the .NET Windows Forms report viewer and the .NET Web Forms report viewer, consult the Crystal Reports 9 documentation installed into the MSDN help collection.

Building Advanced Web Applications

The Simple Web Applications scenario focused on getting reports onto the Web and providing a basic level of customization via parameter fields, record selection formula, and database logon credentials. Whereas that will meet the needs of many, some developers want to build more interactive applications that create reports on-the-fly, modify report layout and structure, and other similar actions. These kind of applications provide a higher level of analysis and ad hoc capabilities. To meet these needs, in addition to the Report Viewers in COM, .NET, and Java, Crystal Reports 9 comes with a powerful Report Application Server SDK.

The Crystal Enterprise Report Application Server is designed for the Web. It is composed of two components: the report processing server and the SDK. The SDK is provided in COM, .NET, and Java platforms. These two components can reside on the same machine, but they can also be separated into two tiers. This means that the overhead of report processing can be offloaded from the Web server to a dedicated reporting server, while still retaining a rich SDK on the Web server. The SDK communicates via open TCP/IP protocols with the Report Application Server. This section focuses on various scenarios with the Report Application Server SDK.

Because the SDK needs to communicate with a Report Application Server, it is designed using a *model-view-controller (MVC)* pattern. The MVC pattern is an established pattern for software development and is in use in common applications such as Microsoft Word and Excel. An MVC pattern defines a model, a view, and a controller as three independent pieces of an application. The model represents the data—in this case, the actual report document. The controller represents the mechanism for modifying the data held in the model—in this case, manipulating the report. Finally, the view represents the developer's application, which provides a visual representation of that data usually using one of the report viewers. The naming of the various objects in the Report Application Server SDK indicates their place in the MVC architecture.

Although the Report Application Server SDK is provided in COM, .NET, and Java, the object model is exactly the same; therefore, the following code examples will be mixed between VBScript (ASP), Java, C#, and VB.NET (.NET).

To start, let's look at a very simple example of using the Report Application Server SDK (see Listing 24.3).

LISTING 24.3   Using the RAS SDK via Active Server Pages

```
<%

Option Explicit

' Open the Report
Dim Report
Set Report = CreateObject("CrystalClientDoc.ReportClientDocument")
Report.Open "C:\Temp\Sorts.rpt"

' Retrieve the customer name field object
Dim field, fieldIndex
fieldIndex = Report.Database.Tables(0).DataFields.Find("Customer Name", 0)
Set field = Report.Database.Tables(0).DataFields(fieldIndex)

' Create a new sort based on the customer name field
Dim sort
Set sort = CreateObject("CrystalReports.Sort")
sort.SortField = field

' Remove the sort previously defined in the Report file
Report.DataDefController.SortController.Remove(0)

' Add the new sort
Report.DataDefController.SortController.Add 0, sort

Dim viewer
Set viewer = CreateObject("CrystalReports.CrystalReportViewer")
viewer.ReportSource = Report.ReportSource

viewer.ProcessHttpRequest Request, Response

%>
```

This example is quite simple because it only opens the report and changes the field that the report is sorted on. Let's examine the code in a bit more detail to fully understand how the RAS SDK works. You'll notice that the Database object is used to retrieve one of the database fields defined in the report. The Database object and other objects suffixed with Definition, such as DataDefinition and ReportDefinition, represent the model piece of the MVC architecture. If all you needed to do was retrieve the definition of the report—such as what database is being used, what fields are where on the report, or other similar things—you need only use the Definition objects. However, in most cases, changes are needed to be made. Any necessary data changes need to be made via the controller.

There are several Controller objects in the RAS SDK. In the preceding example, the `SortController` is being used. First, it is being used to remove the first (and in this case, only) sorting defined in the report. Next, the `SortController` is being used to add the new sorting. This style of programming is consistent across the RAS SDK.

With the power to modify the report in many ways, you can imagine how your Web-based application can evolve from simply projecting a report onto a Web page to building a highly interactive ad hoc reporting application.

Summary

In this hour, you have learned a bit about the history of Crystal Reports developer tools and what is currently available in Crystal Reports 9. For the desktop developer, the Report Designer Component provides the richest SDK available, giving the developer the ability to design reports from within the Visual Basic development environment, manipulate, print, and export them using the object model, and display them using the ActiveX report viewer.

24

For developers using the Web to deliver reports, report viewers are available for the COM, .NET, and Java platforms. These report viewers render any report to HTML and thus provide a zero-client report delivery solution. If and when developers want more control over the report and have more of a need for interactive applications, a Report Application Server SDK is also available in the same three platforms that can be used to build advanced Web applications.

This hour has just been an introduction to the developer tools in Crystal Reports 9: There is much more to learn. A good place to start is the Crystal Reports documentation, both printed and electronic. In addition, the Technical Support site found at `http://support.crystaldecisions.com` has many sample applications and technical briefs on Crystal Reports developer tools. Use that site as another resource.

Workshop

The quiz questions and activities are provided for your further understanding of the current hour's topics.

Quiz

1. What are the three application development scenarios Crystal Reports 9 is targeted toward?
2. What are the three components that compose the Report Designer Component?
3. What development platforms is Crystal Reports 9 targeting for Web applications?

Quiz Answers

1. Crystal Reports 9 is targeting toward three scenarios: Desktop Application, Simple Web Applications, and Advanced Web Applications.

2. The three components that compose the Report Designer Component are the Visual Basic Report Designer, the Object Model, and the ActiveX Report Viewer.

3. For Web-based applications, Crystal Reports 9 is targeting the COM (ASP), .NET (ASP.NET), and Java (JSP) development platforms.

Activities

To ensure that you are comfortable with the topics discussed in this hour, try to perform the following tasks:

- Build a Visual Basic application that prompts the business user with an InputBox for the name of the country he would like to see data for. Then display a report based on the Xtreme Sample Database's Customer table in the ActiveX report viewer.

- Build a simple .NET Application that displays one of the Crystal Reports 9 sample reports on the Web in HTML format.

- Create a Java application that creates a report on-the-fly—based on one of the sample reports' data sources— and adds three fields, then display that report in the Java Interactive Report Viewer.

PART VII

Supplemental Crystal Reports Technologies

APPENDIX A

Crystal Reports for Visual Studio .NET

Crystal Reports for Visual Studio .NET is a custom version of Crystal Reports and provides a comprehensive reporting solution for Visual Studio .NET developers. This version of Crystal Reports is seamlessly integrated with both the Visual Studio .NET development environment (IDE) and the .NET Framework. It is important to note that the Crystal Reports for Visual Studio .NET version is not the same as, or included in, Crystal Reports version 9. Consequently, there might be features and topics covered earlier in this book that are not in the Crystal Reports for Visual Studio .NET version. Crystal Reports version 9 is the latest and most current release of Crystal Reports at the time this book was written.

Who Should Read This Appendix?

This appendix overviews Crystal Report's unique functionality and features in Visual Studio .NET and outlines many of the resources that Crystal Decisions, the company that produces Crystal Reports, offers on its Web site. This material is targeted at developers working within the Visual Studio .NET application development environment, as well as readers interested in obtaining an introduction to this custom version of Crystal Reports.

Overview of Microsoft .NET and Crystal Reports for Visual Studio .NET

Microsoft and Crystal Decisions have a long-standing relationship, and this version of Crystal Reports has been uniquely designed and developed to integrate seamlessly with the Microsoft .NET platform. Crystal Reports was first released in 1992 as a Windows-based report writer, and Microsoft adopted Crystal Reports as the standard for Visual Basic in 1993.[1] Visual Studio .NET now integrates a special version of Crystal Reports, further integrating Crystal Reports for use with all the .NET programming languages, including C#.

Microsoft .NET is an XML Web services platform that enables developers to create programs that transcend device boundaries and harness the connectivity of the Internet. Visual Studio .NET (VS .NET), and the individual tools and languages it contains, is the foundation for building Windows-based components and applications, creating scripts, developing Web sites and applications, and managing source code.[2]

Crystal Reports for Visual Studio .NET is the reporting standard for Visual Studio .NET and is included as part of the Visual Studio .NET developer platform. Crystal Reports for Visual Studio .NET supports XML Web Services, ASP.NET server controls and caching and ADO.NET, and offers a rich programming model and flexible options for customizing and deploying reports. Any Crystal Report created in Visual Studio .NET can become an embedded resource for use in Windows and Web applications as well as Web services.

---

[1] *Strategic Partners: Microsoft,* http://www.crystaldecisions.com/partners/strategic/microsoft/default.asp

[2] *.NET Development,* http://msdn.microsoft.com/library/default.asp

Many of the terms used in this Appendix are specific to the Microsoft .NET solution and/or Visual Studio .NET development environment. For more detailed information on the Microsoft .NET solution, refer to Microsoft's Web site at `http://msdn.microsoft.com/library/default.asp`.

New Terms:

- XML Web Services—A Web Service is a unit of application logic providing data and services to other applications. Applications access Web Services via ubiquitous Web protocols and data formats such as HTTP and XML, with no need to worry about how each Web Service is implemented. Web Services combine the best aspects of component-based development and the Web, and are a cornerstone of the Microsoft .NET programming model.[3]

- ASP.NET—ASP.NET is a set of technologies in the Microsoft .NET Framework for building Web applications and XML Web Services. ASP.NET pages execute on the server and generate markup such as HTML, WML, or XML that is sent to a desktop or mobile browser. ASP.NET pages and ASP.NET XML Web Services files contain server-side logic (as opposed to client side logic) written in Visual Basic .NET, C# .NET, or any .NET compatible language.[4]

- ADO.NET—ADO.NET is an evolutionary improvement to Microsoft *ActiveX Data Objects (ADO)* that provides platform interoperability and scalable data access. Using *Extensible Markup Language (XML)*, ADO.NET can ensure the efficient transfer of data to any application on any platform.[5]

- SOAP—*SOAP (Simple Object Access Protocol)* is a lightweight and simple XML-based protocol that is designed to exchange structured and typed information on the Web. The purpose of SOAP is to enable rich and automated Web services based on a shared and open Web infrastructure.[6]

A

---

[3] *XML Web Services*, `http://msdn.microsoft.com/library/default.asp`

[4] *ASP.NET*, `http://msdn.microsoft.com/library/default.asp`

[5] *"Introducing ADO.NET,"* `http://msdn.microsoft.com/vstudio/techinfo/articles/upgrade/adoplus.asp`

[6] *SOAP, http://msdn.microsoft.com/library/default.asp?url=/nhp/Default.asp?contentid=28000523*

Crystal Reports for Visual Studio .NET provides developers working within Visual Studio .NET a fast, productive way to create and integrate presentation-quality, interactive reports that scale to meet the demands of end users of their applications. This version of Crystal Reports enhances the .NET platform by allowing developers to

- Create reports for Windows, Web, and XML Web Services applications inside Visual Studio .NET.
- Deliver interactive, graphical reports in rich-client, zero-client environments, or any device through an XML Web Services model.
- Save time and write less code by leveraging your existing Crystal Reports and report creation knowledge within your .NET projects

Crystal Reports for Visual Studio .NET Feature Set

The features provided by Crystal Reports for Visual Studio .NET significantly reduce the amount of labor and effort required for data representation in custom .NET applications. These features include

- Business Intelligence Web Services—Gives Visual Studio .NET developers the power to publish Crystal Reports as Business Intelligence Web Services, with just one mouse click.
- Integrated Report Designer—Makes report creation and integration, in any programming language and project type that works with Visual Studio .NET, a *Rapid Application Development (RAD)* experience with presentation-quality results.
- WebForms and WINForms Viewer Controls—Gives Visual Studio .NET developers C# (pronounced "C-sharp") technology to integrate and view reports, and Business Intelligence Web Services, in any project type with a simple drag-and-drop from the development toolbar.
- Run Time Object Model—This native Visual Studio .NET object model provides runtime customization of reports—the ability to resize and reposition objects, as well as pass report parameters and logon credentials.
- ADO.NET Data Set Support—Developers can instantiate ADO.NET data sets at runtime within their application and programmatically set this data set as the source for a Crystal Report file.

- Crystal Enterprise SOAP Connector—Designed to speed report integration, the Crystal Enterprise SOAP Connector allows you to extract managed reports from Crystal Enterprise to use in your .NET applications. For more information on Crystal Enterprise, refer to the Crystal Decisions web site at `http://www.crystaldecisions.com/products/crystalenterprise/default.asp`.

The preceding features are available for any .NET development language. Thus, Crystal Reports for Visual Studio .NET provides developers with increased productivity—there's no need to learn a proprietary language to get results. For example, an accounting firm can use Web services to expose a Crystal Report to its customers over the Web.

Crystal Reports for Visual Studio .NET can rapidly use existing Crystal Reports with just a click of the mouse—leveraging existing assets and report creation knowledge, reducing code, increasing productivity, and saving time. Crystal Reports' powerful report creation and Web capabilities enable developers to experience rapid application development while using any programming language targeting the .NET Framework, as well as carrying forward current development skills without costly and extensive re-training.

Feature Set Comparison—Crystal Reports for Visual Studio .NET and Crystal Reports 9

Crystal Reports 9 extends the power of Crystal Reports Visual Studio .NET. Although Visual Studio .NET integrates a custom version of Crystal Reports that includes many powerful tools, you can also benefit from standalone report design capabilities, faster deployment, and maximum developer efficiency by extending your .NET applications with the additional report creation tools found in Crystal Reports 9 Advanced edition (see Hour 2 for an overview of the various editions available for Crystal Reports 9). Table A.1 displays a reference to many common reporting features and how these two unique versions of Crystal Reports compare.

TABLE A.1 A Feature Comparison of Crystal Reports 9 and Crystal Reports for Visual Studio .NET

Product	Crystal Reports Visual Studio .NET	Crystal Reports 9 Advanced Edition
Rapid Report Design		
Standalone Designer	No (integrated designer)	Yes
Business Intelligence Web Services	Yes	No

TABLE A.1   continued

Product	Crystal Reports Visual Studio .NET	Crystal Reports 9 Advanced Edition
Database Connectivity	Microsoft data sources	Full suite of data sources
OLAP (multidimensional) Reports	No	Yes
Microsoft Excel and Access Add-ins	No	Yes
Report Component Repository	No	Yes
Customizable Report Templates	No	Yes
Unlimited SQL Commands	No	Yes
Custom Functions for sharing formulas	No	Yes
High-Performance Web Reporting		
Out-of-the-Box Web interface for on-demand report access	No	Yes
Report access via WML, RIM, and iPAQ devices	No	Yes
ASP.NET Support	Yes	No
ADO.NET Support	Yes	No
Java Report Viewer	No	Yes
Netscape Viewer plug-in	No	Yes
Comprehensive Formatting and Design Control		
Guidelines and vertical rulers	No	Yes
Integrated geographic mapping	No	Yes

TABLE A.1 continued

Product	Crystal Reports Visual Studio .NET	Crystal Reports 9 Advanced Edition
Interactive Analysis Tools		
Report Alerts	No	Yes
Fully customizable runtime Preview Window	Yes	Yes
Export Formats		
Export to XML	No	Yes
Export to PDF	Yes	Yes
Export to DHTML (HTML 4.0)	Yes	Yes
Export to HTML	Yes	Yes
Export to Microsoft Word and Excel	Yes	Yes
Export to RTF	Yes	Yes
Export to character-separated values, CSV, record style (columns of values), report definition, tab-separated text and values	No	Yes
Report Creation API	No	Yes
Report Integration and Delivery		
Seamless deployment with Crystal Enterprise	Limited	Yes
Easily leverage advanced Crystal Enterprise services	Limited	Yes

A

Ten Reasons to Upgrade to Crystal Reports 9 Advanced from the Crystal Reports for Visual Studio .NET version

Crystal Reports 9 takes reporting in Visual Studio .NET to the next level with innovative new technology for faster report design and enhanced web integration. Here are 10 distinct reasons to upgrade to the Advanced edition:

- Report Application Server with .NET, Java, and COM SDKs—Tightly integrate content into enterprise-wide Web applications without the need for heavy coding of complex data access and formatting routines.
- Runtime report creation and modification—Advanced server-based Java and DHTML viewers let business users view, drill-down, and navigate reports, as well as export, search, and modify reports at runtime.
- Enhanced support for Microsoft Office and mobile users—Let business users easily extract charts, tables, and other report objects from reports and directly insert them into Microsoft Outlook, Word, or Excel documents. With support for Microsoft Smart Tags in Office XP, business users can view, share, and refresh report objects right from within documents. Deliver existing report components via wireless devices including WML phones, RIM, and iPAQ devices using new Report Parts. Reports don't have to be recreated specifically for use within wireless and portal environments.
- Component reuse for faster report design—Design reports faster by storing key report objects—including text objects, SQL commands, bitmaps, and custom functions—in a central library. Objects can be reused, shared, and updated from a single place for faster report design and maintenance.
- Unlimited SQL control—Edit SQL directly for unlimited control over database connectivity. Specify the database connection and create parameterized SQL commands to perform any query your database supports.
- Additional data connectivity and export capabilities—By upgrading to Crystal Reports 9 Advanced edition, you can connect to almost any data, including enterprise data sources (Oracle, IBM DB2, Sybase, Informix, and others), XML, custom JavaBean and COM data providers, and export reports to additional formats such as Excel, Word, XML, Lotus, Text, and others.
- Customizable report preview at design time—Preview reports directly within the designer for faster and more accurate report creation.
- More report design choice—Additional report design and formatting options include Gantt and Gage charts, OLAP reporting, Geographic mapping, and the Formula Wizard.

- Standalone report designer—Separate development from report design to make maintaining reports easier and application integration faster.

- Special Upgrade Pricing—Take advantage of the additional features and enhancements in Crystal Reports 9 with an extra incentive for Microsoft Visual Studio .NET customers. Learn how you can upgrade to Crystal Reports 9 Advanced Edition by visiting the Crystal Decisions Web site at `http://www.crystaldeci-sions.com/tycr/products/crystalreports/`.

Creating Reports in Visual Studio .NET

To assist Visual Studio .NET developers in designing reports, Crystal Reports for Visual Studio .NET provides a collection of Report Experts, extremely similar to the Report Creation Wizards (covered in Hour 4, "Using the Default Report Wizards") available in Crystal Reports 9. The Report Experts will guide the Visual Studio .NET developer through the creation of a variety of reports while handling the details of how the report is created. The available Report Experts create several types of reports, including standard, form letter, form, cross-tab, sub-report, mail label, and drill-down reports, shown in Figure A.1. Figure A.2 displays the Standard Report Creation Expert dialog.

FIGURE A.1

The Crystal Reports Gallery dialog allows Visual Studio .NET developers to access a variety of Report Creation Experts.

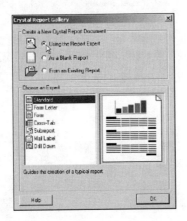

Crystal Reports for Visual Studio .NET is composed of several components. Once a report is set up, either manually or by using one of the Report Experts, developers use the Crystal Reports Designer in Visual Studio .NET to modify, add, and format objects and fields, as well as to format the report layout and manipulate the report design, as shown in Figure A.3. The designer then generates .rpt files. (.rpt is the file extension for a Crystal Report.) Within the Visual Studio environment, these .rpt files are processed by the Crystal Reports engine, which delivers the report output to one of two Crystal Report viewers—a Windows Forms viewer control or a Web Forms viewer control—depending on the type of application the developer specifies. The report viewer then presents the formatted report information to the business user of the application.

The Standard Report Expert is perhaps the most common expert used to create reports.

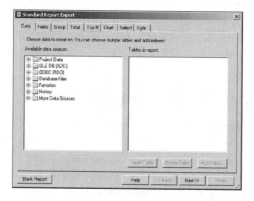

The Crystal Reports for Visual Studio .NET design environment.

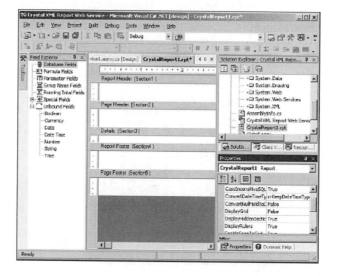

Using Crystal Reports in Web Applications

A developer, using Crystal Reports for Visual Studio .NET, can integrate highly interactive reports into a Web page. Dynamic Web applications are made possible through ASP .NET technology integrated into Visual Studio .NET. Crystal Reports for Visual Studio .NET provides a Web Forms Report Viewer, which is a Web Form (HTML files with embedded Web Controls and code files that contain event-handling logic) that hosts the report. When a client (end business user) accesses such a Web form, the event handler can update and format information in a Crystal Report and send the updated report to the business user of the application.[7]

One of the walkthroughs available on the Crystal Decision's Web site instructs Visual Studio .NET developers how to enable Web page interactivity and how to use ASP .NET and its controls. In this walkthrough, the business user of the application accesses information about countries by first entering a country name into a text box, and then submits the information. The country name is passed to the Web forms viewer control and the report is updated.

Using Crystal Reports with Web Services

Using Crystal Reports for Visual Studio .NET, any Crystal Report created in C# can be published as an "XML Report Web Service" as shown in Figure A.4. A Web service provides methods that are accessible over the Internet to any application, independent of programming language or platform. As an example, an XML Report Web Service could be an excellent mechanism with which business partners could access specific report information. Visual Studio .NET generates a DLL file (dynamic link library) that contains the report and an XML file when a Crystal Report is published as an XML Report Web service. Both files are published to a Web server so that a client machine (business user) can access the report. An XML-based SOAP message passes the data to and from the Web service. When a developer uses Visual Studio .NET to create and publish the Web service, the developer can associate the Web service to either a Windows or a Web application to display the data returned from the Web service.

One of the great things about using a report as a Web service is that it allows companies to exchange corporate information without passing the actual data. Rather than opening up your database to a partner, you can build a report off it and have the report exposed as a Web service. The report is still executed at the host company, alleviating any security issues, but the partner consuming the report can benefit from the insight it provides.

Again, Crystal Decisions provides a good example, via a walkthrough, of the steps necessary to familiarize developers with implementing a report as a Web service.

A

---

[7]*Developer Zone, Hot Downloads (Crystal Reports for Visual Studio .NET Walkthroughs).*
`http://www.crystaldecisions.com/products/dev_zone`

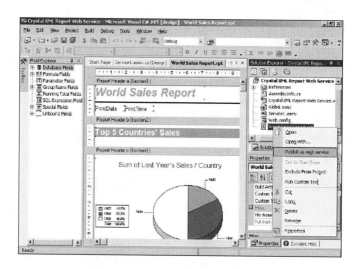

FIGURE A.4

Crystal Reports can be published as a Web Service within the Visual Studio .NET design environment.

To truly understand the value and implementation of a Crystal Report Web service, it's useful to consider a common scenario. Let's assume that company A has a large regional distributor network and needs to share sales information with these distributors on a regular basis and has built a sales report used internally to understand this information. Company A would like to use this same report to serve external audiences. The following example provides an illustration of how company A can build an XML report Web services application to enable business partners to access relevant information:

1. Click New Project on the Start page.
2. Select Visual Basic Projects and then ASP.NET Web Service.
3. Click OK. Provide a new project name, and then click OK. Visual Studio .NET will open up your new project.
4. Right-click on the "name" of your new project.
5. Select Add and then Add New Item.
6. Select Crystal Report from the menu.
7. Either select an existing Crystal Report or create a new Crystal Report.
8. Assuming that you select an existing report, select the World Sales Report.
9. Right-click on the report you just added and select Publish as Web Service.
10. Select Build and then Build Solution.

Company B (business partner of company A) builds a C# Windows application within Visual Studio .NET that consumes the XML report Web service created by company A:

1. Right-click on Solution and select Add and then Add new project.

2. This time, select Visual C# Projects and then Windows Application.

3. IMPORTANT—Set this project as your Startup Project by right-clicking on the name of this new application and selecting Set as Startup Project.

4. Copy the location of the new Crystal Report .asmx file created earlier by clicking on it and selecting Copy.

5. In the new project, select References and then Add Web Reference.

6. Paste the location of the item copied in step 4 into the top Address box and click Enter.

7. When the page comes up, select Add Reference—a new Web Reference should be visible in the Solution Explorer.

8. Go to the toolbox and drag the Windows CrystalReportsViewer.

9. Select Dock from the Properties area.

10. Double-click on the form and view the code.

11. Locate InitializeComponent(); and space down two spaces.

12. Enter this line of code: `crystalReportViewer1.ReportSource = new local-host.<NAME OF CRYSTAL WEB SERVICE>();`.

13. Select Save All, Build, Build Solution, Debug, and then Start without Debugging.

14. The application will build and display after 20 seconds.

15. The resulting report even supports drill-down, export, and printing capabilities.

Additional Resources on Crystal Reports for Visual Studio for .NET

Crystal Decisions offers resources for developers working in Visual Studio .NET at their Web site, `http://www.crystaldecisions.com/products/crystalreports/net`. The site offers report and application samples, technical briefs, an online newsletter, a multimedia product demo, discussion forums, a developer's zone, licensing information, walkthroughs, and an overview of Crystal Reports in Visual Studio .NET. The walkthroughs include integrating and viewing Web reports through Windows applications, creating interactive reports in Web applications, exposing Crystal Reports through Web services, and reporting from ActiveX Data Objects (ADO) .NET data.[9] Crystal Decisions also provides technical support for Crystal Reports C# developers via email or phone.

---

[9] *The walkthroughs on the Crystal Decisions Web site were tested using C# in Visual Studio .NET.*

- To learn more about Crystal Reports for Visual Studio .NET, including technical details, visit `http://www.crystaldecisions.com/products/crystalreports/net`

- For more information about server software expansion packs for Crystal Reports for Visual Studio .NET, visit
`http://www.crystaldecisions.com/products/crystalreports/net/licensing.asp`

- For more information about Crystal Reports 9, visit `http://www.crystaldecisions.com/tycr/products/crystalreports/`

- For more information about Crystal Decisions' selection of public, on-site and computer-based training (CBT) courses, visit
`http://www.crystaldecisions.com/tycr/services/`

- A technical white paper on Crystal Decisions XML Report Web Services can be found on Microsoft's Web site at `http://msdn.microsoft.com/msdnmag/issues/02/05/Crystal/Crystal.asp`

APPENDIX B

Common Crystal Reports FAQs and Tips

If you've made it this far into the book, it means that you're looking for some extra tips or have worked with Crystal Reports enough to have additional questions. We've provided this appendix as a reference for some of the common questions we get from report designers and developers, both novice and advanced.

This appendix will help you find the resources you need to be successful in your endeavors with Crystal Reports.

In this appendix, we cover

- Report design FAQs and resources
- Common report distribution questions
- Resources for additional support

Report Design FAQs and Resources

Undoubtedly one of the best resources for additional information on report design is the Technical Briefs section of the Crystal Decisions support Web site:

```
http://support.crystaldecisions.com/tycr/library/kbase.asp
```

One of the more useful briefs is a whitepaper (cr_sample_rpts_desc.pdf) that provides a listing of sample reports that demonstrate report design concepts. We encourage you to make use of all the various resources available on the Internet, including the Crystal Decisions Web site, to help you with your report design efforts.

As for the rest of this section, we've taken some common report design questions that we often get from novice to intermediate report developers and included them here. Some of the more common report design questions include

- Q. How can I troubleshoot potential database driver connectivity issues between multiple PCs?

  A. Use a utility available from Crystal Decisions, called Modules, to troubleshoot database connectivity issues between multiple physical PCs.

- Q. How do I change the page size of a Crystal Report to give myself more room for additional columns?

  A. Use a different printer driver, even if the physical printer for the driver isn't present. Crystal Reports allocates "space" in the report based on the printer driver specified. This is also important to keep in mind when you plan on distributing a report to other users because they will need this printer driver.

- Q. Why do I lose formatting of things like maps when I save the report?

  A. More than likely, you aren't saving the report with Data, something you can specify by selecting the Save Data With Report option from the File menu.

- Q. How do I specify the exact size of an object in a Crystal Report?

  A. Right-click an object in a Crystal Report and choose Object Size and Position.

- Q. Why is the Select Distinct Records option sometimes unavailable?

  A. The Select Distinct Records command is unavailable when a report contains a memo field, an OLE object, or a hyperlinked object. Try placing these types of fields in a linked subreport, rather than the main report.

- Q. Can Crystal Reports use Stored Procedures?

  A. Yes, this can be enabled by properly specifying the Report Options settings from the File menu.

- Q. Can I group on the same field more than once in a Crystal report?

  A. Yes, but after you group on the actual field, try creating a formula off of the field. Then create the next group using the formula field.

- Q. In older versions of Crystal Reports, I had trouble using memo fields longer than 254 characters. Is this still the case?

  A. Crystal Reports support for memo field has changed for the better in version 9, with support for memo field longer than 254 characters, which can also be used in formulas.

- Q. Can Crystal Reports report off of data sources such as ADO recordsets?

  A. Yes, Crystal Reports can connect to active data produced by objects such as a .dll for reporting.

- Q. When trying to convert a date, what do errors like "a date is required here" mean?

  A. This typically indicates that you are returning your date/time fields in the wrong format based on the formula you have written.

A number of FAQ resources are available on the Crystal Decisions Web site. Refer to the section on Resources for Additional Support found in this appendix for more details.

Common Report Distribution Questions

When distributing reports with Crystal Reports, it's safe to assume that you'll be using one of a number of mechanisms, including

- A management/distribution system such as Crystal Enterprise
- A custom Web or Windows application using a Crystal Reports or Report Application Server SDK
- A compiled report
- Email or other manual distribution mechanisms

Although you can distribute reports through a thick client Windows application using the free Crystal Reports runtime libraries and components, server-based or Web-based applications might require additional licensing. Review the licensing information available on the Crystal Decisions Web site to understand how licensing might impact your applications.

B

One of the most interesting points to note about sharing Crystal Reports and the most common issue found across all mechanisms for sharing Crystal Reports is that the data source(s) are improperly configured—most often when it involves moving a report from a developer's desktop to a report processing server. The same data source connectivity method needs to be created on the server because it is on the workstation where the report was designed.

Second only to that is the issue of conflicting .dlls, or multiple copies of Crystal Reports files on the same physical PC. This shouldn't be surprising because different versions of Crystal Reports, and its associated viewing files, are bundled in so many different third-party applications.

Crystal Enterprise

Crystal Enterprise actually handles the delivery of reports without additional effort from application developers or report administrators. This does not exclude the possibility of running into issues when viewing reports, however. If you want more detailed information on Crystal Enterprise, refer to Hour 23, "Distributing Crystal Reports." You can also find more information on Crystal Enterprise at the Crystal Decisions Web site:

```
http://www.crystaldecisions.com/tycr/products/crystalenterprise/
```

A few of the main benefits in using Crystal Enterprise to distribute and share your reports include

- Centralized management of all your organizational reports—both relational and multidimensional reports
- Secure access to all corporate reports
- Zero-client Web delivery of reports
- Centralized data source connectivity mechanisms
- Reduced data access and client support issues across the organization
- Robust and scaleable Enterprise-ready architecture

The best advice we can give you if you run into report viewing errors or issues when using Crystal Enterprise to distribute your reports is to try different types of viewers to narrow down the problem. For example, if you are using the DHTML viewer in ePortfolio (one of the many Crystal Enterprise "client" applications for business users) and find some report formatting issues, try changing your preferences to the ActiveX or Java viewers.

This will give you a good indication whether the report itself is formatted incorrectly, or the report viewer you are using is the root of the issue.

Additionally, an index to any whitepapers or guides to Crystal Enterprise can be found on the Crystal Decisions Web site at

```
http://support.crystaldecisions.com/tycr/docs/
```

Custom Web or Windows Application

Regardless of the approach used to share a Crystal Report, we can make a few common assumptions about all applications: You are using SDK components of some kind, either the *RDC (Report Designer Component)* or *RAS (Report Application Server)*. We also know that you need a report viewer, which comes in different "flavors" such as, but not limited to, DHTML, ActiveX, and Java.

You might even be using the Crystal Offline Viewer, which is a more robust report viewer application that must be installed on a business user's desktop PC in order to view Crystal Reports files offline. Although many organizations now prefer the use of the DHTML viewer, because it is not installed in any way on a desktop PC, viewers such as the ActiveX viewer still prove useful for many applications.

Distributed Components

One major advantage of the ActiveX viewer is that it is a "distributable" component that many Microsoft Visual Basic developers include in their applications, which enables the viewing of Crystal Reports. Other common distributable components in corporate applications include additional *RCAPI (Report Creation API)* files that enable not just the viewing of Crystal Reports, but the actual modification of reports as well.

Regardless of the application development environment, the Crystal Reports runtime files required for distribution with your application are dependent on the following:

- How the Crystal Reports engine is accessed
- The types of data used for the reports
- Whether or not you will export data
- Additional components such as charts, maps, formula language functions, and so on that might be used

If you've developed an application using any processing or viewing components of Crystal Reports prior to version 9, some update work will be required. Why? Because a new Print Engine is used in Crystal Reports 9, which means that older runtime components shipped in Visual Studio version 6 and earlier won't understand what to do with the report.

One of the common tasks you'll undertake is updating your application to include the newer distributed components included with Crystal Reports 9. Crystal Reports 9 includes a help file that details which files to distribute with your application. To locate this information, search the help file (Runtime.chm) for details.

Additionally, because the ActiveX viewer is the most common distributed Crystal Reports component with Windows applications, it's helpful to know a few of the most common issues that can arise with it. For detailed troubleshooting information, you can download the "Crystal_Web_Viewer_for_Actx.pdf" by searching by filename at

```
http://support.crystaldecisions.com/tycr/docs
```

As for some of the more common issues with the ActiveX viewer in applications, the two that surface the most are as follows:

- The container directory for the ActiveX viewer is incorrectly configured on the Web server for your application.
- An older version of the ActiveX viewer is already installed on the end user's desktop.

Distributed Components with Visual Studio.NET

Additionally, some of you might have questions about the version of Crystal Reports that comes with Microsoft Visual Studio.NET. The release of the Visual Studio.NET version still provides the ability to embed runtime report processing and viewing capability in a windows application—the Windows Forms Viewer, for example, developed in any .NET language, such as C# or VB.NET. Refer to Appendix A, "Crystal Reports for Visual Studio.NET," for more information on, and a feature comparison of, Crystal Reports for Microsoft Visual Studio.NET.

When developing applications with VS.NET and Crystal Reports, it's important to consult Crystal Decisions to make sure that you are within the terms of the End-User License Agreement.

Compiled Reports

Compiled reports are a report distribution feature in earlier versions of Crystal Reports. It provided a way for reports to be "wrapped" inside an executable that would allow interaction with the report and not require any installed Crystal Components.

Compiled Reports are no longer considered a very efficient or robust way to distribute reports, and many Crystal Reports users find that this method doesn't work well in large deployments. The files and documentation required for compiled reports are not on the Crystal Reports CD, but you can find them on the Crystal Decisions Web site.

If your application still uses compiled reports, refer to the Crystal Reports 9 help file for information on where to download support for compiled reports.

You can also visit the Crystal Decisions Web site under the updates section:

    http://support.crystaldecisions.com/tycr/updates/

Manual Report Distribution

Many applications use the RDC to create Crystal Reports automatically, such as to export the report to a specific format, Microsoft Word for example, and then email the report out to a large number of users. Although this is still a perfectly acceptable solution for report distribution, Crystal Reports 9 has additional licensing considerations for distributing reports in this manner.

Make sure to consult with Crystal Decisions for more information on licensing. Licensing issues should always be considered before developing and deploying any report distribution solution.

You might also consider using the Crystal Offline Viewer, which allows an end user to view Crystal Reports with saved data in an "offline" mode, where the end user can still perform tasks such as drilling down on charts and re-sorting data. If you are using Crystal Enterprise, you might already use this within your organization. If not, it's highly recommended as an easy-to-use offline report viewing solution.

Resources for Additional Support

B

Crystal Decisions keeps an up-to-date knowledge base and whitepaper library for additional support. You can find that online at

    http://support.crystaldecisions.com/tycr/library/kbase.asp

Product Registration

Registering your Crystal Reports software allows you to get the full benefit from your product purchase. By registering your copy of Crystal Reports, you will also receive

- Free technical support by phone or email for 60 days
- *Ask Crystal*, a natural-language search tool to help you navigate our extensive support site
- Online Knowledge Base, with more than 5,000 archived technical articles covering a range of topics

- White papers, product updates, sample applications, and more
- Newsletters and product updates

Crystal Consulting and Training

Does your organization need a little help with your report writing efforts? The Crystal Services group within Crystal Decisions designs and delivers reporting solutions to give customers advanced decision-making ability. The Crystal Services group offers a wide range of consulting services, including

- Strategy Services—Includes Enterprise Reporting assessments, Enterprise upgrades, and Proof-of-Concepts
- Deployment Services—Includes QuickStarts and upgrades
- Design Services—Includes eReports/eCubes (remote report and cube design), report writing, and Web architecture and design services
- Integration Services—Includes system auditing and long-term consulting support

In addition to consulting services, the Crystal Services group offers flexible options to meet your training needs, including both instructor-led courses and Computer Based Training (CBT) modules. The following sections provide more details on these training offerings. For more information on Crystal Services, visit the following site at

```
http://www.crystaldecisions.com/tycr/services/
```

Crystal Certified Training Centers—Core Crystal Reports Offerings

Crystal Decisions' instructor-led courses include

- Report Design I—This two-day course is designed for the novice Crystal Reports user who needs to quickly become proficient in creating and modifying reports. Some of the topics include planning a report, creating a basic report, record selection, sorting, grouping and summarizing, charting, and formulas such as basic calculations and running totals. Much of this material is also covered here in this book.
- Report Design II—This two-day course is designed to build on the topics learned in Report Design I—to increase report design skills and further discover the reporting power of Crystal Reports. Along with hands-on practice, the course covers grouping options, formulas (such as variables and functions), geographical mapping, parameters, cross-tabs, and report distribution.

- Report Design III—This one-day course is designed to further increase report design skills by concentrating on advanced topics. Along with hands-on practice, the course covers architecture, report design and Structured Query Language (SQL), advanced formula creation (such as arrays and control structures), sub-reports, and an XML overview as it relates to Crystal Reports.

eLearning—Computer Based Training

Crystal Decisions offers interactive self-learning via self-paced CBT for Crystal Reports. Directly from your desktop, using a familiar Web browser interface, you can select more than 60 animated interactive lessons at a pace that you can control. Each lesson contains task-specific animations that walk you through report creation and design. Whether you need to supplement hard copy material (such as this book) or instructor-led courses, dynamic CBT modules provide you with another flexible learning option.

Additional Web Resources

Additionally, some useful Web sites include

- Top 10 KBase articles

  `http://support.crystaldecisions.com/tycr/fix/topkb.asp`
- Top 10 downloads

  `http://support.crystaldecisions.com/tycr/fix/topdownloads.asp`
- Top 10 technical briefs

  `http://support.crystaldecisions.com/tycr/fix/toptech.asp`
- Crystal Reports product information and demos

  `http://www.crystaldecisions.com/tycr/products/crystalreports/`
- Crystal Enterprise product information

  `http://www.crystaldecisions.com/tycr/products/crystalenterprise/`
- Crystal Analysis product information

  `http://www.crystaldecisions.com/tycr/products/crystalanalysispro/`
- Crystal Decisions product family information

  `http://www.crystaldecisions.com/tycr/products/`
- Crystal Services— Training and Consulting

  `http://www.crystaldecisions.com/tycr/services/`
- Crystal Decisions product registration

  `http://www.crystaldecisions.com/tycr/register/`
- Crystal Decisions online store

  `http://www.crystaldecisions.com/tycr/store`

B

The Developer Zone

Additionally, the Developer Zone is a new addition to the Crystal Decisions Web site. It caters specifically to application developers, rather than report developers. Whether Microsoft Visual Basic, Visual Studio.NET, or even Java is your preferred development language or environment, the Developer Zone has all kinds of code samples and applications.

Some of the top content in the Developer Zone includes how to report off of XML data sources, how to develop Crystal Enterprise applications, and Visual Studio.NET application development.

You can find the Developer Zone at

```
http://www.crystaldecisions.com/tycr/products/dev_zone/
```

Additional Crystal Reports and Utilities

Make sure to check the Crystal Decisions Web site for Crystal Report management utilities, not just whitepapers and knowledge base articles.

The Crystal Decisions technical support team publishes different utilities from time to time that might help you in your endeavors. Additionally, several different types of sample Crystal Reports are published on the Crystal Decisions Web site.

INDEX

C

How can we make this index more useful? Email us at indexes@samspublishing.com

I

icons, Insert Subreport, 306
IIS (Internet Information Server), 419
images, Repository, 338
implementing parameter fields, 253
In-Place Subreports, 311-313
indirect access drivers, 51
INIT command, 421
Inner join, 61
Insert Cross-Tab button, 277
Insert Cross-Tab tab, 277
Insert Group dialog box, 97, 119, 123, 160
Insert menu, 45
Insert Subreport dialog box, 305
Insert Subreport icon, 306
Insert Summary dialog box, 98, 172
Insert Tools toolbar, 44
inserting
    groups of data in reports, 119-121
    report sections, 180-185
install-on-demand, 35, 53
installed programs, locating, 40-41
installing Crystal Reports 9, 33-35
    Custom installation, 35-39
    Typical installation, 35-37
integration, Crystal Reports, 17-19
Internet Information Server (IIS), 419
IT maintenance, report distribution, 414

J

Java
    data sources, 396-397
    Web reporting, 439-441

Java Data Source driver, 392
Java Report Viewer, 440
Joining multiple tables, 406
joins, 61

K-L

KBase Web sites, 471
keyword searches, 325

labels
    cross-tab summaries, 284
    OLAP Expert, 382
Labels tab, 382
languages
    formulas, 195, 320
        Basic syntax, 320-321
        brackets, 321
        characters, 322
        Crystal syntax, 320-321
    SQL, 402
        aliasing, 406-407
        fields, 407
        grouping, 408-409
        records, filtering, 404-405
        records, sorting, 405-406
        SELECT statement, 402-404
        tables, 406
        union queries, 408
layering, report objects, 160-164
Layers menu, 240
layout buttons, 225, 233
legacy mainframe data, 392
libraries, user function library, 292
lines, formatting reports, 263-265
Link dialog box, 71
Link tab, 61, 309

compiled, 468-469
creating, 95-104
creating in Visual Studio .NET, 457-458
data, drill-down reports, 125-127
Details section, 127-129
    filtering, 132-135
    grouping, 118-125
design, 334
design FAQs, 464-465
details, 95
distribution, 465-466
    compiled reports, 468-469
    components, 467-468
    Crystal Enterprise, 466-467
    custom Web or Windows, 467
    manual reports, 469
drill-down, 125-126
    creating, 126-127
    Details section, 127-129
formatting, 262
    applying from other fields, 269-270
    boxes, 263-265
    conditional, 269-270
    Formatting toolbar, 262
    hyperlinks, 268
    lines, 263-265
    Tooltips, 262-263
    vertical text, 266-268
formulas, 95
groups, 94
links, 94
manual, 469
mapping out, 91-92
maps
    Layers menu, 240
    modifying, 240
    panning, 241
    positions, 240

Resolve Mismatch dialog box, 240
    sizes, 240
    zooming, 241
parameters, 95
planning, 22, 88-89
    charts, 23
    considerations, 89-91
    consumer needs, 89-91
    consumers, 23
    due dates, 91
    objectives, 23
    result requirements, 90-91
repositories, 59
reusing, 346
sort orders, 95
SQL, 57-59
stored procedures, 56-57
storyboards, 92
    requirements, 92-94
styles, 377
    two-variable OLAP Chart, 379-380
subreports, 304
    formatting, 307
    In-Place, 311-313
    linked versus unlinked, 308-311
    nested, 317
    On-Demand, 311-313
    troubleshooting, 304-305
    usage, 304-308
    variables, 313-315
summaries, 95, 139
    grand totals, 139-140
    groups, 140-142
    running totals, 142-144
tables, 55-56, 94
views, 56
Web-enabling, 419
Reports section, 41

W

Web
  applications, 437
    advanced, 443-445
  custom, 467
  reporting
    .NET, 441-443
    ASP, 437-439
    ASP.NET, 441
    Java, 439-441
**Web applications, Crystal Reports,
458-459**
Web report distribution, 415-418
  Crystal Enterprise Standard, 418-428
    URL-based commands, 427-428
  RAS, 428-429
  RDC, 428-429
Web services, Crystal Reports, 459-461
Web Sharing and Alias dialog box, 419
Web Sharing tab, 419
Web sites
  Crystal Analysis, 471
  Crystal Decisions, 399, 415, 433, 462,
    466, 469, 471
  Crystal Decisions Web Services, 462
  Crystal Enterprise, 471
  Crystal Reports, 453, 471
  Crystal Reports 9, 462
  Crystal Reports 9 Advanced Edition, 457
  Crystal Reports for Visual Studio .NET,
    462
  Crystal Services, 470-471
  Developer Zone, 472
  KBase, 471
  Sams Publishing, 171
Welcome dialog box, 34, 41
Window menu, 46
windows

Field Explorer, 79
Report Explorer, 79
Repository Explorer, 79
Windows applications, 467
wizards
  Cross-Tab, 277-278
  Crystal Reports Installation, 35
  Crystal Reports Setup, 34-35
  OLAP, 369-370
  OLAP Report Creation, 369, 377
  Publishing, 425
  Registration, 37
  Report, 41, 66, 306, 338
  Report Expert, 41
  Standard Report Creation, 67-78

X-Z

XML data sources, 398-399
Xtreme Sample Database, 54

zooming, maps, 241